Transactions of the Royal Historical Society

SIXTH SERIES

XXIII

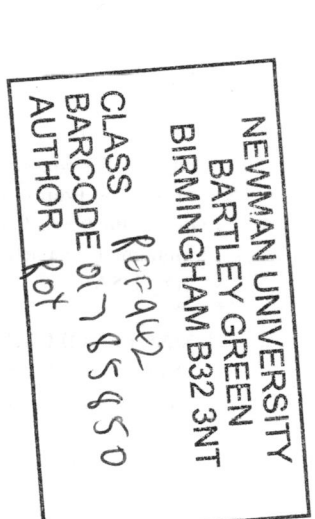

CAMBRIDGE
UNIVERSITY PRESS

Published by the Press Syndicate of the University of Cambridge
The Edinburgh Building, Cambridge CB2 8RU, United Kingdom
32 Avenue of the Americas, New York, NY 10013-2473, USA
477 Williamstown Road, Port Melbourne, VIC 3207, Australia
C/Orense, 4, Planta 13, 28020 Madrid, Spain
Lower Ground Floor, Nautica Building, The Water Club,
Beach Road, Granger Bay, 8005 Cape Town, South Africa

First published 2013

A catalogue record for this book is available from the British Library

ISBN 9781107063860 hardback

SUBSCRIPTIONS. The serial publications of the Royal Historical Society, *Royal Historical Society Transactions* (ISSN 0080-4401) and Camden Fifth Series (ISSN 0960-1163) volumes, may be purchased together on annual subscription. The 2013 subscription price, which includes print and electronic access (but not VAT), is £142 (US $ 237 in the USA, Canada, and Mexico) and includes Camden Fifth Series, volumes 43 and 44 and Transactions Sixth Series, volume 23 (published in December). Japanese prices are available from Kinokuniya Company Ltd, P.O. Box 55, Chitose, Tokyo 156, Japan. EU subscribers (outside the UK) who are not registered for VAT should add VAT at their country's rate. VAT registered subscribers should provide their VAT registration number. Prices include delivery by air.

Subscription orders, which must be accompanied by payment, may be sent to a bookseller, subscription agent, or direct to the publisher: Cambridge University Press, The Edinburgh Building, Shaftesbury Road, Cambridge CB2 8RU, UK; or in the USA, Canada, and Mexico: Cambridge University Press, Journals Fulfillment Department, 100 Brook Hill Drive, West Nyack, New York, 10994-2133, USA.

SINGLE VOLUMES AND BACK VOLUMES. A list of Royal Historical Society volumes available from Cambridge University Press may be obtained from the Humanities Marketing Department at the address above.

Printed and bound by CPI Group (UK) Ltd, Croydon, CR0 4YY

CONTENTS

Transactions of the RHS 23 (2013), p. 1 © Royal Historical Society 2013
doi:10.1017/S0080440113000017

EDITORIAL NOTE

The customary schedule of papers read at the Society's meetings is supplemented by papers from our regional meetings and symposia, comprising Peter Borsay's paper given at the symposium at the University of Glamorgan on 'Visualising the Seaside' in November 2011, Phil Withington's paper given at the University of Sheffield in April 2012 and two papers by Ian Talbot and Harshan Kumarasingham given at a regional visit to the University of Southampton in October 2012. We are also delighted to include the essay by Levi Roach, the winner of the Alexander Prize.

Transactions of the RHS 23 (2013), pp. 3–35 © Royal Historical Society 2013
doi:10.1017/S0080440113000029

TRANSACTIONS OF THE
ROYAL HISTORICAL SOCIETY
PRESIDENTIAL ADDRESS

By Colin Jones

FRENCH CROSSINGS IV: VAGARIES OF PASSION AND POWER IN ENLIGHTENMENT PARIS

READ 23 NOVEMBER 2012

ABSTRACT. This paper examines female libertinism in eighteenth-century France, highlighting the hybrid identity of actress, courtesan and prostitute of female performers at the Paris Opéra. The main focus is on the celebrated singer, Sophie Arnould. She and others like her achieved celebrity by moving seamlessly between these three facets of their identity. Their celebrity also allowed them to circulate within the highest social circles. Feminists of the 1790s such as Olympe de Gouges and Théroigne de Méricourt had pre-Revolutionary careers that were very similar to those of Arnould. It is suggested that understanding this kind of individual in Ancien Régime France can help us to identify a neglected libertine strand within Enlightenment culture, that merged into proto-feminism in the French Revolution. The paper offers a new approach to some of the origins of modern French feminism.

A woman, nearly naked, with heavily rouged cheeks, strolls alongside an elegantly dressed man (Figure 1). The man carries a long torch, set at an angle which would not have posed very much of an interpretative problem for good Dr Freud. The image comes from the unusual book of comic drawings, the *Livre de caricatures tant bonnes que mauvaises*, by the Parisian luxury embroiderer, Charles-Germain de Saint-Aubin, that provides a kind of visual chronicle of Parisian life in the middle decades of the eighteenth century. The caption reads: 'breaker of porcelain at the home of the Farmer General, vilm . . ., or, la Deschamps, notorious courtesan'.[1]

---

[1] Charles-Germain de Saint-Aubin, *Livre de caricatures tant bonnes que mauvaises*, fo. 304. See www.waddesdon.org.uk/collection/special-projects/st.-aubin (call-mark 675.304) (last accessed 3 June 2013). For the work generally, see Colin Jones, 'French Crossings. II. Laughing over Boundaries', *Transactions of the Royal Historical Society*, 21 (2011), 1–38.

Figure 1 (Colour online) Charles-Germain de Saint-Aubin, *Casseuse de Porcelaine, chez le fermier Gal de Vilm . . .*, 1753–64?; watercolour, ink and graphite on paper; 187 × 132 mm; Waddesdon, The Rothschild Collection (The National Trust); acc. no. 675.304. Imaging Services Bodleian Library © The National Trust, Waddesdon Manor.

Using a report written by a police spy, we can clarify just what this incident involved.[2] In late March 1756, Deschamps and a female friend went to dine at the superb neo-classical residence on the north-western edge of the city owned by a wealthy farmer general (not Vilmorin in fact), one Gaillard de la Bouexière and a male friend.

> The dinner was splendid and gay ... The gentlemen got up to take a stroll in in the garden ... To pass the time, the ladies amused themselves by breaking the porcelain, not only all that was left on the table but also what was on the fireplace ... in the end there only remained two cups. Into these the ladies were saucy enough to deposit the digestion of their dinner.

> On returning [from his walk], M. de la Bouexière was not long in noticing the charming action of these ladies, but pretending to be in no way put out he applauded it. In this he went one better than the demoiselle Deschamps who was dying to say that this was nothing for a millionaire like him. In short, they resumed at table and having got rid of the two cups, passed to liqueurs.

Later that evening, the two women were stripped naked, at which point 'the gentlemen had their servants, carrying torches, lead the women to their carriage whence they returned to their homes'. Next morning, Madame Deschamps wrote to her host requesting that he return her clothes, jewels and diamonds. He acceded to the wish, with the exception of her clothes, notably an expensive satin dress with silver and chenille embroidery, of which he made a bonfire.

This gamey anecdote played to the scatological tastes of Charles-Germain de Saint-Aubin: shit in the coffee-cups was definitely his style of humour.[3] Madame Deschamps, 'famous courtesan', was, like many of her type, an actress in the Paris theatre, a topic for which Charles-Germain showed much interest too. She appears elsewhere in the book, notably in a snuffbox lid of his design which was given to her by one M. de Saint-Albin (Figure 2). Charles de Saint-Albin, archbishop of Cambrai, was the illegitimate son of the regent, the duke of Orleans, and an actress (appropriately enough), and he was notorious for leading a scandalous life. If we only knew more about the snuffbox transaction, we might have discovered what the bishop really did say to the actress. We do know, however, a good deal about Madame Deschamps, who was far less obscure to Parisian contemporaries than she is to us. She left traces, and not only in the porcelain.[4]

---

[2] Camille Piton, *Paris sous Louis XV: rapports des inspecteurs de police au Roi* (5 vols. in 3, Paris, 1910–14), V, 132–5.

[3] For scatology in the *Livre de caricatures*, see esp. Jones, 'French Crossings. II', esp. 29ff.

[4] Waddesdon call-mark 675.192. Much about Deschamps's life can be gleaned from the police inspector reports in Piton, *Paris sous Louis XV*, and (for the early 1760s) in *Journal des inspecteurs de M. de Sartines*, 1e série, 1761–4 (Paris, 1863). There is a good biographical sketch drawing on these and other primary source materials in Erica-Marie Bénabou, *La prostitution et la police des moeurs au XVIIIe siècle* (Paris, 1987), 369–77 (see *ibid.*, 209, for La Bouexière's

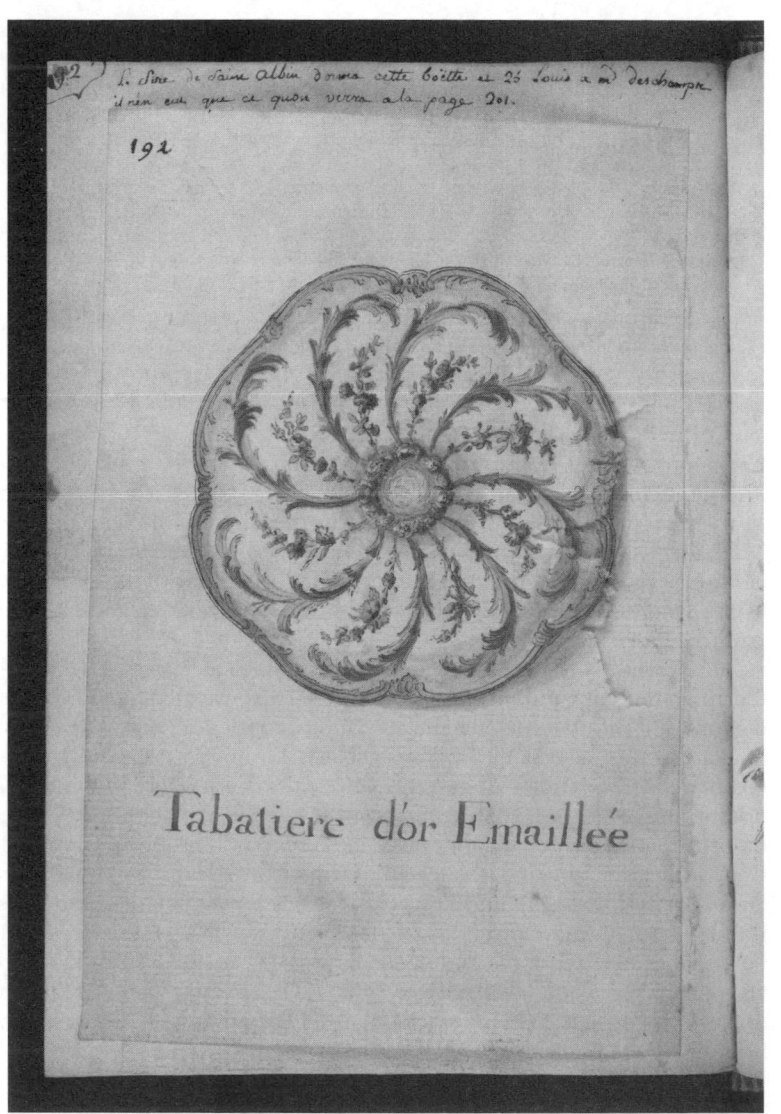

Figure 2 (Colour online) Charles-Germain de Saint-Aubin, *Tabatiere d'or Emaillée*, *c.* 1740 – *c.* 1775; watercolour, ink and graphite on paper; 187 × 132 mm; Waddesdon, The Rothschild Collection (The National Trust); acc. no. 675.192. Imaging Services Bodleian Library © The National Trust, Waddesdon Manor.

Madame Marie-Anne Deschamps, née Pagès, was an actress, a courtesan and a prostitute. Born in 1730, she was the daughter of a Parisian lady's shoemaker, but left this humble background in her early teens to launch herself into the world of prostitution. By the time of her death in 1764, songs had been written about her and gossip retailed about her, while *philosophes* had puzzled over her, police spies had kept an eye on her and moralists and cultural commentators had proved more than willing to be shocked by her. A period as dancer at the Opéra-Comique in the 1740s had led to her becoming a member of an acting troupe attached to the French army in the War of Austrian Succession. Here, first, she married a ne'er-do-well actor Deschamps. Second, in swift succession, she became the lover of the French commander, the comte de Clermont. When the comte returned to his established mistress, Madame Deschamps returned to Paris, the chorus of the Opéra, and a life of sexual adventure and social climbing. By 1754, the Paris police was identifying her as one of the two 'most dazzling whores in the whole of Paris'.[5]

The comte de Clermont was one of no fewer than five princes of the royal blood to whom the shoemaker's daughter became lover. One of them, the raddled voluptuary, the prince de Conti, was said to have performed the act of love with her no fewer than twelve times in a single night. For the rest of his life, allegedly, Conti worshipped at the shrine of the number 12, which he had embroidered to his shirts, hats and handkerchiefs, embossed on his breeches' buttons, and so on. As well as dipping into royalty, 'La Deschamps' also broke through into the world of the farmers-general, the billionnaires of the day, by allegedly spending a night with the high financier Villemur for 100 louis. But she soon moved – in the professional argot – from retail to wholesale, abandoning passing flings for establishment as a kept woman.[6]

There would be some rocky moments for Madame Deschamps over the next decade or so, notably when she was between lovers, who besides princes and financiers included old nobles and strapping young army officers with the occasional Jewish banker, foreign aristocrat, English gentleman, ambassador and archbishop thrown in. Such was the demand for the services of this 'veritable Messalina' (as a police spy called her) that she was known to break off love-making half-way through and demand

---

residence). See too the older G. Capon and R. Yve-Plessis, *Fille d'Opéra, vendeuse d'amour. Histoire de Mademoiselle Deschamps (1730–64)* (Paris, 1906).

[5] Capon and Yve-Plessis, *Fille d'Opéra*, 137, 141–2.

[6] G. Capon and R. Yve-Plessis, *La vie privée du prince de Conty, Louis-François de Bourbon (1717–76)* (Paris, 1907), 87. The account of her life given here draws on the sources cited above, n. 4. The other princes of blood besides Conti and Clermont were Orléans, La Marche and Charolais. For Villemur, see Piton, *Paris sous Louis XV*, V, 98, 390 and *passim*; and for 'retail', *ibid.*, V, 106. For the argot of Parisian prostitution, see Bénabou, *La prostitution et la police des moeurs*, 212–14, 331ff.

higher payment from clients she adjudged too ugly. Her taste for female partners, however, complicated and partly compromised her reputation.[7] This was also affected by spells of gonorrhoea, which were not brilliant for trade, and also involved the administration of a ghastly, mercury-based treatment. Spasmodically, too, her husband appeared on the scene to cramp her style, as financial leech or physical bully, and sometimes both.

In April 1760, she fell on particularly hard times.[8] The Seven Years War was damaging luxury spending in Paris and reducing the clientele for sexual services. Deschamps decided to sell off her porcelain (coincidentally enough): Vincennes, Sèvres, Meissen, the very finest international brands. (But she kept her carriage, which was one of the most ostentatiously luxurious vehicles to be seen in Paris, as well as her diamonds.) The queues of individuals and carriages at the sale of her effects stretched out from her hôtel and down the street. People lingered to ogle and some to buy the stupendous wealth on display, 'fruit of debauchery and prostitution', as one irate contemporary put it, in this 'enchanted palace' fit for a prince (that even boasted English water-closets). Two decades later, the literary chronicler Grimm still remembered with awe this occasion inspired by 'one of the most illustrious courtesans of the age'.[9]

The bubble burst. In 1762, with war still dragging on, Madame Deschamps, plagued by recurrent venereal disease, had fallen so deeply in debt that she fled the city for Italy to lie low. When she returned in 1763, it was incognito, sick, thin and frail, and with growths on her knees, a just reward for her vices, said the devout. In January 1764, the police reported the death of 'La Deschamps', 'so notorious for her debauchery, her luxury and by the excessive price she set on her favours'.[10] She was thirty-four years old. In her final illness, she was said to have turned to a life of piety and repentance. William Hogarth could not have plotted it better.

This was a career spent crossing boundaries, social and sexual, that was so extraordinary that it prompted – and prompts – serious reflection.

---

[7] Capon and Yve-Plessis, *Fille d'Opéra*, 179 (Messalina); Dufort de Cheverny, *Mémoires*, ed. J. P. Guicciardi (Paris, 1990), 278 (ugly lovers); and Piton, *Paris sous Louis XV*, V, 135–6 and *passim* (lesbianism).

[8] The outline of the narrative can be followed in police reports in *Journal des inspecteurs de M. de Sartines*, and in Charles-Simon Favart, *Mémoires et correspondance littéraire, dramatique et anecdotique* (3 vols., Paris, 1808), II, 13–18, inc. footnotes. For the early 1760s as hard times for prostitutes, see Bénabou, *La prostitution et la police des moeurs*, 341, 349.

[9] [Edmond-Jean-François Barbier], *Chronique de la Régence et du règne de Louis XV, ou Journal de Barbier* (8 vols., Paris, 1857–66), VII, 246–7; [Grimm], *Correspondance littéraire, philosophique et critique de Grimm, Diderot, Raynal, Meister, etc*, ed. Maurice Tourneux (16 vols., Paris, 1877–82), XII, 312 (Sept. 1779). For another backward glance on her memory, see Pierre Manuel, *La police de Paris dévoilée* (2 vols., Paris, Year II = 1794), I, 124, II, 169.

[10] Bénabou, *La prostitution et la police des mœurs*, 376; Capon and Yve-Plessis, *Fille d'Opéra*, 193.

Deschamps was a 'prodigy', of whose wealth and independence any decent woman would be jealous, wrote one author. 'One of the seven wonders of the [modern] world', opined another. Women of bad morals like her, thought the Russian visitor Denis Fonvizine, covered in diamonds from head to toe, made Paris a city 'which gives nothing away to either Sodom or Gomorrah'.[11] And some twenty years after the death of 'la Deschamps', the writer and dramatist Louis-Sébastien Mercier (whose father, coincidentally enough, had rented rooms to her for select dinner parties) pondered on her fate less in terms of divine retribution than of the swings and roundabouts of fortune:

> Who can really tell why the late Mademoiselle Deschamps reached this level of opulence which permitted her the insolent luxury of putting paste jewels around her horses' harnesses and edging her commode with English lace draft-excluders? Another girl from the Opéra dies leaving huge effects and a considerable estate. Was she more beautiful or wittier than any other? No, issued from the lowest class of the people, she had in her support the favours of that ineffable destiny which raises, brings down, maintains and overthrows both ministers and whores (*ministres et catins*).[12]

As historians, we are well used to following the fates and fortunes of statesmen – Mercier's '*ministres*'. We are less habituated to doing the same with *catins*. But sex and passion are as much within our remit as historians as politics and power. In this paper, my focus will be on *catins*.

I have organised my set of Presidential Addresses around the theme of 'French Crossings', and here is an identity, an identity (or, more correctly, a suite of interrelated identities – actress, courtesan, prostitute) which contemporaries called 'libertine', and whose very essence was crossing social and sexual boundaries.[13] Because human, sexual desire was involved, libertine identity frequently shuttled back and forth between fixed social roles and role-playing, between truth and fiction. With such

---

[11] De Chevrier, *Le Colporteur* (Paris, 1762), 97 (prodigy); Bénabou, *La prostitution et la police des mœurs*, 334 (citing La Morandière: seven wonders); Denis Fonvizine, *Lettres de France (1777–8)* (reprint edn, Oxford, 1995), 127 (Sodom).

[12] Louis-Sébastien Mercier, *Le tableau de Paris*, ed. Jean-Claude Bonnet (Paris, 1994), II, 17. For Mercier's father, see Piton, *Paris sous Louis XV*, 117. The premises were on the Rue Bellefonds.

[13] There has been a revival of interest on libertinage in recent years, most of it highlighting aristocratic men. See, for example, Patrick Wald Lasowski, *L'ardeur et la galanterie* (Paris, 1986); Michel Delon, *Le savoir-vivre libertin* (Paris, 2000); Didier Foucault, *Histoire du libertinage des goliards au marquis de Sade* (Paris, 2007); and Olivier Blanc, *L'amour à Paris au temps de Louis XVI* (Paris, 2002). A more open approach is offered in *Libertine Enlightenment. Sex, Liberty and Licence in the Eighteenth Century*, ed. Peter Cryle and Lisa O'Connell (2004). For women, see also Olivier Blanc, *Les Libertines: plaisir et liberté au temps des Lumières* (Paris, 1997), and *Femmes et libertinages au XVIIIe siècle: ou les caprices de Cythère*, ed. Anne Richardot (Rennes, 2003). A recent return to the history of prostitution is *Prostitution in the Eighteenth Century: Sex, Commerce and Morality*, ed. Markman Ellis and Ann Lewis (2012). See esp. Ann Lewis, 'Classifying the Prostitute in Eighteenth-Century France', in *ibid.*, 17ff, for a thorough review of the range of practice in this domain.

a figure in the public imagination, one never knew where reality ended and fancy began. Finally, this is also a story in which, as Mercier devined, fate takes a role. There was much that was unpredictable and arbitrary about these crossings.

My first published article, in *History Workshop Journal*, was on prostitution in eighteenth-century Montpellier.[14] This was in 1978, a moment when the author of any article on the history of women felt that she or he was making a political statement and putting in place a contribution to a meta-narrative that had been hidden from History with a capital H.[15] A journal for socialist and feminist historians as *History Workshop* proclaimed itself seemed the obvious place. My main area of expertise at that time was the French Revolution. Yet if I look now at the textbooks on the Revolution that I used and that I recommended to my students at that time, there was simply no mention at all of the key themes of women's history. If women were even mentioned in textbooks on the French Revolution, it was Marie-Antoinette and Charlotte Corday who predominated (with the occasional walk-on part given to Madame Defarge, Charles Dickens's fictional *tricoteuse* from *A Tale of Two Cities*).

Go now to the textbooks, and things are very different. Now, the role that women played in the early stirrings of modern feminism in the Revolutionary decade is freely acknowledged. Now, no textbook worth its salt could *not* mention the figures most prominent in this development, sisters of England's Mary Wollstonecraft (author of the *Vindication of the Rights of Women* (1792)): Olympe de Gouges, author of the *Declaration of the Rights of Women* (1791), which sought to extend to women the rights outlined in the 1789 Declaration of the Rights of Man. Or Etta Palm, the Dutch feminist, author, activist and sometime diplomatic spy. Or Théroigne de Méricourt, frenzied cross-dressing street-fighter. Or Claire Lacombe, founder of the shortlived Society of Revolutionary Republican Women, arguably the first feminist political club in world history.[16]

---

[14] Colin Jones, 'Prostitution and the Ruling Class in Eighteenth-Century Montpellier', *History Workshop*, 6 (1978), 7–28.

[15] Representative of this moment in the feminist history of women were works with titles like Sheila Rowbotham, *Hidden from History: 300 Years of Female Oppression* (1974), and *Becoming Visible: Women in European History*, ed. Renate Bridenthal and Claudia Koonz (Boston, MA, 1977). Fundamental, in terms of the French Revolution, was Olwen Hufton, 'Women in Revolution, 1789–96', *Past and Present*, 53 (1971), 90–108. For an overview of Hufton's feminist history, see Colin Jones, 'Olwen Hufton's "Poor", Richard Cobb's "People" and Notions of the *Longue Durée* in French Revolutionary Historiography', in *The Art of Survival: Gender and History in Europe, 1450–2000*, ed. Ruth Harris and Lyndal Roper, Past and Present Supplement 1 (Oxford, 2006), 78–103. Another work of this earlier generation is *Women in Revolutionary Paris, 1789–95*, ed. Darleen G. Levy, Harriet B. Applewhite and Mary D. Johnson (Urbana, 1979).

[16] Olivier Blanc, *Marie-Olympe de Gouges, une humaniste à la fin du XVIIIe siècle* (Paris, 2003); Joan W. Scott, *Only Paradoxes to Offer. French Feminists and the Rights of Man* (1996), focused on

Yet there was no sort of victory for these militant women in the 1790s, or else only a very poignant and pyrrhic one. The bigger story for women in France in that decade was not these early stirrings of modern feminism but their ruthless suppression. Claire Lacombe merely disappeared from view following a period in gaol, but Olympe de Gouges and Etta Palm were guillotined and Théroigne de Méricourt was beaten up, went mad and ended her life in a lunatic asylum. The republican compact of the 1790s sidelined women; and the Napoleonic Code would confirm their enclosure within a 'separate sphere' that was set to last.[17] The cosy domesticity which Dickens's Charles Darnay and Lucy Manette return to after their trials in Paris under the Terror was clearly the best that women could hope for. For women, the Revolution was the best of times, the worst of times (more the latter than the former, in fact).[18]

Neither of these emergent eighteenth-century narratives – stirrings of feminist modernity, imposition of separate sphere ideology – seems to have much of a place for the Madame Deschamps of this world. Historians train the spotlight in France on the *salonnières*, cultivated and well-connected (and very self-effacing) women who operated the salon sociability which helped power the Enlightenment, and who were very much the blood-sisters of the bluestockings, rational Dissenters and other *femmes savantes* prefiguring and overlapping with Mary Wollstoncraft on this side of the Channel.[19] A *salonnière*, or indeed, in England, a Mary Wollstonecraft, would have died of social mortification at the thought of allowing a Madame Deschamps into their homes. They would have seemed to have come from different planets. If one is searching for the origins of feminism and modernity, then, the assumption is that they will not be found among denizens of the world's oldest profession.[20]

Olympe de Gouges; Olivier Blanc, 'Etta-Lubina-Johana d'Aëlders, Mme Palm', in *idem, Les libertines;* Elisabeth Roudinesco, *Théroigne de Méricourt. Une femme mélancolique sous la Révolution française* (Paris, 1989); and Dominique Godineau, *Citoyennes tricoteuses. Les femmes du peuple à Paris pendant la Révolution française* (Paris, 1988). The literature on women and the French Revolution over the last quarter-century is too long to be listed here.

[17] Joan Landes, *Women and the Public Sphere in the Age of Democratic Revolution* (Ithaca, 1988); René Robaye, 'Code, droit et société bourgeoise en 1804', in *Vers un ordre bourgeois? Révolution française et changement social,* ed. Jean-Pierre Jessenne (Rennes, 2007).

[18] See Colin Jones, 'French Crossings I. Tales of Two Cities', *Transactions of the Royal Historical Society,* 20 (2010), 1–26.

[19] For France, see Dena Goodman, *The Republic of Letters. A Cultural History of the French Enlightenment* (Ithaca, 1994); and for England, Elizabeth Eger, *Bluestockings. Women of Reason from the Enlightenment to Romanticism* (Basingstoke, 2010).

[20] Besides works cited above, nn. 15 and 17, see esp. Barbara Taylor, *Mary Wollstonecraft and the Feminist Imagination* (Cambridge, 2003); *Women, Gender and Enlightenment,* ed. Sarah Knott and Barbara Taylor (2005), see, though, the essay by Felicia Gordon, cited below, n. 89; and Karen O'Brien, *Women and Enlightenment in Eighteenth-Century Britain* (Cambridge, 2009).

In this paper, I want to try to unsettle this consensual assumption, and to remedy this lack of interest in high-class courtesans and prostitutes by historians of feminism (and indeed historians *tout court*). In doing so, I shall not be drawing as heavily as I would have liked on the life of our Madame Deschamps. As historians, we can only get so far with Madame Deschamps. She exists as a phenomenon, a sexual meteor observed and remarked on with awe and wonder by Parisians and *philosophes*. Yet apart from some entanglements she had with the police and the law, it is difficult to get a real sense of what she was like and what she made of her position in life. How should we even interpret the episode with which I began? Shitting in a millionaire's coffee-cup might, I suppose, be seen as a playful if bizarre act of class resistance.[21] Or should we simply write it off as an aesthetic judgement of the quality of her host's china-ware? Sèvres does affect some people that kind of way. Who can tell? In order to explore her world and the identities her type embodied, I am choosing to look elsewhere, and to criss-cross her life story with that of a woman with a similar cultural identity and social profile, about whose life and thoughts we know far more, Sophie Arnould (Figure 3).

One of Sophie Arnould's contemporaries dubbed her 'the doyenne of *catins*' or whores. The Goncourt brothers, who wrote what is still the best study of her, were more sympathetic: 'They are rare and scattered at long intervals across history, those women who while they are alive are the scandal of their age and who once dead are its smile'. The title of the present paper, 'vagaries of Enlightenment passion and power' fits Sophie Arnould like a glove.[22]

---

[21] This is in fact the approach taken in Pamela Cheek, *Sexual Antipodes. Enlightenment Globalisation and the Placing of Sex* (Stanford, 2003), see esp. 214 n. 99.

[22] The excellent biographical treatment of Arnould by the Goncourt brothers is surprisingly short on detail on her theatrical and wider social life while she was at the height of her fame. Edmond and Jules de Goncourt, *Les actrices du XVIIIe siècle. Sophie Arnould, d'après sa correspondance et ses mémoires inédits* (Paris, 1893), see 13 for the quotation. There is also a very well-researched recent popular biography by Rodolf Trouilleux, *N'oubliez pas Iphigénie: biographie de la cantatrice et épistolière Sophie Arnould, 1740–1802* (Grenoble, 1999). Unfortunately, although an impressive list of sources is given there are no footnotes, making it very difficult to align data and sources. The source-list has, however, provided some good leads, notably in the Archives Nationales (AN). Much the same problem applies to the also otherwise rich popular biography by André Billy, *La vie amoureuse de Sophie Arnould* (Paris, 1929). Sophie Arnould was a sufficiently high-profile figure to have left much information and many anecdotes about her. She and her lover Lauraguais are among the most heavily cited individuals in contemporary journalism: *Le règne de la critique. L'imaginaire culturel des 'Mémoires secrets'*, ed. C. Cave (Paris, 2010). Cf. *Mémoires secrets, dits de Bachaumont*, ed. Christophe Cave and Suzanne Cornand (36 vols. in 5, Paris, 2009). Besides these sources, I have drawn on her 'dossier d'artiste' in the Archives de l'Opéra (AOp.). The latter also include a series of letters, mainly from the 1770s (LAS Arnould/1–31), and what seems to be the early parts of an autobiography which in some (but far from all) details corresponds to that cited by the Goncourts (LAS Arnould 32: inc. 'Morceaux détachés ou supplément à la partie des

Figure 3 (Colour online) Jean-Baptiste Greuze, *Portrait of a Lady*, c. 1786. By kind permission of the Trustees of the Wallace Collection.

Sophie Arnould, who was born in 1740, ten years after Deschamps, and who died in 1802, shared the same hybridic, composite, libertine identity. Deschamps was a dancer in first the Opéra-Comique and then the Opéra; Arnould was a singer, a star singer in fact, in the Opéra. They were both

mémoires de mademoiselle Arnould écrits par elle-même'). The 'doyenne of catins' phrase comes from verse cited in Marquis de Bombelles, *Journal*, I: *1780–4* (Geneva, 1978), 62.

courtesans with a series of high-placed lovers. Deschamps was a brilliant success in this respect, notching up a great deal of blue blood; for Arnould it was more an ancillary role. Finally, they both had at least some part of a foot in the world of prostitution. As actresses (I will use the generic term), it was difficult not to. As *philosophe* Denis Diderot remarked, 'an actress who is a respectable woman is such a rare phenomenon'. Jean-Jacques Rousseau was in full-throated agreement – the existence of actresses was a tissue of artifice. The talent of actors for Rousseau was 'the art of counterfeiting oneself, of taking on another character from one's own, of appearing different from what one is'. The profession of acting, similarly, was 'the trade of pretending to be someone else and in which one puts oneself publicly on sale'. In essence, an actress prostituted herself and should therefore be viewed as a prostitute. Like other 'public women' whom Rousseau had in his sights (prostitutes, female court instriguers, *salonnières*), the lack of transparency at the heart of an actress's being cut her off from both nature and virtue. The very few actresses who guarded their chastity were said to be preserving *une vestalité miraculeuse* ('a miraculous vestality').[23]

Madame Deschamps was a supernumerary dancer in the Opéra known at the time as a *garde-cote* – a coast-guard. The name came from the fact that she mainly stood at the back of the stage looking pretty against marine or nautical backdrops (Figure 4).[24] Sophie Arnould in contrast was one of the Opéra's most brilliant female soloists (Figure 5). After allegedly having her voice commended by Madame de Pompadour, Louis XV's mistress, Arnould entered the Paris Opéra company in 1757 and within a year had acceded to principal roles and was causing a sensation.[25] It was less the strength of her voice than its sweetness and purity that was praised, but most of all her qualities as a dramatic actress. The veteran dramatist Charles Collé remarked at the very start of her career, 'I have never seen another actress who brought together as much grace, virtue, feeling, nobility of expression, and such fine posture, intelligence and warmth.' Shortly after this, the visiting English actor, the great David Garrick,

[23] Denis Diderot, *Paradoxe sur le comédien*, ed. Ernest Dupuy (Paris, 1902), 147. Rousseau's views are trenchantly put in his 'Lettre à M. d'Alembert sur les spectacles'. This came out in 1758, the very year that Sophie Arnould began her career. Cf. Landes, *Women and the Public Sphere*, esp. 74–6. 'Vestalité miraculeuse' was a term used by police inspectors: Bénabou, *La prostitution et la police des moeurs*, 109.

[24] Capon and Yve-Plessis, *Fille d'Opéra*, 20. Figures 4 and 6 are drawn from a compendious set of drawings of costumes in the Paris Opéra by Louis-René Boquet, the Opéra's costume designer. There are a number of Sophie Arnould, but none of the parts in plays that we know Deschamps played in. Figure 4 is thus only typical of the genre.

[25] Arnould's early life can be followed in Goncourt, *Sophie Arnould*, 14ff, and AOp., LAS Arnould 32. Both accounts, as Goncourt notes, are full of stories, many no doubt apocryphal.

Figure 4 (Colour online) Louis-René Bouquet, costume of 'begère', from Chamfort, *Palmire*, 1765. © Bibliothèque nationale de France.

Figure 5 (Colour online) Louis-René Bouquet, costume from Montcrif, Zelindor, roi des Sylphes, 1766, 1769. © Bibliothèque nationale de France.

pronounced her the singer of her generation and the only cantatrice who touched his heart.[26]

---

[26] *Journal et mémoires de Charles Collé*, ed. Honoré Bonhomme (3 vols., 1868), II, 147; David Garrick is cited in Goncourt, *Sophie Arnould*, 39.

Arnould dominated the French stage through the 1760s. One of her finest roles was as Thisbe in Francoeur and Rebel's opera *Pyrame et Thisbe* which played in 1759 (coincidentally, Madame Deschamps also appeared in performances of this, as both an Asian woman and an aerial sprite) (Figure 6).[27] The artist Carmontelle painted Arnould in this role, at a moment of heightened pathos, which drew the audience's tears (Figure 5). The gesture of the uplifted eyes seems to have been picked up by the pastellist Quentin de La Tour in a portrait of her which has been lost but of which we have an engraving by Bourgeois de la Richardière. The great sculptor Houdon (Figure 7) drew on the same source in his bust of her in 1775, which evoked her role in one of the greatest final performances of her life in Gluck's *Iphigénie en Aulide*, which played in 1774, and which helped seal the acceptance of Gluck's operas in the city.[28]

Arnould later recalled that a copy of the bust, standing on her mantelpiece, had saved her life when, during the reign of Terror in the 1790s, her home was raided by a group of radical sans-culottes wishing to interrogate a *ci-devant* who prior to 1789 had enjoyed strong aristocratic connections. She managed to overcome their suspicions when they spotted this statue – and took it to be a bust of the radical journalist Marat. The famous portrait of the death of Marat by David notwithstanding, Marat was notorious for being not just extremely ugly but also physically repulsive. So to be mistaken for him was, as she put it, 'not galant'. But at least it had saved her life. Yes, she assured them as she waved them off and out, as an actress she had often been *sans culotte* under the Ancien Régime and as for the Rights of Man, she really knew them all by heart ... [29]

This exchange highlights a particular facet of Arnould's character that explains the reputation which contributed to her celebrity in the Ancien Régime: her wit. She was a diva all right – a singer acknowledged as among the most brilliant of the age, who was always threatening to walk out of the Opéra, who turned up late (or not at all) for rehearsals, who corpsed and went off-script at key moments so as to trigger audience

---

[27] Arnould's performance is commented on in [Grimm], *Correspondance littéraire*, III, 477. See the list of Deschamps's performances in Capon and Yve-Plessis, *Fille d'Opéra*, 211ff. Both women feature in songs and ditties featured in the Chansonnier Maurepas: see *Recueil Clairambault-Maurepas, Chansonnier historique du XVIIIe siècle*, ed. E. Raunié (10 vols., Paris 1879–84), VII–IX, *passim*.

[28] See Anne Poulet, *Jean-Antoine Houdon, Sculptor of the Enlightenment* (Chicago, 2003), 96–103. Olivier Blanc has stated that the original was by Leclercq not de la Tour: Olivier Blanc, *Portraits de femmes. Artistes et modèles à l'époque de Marie-Antoinette* (Paris, 2006), 297. For Sophie Arnould's success of the role in *Iphigénie*, see Goncourt, *Sophie Arnould*, 92–3.

[29] *Galerie théâtrale. Collection de 144 portraits des principaux acteurs et actrices qui ont illustré la scène française depuis 1552 à nos jours* (2 vols., Paris, 1873), I, 3. I have preferred this to the slightly less colourful version of the incident given in Goncourt, *Sophie Arnould*, 155. See too [Fayolle], *Esprit de Sophie Arnould* (Paris, 1813), 14.

Figure 6 (Colour online) Portrait of Mademoiselle Sophie-Arnould in the opera *Pyrame et Thisbe*, by Carmontelle (Louis Carrogis). © RMN-Grand Palais (domaine de Chantilly)/Rene-Gabriel Ojéda.

Figure 7 (Colour online) Sophie Arnould in the role of Iphigénie, by Jean Antoine Houdon. © RMN-Grand Palais (Musée du Louvre)/Gérard Blot.

laughter, who set her own, erratic tempi for her arias, and so on. But in an age of wit, her lightning verbal facility embellished her reputation. She was one of extremely few Enlightenment figures, male or female, to have a book of her witticisms published.³⁰ One has to confess, with some sadness, that the brilliant cerebral ingenuity there on show rarely raises a smile or a laugh in our own day.³¹ Her humour was too often directed at specific targets in the theatre or the world of courtesans or else highlight puns and word-play that do not translate very easily. Her reputation, however, was very widely recognised as often sparkling, invariably direct and not infrequently quite filthy. The sans-culotte quip mentioned above is a case in point. Punning on the meaning of the term, it nominally referred to the radical Parisians who wore trousers rather than genteel breeches or *culottes*. But *culottes* also meant lady's knickers and these had been the subject of quite a storm at the Opéra under the Ancien Régime. The tendency for ballerinas to perform increasingly high jumps in skirts that became shorter and shorter instigated a police decree forbidding performers going on stage without wearing knickers.³² The men in the front row were getting over-excited at this absence of women's *culotte*: public morality was under threat. Quondam *sans culotte* Sophie Arnould would have expected us to have understood all that, if we were to be up to her benchmark of wit. There are other examples of her direct and earthy humour where one can catch the drift more easily. Convened to speak to her fellow actresses in the Opéra about an order from Louis XV that threatened them all with disciplinary action if they failed to be less flagrant and ostentatious in their sexual liaisons in the future, Sophie's double-entendre was to the point, and a bit more: 'Ah! *mes amies*. We're fucked.'³³

Arnould had established her reputation for wit, earthy and otherwise, early in her career. Her family had been desperately trying to keep their Sophie pure by making her live at home while she served her apprenticeship at the Opéra. One night, however, she ran off with a lodger. The lodger had been in disguise. He was the comte de Lauraguais, one of the most dashing and eccentric of Enlightenment intellectuals.³⁴ On the night of their elopement, Lauraguais revealed his identity to

---

³⁰ *Arnoldiana ou Sophie Arnould et ses contemporains* (Paris 1813); and cf. [Fayolle], *Esprit de Sophie Arnould*.

³¹ The failure of humour to travel is considered in Jones, 'French Crossings. II'.

³² For the underwear story, Marie José Kerhoas, 'Les dessins de costumes de scène de 1750 à 1790 dans les collections patrimoniales françaises' (doctoral thesis, Université de Tours, 2007), 18; cf. Mercier, *Tableau de Paris*.

³³ 'Ah, mes amis, nous sommes foutues', *Anecdotes échappées à l'Observateur anglais et aux Mémoires secrets en forme de correspondance* (2 vols., 1788), I, 23–4. Another coarse shaft of wit may be found at *Mémoires secrets*, I, 209.

³⁴ Paul Fromageot, 'Les fantaisies littéraires, galantes, politiques et autres d'un grand seigneur: le comte de Lauraguais (1733–1824)', *Revue des études historiques*, 79 (1914), 14–56, provides a summary overview. See too Goncourt, *Sophie Arnould*, esp. 32–40, 46–7, 54ff. For Arnould's life as a mother, see Maurice Dumoulin, *Sophie Arnould, mère de famille* (Paris, 1911). There is a good account of the relationship in Blanc, *L'amour à Paris*, ch. 12, 182–90.

Sophie and explained that unfortunately he would not be able to marry her. He was of ducal rank: some boundaries in Ancien Régime France were simply uncrossable. Also, he was already married. This set the tone for the extraordinary vagaries of their relationship throughout the rest of her life. Three children emerged from a relationship quite as passionate as it was stormy. 'Monsieur de Lauraguis has given me two million kisses', she sighed towards the end of her life, 'and made me shed four million tears'. 'Ah! The good old days!', she sighed with pathos and irony in her later years as she recollected her brilliant if star-crossed career. 'I was so unhappy.'[35]

After one huge row, in 1762, when Lauraguais had gone off to stay with Voltaire near Geneva, Sophie took spectacular action. In a letter that circulated widely through the Parisian news-sheets, she addressed him:

> I do not understand what you are doing. You have left me alone and abandoned. I am using my liberty – that liberty so precious to the *philosophes* – to do without you. Don't take it ill that I am tired of living with a madman who has dissected his own coachman and wanted to be my accoucheur with the aim of dissecting me too. Forgive me if I protect myself from your encyclopaedic lancet.[36]

The letter was placed in a coach, and sent round to his Parisian residence. On the back seat of the coach were all the diamonds that he had given her – plus the two children she had by then borne him. The latter gesture scandalised all of Paris. The presumption of a courtesan and actress brandishing claims to liberty as regards her illegitimate offspring was shocking in the extreme. Even Diderot, hardly the most prudish of the *philosophes*, adjudged her a 'little tramp' and 'a little monkey'.[37] She had broken a sacramental relationship by abandoning her children. Lauraguais's put-upon wife had to tolerate three days of her husband sobbing on the sofa at being abandoned by his mistress, yet she actually looked after the children for a period of months. This motherly gesture by the wronged wife won far warmer public support.[38] In the end, Lauraguais returned to Arnould, set up an allowance for the children and their mother, she resumed maternal duties, and they even had another child together. But although their friendship remained, this began a period when, while retaining his friendship, she moved away from him

---

[35] Goncourt, *Sophie Arnould* 46 (kisses); *Chef-d'oeuvres politiques et littéraires de la fin du XVIIIe siècle* (3 vols., Paris, 1788), III, 133 (good old days).

[36] Goncourt, *Sophie Arnould*, 48–9n, gives the transcription, which is widely available elsewhere.

[37] Diderot, *Oeuvres: Correspondance*, ed. L. Versini (Paris, 1997), 362, 365, 371.

[38] The generosity of Lauraguais's wife as regards the children emerges from documents concerning the separation of the Lauraguais couple. AN Y14811 (5 Feb. 1763) and Y14812 (24 Mar. 1763). The couple's servants testified about Lauraguais's sobbing. See too the favourable comment on Mme de Lauraguais in André Morellet, *Lettres. Tome 1 (1759–85)* (Oxford, 1991), 181.

and started to pass through a series of high-profile liaisons. They lived stormily ever after.

Lauraguais was a fascinating, impassioned character to be involved with. The scientific dabbling which Sophie's letter mentions was an inveterate characteristic. Elected to the Académie des Sciences in 1758, he remained an academician till his death in 1824, and boasted a long list of crazes and hobby-horses. Under the Ancien Régime, these included chemistry, porcelain manufacture, horticulture, medicine, as well as anatomy and midwifery (if we are to believe the note from Sophie). He defended smallpox inoculation against the university consensus, and was gaoled for his pains (Sophie helped to get him a royal pardon). His interests stretched widely beyond science too: he also had an anglophilic passion for horse-racing, collecting, political economy and theatre (he was credited with clearing the stage of public seating).

Their relationship was on and off, off and on. At one time when Lauraguais resented that Sophie was staying faithful to her current lover, the prince d'Hénin ('the king of bores', according to the baronne d'Oberkirch), he summoned a group of physicians from the Paris Medical Faculty, and put to them the theoretical proposition that it was medically possible to die of boredom. When they gave learned assent to the proposition, Lauraguais immediately tried to get the Paris police to arrest the poor prince for the attempted murder of his mistress.[39] Setting up a trial for murder by boredom. This was a characteristic Lauraguais stunt, that set the city talking.

Arnould's sexual availability and also her relationship with Lauraguais and others of his ilk gave her access to a wide gamut of intellectuals and theatre-goers from the social elite. In an autobiographical fragment, she highlighted the place of men of letters in the career that she had chosen.

> I dedicated myself to the world, as soon as my existence ceased belonging to my family. I belonged to the king, sovereign protector of the theatre; I belonged to the public, passionate lover of frivolous pleasures; and I belonged above all to men of letters whose creative talent nurtures and sustains the theatre. We all know how much power these gentlemen wield in the coffee-houses, the newspapers and the salons.[40]

Sophie was highly successful in playing men of letters to get her name in the papers. Indeed, she and the comte de Lauraguais were among the most frequently cited figures in Parisian cultural commentaries, far surpassing any of the *philosophes*.[41] A woman of her standing would neither

---

[39] Goncourt, *Sophie Arnould*, 83; *Mémoires de la baronne d'Oberkirch sur la cour de Louis XVI et la société française avant 1789*, ed. Suzanne Burkard (Paris, 1989), 183. For the Abbé Galiani's comments on the incident, see Fernando Galiani and Louise d'Épinay, *Correspondance* (5 vols., Paris, 1992–7), II, 116.

[40] AOp., LAS Arnould 32, fo. 3: autobiographical fragment. For the meaning of 'belong[ing] to the king', see below.

[41] See above, p. 21.

dream of entering a coffee-house, nor stand much of a chance of being invited into Paris's classier salons. So, instead, she held court herself. Her residence on the cul de sac du Dauphin near the Louvre (the same street, coincidentally, where Madame Deschamps had been born) became a kind of breezy and bawdy meeting-point for writers and playwrights, wits and jokers, intellectuals and artists.[42] Figures from the leading ranks of the theatre and the *philosophe* movement such as Marmontel, Helvétius, Neufchateau, Linguet, Favart, Dorat and Beaumarchais were regulars (and, improbably, Jean-Jacques Rousseau an occasional guest).[43] Other figures from the intellectual world also attended, such as the brilliant young architect Bélanger (who became her lover in the early 1770s), plus a flotilla of up-and-coming marquis, including the prince de Ligne.[44] There were artists too: Greuze, who painted her portrait,[45] Carmontelle, Houdon and others. 'People say', reported a journalist, 'that Mlle Arnould is not out of place in good company because in her home even bad company becomes good.'[46] Her quips and her repartee became stock items in the newspaper columns of the day. In 1778, she was honoured to receive a personal visit from Voltaire on the great man's swansong return to Paris, an extraordinary accolade from the patron saint of Enlightenment. Characteristically, she swapped quips with him.[47]

Although Sophie Arnould's home never received the kind of public scrutiny that Madame Deschamps enjoyed, it is clear that it too was impressive. She was an avid visitor and purchaser at auction sales. Gabriel de Saint-Aubin (Charles-Germain's brother) captured her visually at one such event, characteristically cracking a joke.[48] She was a woman of taste who had a passion for collection. The sale of many of her possessions in 1778 would reveal paintings by Sébastien Ricci, Salvator Rosa, Boullogne

[42] For the Arnould salon, see e.g. Goncourt, *Sophie Arnould*, 121–2.

[43] For Rousseau's involvement, see his *Correspondance*, ed. R. A. Leigh (52 vols., Oxford, 1981–98), XXVIII, 322.

[44] For the Bélanger relationship, see Jean Stern, *François-Joseph Bélanger, architecte des Menus-Plaisirs, premier architecte du comte d'Artois* (Paris, 1930), and Roger Wahl, *La folie de Saint-James, notamment d'après les 'secrets' de Bachaumont* (Paris 1955). For de Ligne, see Prince Charles-Joseph de Ligne, *Fragments de l'histoire de ma vie*, ed. Jérôme Vercruysse (2 vols., Paris, 2000), I, 194, 291n.

[45] The Wallace Collection owns what is often adjudged to be a portrait by Greuze of Sophie Arnould (call-mark P403). This is shown here, Figure 3. However, the painting is classified currently as 'Portrait of a Lady'. Another portrait by Greuze (P413) is adjudged to be of Sophie Arnould.

[46] Cited in Trouilleux, *N'oubliez pas Iphigénie*, 84; Goncourt, *Sophie Arnould*, 122n.

[47] For the Voltaire visit, *Lettres historiques, politiques et critiques sur les événemens qui se sont passés depuis 1778 jusqu'à présent* (18 vols., Paris, 1788–94), I, 48–9; and Goncourt, *Sophie Arnould*, 123n.

[48] *Gabriel de Saint-Aubin, 1724–80*, ed. Colin B. Bailey (New York), 280–1.

and Boucher, Beauvais tapestries and enough cupboardsful of choice porcelain to rejoice the iconoclastic heart of a Madame Deschamps.[49]

Sophie Arnould lived a life of extraordinary freedom and material pleasures compared with the fortunes of other women in this period. The protection and patronage of well-placed lovers counted for a lot in this, as did the care she took to cultivate a media image. So too did her status as what was called a *fille du roi* (a 'king's girl' might be one way of putting it). The women attached to the Paris Opéra enjoyed an important set of privileges. As Mercier regretfully noted, a young woman had only 'to set her foot on the boards (*planches*) of the Opéra' to escape paternal or marital authority or even normal policing procedures. A *fille du roi* received the *privilège des planches*, the liberty of the boards. The monarch stood *in loco parentis*, and their special royal protection was symbolised by the fact that they took orders from the (improbably named) Gentlemen of the Bedchamber.[50] As one of the indignant creditors of Arnould's former colleague, Madame Deschamps, expostulated, this was 'a world like no other [in which] nature, and paternal and marital power have lost their rights'.[51]

Royal protection allowed these women to engage in illicit sexual relationships without the kind of police repression that was the rule for normal Parisian prostitutes. In fact, the police gave them a wide berth so that they could concentrate on common prostitutes. Suspicious of too much boundary-crossing, the police also liked the idea that aristocratic vice could be kept segregated from plebeian virtue. The wider context probably counts for something here: from the middle decades of the century, King Louis XV was becoming a serial sexual predator, and from 1768 had as his official mistress a woman, Madame du Barry, who was widely believed once to have been a denizen of the finest brothels.[52] This set an example of loose morals that was eagerly followed by the Gentlemen of the Bedchamber, a louche crowd at the best of times. This may also help to explain that the usual rite of passage on entry to the Opéra, in many cases of girls in their early teens, was defloration. This was very

---

[49] For the sale inventory, see Emile Dacier, *Catalogues de ventes et livrets de salons illustrés par Gabriel de Saint-Aubin* (11 vols., Paris, 1909–21), VIII: *Natoire et Arnould (1778)*.

[50] The system is well described in Bénabou, *La prostitution et la police des moeurs*, 109ff ('Les "demoiselles de spectacle"' (Mercier is cited at 110). See too Gaston Maugras, *Les comediens hors la loi* (Paris, 1887), inc. 216ff, specifically on Arnould; and 'Mémoires de J. C. P. Lenoir' (1790), in Vincent Milliot, *Un policier des Lumières* (Paris, 2011), 505.

[51] This was the architect and designer Blanchard who launched a suit against her for unpaid bills in 1760. See Capon and Yve-Plessis, *Fille d'Opéra*, 162–5.

[52] For an overview of the king's sex-life and his illegitimate offspring, see M. Antoine, *Louis XV* (Paris, 1989), 484ff, 507ff, 842ff; and for Mme du Barry, 886ff. For the public scandals aroused by tales of the private lives of king and courtiers, see Sarah Maza, *Private Lives and Public Affairs. The Causes Célèbres of Pre-Revolutionary France* (Berkeley, 1993); and *Dictionnaires des vies privées (1722–1842)*, ed. Olivier Ferret et al. (Oxford, 2012).

often at the hands of the ballet-master of the institution – from 1748 to 1768, this was the famous dancer Jean-Barthélemy Lany, notorious for having sold his own sister into prostitution.[53] Sophie Arnould's parents, who tried to keep their daughter chaste, were easily thwarted by predatory aristocratic galants such as the comte de Lauragauais, and they had no recourse either against that daughter if she had the *privilège des planches*.

The plot of Beaumarchais's (and Mozart's) *The Marriage of Figaro* (1784), revolves, as we all know, around the wish of Count Almaviva to enjoy the feudal right of the first night with his servant Susannah before she can consummate her marriage with her Figaro. No historian takes seriously any more the idea that such a *droit de seigneur*, or *droit de cuissage*, existed as part of the feudal system in France in the late eighteenth century (or indeed probably ever). That was sheer fantasy.[54] But such a privilege of the first night was very precisely what was systematically claimed by the predatory managers of the Opéra.[55] A man of the theatre like Beaumarchais could simply not be unaware of the practice: he was a close friend of Sophie Arnould (and indeed an early lover of the precociously promiscuous daughter of her fellow artiste, Madame Deschamps).[56]

One author, writing in 1752, set out how things worked once virginity had been disposed of:

> A girl only has to be young to be presented to the eager eyes of the public dressed in the costume of the chorus or decked out by the wardrobe. They arrive on the stage, stay there two hours doing nothing and walk out covered in eulogies ... This dumb [but beautiful] actress attracts the attention of a young foreigner or an old financier. She gathers she pleases him, she is offered rent for several months which she accepts; there are some discussions and haggling and a price is fixed; she becomes a kept woman.[57]

This crucible of operatic talent thus became, as another author put it, 'a sanctuary consecrated to the sons of Venus and an asylum for libertinage in which by means of royal privilege vice is shielded from the punishment it

---

[53] Of Lany's claims on Madame Deschamps, police spies noted that paying the *droit d'entrée* 'cost her little, for she was already well broken in': Piton, *Paris sous Louis XV*, v, 98. See too *ibid.*, v, 122. This could have been true of others: see for example the police comment on the possibility of a potential mistress at the Opéra being a virgin: 'la chose n'est pas impossible; elle n'est pas française'(!): *ibid.*, III, 190. On the whole sexual ecology of the Opéra, see Robert Muchembled, *Les ripoux des Lumières. Corruption policière et révolution* (Paris, 2011), esp. 279ff, and Lennard R. Berlanstein, *Daughters of Eve: A Cultural History of French Theatre Women from the Old Regime to the Fin de Siècle* (2001), esp. ch. 2, 33ff.

[54] Alain Boureau, *Le droit de cuissage. La fabrication d'un mythe, XIIIe–XXe siècles* (Paris, 1995).

[55] In this, they were following the example of pimps generally: see 'Instructions pour un homme qui veut devenir ... maquereau', in *Correspondance de Mme Gourdan, dite la Comtesse* (orig. 1783), ed. Jean Hervez (Paris, 1967), 185: 'il ne faut pas oublier qu'on a droit de cuissage'.

[56] Cf. Maurice Lever, *Pierre-Augustin Caron de Beaumarchais* (3 vols., Paris, 1997), I, 34, 293, etc. For Beaumarchais and Deschamps the younger, see Piton, *Paris sous Louis XV*, III, 201. Beaumarchais comes up frequently in the biographies of Arnould and in the *Arnoldiana*.

[57] [F. A. Chevrier], *Les ridicules du siècle* (1752), 65.

deserves' or else 'an inexhaustible pool of public incontinence, a harem, a bazaar in which the Empire's grandees procure their slaves'.[58] Effectively, the Opéra was a prostitute training ground and support group operating under royal protection.

The *filles d'Opéra* were thrust towards wealthy lovers by the economics of a career in theatre. A police enquiry in the early 1750s on the marital state of women attached to the Opéra revealed that, of those between the ages of seventeen and forty, all but two had a lover – and the two who did not, the police recorded, were 'extremely ugly'.[59] Over the ten years of her rather erratic service in the chorus of the Opéra, Madame Deschamps earned wages amounting in total to 66 livres (three eighteenth-century pounds sterling). Yet, on one occasion when she needed to make an impression, she turned up for work with a dress covered in 100,000 livres of diamonds and shoe-buckles estimated at 20,000 livres.[60] Diamonds really were a girl's – that is, a *catin*'s – best friend. Sophie Arnould was one of the stars of the company, but her annual salary was, with supplements, only around 4,000 livres, roughly that of a middling lawyer.[61] She too, needless to say, lived way beyond the station her salary commanded. In such cases, lovers filled the gap.

The singers of the Opéra were thus caught up in a spider's web of sexual libertinage dominated by the very wealthiest males in court and urban society, from princes of the Blood and old nobles to bankers and financiers through to members of the administrative, military and indeed ecclesiastical elites. Louis XV, who set the tone for this, did his best to keep his own sexual affairs private.[62] With the aristocracy, a quite different set of values obtained. No secrecy here. On the contrary. They lived a life of conspicuous consumption, in which the display of a mistress covered in diamonds from top to toe, living in splendour in her own apartment and riding about town in the fanciest of carriages redounded to the credit in which they were held by their peers and, allegedly, their inferiors too. In this distinctive sexual ecology, opera dancers and singers were prime meat. Realising that their asset was volatile, the men often allowed their mistresses to take ancillary lovers secretly and on the side

---

[58] *Le Vol plus haut, ou l'espion des principaux théâtres de la capitale* (Memphis, 1784), 21 (sanctuary); D. L. Turmeau de la Morandière, *Représentations à M. le Lieutenant Général de Police de Paris sur les courtisanes à la mode et les demoiselles du bon ton* (Paris, 1760), 11.

[59] Bénabou, *La prostitution et la police des moeurs*, 110.

[60] For this incident, whose telling was much replicated, see Piton, *Paris sous Louis XV*, V, 120.

[61] Bénabou, *La prostitution et la police des moeurs*, 371 (Deschamps), 339 (general salary levels). The comparison with a lawyer is from Berlanstein, *Daughters of Eve*, 30. Cf. Goncourt, *Sophie Arnould*, 116–19. For the Opéra incident, see Piton, *Paris sous Louis XV*, V, 96.

[62] Louis XV was probably moved this way by the disruptive political influence caused by Louis XIV's decision to legitimize his illegitimate children. See above, n. 52.

so long as they themselves stayed the 'Monsieur', as it was called, the main man.[63] Even so, they did risk ridicule by being made a fool of by their mistresses (especially given the goldfish bowl atmosphere in which these relationships took place). One imagines that the financier Gaillard de La Bouexière and his soiled coffee-cups would say amen to that.[64] Although the cards were stacked against the women, they also retained leeway because the men involved often fell in love with their mistresses, and did the silly things that lovers do.

Having lost her chastity on entering their profession, a *fille d'Opéra* forewent any chance of a respectable life. Unsurprisingly, most had an eye on the main chance and used their status as sexual free agents to their advantage, often affecting a cynical and hard-headed approach to their sexual business. Physical attraction did not rule out the need for business sense: on the contrary in fact. Self-auctioning for favour between two rival male bidders was not uncommon, for example. The women would drag their lovers to the notary, to regularise establishment costs and monthly allowances and other perks.[65] This was all the more understandable in the context of the risks and dangers that were part of their working conditions. The fact that both Deschamps and Arnould were faced with bankruptcy on several occasions during their career shows that their situation involved living at the limit of or beyond their means. This left them highly exposed when relationships terminated and the money dried up.

Furthermore, although the status of opera singers as *filles du roi* spared them some of the indignities which were still routinely meted out to actresses, they were tarred with the same brush. The church formally held that actresses were living in a state of sin which precluded them from receiving the sacraments. 'Any mother would prefer her daughter in the grave rather than on the stage', had been Bishop Bossuet's cheerfully categorical statement – which was not so very far from the view of Jean-Jacques Rousseau in fact.[66] Unless they formally renounced their status, actresses could not marry either, or have their children baptised as normal offspring. If they died, they would not receive a proper burial nor be buried in consecrated soil. These archaic prohibitions were in some respects worse than the treatment meted out to African slaves in

---

[63] The argot among courtesans: Bénabou, *La prostitution et la police des moeurs*, 331.

[64] Piton, *Paris sous Louis XV*, is absolutely full of examples of love's follies.

[65] Bénabou, *La prostitution et la police des moeurs*, 332ff, and Muchembled, *Les ripoux des Lumières*, 281, 289, for such arrangements. For the example of Sophie Arnould and the prince d'Hénin, see Goncourt, *Sophie Arnould*, 68n; and Berlanstein, *Daughters of Eve*, 51. See too examples in Piton, *Paris sous Louis XV*, III, 282, V, III, etc.

[66] Maugras, *Les comédiens hors la loi*, 186ff; for Bossuet, see Paul Friedland, *Political Actors. Representation, Bodies and Theatricality in the Age of the French Revolution* (Ithaca, 2002), 18. For Rousseau, see above, p. 13.

France's Caribbean colonies.[67] Yet they were fully upheld over the century. Archbishop de Saint-Albin, for example, one of Madame Deschamps's clients as we have seen, and on police files as a sexual voyeur, was an utter rigorist in this regard.[68]

In addition, the *filles d'Opéra* had hovering over them the most ignominious and humiliating of disgraces. On one occasion, after refusing to perform at the royal court at Fontainebleau, Sophie Arnould was within a whit of being imprisoned by a *lettre de cachet* issued by Louis XV's mistress, Madame du Barry. She would have gone to La Salpêtrière, the grim section of the Paris Hôpital Général, where common street-walkers were sent for treatment for syphilis. We know from the traces of her correspondence that survive that she feared ending her days as a down-and-out within this hospital-cum-poorhouse for which, she ironised, 'she did not have much esteem'.[69] Madame Deschamps, by the same token, only avoided imprisonment for debts in 1760 by fleeing Paris and she died in misery four years later in her mid-thirties. Those who flew so high always risked having their wings burned and crashing spectacularly to earth.

Having the *privilège des planches* offered women like Madame Deschamps and Sophie Arnould a degree of protection within the elite Parisian bubble where anything went in terms of sexual frolics; but not enough to avoid them having nightmares about being treated as common prostitutes rather than as high-class courtesans. Both Arnould and Deschamps may well have witnessed the traditional treatment meted out to the most ignominious Parisian prostitutes and procuresses: being paraded through the streets seated backwards on an ass with a crown of straw on their heads and placard round their necks.[70] Being led in a cart through Paris to be transported to a port city and thence banished to Louisiana was another means of deterrence. These traditions of exemplary punishment were dying out in fact, but were still there in the 1750s, and remained in the imagination much longer. And the practice of shaving the heads of imprisoned prostitutes was actually reimposed later in the century. Some of Paris's estimated 20,000–25,000 prostitutes spent their last days in the few magdalen shelters for repentant prostitutes. Some moved onwards

---

[67] David Geggus, private communication.

[68] Maugras, *Les comediens hors la loi*, 211. For the voyeurism, see Piton, *Paris sous Louis XV*, V, 310–11. See above, p. 5.

[69] The La Salpetrière episode is recorded in *Mémoires secrets*, II, 1242. Cf. Goncourt, *Sophie Arnould*, 73–4; and Maugras, *Les comédiens hors la loi*, 222ff. For the Hôpital Général as punishment, see Bénabou, *La prostitution et la police des mœurs*, 414ff. For Arnould's concerns about her end, AOp., LAS Arnould, 3: [if she does not receive aid], 'il me faudra aller mourir à l'Hôpital, et je n'ai pourtant pas une grande estime pour ce château'.

[70] The range of punishments is detailed in Bénabou, *La prostitution et la police des moeurs*: see esp. 19ff (ch. 1, 'La répression'), 63–5, 79ff, 85ff. See too Mercier, *Tableau de Paris*, II, 15–19.

and upwards – into management so to speak – and became procuresses or brothel-keepers. Most seem to have died in penury, however, many in the gutter, some in the final stages of syphilitic illness. [71]

Sophie Arnould was shrewd enough to realise that the highlife had to end and that she had to take precautions against the day that it did. Even in the mid-1760s, critics were complaining that her voice had lost its strength, and that she produced a wheezy effect: 'the most beautiful asthma I ever heard' was the Abbé Galiani's still admiring comment on her singing.[72] She made a comeback in the 1770s and her Iphigénie in 1774, as mentioned, was one of her career highlights. By then, she was mistress of the up-and-coming architect Bélanger. But a few years later, not only had that affair had fallen through, Sophie Arnould was also losing control of the media image that had always won her a favourable reception among Parisian opinion. This was partly about diva rivalries within the Opéra and partly due to a battle between rival literary cabals. Also significant was the sexual relationship that she formed with a group of other singers in the Opéra, notably one of the new generation of Opéra stars, Mademoiselle de Raucourt, who became a rallying point for lesbianism. A wave of salacious and highly critical newspaper reports highlighted the scandal and damaged Sophie's reputation.[73]

Partly too, however, Sophie Arnould was just getting old – old for life as a *fille d'Opéra* in any case. She was in her thirties, and her looks were fading faster than her voice. Women such as she, she admitted 'were like weathercocks; they only stop when they get rusty'.[74] She was getting rusty. She stopped. Voltaire's visit to her home in 1778 was a crowning glory. She was already winding up her affairs for retirement with a sale of her finest possessions. She took formal retirement from the Opéra, with a royal pension of 4,000 livres a year. It was said she was occasionally called out for private performances at Versailles, where the new queen, Marie Antoinette, was a fan. Her louche salon-like gatherings continued.

---

[71] In 1778, *la tonte* (head-shaving) was reimposed: Bénabou, *La prostitution et la police des moeurs*, 62–3. Restif de la Bretonne guessed 20,000 prostitutes in the 1780s, and Bénabou endorses this approximate figure (p. 323). For magdalen shelters, *ibid.*, 89ff; and for the dangers of venereal disease, *ibid.*, esp. ch. 8 ('Le "danger vénérien": un mythe collectif?'), 407ff.

[72] [Grimm], *Correspondance littéraire*, IX, 16 (May 1770: asthma). On the decline of her career, Goncourt, *Sophie Arnould*, 98–9; C. Pougin de Saint-Aubin, *Correspondance littéraire de Karlsruhe (1766–8)*, ed. J. Schlobach (Paris, 1995), 16 Sept. 1766; Jean-François La Harpe, *Correspondance littéraire* (4 vols., Paris, 1801), I, 418; *Mémoires secrets*, I, 480 (16 June 1765), II, 636 (4 Dec. 1766), II, 839 (1 Jan. 1768), II, 1073 (5 Feb. 1769), etc.

[73] For the whole Raucourt farrago, see the very outdated but still useful Jean de Reuilly, *La Raucourt et ses amies. Étude historiques des moeurs saphiques au XVIIIe siècle* (Paris, 1909). For primary sources, consult *Le vol plus haut*, 45ff; *Anecdotes échappées*, 185; [Grimm], *Correspondance littéraire*, VI, 159; and *Mémoires secrets*, V, 35–7. And cf. Goncourt, *Sophie Arnould*, 82–4.

[74] *Arnoldiana*, 137.

Her quips and one-liners were still quoted in the news-sheets. But she effectively retired from singing in public.[75]

Private life proved hard for her. She was not in the gutter but in the final years of her life she came close to it. Her life was tough.[76] The Revolution of 1789 brought a massive reduction in her state pension due to political upheavals and monetary fiasco. She sent her sons to the Jacobin Club, of which she was an avowed enthusiast (though she later switched her sympathies to Bonaparte). One son went on to do well in the army, while the other became a government clerk.[77] But the break-up of her daughter's marriage and then her daughter's death meant that Sophie became a child-burdened single grandparent.

Artistic talent, good looks, sex and singing plus substantial media savvy had been the means by which Sophie Arnould had achieved glory, adoration, adulation and social promotion to celebrity level. These had gone; but the friendship networks that had supported them survived; and they proved vital. She proved adept at milking assistance out of ex-lovers. The prince d'Hénin died at the guillotine but remembered her in his will. Lauraguais was a constant support. So was Bélanger, with whom she remembered 'happy days and happy nights'. 'I can now no longer count on either your head or your cock', she wrote to him on one occasion, with characteristically tender coarseness, 'but I tell you that I do count and will count eternally on your heart'. Bélanger and his wife, ex-Opéra star Anne-Victoire Dervieux, were generous in her support too.[78]

Fortunately, too, one of Sophie's young enthusiasts in the 1770s, François de Neufchâteau, became minister of the interior in the late 1790s and he fixed her up with an upgraded pension from the Opéra plus lodgings in central Paris.[79] But by then she was very ill, seemingly with cancer of the rectum. She bore her last bouts of illness with stoicism and dignity and some characteristic humour to boot. She now paid for men to look up her skirt, she complained after a visit from the doctors; it had been very different in earlier days. Now, 'thin as a spider', she could only 'sit on my arse like an old monkey' or walk 'with all the elegance and speed of a

---

[75] She alleged she was being convoked to Versailles down to 1788: Goncourt, *Sophie Arnould*, 95. For her retirement arrangements, *ibid.*, 99–100, 111–12, 116.

[76] The correspondence at AOp., LAS Arnould, 1–28, shows her struggling to cope with reduced income and lavish expenditure in the 1770s. The last 150 pages of Goncourt, *Sophie Arnould*, are composed of letters mainly from and sometimes to Arnould from 1789 to her death showing real distress.

[77] Goncourt, *Sophie Arnould*, 194 (sons at Jacobin Club). For one son, see A. Chuquet, 'Constant de Brancas, le fils de Sophie Arnould', in *idem*, *Études d'histoire. 4ᵉ série. Roture et noblesse dans l'armée royale* (Paris, 1911). The other was arrested in early 1794 but soon released and he became a clerk of the Committee of Public Safety: AN F7 4615.

[78] Blanc, *L'amour à Paris*, 185 (Hénin); Goncourt, *Sophie Arnould*, 143.

[79] For her pension, see AN O1 404 (Arnould); Goncourt, *Sophie Arnould*, 179–80. The award letter from Neuchâteau is mentioned in her inventory: AN MC ET VII 561.

tortoise'. As 'poor as a church mouse', she felt that 'love, pleasure and springtime' had all gone out of her life forever, and adjudged herself 'too old for love, but too young to die'.[80] Yet die she did, in 1802, aged sixty-two. On her mantelpiece, fittingly enough considering this final chapter of her life, the executors of her will found 'a small statue representing Love and Friendship'. It was, they noted, 'slightly cracked'.[81]

'Let us hope we have no more tyrants [she was referring to Robespierre] and no more ministers to combat' wrote, in one of her final letters, this rather extraordinary libertine whose life had combined the identities of actress, courtesan and prostitute. Mercier, as we noted above, had evoked the vagaries of fate and fortune for *ministres et catins*.[82] The ever-passionate *doyenne des catins* had been in terminal free-fall in the Revolutionary decade, victim of the political vagaries of *ministres* and tyrants. *Ministres* always tend to win out over *catins*.

The French Revolution was hard for single women. Olwen Hufton taught us this many years ago, although she also noted their resilience, which was certainly a feature of the last decades of Sophie Arnould's life.[83] It is tempting to leave the story there. Yet if this particular actress and courtesan hit the rocks in the Revolutionary maelstrom, far away from the sparks of proto-feminist action, other women with her kind of profile spectacularly did not. For let us go back to the four foundational French feminists of the 1790s that I highlighted earlier and scratch the surface of their pre-Revolutionary identities. In fact, although reading current historiography one would scarcely suspect the fact, these younger women were very similar to Sophie Arnould.[84] Olympe de Gouges, woman of the theatre to her finger-tips, was a published and performed dramatist who ran her own private company in which we can expect her to have acted. Etta Palm came to Paris in the 1780s and lived the life of as a courtesan. Théroigne de Méricourt was courtesan and concert cantatrice. Claire Lacombe was a provincial actress.[85]

So, in other words, these founding parents of French feminism all had a libertine identity prior to the Revolution which echoed that of Sophie Arnould, the actress, cum courtesan, cum prostitute, who is at the heart of this paper. Maybe it is all a glorious coincidence, and certainly

---

[80] Goncourt, *Sophie Arnould*, 238 (skirts), 174 (spider), 251 (monkey, tortoise), 206 (church mouse, springtime), 204 (too young to die).

[81] AN MC ET VII 561 (8 Nov. 1802). Curiously, an abortive inventory had been started but not completed on the same day: AN MC ET IV 938.

[82] Goncourt, *Sophie Arnould*, 155; for Mercier, see above, p. 12.

[83] Notably in her 'Women in Revolution' and in *Women and the Limits of Citizenship in the French Revolution* (Toronto, 1992).

[84] Blanc, *Les libertines*, does recognise the strand of libertinism. But he does not link it to proto-feminism as here.

[85] See the list of works at n. 15.

against these four women one could probably dredge up some dreary counter-examples. But my instinct as a historian is to say that it was more than coincidence. And that the experience of being an actress and courtesan in pre-Revolutionary France could – and emphatically, in these four high profile cases, did – predispose women in this position into an understanding of and then into a radical critique of the values of the system under which they lived. Such women might float voluptuously in the ether of their own celebrity, it is true, and buy into the values of their aristocratic patrons. But they did so while also being well aware that the conditions under which they operated were in some ways worse than that of Caribbean slaves, and in others more demeaning than that of Figaro's Susanna. And they also knew that if things went badly, their career trajectory would be like falling off a cliff and that they could end their days in a grim shaven-headed world of common street-walking that was treated roughly and toughly, brutally and expeditiously, by the Parisian police.[86]

I am arguing that the contrast between the extremes of life as an eighteenth-century actress – the *splendeurs et misères d'une courtisane* if you like (to adopt the title of one of Balzac's novels)[87] – was instrumental in driving women like Olympe de Gouges, Etta Palm, Théroigne de Méricourt and Claire Lacombe into a radical position of proto-feminism. Furthermore, viewing these women as a kind of female libertine and proto-feminist wave goes broadly with the grain of much recent scholarship on libertinage. Instead of seeing this phenomenon as essentially male and focused on writings, libertinage is increasingly viewed as cross-gender, multiform and incorporating practices as well as discourses.[88] While women like Sophie Arnould had probably never read the pre-Revolutionary proto-feminist texts that in much of the current historiography provide the guidelines for contemporary analysis of the emergence of feminism, she would have felt more than at home in libertine company had she been in the prime of her life in the 1790s.

We have perhaps lost sight of this libertine strand within early Western feminism. Yet even if the reach of the notion of libertinage is expanding in the scholarship, the characteristics of feminism are if anything shrinking. Class and respectability still functioned as a block on communication on both sides of the Channel. The highly limited role in France of women even in the salons they ostensibly ran has

---

[86] See above, p. 28.

[87] The name of Sophie Arnould is often evoked in Balzac's novels in fact as a token of a lost Ancien Régime world of wit and elegance. References to her in *Sarrasine, La Cousine Bette, Scènes de la vie parisienne* and *Physiologie du mariage* may be recovered through Frantext/ARTFL.

[88] See esp. *Libertine Enlightenment*, ed. Cryle and O'Connell, 2ff.

been widely acknowledged. And recent scholarship has underlined how difficult it proved for proto-feminists in England to escape from the hegemony of politeness and the hardening of separate spheres ideology. Firmly embedded within the domestic sphere, English feminists seem also to have been disproportionately influenced by religion, which was more likely to prove a divisive rather than a unifying force. It certainly cut them off from their French sisters. The libertine French feminists I have identified would probably have struggled in the company of precious *salonnières* and *femmes savantes*. They would have been out of their depth with the pious bluestockings and rational Dissenters who crowd the present historiographical landscape of eighteenth-century English feminism.[89]

The gap between the two sides was all the more difficult to bridge once the Revolution got under way. The putative excesses of feminist viragoes and *tricoteuses* were endlessly highlighted by English counter-revolutionary propagandists from Edmund Burke onwards.[90] This made it difficult for English feminists to hold on to support for revolutionary principles with which many at least sympathised. Mary Wollstonecraft for one was open to libertine views, but still in the 1790s saw the theatricality and sensuality of the French as the defects which made them unable to achieve the noble aims of their Revolution.[91] She was as tough on the play-acting of coquettish women as she was on what she saw as the false gallantry of polite males. She certainly would have found it strategically disastrous, in 1790s England, to be thought to be standing shoulder-to-shoulder with such passionate, theatrical, full-blooded libertine women as Sophie Arnould and her kind (and indeed she herself may have found the very prospect fairly horrifying anyway).

Accepting the existence of this largely unsuspected libertine strand within the early history of French feminism also, finally, helps to explain the venom which characterised the opponents of feminism, even on the radical Left in France throughout the 1790s. It counted massively against these arch-proponents of the feminist cause that they could be and were viewed as actresses and prostitutes. For after some deceptively benign and tolerant beginnings, the Revolution was kind to neither sort.

Prostitutes, first, were seen as an affront to the bourgeois domestic order which the Revolution wished to establish. An early, benign tendency to see them as victims of aristocratic lust soon shifted towards a harsher view

---

[89] Felicia Gordon, 'Filles Publiques or Public Women: The Actress as Citizen', in *Women, Gender and Enlightenment*, ed. Knott and Taylor, stands out from the collection by highlighting the link between acting, libertinism and politics.

[90] Besides the works cited above, see T. Furniss, 'Mary Wollstonecraft's French Revolution', in *Cambridge Companion to Mary Wollstonecraft*, ed. C. L. Johnson (Cambridge, 2002).

[91] *Ibid.*, 70; Taylor, *Mary Wollstonecraft*, esp. 198ff, for a discussion of libertinism.

and condemnations of sleeping with enemies of the Revolutionary cause, especially once war and terror were under way.[92] There were round-ups of Parisian prostitutes from autumn 1793 onwards. The one that occurred on the day before the overthrow of Robespierre (26 July 1794/8 Thermidor Year II in the Revolutionary Calendar) roundly declared that 'Virtue is the order of the day' – not the best banner for prostitution to flourish under.[93] Even after the fall of Robespierre, moreover, the prostitute's lot did not improve much. Indeed, such women were increasingly under attack for spreading venereal diseases within the Revolutionary armies.

The attack on prostitutes could only be an attack on courtesans and actresses as well, since the three identities had been so closely associated under the Ancien Régime. In some ways, theatre boomed in the Revolutionary decade: a thousand new plays were written, for example, and fifty new theatres were opened.[94] Yet the status and security of actors and actresses were highly fragile. Reflecting the long-standing religious prejudices against them, it remained unclear whether male actors even were justified to vote or have civil rights. In 1791, the great Revolutionary actor Talma chose to renounce his profession and declare himself of bourgeois status before marrying his mistress and allowing their children to have full civil rights and to be baptised (he resumed as an actor no sooner was the water on his babies' heads dry).[95] As the Revolution became increasingly radical, moreover, just being an actor was problematic. Most of the celebrated actors of the Comédie-Française were imprisoned in late 1793, and only released after the fall of Robespierre.

What made the acting profession particularly suspect in the Terror was the acceptance within Jacobin ideology of the Rousseau-ist critique of theatre developed since the 1750s. Actors and actresses were seen as simply not conforming to the Revolutionary values of transparency. At some level, if one was performing a Revolutionary identity one was in essence a counter-Revolutionary. 'The princesses of the theatre are no better then the princesses of Austria', Robespierre had once proclaimed. 'Both are equally depraved and both should be treated with equal severity.'[96] For

---

[92] Bénabou, *La prostitution et la police des moeurs*, 502ff. See too the works by Susan P. Conner: 'Politics, Prostitution and the Pox in Revolutionary Paris, 1789–99', *Journal of Social History*, 22 (1988), 221–40; 'Public Virtue and Public Women: Prostitution in Revolutionary Paris', *Eighteenth-Century Studies*, 28 (1994); 'Napoleon's Courtesans, Citoyennes and Cantinières', *Members' Bulletin of the Napoleonic Society of America*, 73 (2003), 21–5.

[93] Bénabou, *La prostitution et la police des moeurs*, 428.

[94] S. Maslan, *Revolutionary Acts: Theatre, Democracy, and the French Revolution* (Baltimore, 2005), 15. Also on Revolutionary theatre, see E. Kennedy, *A Cultural History of the French Revolution* (New Haven, 1989); and F. W. J. Hemmings, *Theatre and State in France, 1760–1905* (Cambridge, 1994). Cf. Friedland, *Political Actors*.

[95] M. Carlson, *The Theatre of the French Revolution* (Ithaca, 1966), 80.

[96] Maximilien Robespierre, *Oeuvres complètes* (11 vols., Paris, 1910–2007), X, 101. My thanks to Jeremy Jennings for locating this reference.

performance signified insincerity and artificiality, not truth and virtue. Revolutionary sincerity was supposed to come from the heart. Jacobin ideology was fixated on rooting out evil intentions behind the masks of insincerity – and actors were viewed as suspect as counter-revolutionaries because they performed sincerity and revolutionary commitment. The kind of hybrid identity of performance – and performance of identity – that women like Sophie Arnould, Etta Palm, Olympe de Gouges or Claire Lacombe had had freedom to practise, and which allowed them to cross from courtesan to actress to prostitute, was profoundly un-Jacobin and ultimately un-Revolutionary. Sad to relate, the Revolution was for them the moment that this type of crossing of identities had to stop. Quite as much as their English counterparts, they and their kind were contained within a bourgeois domestic order where crossing was not an option. And in a series of lectures devoted to French crossings, what better moment at which to stop. As now I have.

Transactions of the RHS 23 (2013), pp. 37–73 © Royal Historical Society 2013
doi:10.1017/S0080440113000030

ENTRUSTING WESTERN EUROPE TO THE CHURCH, 400–750*

By Ian Wood

READ 3 FEBRUARY 2012

ABSTRACT. Although there had been substantial donations to the church in the course of the last two centuries of the Roman Empire, the amount of property transferred to the episcopal church and to monasteries in the following two and a half centuries would seem to have been immense. Probably rather more than 30 per cent of the Frankish kingdom was given to ecclesiastical institutions; although the Anglo-Saxon church was only established after 597, it also acquired huge amounts of land, as did the churches of Spain and Italy, although the extent conveyed in the two peninsulas is harder to estimate. The scale of endowments helps explain the occasional criticisms of the extent of church property, and also the secularisations and reallocation of church land, and indeed suggest that the transfer of property out of the control of the church in Francia and England in the eighth century may have been greater than is often assumed. The transfer of land should probably also be seen as something other than a simple change of ownership. Church property provided the economic basis for cult, for the maintenance of clergy, who were unquestionably numerous, and for the poor. In social and economic, as well as religious terms, this marked a major break with the Classical World.

In 1850, the German legal historian Paul Roth published his *Geschichte des Beneficialwesens*, one of the seminal works on the origins of feudalism, which, for him, lay in the secularisation of ecclesiastical land by the early Carolingians.[1] In order to justify this claim he set about estimating the amount of land held by the Frankish church at the start of the eighth century; his conclusion was that around a third of Francia was in

---

* I would like to thank Peter Brown, Mayke de Jong, Penny Goodman, Rosamond McKitterick, Walter Pohl, Helmut Reimitz, and Pauline Stafford for commenting on earlier drafts of this paper. I am also indebted to John Hunt for transforming my maps into something professional.

[1] Paul Roth, *Geschichte des Beneficialwesens von den ältesten Zeiten bis ins zehte Jahrhundert* (Erlangen, 1850), 246–76. There is an acute assessment of Roth's position in the development of the subject in Carl Stephenson, 'The Origin and Significance of Feudalism', *American Historical Journal*, 46, 4 (1941), 788–812. For Roth himself, see the entries by K. von Amira, *Allgemeine Deutsche Biographie*, LIII (Berlin, 1907), 538–49; and A. Thiel, *Neue Deutsche Biographie*, XXII (Berlin, 2005), 108–9.

ecclesiastical hands at the end of the Merovingian period.[2] It is an estimate that was questioned in 1911 by Emile Lesne in the first volume of his great study of ecclesiastical property in France, although the Frenchman was prepared to accept that the church held a third of the land that was under cultivation.[3] Fifty years later, in 1961, David Herlihy attempted to reconcile this figure with his own view that the period between 751 and 825 saw the church's possessions increase from 10 to 30 per cent of the Christian West, by arguing that different kinds of ownership were involved.[4] Perhaps a more significant difference between the two figures is the fact that Roth was talking about Francia alone, whereas Herlihy was talking about Western Europe – and there are extensive areas even within and on the fringes of the Merovingian world, including parts of the Rhineland and Bavaria, where the transfer of land to the church was more a feature of the eighth and ninth centuries than of an earlier period.[5]

Roth's book has been largely forgotten,[6] and his argument about the origins of feudalism has been rendered obsolete by the vast discussion of that subject that has followed.[7] It may well be that he had been oversensitised to the fate of church land as a result of the Napoleonic secularisations, which had been introduced into Germany following the Treaty of Luneville in 1801. Coming from Catholic Munich, this was an

---

[2] Roth, *Geschichte des Beneficialwesens*, 253: 'so wird man den oben aufgestellte Berechnung, dass zu Anfang des achten Jahrhunderts ein Drittheil alles gallischen Grundbesitzes Kirchengut war, gewiss nich übertrieben finden'.

[3] E. Lesne, *Histoire de la propriété ecclésiastique en France* (6 vols., Lille, 1910–43), I, 224: 'On l'a evalué quelquefois au tiers du sol des Gaules. Ce calcul, qui ne repose sur aucune base solide, fait sans doubt aux églises et aux monastères un part trop large. Une vaste étendue du territoire de la Gaule mérovingienne reste en friche. Les moines sont très loin d'avoir pris entière possession de ce sol sans maître qui est censé appartenir au fisc. Mais si l'on fait seulement état des terres exploitées et productives, on admettra facilement que l'Église en ait pu détenir la tierce partie.'

[4] D. Herlihy, 'Church Property on the European Continent 701–1200', *Speculum*, 36 (1961), 81–105, at 87–9. Herlihy provides a useful summary of those who believed that the Carolingian period saw a rapid expansion of church property (Mauer, Lamprecht and von Inama-Sternegg) as against those who argued for a steady growth beginning earlier (Dopsch, Halphen, Bloch and Lot).

[5] For the Rhineland: M. Innes, *State and Society in the Early Middle Ages: The Middle Rhine Valley, 400–1000* (Cambridge, 2000), 40–50; for Bavaria: S. Wood, *The Proprietary Church in the Medieval West* (Oxford, 2006), 33–48.

[6] See P. Fouracre, 'The Use of the Term *Beneficium* in Frankish Sources: A Society Based on Favours?', in *The Languages of Gift in the Early Middle Ages*, ed. W. Davies and P. Fouracre (Cambridge, 2010), 62–88. The conflict between Roth and Georg Waitz is recalled in B. Kasten, 'Economic and Political Aspects of Leases in the Kingdom of the Franks during the Eighth and Ninth Centuries: A Contribution to the Current Debate about Feudalism', in *Feudalism, New Landscapes of Debate*, ed. S. Bagge, M. H. Gelting and T. Lindkvist (Turnhout, 2011), 27–55, at 27.

[7] Not least S. Reynolds, *Fiefs and Vassals. The Medieval Evidence Reinterpreted* (Oxford, 1994).

issue of which he must have been keenly aware. It may be, however, that Roth's observations on ecclesiastical property-holding have been unjustly neglected, and that they might tell us more about general European developments than has been acknowledged. Indeed, it is possible that his conclusions on the extent of church land might be rather more important than his own argument recognised, for the transfer of a third of the land mass of Francia could have had implications far beyond the issue of the questionable origins of feudal tenure; the entrusting of so large a part of the late and post-Roman world could have amounted to a social and economic, as well as a religious, revolution.

I shall, therefore, begin by reassessing the evidence for the amount of property transferred to God and the saints, which is how contemporaries would have understood ecclesiastical institutions, in Gaul and Francia from the fifth to the eighth centuries, before looking at the information from other parts of Western Europe in the post-Roman period. Having attempted a very rough estimate of the scale of church landholding up to the early eighth century (and, given the nature of the evidence, which is extremely patchy, and often comes from biased sources, anything other than a rough estimate is impossible), I shall look at what the transfer of land to churches might actually have entailed, and ask what that might imply for early medieval society and its economy – and thus I shall try to explore the extent to which Christianisation should be seen as affecting the development of Europe outside what is frequently cordoned off as the religious sphere.[8] I shall also attempt to provide some explanation for the tendency among historians, from the nineteenth century down to the present day, to leave the church out of discussions of the early medieval economy, despite Roth and the arguments he engendered, for the problem is historiographical as much as historical. I shall say little about politics, although the period from the fourth to the eighth centuries witnessed a transformation of politics, and not just because of the break-up of the Roman Empire into the successor states, but also because of the increasing involvement of the aristocracy in the church hierarchy and the developing political influence of bishops, abbots and holy men.[9] This undoubtedly had a major impact on many aspects of life in Western Europe, and is not unrelated to the question of the transfer of land. The rising political power of the church has, however, been rather more fully

---

[8] But see now P. Brown, *Through the Eye of a Needle. Wealth, the Fall of Rome, and the Making of Christianity in the West, 350–550 AD* (Princeton, 2012).

[9] C. Rapp, 'The Elite Status of Bishops in Late Antiquity in Ecclesiastical, Spiritual and Social Contexts', *Arethusa*, 33 (2000), 379–99; R. van Dam, 'Bishops and Society', in *Cambridge History of Christianity*, II: *Constantine to c .600*, ed. A. Casiday and F. W. Norris (Cambridge, 2007), 343–66.

recognised than has the acquisition of property, and it is land that forms the core of the present argument.

In making his assessment, Roth cited the evidence of a number of leading monasteries. He reckoned St Denis to be the richest church in Francia – although the fragmentary state of its charters means that this is no more than a hypothesis. There are plausible records for the donation of 36 *villae* to the monastery between 625 and 726,[10] and 46 *loca* were restored to the abbey by Pippin III in 751.[11] These can only have been a fraction of the total holdings. For Roth, St Wandrille had 4,288 *mansi*, or estates, after the secularisations of the eighth century, leading him to estimate its earlier holdings at 7,000 *mansi*. St Germain-des-Prés held 8,000 *mansi* at the start of the ninth century – amounting, according to Guérard, the editor of the monastery's polyptych, to 429,987 hectares (not much short of 1 per cent of the present extent of France); St Riquier, Roth thought, must have been comparable; Luxeuil held 15,000 hectares in the time of Charlemagne; and Fulda owned 15,000 *Hufen* (*villae*).[12] Not all of these figures will stand up to scrutiny; for instance, St Wandrille would seem only to have held 3,964 *mansi*, including those that had been alienated as *precaria* to secular figures.[13]

Yet, if we have to downgrade some of Roth's figures, there are others to be added. In addition to the group of monasteries he looked at, there were a number of other well-endowed houses, among them Chelles, Faremoutiers and Corbie, which was granted a considerable amount of forest land at its foundation, and continued to receive benefactions.[14] In 739, the Provençal aristocrat Abbo gave an enormous amount of property, made up of estates of all sizes, scattered through much of Francia, to his new foundation of Novalesa, now within the borders of Italy, but then in

[10] For the early charters of St Denis, L. Levillain, 'Études sur l'abbaye de Saint-Denis à l'époque mérovingienne', part 1, *Bibliothèque de l'École de Chartes*, 82 (1921), 5–116, part 2, *ibid.*, 86 (1925), 5–99, part 3, *ibid.*, 87 (1926), 20–97, 245–346, part 4, *ibid.*, 91 (1930), 5–56, 264–300; D. Ganz and W. Goffart, 'Charters Earlier than 800 from French Collections', *Speculum*, 65 (1990), 906–32, at 912–14. For the early Carolingian charters of St Denis: R. McKitterick, *Charlemagne. The Formation of a European Identity* (Cambridge, 2008), 197–9. 36 *villae* were given to the monastery between 625 and 726 according to the charters accepted by Pertz as authentic (*Diplomata Imperii*, 1, ed. G. H. Pertz, Monumenta Germaniae Historica (MGH) (Hannover, 1872), 10, 18, 34, 35, 64, 67, 75, 84, 87, 94); M. Roper, 'Wilfrid's Landholdings in Northumbria', in *Saint Wilfrid at Hexham*, ed. D. P. Kirby (Newcastle upon Tyne, 1974), 61–79, at 77 n. 28.

[11] Roper, 'Wilfrid's Landholdings in Northumbria', 65, 77 n. 29.

[12] Roth, *Geschichte des Beneficialwesens*, 249–51.

[13] The error was that of the author of the source and not Roth's: *Gesta Abbatum Fontanellensium*, 11, 3, *Chronique des abbés de Fontenelle*, ed. P. Pradié (Paris, 1999); I. N. Wood, 'Teutsind, Witlaic and the History of Merovingian *Precaria*', in *Property and Power in the Early Middle Ages*, ed. W. Davies and P. Fouracre (Cambridge, 1995), 31–52, at 38–9.

[14] L. Levillain, *Examen des chartes mérovingiennes et carolingiennes de l'abbaye de Corbie* (Paris, 1902), 42, 45–8, 199, 214–17; Roper, 'Wilfrid's Landholdings in Northumbria', 65.

the Frankish kingdom.[15] He had amassed this from thirty-four different people.[16]

Alongside the rich foundations, we need to factor in the numerous small communities. The number of Merovingian monasteries was considerable (Figure 1). In 1976, Hartmut Atsma estimated that there were around 220 in Gaul at the end of the sixth century, divided evenly between the north and south of the region; he reckoned that by the early eighth century there were around 550, of which over 330 were in the north, meaning that the seventh century had seen around 230 new foundations in the north and 90 in the south.[17] Moreover, in general, northern foundations tended to be very much more lavishly endowed than their southern counterparts.[18] And not only were they well endowed at the moment of foundation, but the cartularies of such houses as St Gallen, Wissembourg and Fulda show that they continued to attract donations, not least from laymen and women. The transfer of land to monastic houses in the Merovingian period must, therefore, have been very sizeable.

But it is the episcopal holdings that radically strengthen Roth's case. Indeed, in merely noting that there were 112 bishoprics in Francia, he rather undersold his hand, and not just because Louis Duchesne reckoned there were 130 dioceses in *l'ancienne Gaule*.[19] Every bishop controlled a substantial amount of land that had been given to the church, much of it no doubt in small bequests.[20] Charters and wills, almost all of them, admittedly, preserved in later copies, and episcopal *Gesta*, or diocesan histories, give us some indication of the possible scale of episcopal donations to churches, some of which, of course, were monastic. There are twelve wills of the Merovingian period, all of which transfer land to one church or another. Four of them, those of Caesarius,[21] Remigius of Rheims and Bertram and Hadoind of Le Mans, are episcopal.[22] Three of these were preserved in diocesan histories dealing with the Merovingian

---

[15] P. Geary, *Aristocracy in Provence* (Stuttgart, 1985), 1. Geary does not attempt to estimate the amount of land actually held by Abbo: *ibid.*, 84.

[16] *Ibid.*, 84.

[17] H. Atsma, 'Les monastères urbains du Nord de la Gaule', *Revue d'Histoire de l'Église de France*, 62 (1976), 163–87, at 168.

[18] P. Brown, *The Rise of Western Christendom*, 2nd edn (2003), 254; see also 221, 227.

[19] Roth, *Geschichte des Beneficialwesens*, 253; L. Duchesne, *Les fastes épiscopaux de l'ancienne Gaule* (3 vols., Paris, 1894–1915).

[20] See Council of Orléans, I (511), cc. 5, 15, and Council of Carpentras (527), ed. J. Gaudemet and B. Basdevant, *Les canons des conciles mérovingiens (VIe–VIIe siècles)*, Sources Chrétiennes 353–4 (Paris, 1989).

[21] *Césaire d'Arles, Œuvres monastiques*, I: *Œuvres pour les moniales*, ed. A. de Vogüé and J. Courreau, Sources Chrétiennes 345 (Paris, 1988), 360–97.

[22] U. Nonn, 'Merowingische Testamente: Studien zum Fortleben einer römischen Urkundenform im Frankenreich', *Archiv für Diplomatik*, 18 (1972), 1–129; Geary, *Aristocracy in Provence*.

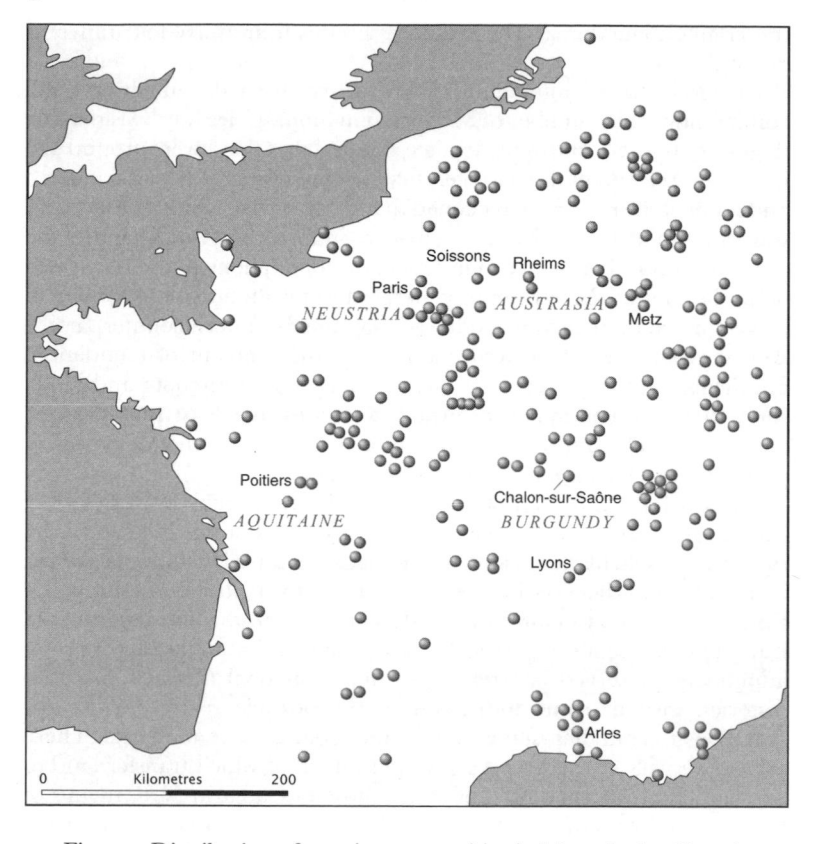

Figure 1 Distribution of ascetic communities in Merovingian Francia

and Carolingian periods, which provide crucial evidence, depicting, as they do, the steady build up (and loss) of ecclesiastical land. For instance, Flodoard's tenth-century *History of the Church of Rheims* includes a version of the will of Remigius, although a more authentic text, listing fewer properties, is contained in Hincmar's ninth-century *vita* of the saint.[23] Remigius, as the bishop who baptised the Merovingian King Clovis, has a particular historical importance, but he appears not to have been especially wealthy.[24] Certainly, his wealth does not compare with that of Bertram, whose testament, along with that of Hadoind, is conserved in

[23] Hincmar, *Vita Remigii*, c. 32, ed. B. Krusch, MGH, SRM 3 (Hannover, 1896).
[24] M.-C. Isaïa, *Remi de Reims* (Paris, 2010).

the *Actus pontificum Cenomannis in urbe degentium*.[25] The extraordinary will of Bertram, from 616, disposes of around 120 units of property, including 74 *villae* and 45 smaller settlements, scattered across most of the length and breadth of the Merovingian kingdom, amounting in all, in the estimate of Cabrol and Leclerq, to some 300,000 hectares;[26] that would seem to be a little over a half of 1 per cent of the land mass of Francia. Even in the Roman period, there had been vast disparities in the wealth of individual dioceses;[27] gifts such as Bertram's must have led to yet more inequality.

The scale of Bertram's landholdings far exceeds that set out in any other surviving Merovingian will, even though he was not a member of the highest aristocracy; much of his wealth derived from his loyalty to Chlothar II.[28] One cannot regard his endowment of the church of Le Mans as being in any way ordinary, though he was surely not the only churchman to be rewarded for loyalty to a king. More important, we should remember that bishops were expected to give property to the churches over which they presided. This is most apparent from a tale in Gregory of Tours, who recalls that his uncle, Nicetius of Lyons, left nothing to the basilica in which he was buried, much to the disgust of the priest, who complained bitterly when the deceased bishop's will was made public. Shortly after, the dead saint appeared, explained that in bequeathing his body to the church he had given his most valuable possession, and, having pummelled the priest's throat, vanished.[29] Clearly there was an expectation that bishops would endow their funerary churches, even if they left nothing to any other church.

We can get some impression of the bequests not only from the diplomatic evidence, but also from various saints' Lives and diocesan histories. In addition to those already mentioned, there is the *Gesta Pontificum Autissiodorensium* which provides particularly detailed descriptions of the property and goods left to the church by

---

[25] *Actus pontificum Cenomannis in urbe degentium*, ed. G. Busson and A. Ledru, Archives historiques du Maine, 2 (Le Mans, 1901), 101–41; also F. Cabrol and H. Leclerq, *Dictionnaire d'archéologie chrétienne et de liturgie*, X (Paris, 1931), cols. 1490–152; M. Weidemann, *Das Testament des Bischofs Berthramn von Le Mans vom 27. März 616* (Mainz, 1986); W. Goffart, *The Le Mans Forgeries* (Cambridge, MA, 1966), 263–4.

[26] The most recent description of the territory is to be found in Weidemann, *Das Testament des Bischofs Berthramn*, 79–81; the assessment of scale comes from C. Leclercq, 'L'épiscopat de saint Bertrand', in Cabrol and Leclerq, *Dictionnaire d'archéologie chrétienne et de liturgie*, X, col. 1495: 'l'évêque possédait peut-être plus de 300,000 hectares, la moitié d'un département français comme celui de la Sarthe, y compris des maisons au Mans, à Jublains, à Paris et à Bordeaux'.

[27] A. H. M. Jones, 'The Western Church in the Fifth and Sixth Centuries', in *Christianity in Britain 300–700*, ed. M. W. Barley and R. P. C. Hanson (Leicester, 1968), 9–18, at 11–12.

[28] Weidemann, *Das Testament des Bischofs Berthramn*, 86–92.

[29] Gregory of Tours, *Liber in Gloria Patrum*, VIII 5, ed. B. Krusch, MGH, SRM 1, 2 (Hannover, 1885).

Bishops Desiderius and Hainmar.[30] It also provides an account of the secularisation of the property of the church of Auxerre under Charles Martel and Pippin III, as a result of which the bishop was left with only a hundred *mansi*.[31] The *Life of Desiderius of Cahors* contains both a citation of part of the saint's will, and also the text of a *donatio*, which conferred 91 *villae* or portions of them (a figure similar to that of Bertram's donation) to various churches, including the monastery in which the bishop wished to be buried.[32]

Once again, however, we are not just dealing with the property conveyed by two or three remarkably rich individuals. To judge from the twenty-three Frankish dioceses for which we have episcopal lists, the average number of bishops per diocese in the period from the mid-fifth to the mid-eighth century was around twenty, which at 130 dioceses makes more than 2,500 appointments.[33] If every bishop left even a small number of estates to his church, that would have added up to a considerable amount of property. While some bishops may, like Nicetius, have left little or nothing (though he may well have endowed churches other than that where he was buried), the *Life of Desiderius of Cahors* shows that Bertram of Le Mans was not unique in his generosity.

In addition to the land held by the bishops and monasteries of Merovingian Francia, there was also the apparently extensive patrimony held by the papacy in southern Gaul. We learn of this particularly from Gregory the Great's dealings with his agents in Provence, Candidus and the *patricius* Dynamius, who was specifically entrusted with oversight of the papal estates of the region, and who is known to have sent 400 *solidi* raised from those estates to the pope.[34] This is a considerable sum, and suggests that the bishops of Rome held a sizeable amount of land in the region.

These details imply extensive ecclesiastical landholding, and they do so without reference to the problematic issue of the private churches, *oratoria in agro proprio*, which should no doubt be understood as the property of the estate owners, but which were also dedicated to God.[35] Yet, even

---

[30] *Gesta Pontificum Autissiodorensium*, cc. 20, 27, ed. M. Sot, *Les gestes des évêques d'Auxerre* (2 vols., Paris, 2006).

[31] *Ibid.*, c. 32.

[32] *Vita Desiderii*, cc. 30, 34, ed. B. Krusch, MGH, SRM 4 (Hannover, 1902).

[33] Duchesne, *Fastes épiscopaux*, I, 3–4, lists the episcopal lists. See also S. Liger, 'L'écrit à l'époque merovingienne d'après la correspondance de Didier, évêque de Cahors (630–55)', *Studi medievali*, 33 (1992), 799–823, at 810, for appointments in the second half of the period.

[34] Gregory I, *Register*, III 33, VI 56, ed. P. Ewald and L. M. Hartmann, MGH, Epp. I (2 vols., Berlin, 1896–9); see also B. Dumézil, 'Le patrice Dynamius et son réseau: culture aristocratique et transformation des pouvoirs autour de Lérins dans la seconde moitié du VIe siècle', in *Lérins, une île sainte de l'Antiquité au Moyen Âge*, ed. Y. Codou and M. Lauwers (Turnhout, 2009), 167–94, at 180–1.

[35] See L. Pietri, 'Les oratoria in agro proprio dans la Gaule de l'Antiquité tardive: un aspect des rapports entre potentes et évêques', in *Aux origines de la paroisse rurale en Gaule*

without including the proprietary churches, it is clear that the Frankish church was very well endowed. If the assessments of the holdings of St Germain and Bertram of Le Mans are correctly calculated as constituting respectively 1 and 0.5 per cent of France, it is difficult to see how Roth's estimate of 30 per cent of Francia being in the hands of the church by the start of the eighth century can be an exaggeration; Lesne's modification, that Roth's assessment could be correct if one limited the calculation to the cultivated area of the kingdom, looks conservative (and in any case one type of land which was held extensively by the northern monasteries was forest).[36] At least for the heartlands of Francia, Roth's estimate looks more likely than Herlihy's.

We can get a glimpse of what this meant for one diocese, if we look back from the Carolingian period. Between 809 and 812, archbishop Leidradus of Lyons wrote to Charlemagne to tell him of his achievements since his appointment in 797; he had restored the cathedral and the episcopal churches as well as the monasteries of his see for as bishop he was responsible for them all, except for those which held specific exemptions. In so doing, he had left the religious free to carry out their duty of performing the divine service[37] – for the churches, monastic and secular, were above all powerhouses of prayer.[38] The liturgy was new, reflecting the Carolingian reforms, but the majority of the houses were old, having been conveyed to God and his saints before the days of Charles Martel. The same must have been true of the forty-three churches to be found in Metz in the days of Chrodegang.[39] Charlemagne's state relied upon the likes of Leidradus, for its administration, its armies and for its religion; underpinning them all was the transfer of property and wealth to the church in the previous 300 years.[40]

méridionale (Ive–IXe siècles), ed. C. Delaplace (Paris, 2005), 235–42. See also the massive survey of Wood, *The Proprietary Church*, 9–244.

[36] C. Wickham, 'European Forests in the Early Middle Ages: Landscape and Land Clearance', *L'ambiente vegetale nell'alto medioevo*, Settimane di Studio 37 (Spoleto, 1990), 479–548, reprinted in idem, *Land and Power. Studies in Italian and European Social History, 400–1200* (1994), 155–99.

[37] Leidradus, *Epistola ad Carolum*, ed. E. Dümmler, MGH, Epp. 4 (Berlin, 1895), 542–4. See M. de Jong, 'Charlemagne's Church', in *Charlemagne: Empire and Society*, ed. J. Story (Manchester, 2005), 103–35, at 103–4.

[38] The phrase comes from Brown, *The Rise of Western Christendom*, 219–31.

[39] T. Klauser, 'Eine Stationsliste der Metzer Kirche aus dem 8. Jahrhunderts, wahrscheinlich ein Werk Chrodegangs', *Ephemerides Liturgicae*, 44 (1930), 162–93; M. Claussen, *The Reform of the Frankish Church. Chrodegang of Metz and the Regula Canonicorum in the Eighth Century* (Cambridge, 2004), 276–86.

[40] For the central position of the church in the Carolingian world, see de Jong, 'Charlemagne's Church'; idem, 'The State of the Church: Ecclesia and Early Medieval State Formation', in *Die frühmittelalterliche Staat – europäische Perspektiven*, ed. W. Pohl and V. Wieser (Vienna, 2009), 241–54; and idem, 'Carolingian Monasticism: The Power of Prayer', in *The New Cambridge Medieval History*, II, c. 700 – c. 900, ed. R. McKitterick (Cambridge, 1995), 622–53.

A more challenging question is whether the extent of ecclesiastical landholding in any other part of western Europe was remotely comparable to that in the Merovingian kingdom. Nowhere else provides us with documentation as rich for the period before the mid-eighth century. One might have expected the church in Italy to have been rather better endowed than that in Francia. The surviving evidence, however, suggests otherwise. By comparison with Atsma's figure of 220 monasteries in Gaul by the end of the sixth century, Jenal knew of only 100 in Italy (Figure 2).[41] At the same time, the evidence implies considerable regional variation.[42] Church holdings were extensive in Rome and in those areas of Italy dominated by the papacy. Whereas elsewhere in Western Europe the churches took some time to acquire substantial estates, the sizeable property-holdings of the papacy began in the reign of Constantine.[43] Although even the papacy lacks a collection of early charters, there is a wealth of evidence in the *Liber Pontificalis* and in papal letters as well as diplomatic texts. In particular, we get a clear impression of the estates held by the popes in the south of Italy and in Sicily (as well as Provence) in the correspondence of Gregory the Great.[44] What is revealed there can only be the tip of an iceberg, for we have no more than a selection of his letters.[45] The patrimony of St Peter in the South has, not surprisingly, been the subject of intensive study.[46] The revenues raised from the papal estates confiscated by the emperor Leo in 731–2, that is those estates which lay within Byzantine Italy, apparently amounted to 113.4 kilogrammes of gold annually.[47] In addition, we hear of presumably extensive estates in

[41] G. Jenal, *Italia ascetica atque monastica: das Asketen- und Mönchtum in Italien von den Anfängen bis zur Zeit der Langobarden (ca. 150/250–604)* (2 vols., Stuttgart, 1995); see Brown, *The Rise of Western Christendom*, 221.

[42] T. S. Brown, *Gentlemen and Officers. Imperial Administration and Aristocratic Power in Byzantine Italy A.D. 554–800* (1984), 190–1.

[43] A. H. M. Jones, *The Later Roman Empire, 284–602: A Social Economic and Administrative Survey* (3 vols., Oxford, 1964), II, 894–910; U. Stutz, *Geschichte des kirchlichen Benefizialwesens von seinen Anfängen bis auf die Zeit Alexanders III*, I (Berlin, 1895; repr. Aalen, 1961), 27–8; for church property in the post-Constantinian period, 24–41.

[44] J. Richards, *Consul of God. The Life and Times of Gregory the Great* (1980), 126–39; Brown, *Gentlemen and Officers*, 195–6.

[45] See R. A. Markus, *Gregory the Great and his World* (Cambridge, 1997), 206–8.

[46] F. Marazzi, *I 'Patrimonia Sanctae Romanae Ecclesiae' nel Lazio (secoli IV–X)* (Rome, 1998); M. Costambeys, 'Property, Ideology and the Territorial Power of the Papacy in the Early Middle Ages', *Early Medieval Europe*, 9 (2000), 367–96; D. Moreau, 'Les patrimoines de l'église romaine jusqu'à la mort de Grégoire de Grand. Dépouillement et réflexions préliminaires à une étude sur le rôle temporel des évêques de Rome durant l'antiquité la plus tardive', *Antiquité tardive*, 14 (2006), 79–93.

[47] M. McCormick, *Charlemagne's Survey of the Holy Land. Wealth, Personnel, and Buildings of a Mediterranean Church between Antiquity and the Middle Ages* (Washington, DC, 2011), 15, 17.

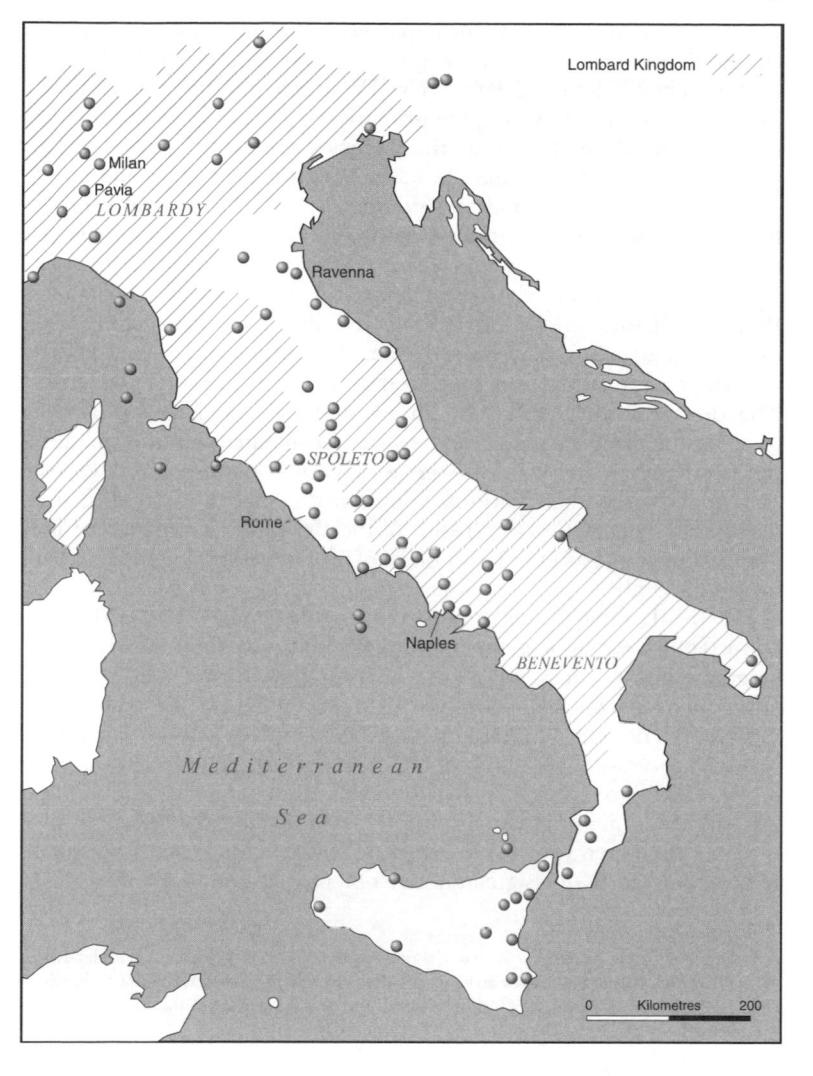

Figure 2 Distribution of ascetic communities in Italy before AD 615

the Cottian Alps which were returned to the papacy in the time of the Lombard King Aistulf.[48]

---

[48] Paulus Diaconus, *Historia Langobardorum*, VI 28, ed. G. Waitz, MGH, Scriptores Rerum Germanicarum (SRG) (Hannover, 1878).

Lagging some way behind the papal see, but nevertheless with extensive landholdings, was the church of Ravenna. Agnellus, writing in the ninth century, cited a letter of Pope Felix IV which implies that its annual income in around 525 was 54 kilogrammes of gold, or 3,000 *solidi*,[49] that is approximately half of what the papacy's confiscated estates yielded two centuries later. Ravenna churches gained considerable amounts of property during the period of Byzantine rule.[50] Among the surviving Ravenna papyri for the period between 476 and *c.* 700 there are two wills and eleven charters which convey property to the churches in Ravenna, and one charter in favour of Santa Maria Maggiore in Rome.[51] Of these, the most striking is a grant of money and estates made in 553 to the Ravenna church. The property lay as far afield as Urbino and Lucca, and produced an annual income of 100 *solidi*.[52] The donors, Ranilo and Felithanc, would seem to have been trying to secure a place in the society of the Exarchate after the failure of the Ostrogothic kingdom.[53] If this explanation for their gift is correct, one might guess that Ravenna's churches gained a good deal from likeminded benefactors as a result of the Byzantine conquest, but they may also have lost substantial amounts of property following the Lombard invasion.

For the Lombard area before the eighth century, the evidence is consistently poor. Bobbio, the most important monastery of the Lombard kingdom, boasts a handful of early charters that are accepted as largely authentic, but which do not give us much detail on the scale of the monastery's holdings,[54] although it has been argued that the estates listed in the *Adbrevationes* of 862 and 883 were predominantly endowments of the Lombard period.[55] By the late ninth century, Bobbio held fifty-six economic units amounting to around 11,605 hectares,[56] which is paltry compared with the holdings of St Germain, which would seem to have been forty times greater. The other great Lombard monasteries,

---

[49] Agnellus, *Liber Pontificalis sive vitae Pontificum Ravennatum*, c. 60, ed. O. Holder-Egger, MGH, Scriptores Rerum Langobardicarum (Hannover, 1878); Stutz, *Geschichte des kirchlichen Benefizialwesens*, 33–4; McCormick, *Charlemagne's Survey of the Holy Land*, 15.

[50] Brown, *Gentlemen and Officers*, 181–3, with nn. 12–13.

[51] J.-O. Tjäder, *Die nichtliterarischen lateinischen Papyri Italiens aus der Zeit 445–700* (3 vols., Lund and Stockholm, 1954–82), I, wills: papyri 4–5, 6; charters in favour of the church of Ravenna: papyri 12, 13, 14–15, 16, 18–19, 20, 21, 22, 23, 24, 27; charter in favour of the church of Rome: papyrus 17.

[52] *Ibid.*, I, papyrus 13; Brown, *Gentlemen and Officers*, 75–6.

[53] Brown, *Gentlemen and Officers*, 61.

[54] *Codice diplomatico del monastero di S. Colombano di Bobbio*, ed. C. Cipolla, I: *Fonti per la storia d'Italia*, 52 (Rome, 1918), 3, 7, 9, 15, 24; see also M. Richter, *Bobbio in the Early Middle Ages. The Abiding Legacy of Columbanus* (Dublin, 2008), 13–23.

[55] *Codice diplomatico*, ed. Cipolla, 63; Richter, *Bobbio*, 126.

[56] Richter, *Bobbio*, 126, 134.

Farfa, Nonantola and Brescia, are eighth-century foundations,[57] and fit Herlihy's model of an expansion of ecclesiastical property-holding after 750. In general, early monastic foundations in Lombard Italy seem to have been relatively poor and small scale;[58] a monastery might boast no more than one mass priest and a clerk,[59] which perhaps indicates a proprietary foundation, though there certainly were larger institutions, since a law of Aistulf talks of monasteries with more than fifty monks.[60] One such may have been the monastery of Mezzano, which was powerful enough to challenge Bobbio over the ownership of land.[61] Perhaps more important, there were clearly a number of smaller institutions, many of which would be transferred to larger houses or bishoprics in the eighth century.[62] We may get some idea of these from the growing record of early medieval sculpture noted in Italian churches, for this points to numbers of endowments that are otherwise unattested in our sources.[63] It can be no more than a guess, but in the seventh century while the church may well have held a high percentage of the territory of Byzantine Italy, it would seem to have owned a much smaller proportion of the land of the Lombard kingdom and duchies. Information relating to the monasteries of Farfa, Brescia, Nonantola and Montecassino, as well as the charters from Lucca, suggest a significant increase in the eighth.

The evidence for Visigothic Spain is less satisfactory than for Lombard Italy, although it has been claimed that the seventh century marked the flowering of Spanish monasticism.[64] The most recent study of early medieval monasticism in the peninsula, which is concerned with surviving architecture, lists a mere eighty-six sites (Figure 3),[65] not all of which were in operation before the eighth century, although, equally, there were plenty of monasteries which have left no archaeological trace. Beyond the monastic source material, there is a fascinating parish list from the Suevic region of the north-west,[66] and councils do give an indication of parish

---

[57] For the endowment of Farfa, M. Costambeys, *Power and Patronage in Early Medieval Italy. Local Society, Italian Politics and the Abbey of Farfa, c. 700–900* (Cambridge, 2007), 70–86.

[58] Brown, *The Rise of Western Christendom*, 222.

[59] Wood, *The Proprietary Church*, 166.

[60] *Ahistulfi leges*, 19, ed. C. Azzara and S. Gaspari, *Le leggi dei Langobardi. Storia, memoria e diritto di un populo germanico* (Rome, 2005), 290–3; Wood, *The Proprietary Church*, 167.

[61] Richter, *Bobbio*, 95–6, 110–11.

[62] Wood, *The Proprietary Church*, 65.

[63] See the *Corpus della scultura altomedievale*, published by the Centro Italiano di Studi sull'alto medioevo.

[64] F. J. Moreno Martín, *La arquitectura monástica hispana entre la Tardoantigüedad y la Alta Edad Media*, BAR, International Series 2287 (Oxford, 2011), 20.

[65] *Ibid.*, 691–2.

[66] *Parochiale Sueuum* (569), ed. P. David, Corpus Christianorum Series Latina (CCSL) 175, *Itineraria et alia Geographica* (Turnhout, 1965), 411–20; see P. C. Díaz, 'Monasteries in a

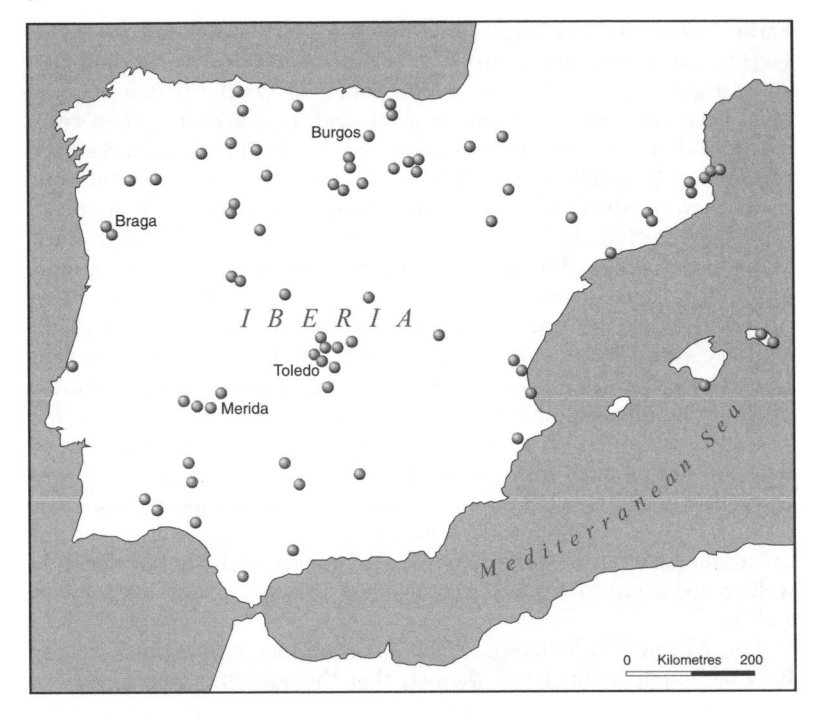

Figure 3 Distribution of ascetic communities in Visigothic Spain

funding.[67] Some of the *pizarras visigodas*, Visigothic slate documents, may well relate to ecclesiastical estates,[68] but there are no early charters to help us understand the scale of ecclesiastical holdings. The absence of documentation for much of the peninsula can, of course, be linked to the disruption caused by the long period of Islamic rule, although this did not lead to the total collapse of monasticism in the south,[69] and it scarcely explains the lack of information for a northern diocese like Lugo. Visigothic law, secular and ecclesiastical, sheds light on some property issues, but for the most part the land that attracted the attention of the

Peripheral Area: Seventh-Century Gallaecia', in *Topographies of Power in the Early Middle Ages*, ed. M. De Jong, F. Theuws and C. van Rhijn (Leiden, 2001), 328–59, at 334, 348–50.

[67] Council of Toledo, I, c. 19, IV, c. 33, and Council of Braga, II, c. 5, ed. J. Vives, *Concilios visigóticos e hispano-romanos* (Barcelona, 1963); Jones, 'The Western Church in the Fifth and Sixth Centuries', 11–12.

[68] I. Velázquez Soriano, *Las pizarras visigodas: edición crítica y estudio* (Murcia, 1989).

[69] Moreno Martín, *La arquitectura monástica hispana*, 20.

legislators was fiscal rather than ecclesiastical.[70] There are, however, some indications that ecclesiastical land was substantial enough to be under threat. Thus, the provincial Council of Lérida in 546 legislated against laymen attempting to withdraw from episcopal jurisdiction monasteries which they had founded, suggesting some battle over proprietary rights.[71]

A further issue gives us a different perspective on the donation of land to God and his saints. The first two clauses of the *Regula communis*, composed around 660, either by Fructuosus of Braga or possibly in his circle, talk of family monasteries and communities made up of bands of serfs, lacking episcopal control.[72] A text from around the same time, Valerius of Bierzo's *De genere monachorum*, refers to monasteries that were little more than peasant communes.[73] The houses mentioned in the *Regula communis* would seem to be proprietary churches, which we left to one side in Francia. The peasant communes may be a rather different matter. Even so, the evidence of the *Regula communis* and the *De genere monachorum* appears to suggest the dedication of land to God, but not, apparently, under the control of the established church.

More orthodox were the foundations of Fructuosus himself, recorded in his *vita*, which was once attributed to Valerius. Among them were Compludo, near Astorga, and Nono, in the region of Cadiz. The latter was apparently of unusual size, and was so popular that the local military commanders had to intervene to prevent the area from being denuded of potential soldiers.[74] There would seem to be an allusion here to the explicit exemption from military service granted to monks by Visigothic law.[75] We can, therefore, be sure that there were sizeable monasteries, but unfortunately for any detail we can only turn to the *Life of Fructuosus*. We even lack source material for the monastic foundations of the capital Toledo.

Nor do we know much about the wealth of the great episcopal churches of Toledo or Seville, but for that of Mérida we have the evidence of the

[70] P. D. King, *Law and Society in the Visigothic Kingdom* (Cambridge, 1972), 62–4.

[71] Lérida (546), c. 3, ed. Vives, *Concilios visigóticos e hispano-romanos*; Wood, *The Proprietary Church*, 15.

[72] *Regula communis*, cc. 1, 2, ed. J. Campos Ruiz and I. Roca Melia, *Reglas monasticas de la España: santos padres españoles*, II (Madrid, 1971).

[73] *Anécdota Wisigothica*, I: *Estudios, ediciones de textos literarios menores d época visigoda*, ed. M. C. Diaz y Diaz (Salamanca, 1958), 56–61.

[74] *Vita Fructuosi*, cc. 3, 14, ed. F. C. Nock (Washington, DC, 1946); see *Lives of the Visigothic Fathers*, ed. A. Fear (Liverpool, 1997), 136–8. For comparison with Anglo-Saxon England, see P. Sims-Williams, *Religion and Literature in Western England, 600–800* (Cambridge, 1990), 126–30.

[75] *Leges Visigothorum*, 9, 2, 8–9, ed. K. Zeumer, MGH, Leges 1 (Hannover, 1902); *Lives of the Visigothic Fathers*, ed. Fear, 138 n. 62, draws a parallel with chapter 10 of the edict of the emperor Maurice.

Vitas Patrum Emeretensium, which explains at considerable length how the diocese became the wealthiest in Spain. This came down to the medical skills of Bishop Paul, who removed a dead foetus from the womb of a senator's wife, thus saving her life; the couple, the richest in Lusitania, were so grateful that they conveyed all their wealth to the bishop, who in turn left it to his nephew and successor, Fidelis, who eventually conferred the complete estate to the church of Mérida.[76] This single benefaction was supposedly greater than all the rest of the ecclesiastical property of the city.

The *Vitas Patrum Emeretensium* does not allow us to quantify the scale of the possessions of the diocese, although it indicates that the territory left by Paul and Fidelis was very considerable. Perhaps more important, the text draws attention to the extent to which church landholding in Spain (as indeed elsewhere)[77] varied from region to region, while the evidence of the *Vita Fructuosi* and the *Regula communis* shows that while there may have been a considerable number of monasteries in the north, they were not necessarily under the control of the bishop.

The evidence for Anglo-Saxon England presents a picture that in some ways is similar to Spain; indeed, the critical picture of monasticism to be found in the *Regula communis* has been compared with certain aspects of English monasticism.[78] In other respects, however, the image presented by the Anglo-Saxon material recalls the situation in Francia, which is all the more surprising given that the Christianisation of the Anglo-Saxon kingdoms essentially began with the arrival of Augustine in Kent, meaning that (while there may have been some continuity in ecclesiastical landholding in the West)[79] the history of the English church really begins a good two and a half centuries after that of Gaul. In addition, because of the collapse of Roman traditions of property-holding, the permanent endowment of churches involved a change in land tenure.[80] Yet there are intriguing parallels between Francia and Anglo-Saxon England, not least because secularisation was an issue in both regions in the early eighth

[76] *Vitas Patrum Emeretensium*, ed. A. Maya Sánchez, CCSL 116 (Turnholt, 1992), cc. 4, 2 and 4 (*Lives of the Visigothic Fathers*, ed. Fear, c. 2, 16–18, and c. 4, 2–4).

[77] Jones, 'The Western Church in the Fifth and Sixth Centuries', 11–12.

[78] Sims-Williams, *Religion and Literature*, 127–9; see also P. Hunter Blair, *The World of Bede* (1970), 136; and J. Hillgarth, 'Popular Religion in Visigothic Spain', in *Visigothic Spain. New Approaches*, ed. E. James (Oxford, 1980), 3–60, at 47.

[79] For the problematic charter documents, see W. Davies, *An Early Welsh Microcosm* (1978), and *idem*, *The Llandaff Charters* (Aberystwyth, 1979), with the review by P. Sims-Williams, *Journal of Ecclesiastical History*, 33 (1982), 124–9.

[80] P. Wormald, *Bede and the Conversion of England. The Charter Evidence*, Jarrow Lecture (Jarrow, 1984), reprinted in *idem*, *The Times of Bede* (Oxford, 2006), pp, 135–66. For bookland, see, with more extensive citation of the literature, Wood, *The Proprietary Church*, 152–60.

century.[81] Not that England seems to have experienced anything like the secularisation of ecclesiastical property witnessed in Francia in the days of Charles Martel. Even so, Bede claimed that too much property had been transferred to monasteries (many of which he regarded as bogus), with the result that the Northumbrian kingdom was in danger of not being able to provide for its warriors[82] – a parallel complaint to that raised against Fructuosus's foundation of Nono. That a cleric, and one of Bede's stature, could make such a claim is a clear indication that a considerable amount of land had been donated to the church, although particularly to proprietary churches – for Bede thought that the episcopal church was under-endowed to carry out its pastoral duties.[83]

For the endowment of Northumbrian monasteries, our evidence is almost exclusively to be found in the narrative sources. Wearmouth's original landholdings amounted to 70 hides, according to Bede, and 50 according to the author of the anonymous *Life of Ceolfrid*.[84] Jarrow was founded with 40 hides.[85] By the time that Abbot Ceolfrid retired and set off for Rome in 716, the joint-monastery possessed 150 hides.[86] The hide, which varied in actual acreage, was supposedly enough land to support one family.[87] This was a sizeable and well-endowed community, although its landholdings were not remotely comparable with those of the more important Frankish monasteries that we have considered.[88] Ripon initially received the rather smaller amount of 30 hides,[89] though this was subsequently increased by a major grant of territory around the Ribble, *Ingaedyne* (perhaps the area round Yeadon), Dent and Catlow.[90] But even the initial endowment of Ripon was a good deal larger than the

[81] I. N. Wood, 'Land Tenure and Military Obligations in the Anglo-Saxon and Merovingian Kingdoms: The Evidence of Bede and Boniface in Context', *Bulletin of International Medieval Research*, 9–10 (2005), 3–22.

[82] Bede, *Epistola ad Ecgbertum*, cc. 10–11, ed. C. Plummer, *Venerabilis Baedae Opera Historica* (Oxford, 1896).

[83] See the discussion in J. Blair, *The Church in Anglo-Saxon Society* (Oxford, 2005), 100–17; Wood, *The Proprietary Church*, 152.

[84] Bede, *Historia Abbatum*, 4, ed. Plummer, *Baedae Opera Historica; Vita Ceolfridi*, c. 7, in *ibid.*

[85] Bede, *Historia Abbatum*, 7; *Vita Ceolfridi*, c. 11.

[86] *Vita Ceolfridi*, c. 33.

[87] T. M. Charles-Edwards, 'Kinship, Status and the Origins of the Hide', *Past and Present*, 56 (1972), 3–33.

[88] For an assessment: I. N. Wood, 'La richesse dans le monde de Bède le Vénérable', in *Les élites et la richesse*, ed. J.-P. Devroey, L. Feller and R. Le Jan (Turnhout, 2010), 221–31, at 227; the estates of Wearmouth-Jarrow would cover about 1/2800th of England, perhaps 1/700th of Northumbria, compared with St Germain's near 1 per cent of Francia.

[89] Stephanus, *Vita Wilfridi*, c. 8, ed. B. Colgrave, *The Life of Bishop Wilfrid by Eddius Stephanus* (Cambridge, 1927). See Roper, 'Wilfrid's Landholdings in Northumbria', 61–79.

[90] Stephanus, *Vita Wilfridi*, c. 17. For the identification of *Yngaedyne*, however, see *West Yorkshire: An Archaeological Survey to A.D. 1500*, ed. M. L. Faull and S. A. Moorhouse (Wakefield, 1981), 183; for the Ripon estates, Roper, 'Wilfrid's Landholdings in Northumbria', 61, 70.

10 hides of Wilfrid's first foundation at *Ætstanford*,[91] though this was the same amount as that allocated by Oswiu to each of the twelve monasteries he founded as a thank-offering following his victory over Penda at the battle of the Winwæd.[92] Unfortunately, Bede does not comment on the endowment of Lindisfarne. Later sources indicate that the community of St Cuthbert had very extensive landholdings, but how much of this had been acquired before the Viking period is unclear.[93] Equally, we do not have any idea of the scale of the early endowment of Whitby, or even Wilfrid's Hexham, although it was founded on a portion of the dowry of Queen Æthelthryth.[94]

As in Francia, ecclesiastical property should not just be assessed in terms of the wealth of the great monasteries and bishoprics. Indeed, Bede's *Letter to Ecgbert* implies that it was not the endowments of these that had depleted the resources available to the king and his warriors, but rather small family communities, essentially proprietary foundations. For the numbers of minor houses and their whereabouts, we rarely have documentary evidence, although it has been suggested that early Anglo-Saxon sculpture may be monastic, and it has, indeed, been taken as an indication of the distribution of Anglian monasteries. Certainly, the sculpture is ecclesiastical, and therefore gives us some sense of the spread of church institutions.[95] Ultimately, however, for Northumbria, Bede's statement about the over-endowment of monasteries (and the under-endowment of bishoprics) is our most precious piece of information.

Wilfrid provides a point of entry for the ecclesiastical landholding throughout the Anglo-Saxon world (Figure 4). Apart from his foundations of *Ætstanforda*, Ripon and Hexham, he appears to have been given *Ingetlingum* and Poppleton in Northumbria,[96] as well as holding the dioceses of York, and briefly Lindisfarne. In Mercia he received property, notably at Oundle,[97] and at various times he held the sees of Lichfield

[91] Stephanus, *Vita Wilfridi*, c. 8.

[92] Bede, *Historia Ecclesiastica*, III 24, ed. Plummer, *Baedae Opera Historica*. For a hypothesis as to where these monasteries might have been, see I. N. Wood, 'Monasteries and the Geography of Power in the Age of Bede', *Northern History*, 45 (2008), 11–25, at 17–18.

[93] *Historia de sancto Cuthberto*, 11–10, ed. T. Johnson South (Woodbridge, 2002); E. Craster, 'The Patrimony of St Cuthbert', *English Historical Review*, 69 (1954), 177–99, at 182–4, reckoned that the twelve vills in the Bowmont Valley, fifteen miles round Carlisle, Cartmell and Suthgedling, were early acquisitions: Roper, 'Wilfrid's Landholdings in Northumbria', 64; Blair, *The Church in Anglo-Saxon Society*, 87.

[94] Stephanus, *Vita Wilfridi*, c. 22; Roper, 'Wilfrid's Landholdings in Northumbria', 61.

[95] R. N. Bailey, *Viking Age Sculpture* (1980), 81; I. N. Wood, 'Anglo-Saxon Otley: An Archiepiscopal Estate and its Crosses', *Northern History*, 23 (1987), 20–38, at 21.

[96] Roper, 'Wilfrid's Landholdings in Northumbria', 61. See also G. R. J. Jones, 'Some Donations to Bishop Wilfrid in Northern England', *Northern History*, 31 (1995), 22–38.

[97] Stephanus, *Vita Wilfridi*, c. 65.

Figure 4 Properties held by Bishop Wilfrid

and Leicester.[98] In Wessex, he is supposed to have been given 71 hides at Wedmore and Clewer, estates that he conveyed to Glastonbury. Among other sites he is said to have held in the south-west is Withington. In the kingdom of the South Saxons he held 87 hides at Selsey, as well

---

[98] For what follows, see Roper, 'Wilfrid's Landholdings in Northumbria', 61–2.

as Lidsey, Aldingbourne, Westergate and Northmundham, which were given to him by Nothgitha, sister of King Nothelm. After the conquest of the South Saxons by the West Saxon King Cædwalla his right to Selsey was confirmed and he received in addition 70 hides at Pagham and 10 at Tangmere, both of which he passed to Archbishop Theodore. Cædwalla also gave him a quarter of the Isle of Wight, which amounted to 300 hides.[99] Wilfrid may also have been given Seaford.[100] Although he did not control all of this at any one time, far in excess of 500 hides must have passed through his hands, for Stephanus talks of numerous other donations without providing details. The amount of land held throughout England by Wilfrid at some time in his career (all of which passed to the church) might well have constituted as large a proportion of the territory controlled by the Anglo-Saxons as Bertram held of Francia.

For no other ecclesiastic are we so well informed, though Bede also tells us that the Mercian King Wulfhere gave 50 hides at Barrow to Chad, who took over the see of Lichfield from Wilfrid.[101] Further south, charters provide some evidence. The monastery of Hanbury acquired 50 hides of land,[102] Farnham 60, Bradfield 120 and Minster-in-Thanet 124.[103] In addition, the later evidence of the *Liber Eliensis* suggests that the original endowment of Ely was very substantial, perhaps as much as 600 hides.[104] Unfortunately, we know little about the early landholdings of such major foundations as Peterborough, Malmesbury and Glastonbury,[105] let alone the episcopal church of Wessex, Canterbury or York[106] – though according to Bede the secular clergy of Northumbria were under-endowed. One would be hard pressed to argue from this that the proportion of land in the hands of the church was as high in England as it was in Francia. However, in 1086 the English church received approximately a quarter of the kingdom's land rents;[107] and

---

[99] Stephanus, *Vita Wilfridi*, c. 41; Bede, *Historia Ecclesiastica*, IV 13.

[100] Roper, 'Wilfrid's Landholdings in Northumbria', 62.

[101] Bede, *Historia Ecclesiastica*, IV 3.

[102] For Hanbury, see S. Bassett, 'The Landed Endowment of the Anglo-Saxon Minster at Hanbury (Worcs.)', *Anglo-Saxon England*, 38 (2010), 77–100. Note also that on 77 he calculates that there were at least thirty minsters in the diocese of Worcester by 800.

[103] Blair, *The Church in Anglo-Saxon Society*, 87; Wood, 'La richesse dans le monde de Bède le Vénérable', 227–8.

[104] *Liber Eliensis*, ed. E. O. Blake, Camden Society, third series, 92 (1962), cc. 4, 15, 32; D. Whitelock, 'The Pre-Viking Age Church in East Anglia', *Anglo-Saxon England*, 1 (1972), 1–22, at 7.

[105] For Wilfrid's gift of 71 hides to Glastonbury, H. P. R. Finberg, *The Early Charters of Wessex* (Leicester, 1964), 110–11 nn. 362, 363, 366.

[106] For York, however, see the eleventh-century evidence contained in the York Gospels: S. D. Keynes, 'The Additions in Old English', in *The York Gospels, Roxburghe Club*, ed. N. Barker (1986), 81–99.

[107] J. Goody, *The Development of the Family and Marriage in Europe* (Cambridge, 1983), 127.

while it accumulated considerable amounts of property in the tenth and early eleventh centuries, it had surely lost large numbers of estates in the previous Viking period, when numerous proprietary churches in particular must have fallen by the wayside. The proportion of territory held by ecclesiastical institutions in England before the Viking invasions may not have been radically less than what they held in 1086. What early evidence there is at least implies that they were as well endowed in the south as in the north. It is not therefore surprising that secularisation of church property was every bit as much of an issue in Mercia as it was in Northumbria,[108] and indeed that it would become an issue in Alfredian Wessex.[109]

This very brief tour of ecclesiastical landholding from the fifth to the early eighth centuries has not trespassed into Wales or Ireland, for the simple reason that figures for the period in question are effectively non-existent (although we do know that the original endowment of Iona was reputed to be a paltry 5 hides).[110] For Francia, what evidence there is allows us to conclude that Roth's estimate of Merovingian ecclesiastical landholding may not be wide of the mark; if anything, it is likely to be an underestimate. Churches may have held a comparable, perhaps even larger, proportion of the lands of Byzantine Italy (which included the core territories of the papacy), but ecclesiastical holdings in Lombard Italy, Spain and England were probably on a lesser scale. In considering developments in the ninth century and beyond, one should probably bear these differences in mind. Even so, in Anglo-Saxon England, as in Francia, the amount of property held by ecclesiastical institutions was extensive enough to present a major political problem in terms of ensuring adequate territorial support to maintain an army. In other words, a significant proportion of Western Europe was entrusted to God and his saints in the pre-Carolingian era. Further, much of that land was conferred to the church after the disruption occasioned by the settlement of the barbarians, which had caused huge changes in property ownership, rather than in the Roman period.[111]

---

[108] Boniface, epp. 73–4, ed. M. Tangl, *S. Bonifatii et Lulli Epistolae*, MGH, Epistolae Selectae in Usum Scholarum 1 (Boniface, 1916); Wood, 'Land Tenure and Military Obligations in the Anglo-Saxon and Merovingian Kingdoms'.

[109] J. L. Nelson, '"A King across the Sea": Alfred in Continental Perspective', *Transactions of the Royal Historical Society*, sixth series, 36 (1986), 45–68, at 61, reprinted in *idem, Rulers and Ruling Families in Early Medieval Europe: Alfred, Charles the Bald and others* (Aldershot, 1999).

[110] On Iona: Bede, *Historia Ecclesiastica*, III 4; Roper, 'Wilfrid's Landholdings in Northumbria', 64. See also M. Richter, *Ireland and her Neighbours in the Seventh Century* (Dublin, 1999), 22–3. With regard to Wales, the dating of the earliest of the Llandaff charters is notoriously problematic: see above, n. 79.

[111] M. Innes, 'Land, Freedom and the Making of the Medieval West', *Transactions of the Royal Historical Society*, sixth series, 16 (2006), 39–74; P. Sarris, *Empires of Faith: The Fall of Rome*

The build-up of ecclesiastical property has not gone unremarked. In a challenging book published in 1983, Jack Goody not only drew attention to the fact that the church acquired very substantial property holdings in the early Middle Ages, but he also argued that this resulted from a deliberate ecclesiastical policy. According to Goody, the church's definition of the family, marriage and incest challenged previous marital traditions, which had often seen marriage between close kin, with the result and perhaps the intention that land had been kept within confined kin groups; the fact that such unions were now branded as incestuous undermined the associated patterns of inheritance and facilitated the ecclesiastical acquisition of land.[112] That donations to the church did affect patterns of inheritance is clear; although biological heirs were not ignored, the portion of parental property (perhaps acquired rather than family property) which they inherited was frequently reduced by gifts to God and his saints. However, although ecclesiastical councils have much to say about the acquisition and protection of church property,[113] Goody's explanation for the accumulation of church land attributed far too much intentionality to the process.[114] More significant than the legal restriction of strategies of inheritance was the positive drive to donate to the sacred.[115] Indeed, as Régine Le Jan has argued, the upper classes developed a strategy 'de fonder dans le sacré le pouvoir familial'.[116] At the same time, the fact that Goody traced the development from the Christianisation of the Roman Empire down to the Reformation rather obscured the extent to which the change he documented took place in the pre-Carolingian period. Crucially, however, he put ecclesiastical land at the centre of an interpretation of early European history.

Yet this should not lull us into believing that there was an unregulated transfer of property to churches. There were limitations on how much could be alienated from the family. A quarter of a man's property had to be passed on to his direct heirs, according to the Theodosian

---

to the Rise of Islam, 500–700 (Cambridge, 2011), 55–68. For the earlier transfer of wealth to the church, see Brown, *Through the Eye of a Needle*.

[112] Goody, *The Development of the Family and Marriage in Europe*, esp. 103–56.

[113] Jones, 'The Western Church in the Fifth and Sixth Centuries', 12–13. The evidence for Francia is summarised in O. Pontal, *Die Synoden im Merowingerreich* (Paderborn, 1986), esp. 249–52. A classic statement prohibiting the alienation of church property is Council of Agde (506), c. 7, ed. C. Munier, *Concilia Galliae A.314- A. 506*, CCSL 148 (Turnhout, 1963), 195–6.

[114] For more recent studies of incest legislation, see P. Mikat, *Die Inzestgesetzgebung der merowingisch-fränkischen Konzilien (511–626/7)* (Paderborn, 1994); K. Ubl, *Inzestverbot und Gesetzgebung. Die Konstruktion eines Verbrechens (300–1100)* (Berlin, 2008).

[115] See, for instance, the development of child oblation: M. de Jong, *In Samuel's Image* (Leiden, 1996).

[116] R. Le Jan, *Femmes, pouvoir et société dans le haut Moyen Âge* (Paris, 2001), 107.

Code.[117] Visigothic law protected the family a good deal more, limiting the disposable part of an estate to a fifth, which surely restricted the scale of ecclesiastical property in Spain.[118] Nor did land always remain in the hands of a church, as can be seen from a comparison between the surviving Merovingian charters for St Germain, and the evidence of the monastery's possessions in the Polyptych of Irminon.[119] Biological heirs could and did challenge grants made by their parents to the church;[120] the brother-in-law of Fructuosus asked the Visigothic king, probably Reccared, to give him some property from one of the saint's monasteries so that he could carry out his military obligations;[121] the community of Wearmouth seems to have been terrified that its property would be claimed by the brother of its founder Benedict Biscop.[122] There were, indeed, numerous potential threats to the possession of land once it had been passed to the church. Estates could be transferred from ecclesiastical possession in a variety of different legal ways, as Caesarius of Arles remarked in a letter to Pope Symmachus.[123] As the early sixth-century Council of Clermont complained, men petitioned the king for church property,[124] while a generation later at the third Council of Paris the bishops reiterated their fears about the threats to church land.[125] In addition, there were plenty of threats from hostile neighbours in times of unrest.[126]

In fact it is by no means clear that the church's ownership of the gifts it received was anything like as secure as the conciliar *acta* would have us believe. Shortly after 500, Avitus, bishop of Vienne, wrote to the Burgundian ruler Gundobad, saying 'Whatever my small church has, nay all of our churches, is yours in its substance, since up to now you have

---

[117] *Codex Theodosianus*, II 19, 4 (AD 361), ed. T. Mommsen (Berlin, 1905).

[118] *Leges Visigothorum*, IV 2, 19, IV 5, I, V 2, 4. See Wood, *The Proprietary Church*, 22.

[119] I. N. Wood, *The Merovingian Kingdoms 450–751* (1994), 205.

[120] E.g. *Lex Alamannorum*, I, ed. K. A. Eckhardt, MGH, Leges 5, I (Hannover, 1966). See R. McKitterick, *The Carolingians and the Written Word* (Cambridge, 1989), 66.

[121] *Vita Fructuosi*, c. 3; M. Rouche, *L'Aquitaine des Wisigoths aux Arabes* (Paris, 1976), 371 and 673. See also King, *Law and Society in the Visigothic Kingdom*, 62.

[122] I. N. Wood, 'The Foundation of Bede's Wearmouth-Jarrow', in *The Cambridge Companion to Bede*, ed. S. DeGregorio (Cambridge, 2010), 84–96, at 87–8.

[123] Caesarius, ep. 7, ed. G. Morin, *Sancti Caesarii episcopi Arelatensis Opera omnia nunc primum in unum collecta*, II (Maredsous, 1942); trans. as ep. 7a in W. E. Klingshirn, *Caesarius of Arles: Life, Testament, Letters* (Liverpool, 1994), 90–1.

[124] Council of Clermont, 535, c. 5, ed. Gaudemet and Basdevant, *Les canons des conciles mérovingiens*.

[125] Council of Paris, 556/73, pref., 1–3, ed. Gaudemet and Basdevant, *Les canons des conciles mérovingiens*.

[126] See Lesne, *Histoire de la propriété ecclésiastique*, I, 134, on the history of Bèze.

either guarded it or given it.'[127] At the time he wrote these words, Avitus was caught up in an awkward legal dispute which was being looked into by Gundobad, and which may well have put him on the defensive; even so it is clear that certain kings and rulers regarded ecclesiastical land as being subject to royal demands and to being redistributed by royal command, despite the views expressed by bishops in council.[128]

The best-known example of secularisation is that carried out by the early Carolingians. The seizure of church property is already portrayed as a major issue in sources of the eighth and ninth centuries, not least in a number of visionary texts which present Charles Martel as suffering in hell.[129] It is true that these and other texts, including what is usually thought to be an interpolated version of a letter of Boniface,[130] were intended to warn later Carolingians against taking over ecclesiastical property, and that they therefore reveal as much about late eighth- and ninth-century concerns as they tell us about how much land actually was returned to secular use by Charles Martel.[131] Even so, the evidence from St Wandrille and Auxerre[132] proves that secularisation was a very significant issue.[133] And one may wonder whether in rejecting Roth's figures, Herlihy did not pay enough attention to the reclamation of land from the church in the early eighth century.

Although the age of Charles Martel would seem to have constituted the first great period of secularisation of church property, Boniface, in his denunciation of the policies of the *maior palatii*, makes it clear that he thought the evil had begun a good deal earlier.[134] Lesne acknowledged that secularisation had occurred in the days of Ebroin, Childebert III and Grimoald, in other words throughout much of the late seventh century; and Michel Rouche, citing the *Chronicle of Fredegar*, pushed the challenge to ecclesiastical property rights further back, to the reigns of

---

[127] Avitus, ep. 44, ed. R. Peiper, MGH, AA VI 2 (Berlin, 1883); *Quicquid habet ecclesiola mea, immo omnes ecclesiae nostrae, vestrum est de substantia, quam vel servastis hactenus vel donastis,* trans. D. Shanzer and I. N. Wood, *Avitus of Vienne, Letters and Selected Prose* (Liverpool, 2002), 218.

[128] M. Rouche, '*Religio calcata et dissipata* ou les premières sécularisations de terre d'Église par Dagobert', in *The Seventh Century. Change and Continuity,* ed. J. Fontaine and J. N. Hillgarth (1992), 236–46, at 243.

[129] The fullest assessment of the secularisation remains Lesne, *Histoire de la propriété ecclésiastique,* II; for the visionary material P. Dutton, *The Politics of Dreaming in the Carolingian Empire* (Lincoln, NB, 1994).

[130] Boniface, ep. 73; challenging the idea of interpolation, T. Reuter, '"Kirchenreform" und "Kirchenpolitik" im Zeitalter Karl Martells. Begriffe und Wirklichkeit', in *Karl Martell in seiner Zeit,* ed. J. Jarnut, U. Nonn and M. Richter (Sigmaringen, 1994), 33–59.

[131] P. Fouracre, *The Age of Charles Martel* (Harlow, 2000), 122–6.

[132] *Gesta Abbatum Fontanellensium,* 11, 3, *Gesta Pontificum Autissiodorensium,* c. 32.

[133] See also Fouracre, *The Age of Charles Martel,* 72.

[134] Boniface, ep. 50; see Rouche, '*Religio calcata et dissipata*', 236–8.

Dagobert I and his son Clovis II (thus from the 620s onwards).[135] He even argued that Merovingian kings essentially treated ecclesiastical land in the same manner as fiscal land: 'ils sont des terres publiques', and that was enough to justify Dagobert's secularisations.[136] Moreover, for Rouche, this attitude could be found in Visigothic Spain around the year 600,[137] and he suggested, less convincingly, that it derived ultimately from Roman law.[138]

Some kings felt they could make heavy tax demands on church property; already before 561 Chlothar I demanded a third of all ecclesiastical revenue.[139] There were also plenty of royal complaints about how much the church had amassed, even in the sixth century. One of Chothar's sons, Chramn, had an adviser, Leo, who argued that Saints Martial and Martin (that is their churches) had denuded the royal treasury; another son, Chilperic, who succeeded to the kingdom of Soissons, argued, infamously, that 'my treasury is always empty. All our wealth has fallen into the hands of the church. There is no one with any power left except the bishops. Nobody respects me as king: all respect has passed to the bishops in their cities.'[140] That Chilperic did not embark on a policy of secularisation suggests that not everyone saw church property as being so open to royal or mayoral exploitation as did Dagobert, Clovis II and Charles Martel. Just as their actions, like those of later Anglo-Saxon rulers, do suggest that ecclesiastical land might be brought back into secular use in certain circumstances, the words of Chilperic, and the opinions of Leo, as retold by Gregory of Tours, underline the fact that massive amounts of property had already been conveyed to the church even by the second half of the sixth century.[141]

What is perhaps most difficult to grasp is the relationship between the alienation of land to the church and the desire of family members and of rulers to bring that land back into secular use. At times, we seem to be watching an extraordinarily complicated dance in which the partners move in one direction and then another, and not always the same direction at the same time, yet they continue to hold on to one another. Families,

[135] Rouche, 'Religio calcata et dissipata', 240–3, citing Fredegar, IV 60, 90, ed. B. Krusch, MGH, SRM 2 (Hannover, 1888).

[136] Rouche, 'Religio calcata et dissipata', 243; Lex Alamannorum, 21; Lex Baiuvariorum, I, 13, ed. E. von Schwind, MGH, Leges 5, 2 (Hannover, 1926).

[137] Rouche, 'Religio calcata et dissipata', 244, citing Rouche, L'Aquitaine, 371 and 673, on Fructuosus's brother-in-law wanting land transfered from Fructuosus's monastery to cover military service.

[138] Codex Theodosianus, XVI 10, 12.

[139] Gregory of Tours, Decem Libri Historiarum, IV 2, ed. B. Krusch and W. Levison, MGH, SRM I, 1 (Hannover, 1951).

[140] Gregory of Tours, Decem Libri Historiarum, IV 16, VI 46, trans. L. Thorpe (Harmondsworth, 1974).

[141] Brown, Through the Eye of a Needle, 493.

in giving to the church, did not see their gift as a finite act, but rather as one element in a series of negotiations,[142] as has been shown most fully by Barbara Rosenwein in her study of the tenth-century charters of Cluny, where families and individuals deliberately set out to establish themselves as neighbours of St Peter.[143] To give was to invest in the church, but a donation was also an investment for the souls of the donor and his or her family.[144] At the same time, there could be more immediate benefits: positions for sons and daughters, even a continuing, and secure, land bank on which the family could draw, especially if it negotiated the usufruct of the estate or its use under a tenancy agreement, such as those made *in precaria*. The establishment of a proprietary church was just one of a number of possible channels for giving to God while retaining a major stake in the gift offered. Even if they claimed their land back, as some Merovingian and Anglo-Saxon families did, in making a bequest to the church they had entered into a relationship which placed demands on both sides, drawing together spiritual and economic investment, which also had political ramifications.[145] Secularisation could be structured so as not to break the relationship; there was no need to take land away from a church in perpetuity, but rather bishops and abbots could be persuaded to grant out their property *in precaria* or as benefices (which takes us back to the arguments of Roth), so that the new holder of the property was himself drawn into the patronage networks of a church and its patron saint.[146] The challenges made by kings, kinsmen and by men hostile to the original benefactors ultimately did not check the transfer of property to churches for the simple reason that almost everyone wished to have a favourable relationship with God and his saints.

The endowment of churches, and indeed the subsequent secularisations, are clearly an aspect of church history. These

---

[142] See the discussions prompted by A. Wiener, *Inalienable Possessions. The Politics of Keeping while Giving* (Berkeley, 1992); e.g. F. Theuws, 'Maastricht as a Centre of Power in the Early Middle Ages', in *Topographies of power*, ed. de Jong, Theuws and van Rhijn, 155–216, at 201–5.

[143] B. Rosenwein, *To Be the Neighbor of Saint Peter. The Social Meaning of Cluny's Property, 909–1049* (Ithaca, 1989).

[144] A. Angenendt, '*Donationes pro anima*: Gift and Countergift in the Early Medieval Liturgy', in *The Long Morning of Medieval Europe*, ed. J. R. Davis and M. McCormick (Aldershot, 2008), 131–54. There are significant parallels to be drawn with early Islam; A. M. Carballeira Debasa, *Legados Píos y Fundaciones Familiares en al-Andalus (siglos IV/X–VI/XII)* (Madrid, 2002); I am indebted to Ann Christys for the comparison and the reference.

[145] Well illustrated, for instance, in R. Le Jan, 'Convents, Violence and Competition for Power in Seventh-Century Francia', in *Topographies of power*, ed. de Jong, Theuws and van Rhijn, 243–69.

[146] Wood, 'Teutsind, Witlaic, and the History of Merovingian *Precaria*', 47–8. Roper, 'Wilfrid's Landholdings in Northumbria', 71, sees this as a compromise, but the evidence from St Wandrille scarcely supports this reading.

developments have, however, rarely been presented as a significant aspect of the socio-economic history of the early Middle Ages. In 1963, Arnaldo Momigliano commented that Pirenne, Dopsch and Rostovtzeff had written about the social changes of the late Roman period 'without even discussing the most important of all social changes – the rise of Christianity'.[147] He could have looked further back; Fustel de Coulanges, who placed religion right at the centre of his understanding of the Ancient City, ignored it almost entirely in his study of the early development of French political institutions.[148] Indeed, with few exceptions, there had been a long-standing exclusion of religion from socio-economic studies of the post-Roman period.[149] Some explanation for this may be provided by the lines of development within the relevant historiographies. The seminal French debates of the eighteenth century, which were concerned largely with social structures (which had implications for an understanding of the France of the Ancien Régime), almost all ignored religious issues – and the Enlightenment did not encourage the integration of religion into historical study. An economic dimension was developed by Sismondi in the first half of the following century, but, perhaps not surprisingly, as a Genevan Calvinist he had little to say about early medieval Christianity, something which drew the ire of Alessandro Manzoni. Among secular historians, Italians more than most did emphasise the significance of the church, not least because the papacy was a major factor in debates about the unification of Italy. Yet the main advocates of religious history were to be found in France, and for them – notably Chateaubriand, Ozanam, Montalembert and Broglie – the history of the early Middle Ages was important above all for the models of spirituality it had to offer to a world recovering from the secularism of the Enlightenment and the Revolution. This was a reading that tended not to pause over the social and economic considerations of church history. By contrast, the Germans in the nineteenth century saw the early Middle Ages as providing material for understanding and promoting their own national unity and their primordial constitution; Roth was unusual in placing the church firmly within a debate about supposedly secular issues.

It was the German tradition that won out, not least because it was most deeply embedded in the universities. In the second and third decades of the twentieth century Alfons Dopsch situated his work in a line of German scholarship, though he also acknowledged the overwhelming

---

[147] A. Momigliano, 'Christianity and the Decline of the Roman Empire', in *The Conflict between Paganism and Christianity in the Fourth Century*, ed. *idem* (Oxford, 1963), 5–6. But see now Brown, *Through the Eye of a Needle*.

[148] N. D. Fustel de Coulanges, *Histoire des institutions politiques de l'ancienne France* (6 vols., Paris, 1875–92).

[149] For what follows, see I. N. Wood, *The Modern Origins of the Early Middle Ages* (Oxford, 2013).

importance of Fustel. It is perhaps more surprising that Henri Pirenne left the church to one side; although a Protestant, he had studied with Godefroid Kurth, a deeply committed Catholic.[150] Yet Kurth himself separated his study of settlement from his more pious investigations of Merovingian saints and politics. Despite the influence of Kurth, Pirenne looked up, above all, to the Germans, especially Karl Lamprecht, that is until the impact of the First World War led him (like Fustel after 1870) to want to cut them down to size. There were still scholars who concentrated on the church, again Frenchmen like Henri-Irenée Marrou, but also Christopher Dawson, who in many ways was an heir to the French Catholics of the nineteenth century. However, insofar as anyone attempted to integrate religious and secular narratives, it was the heirs of Gibbon: Bury and Hodgkin. Yet Bury's interests were more political and cultural than economic – and while Hodgkin did discuss religion as a factor in the Fall of Rome (modifying Gibbon's view of the church, and emphasising God's hand in events), and while he also looked at economic factors (as one would expect from a banker), he did not pause to consider the economic impact of Christianity.[151] Momigliano, then, was commenting on a lacuna which had essentially become ingrained in the study of the early Middle Ages; the study of the economy and society did not involve that of religion, and vice versa.

Among social and economic historians' writing, even after Momigliano's comment, there has been a tendency to avoid discussing Christianisation,[152] although religious historians have been rather more inclined to keep an eye on the social (though rarely the more purely economic) aspects of their subject.[153] Political historians have continued

---

[150] A. van Zeebroeck, 'L'âge d'or medieval, un ideal pour une nouvelle chrétienté? La réponse d'un historien engage, Godefroid Kurth (1847–1916)', in *Rêves de Chrétienté. Réalités du monde*, ed. L. van Ypersele and A.-D. Marcelis (Louvain, 2001), 205–19.

[151] T. Hodgkin, *Italy and her Invaders*, II: *The Hunnish Invasion, the Vandal Invasion and the Herulian Mutiny* (Oxford, 1880), ch. 13. Dean Church and Mandell Creighton, however, criticised the lack of focus on ecclesiastical history in vols. I and II, something Hodgkin set out to remedy from vol. III onwards, *Italy and her Invaders*, III: *The Ostrogothic Invasion* (Oxford, 1885), vii.

[152] C. Wickham, *Framing the Early Middle Ages. Europe and the Mediterranean, 400–800* (Oxford, 2005); M. McCormick, *Origins of the European Economy. Communications and Commerce AD 300–900* (Cambridge, 2001) (though in *Charlemagne's Survey of the Holy Land* he puts the church stage centre); B. Ward-Perkins, *The Fall of Rome and the End of Civilization* (Oxford, 2005), 108–9, 148–50, makes rather more of ecclesiastical material in his examination of late antique and early medieval building.

[153] Brown, *The Rise of Western Christendom; idem, Poverty and Leadership in the Later Roman Empire* (Hanover, NH, 2002), and *idem, Through the Eye of a Needle*, do register the relation between religion and the economy. So too some discussions of the social system, and especially the exploitation of land, have emphasised the importance of the church as a property-owner; see J.-P. Devroey, *Puissants et misérables. Système social et monde paysan dans l'Europe des Francs (VIe–IXe siècles)* (Brussels, 2006).

to note the impact of doctrinal debate,[154] but Gibbon, for all his anti-clericalism, still stands relatively isolated among secular historians for his attempt to place the development of the church at the heart of a totalising narrative.[155] Gibbon saw Christianisation as a negative force, sapping the vitality of the Roman state. Leaving aside the judgemental aspect of his argument, it is worth returning to the question of the effect of Christianisation on society. In other words, it is worth returning to Momigliano's observation. Since, as we have seen, a substantial proportion of the landed resources of Western Europe was entrusted to God and his saints in the course of the fifth, sixth and seventh centuries, we need to ask whether this had any significant social or economic impact, or whether it simply marked the transfer of land from one owner to another.

One would like to know whether the needs of the church led to any reorganisation of agricultural production, such as has been argued for early medieval Ireland.[156] Given the fact that monasticism in mainland Europe evolved in part on late Roman villas, abbots may well have simply followed established practice.[157] Unfortunately, for the Merovingian period we are largely dependent on the remarkable Tours documents,[158] and we lack any earlier point of comparison for the West other than the theoretical comments of the *agrimensores*. We do know that churches kept a close eye on their tenants,[159] and legal *formulae*

[154] J. B. Bury, *History of the Later Roman Empire from Arcadius to Irene (395 A.D. to 800 A.D.)* (1889); *idem*, *History of the Later Roman Empire from the Death of Theodosius to the Death of Justinian* (1923).

[155] Some of the Catholic historians who responded to him followed suit; for Ozanam and Dawson see Wood, *The Modern Origins of the Early Middle Ages*. Among 'secular' historians one should, of course, note A. H. M. Jones.

[156] F. Kelly, 'The Relative Importance of Cereals and Livestock in the Medieval Irish Economy: The Evidence of the Law Texts', *L'Irlandia e gli Irlandesi nell'alto medioevo*, Settimane di Studio 57 (Spoleto, 2010), 93–110; W. Davies, 'Economic Change: The Case for Growth', *ibid.*, 111–34. See also C. Doherty, 'The Monastic Town in Ireland', in *The Comparative History of Urban Origins in Non-Roman Europe: Ireland, Wales, Denmark, Germany, Poland and Russia from the Ninth to the Thirteenth Century*, ed. H. B. Clarke and A. Simms, BAR, International Series 255 (Oxford, 1985), 55–63; Richter, *Ireland and her Neighbours in the Seventh Century*, 22–3.

[157] J.-M. Carrié, 'Pratique et idéologie chrétiennes de l'économique (IVe–VIe siècle)', *Antiquité tardive*, 14 (2006), 17–26, emphasises the traditional nature of economic practice in the ecclesiastical economy. See also H. G. Ziche, 'Administrer la propriété de l'église: l'évêque comme clerc et comme entrepreneur', *ibid.*, 69–78; Moreno Martín, *La arquitectura monástica hispana*, 21. Wickham, *Framing the Early Middle Ages*, 259–302, deals with land-management, without distinguishing between ecclesiastical and secular estates.

[158] P. Gasnault, *Documents comptables de Saint-Martin de Tours à l'époque mérovingienne* (Paris, 1975); S. Sato, 'The Merovingian Accounting Documents of Tours', *Early Medieval Europe*, 9 (2000), 143–61.

[159] Devroey, *Puissants et misérables*, 426.

may shed light on some changing tenurial practices,[160] but evidence that allows a detailed reconstruction of estate organisation largely begins in the Carolingian period, by which time developments in the demesne system were underway.[161] In addition to the organisation of individual estates, the richer churches would have been concerned with the management of a very dispersed range of holdings, and here abbots could well have looked to the practices of the late Roman senatorial aristocracy, whose property was even more far-flung.[162] The dispersed nature of the properties of bishops and monasteries must have meant that ecclesiastical institutions needed to transport goods, and we get some glimpse of this in charters, above all those granted to Corbie in 661 and 716.[163] Yet one would like to know whether the involvement of churches in the transportation of goods led to any specific developments in trade and exchange.[164] We can be sure that bishops and monasteries were responsible for minting coin,[165] and also that religious establishments were heavily involved in the economy; it is less easy to say whether this prompted any change in its organisation.

What we can be sure about is that some of the wealth of the church was directed into new channels. Churches would seem to have constituted the major stone constructions of the post-Roman era, however small those of the seventh and eighth centuries were in comparison with what had been erected previously.[166] Among some Germanic groups, wealth which might once have gone into a great potlach burial, like those at Sutton Hoo, seems to have been channelled into churches which could act as mausolea.[167] Once built, there was the matter of their upkeep, to which a quarter of ecclesiastical income was dedicated in Italy.[168]

---

[160] A. Rio, *Legal Practice and the Written Word in the Early Middle Ages. Frankish Formulae, c. 500–1000* (Cambridge, 2009), 228–37.

[161] A. Verhulst, 'La genèse du régime domanial classique en France au haut moyen âge', *Agricoltura e mondo rurale in Occidente nell'alto medioevo*, Settimane di Studio 13 (Spoleto, 1966), 135–60; Devroey, *Puissants et misérables*, 435–41.

[162] That late Roman bishops essentially followed senatorial practices is argued by Ziche, 'Administrer la propriété de l'église'.

[163] T. Kölzer, ed., *Die Urkunden der Merowinger*, MGH, Diplomata Regum Francorum e Stirpe Merovingica (Hannover, 2001), 96 (pp. 246–8), 171 (pp. 424–6).

[164] R. Kaiser, '*Teleonum episcopi*. Du tonlieu royal au tonlieu épiscopal dans les civitates de la Gaule', *Histoire comparée de l'administration*, Beihefte der Francia 9 (Munich, 1980), 469–85, at 469–71; I. N. Wood, 'Monastères et ports dans l'Angleterre des VIIe–VIIIe siècles', in *Échanges, communications et réseaux dans le haut Moyen Âge*, ed. A. Gautier and C. Martin (Turnhout, 2011), 89–100. The distribution of relics is discussed by McCormick, *Origins of the European Economy*, 283–318.

[165] P. Grierson and M. Blackburn, *Medieval European Coinage*, I: *The Early Middle Ages (5th–10th centuries)* (Cambridge, 1986), 100, 139, 173.

[166] See the comparisons in Ward-Perkins, *The Fall of Rome*, 149.

[167] H. Geake, 'Burial Practice in Seventh- and Eighth-Century England', in *The Age of Sutton Hoo*, ed. M. Carver (Woodbridge, 1992), 83–94, at 92.

[168] Lesne, *Histoire de la propriété ecclésiastique*, I, 334.

The performance of the liturgy also required substantial funding. Paul Fouracre has brought home to us the extent to which the need for lighting materials is addressed in charters and immunities of the Merovingian period.[169] Nor should we forget the resources required for the production of major manuscripts: 1,545 high-quality animal skins were needed simply for the three Pandects of the Bible produced at Wearmouth-Jarrow.[170]

More important, however, is the question of human numbers. Gibbon envisaged the east Roman Empire in the fourth century as being swamped by a 'swarm of fanatics', claiming that in Egypt there was even a hope 'that the number of monks was equal to the remainder of the people'.[171] In his considerations of the causes of the Decline and Fall, he claimed that 'the sacred indolence of the monks was devoutly embraced by an effeminate age', while he also claimed that 'the bishops, from eighteen hundred pulpits, inculcated the duty of passive obedience to a lawful and orthodox sovereign'.[172] Nobody would argue that monasticism in the West was anywhere near as popular as Gibbon envisaged it to have been in the East, and Gaul's 130 bishoprics[173] are a small percentage of the overall number of dioceses in the empire.[174] Nevertheless, a significant number of people entered the church. We have a few indications of the numbers of monks in individual communities. The *Vita Clari* lists 1,525 monks divided between twelve communities in the city of Vienne in the seventh century, and claims there were sixty other houses in the diocese.[175] Certainly, there are problems with this text, which was apparently written in the context of the reforming episcopate of bishop Leodegarius (1025–69).[176] The numbers of religious would seem to represent a remarkably high percentage of the total population of the city – especially if we assume

[169] P. Fouracre, 'Eternal Light and Earthly Needs: Practical Aspects of the Development of Frankish Immunities', in *Property and Power*, ed. Davies and Fouracre, 53–81; Jones, 'The Western Church in the Fifth and Sixth Centuries', 3, citing the Council of Braga, II, c. 2.

[170] R. L. S. Bruce-Mitford, *The Art of the Codex Amiatinus*, Jarrow Lecture (1967), 2.

[171] E. Gibbon, *The History of the Decline and Fall of the Roman Empire*, ch. 37, ed. D. Womersley (Harmondsworth, 1994), II, 414, 419. I have not seen E. Wipszycka, *Moines et communautés monastiques en Égypte, IVe–VIIIe siècles* (Warsaw, 2008).

[172] Gibbon, *Decline and Fall*, ch. 38, ed. Womersley, II, 511.

[173] Duchesne, *Fastes épiscopaux*.

[174] For numbers of bishoprics, Jones, 'The Western Church in the Fifth and Sixth Centuries', 9.

[175] *Vita Clari*, c. 2, *Acta Sanctorum* (Brussels, 1863), Jan. I, 55–6. See I. N. Wood, 'Prelude to Columbanus: The Monastic Achievement in the Burgundian Territories', in *Columbanus and Merovingian Monasticism*, ed. H. B. Clarke and M. Brennan, BAR, International Series 113 (Oxford, 1981), 3–32, at 9. See also A. Hauck, *Kirchengeschichte Deutschlands* (Leipzig, 1887–1954), I, 276.

[176] N. Nimmegeers, 'Provincia Viennensis. Recherches sur la province ecclésiastique de Vienne et ses évêques au haut Moyen Âge (Ive–XIe siècles)' (unpubl. Thèse de doctorat, Lyon III, 2011), I, 2, 410–11, sees *Vita Clari* as belonging to reform programme of Leodegarius of Vienne (1025–69).

that they only include the monks and nuns, and leave out their servants, agents and tenants. Yet, so precise are the figures that it is difficult to think where they originated, if not in some early survey. Nor are they out of line with those that we have for other foundations. Writing in the late 1920s, Ulrich Berlière gathered a good deal of evidence relating to the size of monastic communities.[177] Several of them were in the 200s or above: Lérins supposedly held 500 and Jumièges 900![178] Most of Berlière's figures come from late sources, but there is some early evidence. Jonas of Bobbio states that there were 60 monks at Fontaines, one of the least significant of Columbanus's foundations,[179] which makes the 220 monks ascribed to Luxeuil in the *Vita Walarici* plausible.[180] Then there are the early Carolingian figures for Merovingian houses: Angilbert talks of 300 monks and 100 *pueri* at St. Riquier;[181] Adalhard prescribed that there should be between 300 and 400 at Corbie;[182] while Irminon lists 212 at St Germain.[183] All these we may compare with those in the dossier on the Holy Land drawn up for Charlemagne in the early ninth century, which talks of 725 religious in cenobitic institutions. The region, of course, was under Islamic control and this must therefore represent a very much smaller number than there had been in the fifth and sixth centuries.[184] The Frankish figures allow us to say no more than that a sizeable number of people entered the church. Much the same can be argued for England, where we know that the community of Wearmouth-Jarrow numbered 600 in 716 (though this figure, unlike those for Frankish houses, would seem to include servants and labourers as well as monks).[185] For Spain, we have comments on the crowds of monks at the monasteries of Fructuosus, above all Compludo with its army of ascetics drawn from all over the peninsula, and Nono, which led the local *duces* to worry whether they

[177] U. Berlière, 'Les nombres des moines dans les anciens monastères', *Revue Bénédictine*, 41 (1929), 231–61, 42 (1930), 19–42.

[178] Berlière, 'Les nombres des moines', pt 1, 248, 256. For Jumièges, see D. S. Dubusc, *Histoire de l'abbaye royale de St-Pierre de Jumièges*, ed. J. Roth (Rouen, 1882), I, 22; for Lérins, see now M. Lauwers, 'Porcaire, Aygulf et une île consacrée par le sang des martyrs (début du XIIe siècle)', in *Lérins, une île sainte de l'Antiquité au Moyen Âge*, ed. Codou and Lauwers, 444–455, at 453–5. Hauck, *Kirchengeschichte Deutschlands*, I, 276, also lists communities of 300, 500 and 900 monks and nuns.

[179] Berlière, 'Les nombres des moines', pt 2, 20; Jonas, *Vita Columbani*, I 17, ed. B. Krusch, MGH, SRG (Hannover, 1905).

[180] *Vita Walarici*, c. 5, ed. B. Krusch, MGH SRM 4. See Richter, *Bobbio*, 32.

[181] Berlière, 'Les nombres des moines', pt 1, 243; Angilbert, *Libellus de ecclesia Centula*, ed. G. Waitz, MGH, SS 15, 1 (Hannover, 1887), 174–9, at 178.

[182] Berlière, 'Les nombres des moines', pt 1, 242; P. Grenier, *Histoire de la ville et du comté de Corbie des origines à 1400* (Amiens, 1910), 78.

[183] Berlière, 'Les nombres des moines', pt 1, 244; A. Longnon, *Polyptique d'Irminon* (Paris, 1895), I, 187.

[184] McCormick, *Charlemagne's Survey of the Holy Land*, 55.

[185] *Vita Ceolfridi*, c. 33.

could still staff the army.[186] While some Lombard monasteries seem to have been very small, Bobbio is said to have housed 150 monks in 643,[187] and we have Aistulf's law referring to communities of over 50 monks.[188] Nor do such figures include the secular clergy. In any diocesan centre, there would have been a bishop, priests, deacons, subdeacons, exorcists, acolytes and lectors; and then there were priests in subordinate settlements.[189] It would be difficult to guess the numbers involved, but the figures from the diocese of Le Mans suggest that on average just short of ten priests and seven deacons were ordained each year.[190] A priest might well hold office for twenty years or more; multiply that by the 130 dioceses of Gaul, and one is dealing with tens of thousands of clergy in Francia at any one moment. The picture would be replicated in Spain and Italy, if not in England. Thus, a significant minority of the population entered the church. At least part of the revenues and yields of the estates conveyed to God and his saints must have been devoted to feed these men and women.[191] Indeed, a quarter of the wealth of the Italian church was supposedly earmarked for the clergy.[192] Gibbon's sacred indolents are a significant issue.

In addition, the cost of support for the poor, the widows, the orphans and the sick, that fell on the churches of the early Middle Ages, is almost incalculable, although we know from a ruling of Pope Simplicius in 465 that a quarter of the income of Italian bishops was supposed to be devoted to such causes.[193] Elsewhere, the regulations of episcopal expenditure were not so clear, but there was an assumption that a bishop should look

---

[186] *Vita Fructuosi*, cc. 3, 6.

[187] *Codice diplomatico*, ed. Cipolla, 109.

[188] *Ahistulfi leges*, 19.

[189] R. Godding, *Prêtres en Gaule mérovingienne* (Brussels, 2001), 36.

[190] *Ibid.*, 210, 458; *Actus pontificum Cenomannis in urbe degentium*, ed. Busson and Ledru, c. 7 (p. 52): Principius (29 years, 1 month, 21 days) *presbyteros enim sacravit ccv, et levitas atque alios ministros aecclesiasticos quantum necesse praevidit*; c. 8 (p. 59) Innocens (45 years, 10 months, 25 days) *presbyteros enim consecravit cccxviii, et levitas atque alios ministros, quantum necesse fuit*; c. 9 (p. 83) Domnolus (46 years, 11 months, 24 days) *et fecit ordinationes lxxv, presbyteros ccclx, diaconos ccl et reliquos ministros sufficienter*; c. 13 (pp. 182–3) Berarius (26 years, 4 months, 14 days) *fecit ordinationes lxi; sacerdotes ccccv, diaconos ccxxviii, subdiaconos et reliquos ministros sufficienter*; c. 14 (p. 199) Aiglibertus (34 years, 6 months, 11 days) *et fecit ordinationes lxxv, presbyteros ccc, diaconos cccx, subdiaconos xc et reliquos ministros quantum necesse fuit*; c. 15 (p. 224) Herlemundus (26 years, 9 months, 13 days) *et fecit ordinationes xxxviii, presbyteros per diversa loca cclxxxiii, diaconos clxxii, et reliquos ministros quantum necesse tunc temporis erat*.

[191] Godding, *Prêtres en Gaule mérovingienne*, 331–58.

[192] Lesne, *Histoire de la propriété ecclésiastique*, I, 334.

[193] Simplicius, ep. 1, ed. A. Thiel, *Epistolae Romanorum pontificum genuinae et quae ad eos scriptae sunt a S. Hilaro usque ad Pelagium I*, 1 (Brunsberg, 1868), 175–7); Stutz, *Geschichte des kirchlichen Benefizialwesens*, 27–8; Jones, 'The Western Church in the Fifth and Sixth Centuries', 12. See also Gregory I, *Register*, IV 11. See also, Brown, *Through the Eye of a Needle*, 488.

after his flock.[194] Julianus Pomerius, writing around 500, saw donations to the church as being primarily intended for the poor, and it was they who were defrauded, in the eyes of the church councils, by those who stole ecclesiastical property.[195] We do, however, get a very rough indication of one group who would need care in a time of crisis from the statement in John the Deacon's *Life of Gregory the Great*, that 3,000 refugee nuns were registered on the *matricula*, poor lists, of the churches of Rome.[196] Hospitals, which were religious institutions, could be very generously endowed, as in the case of Childebert's *xenodochium* at Lyons.[197] Essentially, a whole range of social services became part of the ecclesiastical budget. In Peter Brown's words, there was a shift 'from "Lover of the City" to "Lover of the Poor"'.[198] To love one's city, and to be its most outstanding patron – the French rather more than the English use the classically derived word evergetism[199] – was a virtue in classical Antiquity; the social demands of the Gospels led to a new set of priorities, effectively moral imperitives, with an eschatalogical backing,[200] the costs of dealing with which fell above all to bishops. This was already true by 450, but the growing benefactions to the church, and the fact that a bishop was expected to set aside a quarter of his revenue for such philanthropy, must have had an increasing impact on the structures of society.

Alongside the religious and pastoral duties of bishops and abbots, one should set the claims of some churches to exemption from taxation, which recur on a number of occasions in the *Histories* of Gregory of Tours.[201] Although the precise chronology of the collapse of the tax system in

---

[194] Lesne, *Histoire de la propriété ecclésiastique*, I, 147, 333–5, 370, 375; Roper, 'Wilfrid's Landholdings in Northumbria', 69.

[195] Julianus Pomerius, *De vita contemplativa*, II 9, Patrolgia Latina (PL), ed. J. P. Migne, 59, cols. 453–4; Lesne, *Histoire de la propriété ecclésiastique*, I, 4; P. Brown, 'From *Patriae Amator* to *Amator Pauperum* and Back Again: Social Imagination and Social Change in the West between Late Antiquity and the Early Middle Ages, ca. 300–600 A.D.' (forthcoming). I am indebted to Peter Brown for allowing me to see this paper in advance of publication.

[196] John the Deacon, *Vita Gregorii*, II cc. 27–30, PL 75, cols. 59–242; Markus, *Gregory the Great and his World*, 121–2; Brown, 'From *Patriae Amator* to *Amator Pauperum*'.

[197] Council of Orléans V (549), c. 15, ed. Gaudemet and Basdevant, *Les canons des conciles mérovingien*, I, Sources Chrétiennes 353; F. Prinz, *Frühes Mönchtum im Frankenreich* (Kempten, 1985), 155.

[198] Brown, *Poverty and Leadership*, esp. 1–44, see *idem*, 'From *Patriae Amator* to *Amator Pauperum*'.

[199] For the relationship between classical evergetism and the building of churches, R. Haensch, 'Le financement de la construction des églises pendant l'antiquité tardive et l'évergetisme antique', *Antiquité tardive*, 14 (2006), 47–58.

[200] For the transition to the Christian economy, see Carrié, 'Pratique et idéologie chrétiennes de l'économique'; also J.-M. Salamito, 'Christianisme antique et économie: raisons et modalité d'une rencontre historique', *Antiquité tardive*, 14 (2006), 27–37; R. Flynn, *Almsgiving in the Later Roman Empire. Christian Promotion and Practice (313–450)* (Oxford, 2006).

[201] Gregory, *Decem Libri Historiarum*, III 25, IX 30

the post-Roman world is still a matter for debate,[202] the collapse itself has plausibly been presented as one of the central developments of the period.[203] Among the forces undermining the old fiscal regime, the claims to exemption made by leading clergy, as they represented the demands of their communities, may well have been significant.

While there was an undoubted change between the fourth and the eighth centuries, it is by looking back to the pagan period that one can most appreciate its scale. The church's acquisition of property and wealth not only expanded from a very low base, but pagan religious centres were in no sense comparable to the Christian churches and monasteries that followed. Roman temples may have been rich in gold, silver and precious objects, but they were rarely endowed with vast estates.[204] Egyptian temples had possessed extensive properties at the time of the Roman conquest, but these were taken over by the state; likewise, Hellenistic Asia Minor originally boasted some temples well endowed with land, but their endowments were either confiscated or directed to new uses after the Roman take-over. In Italy, temples did not have significant landed endowments, and the same was true in Gaul.[205] One may guess that this was the case for the whole of the West. For the Germanic world we do know of sacred groves, though their extent is far from clear, and there is nothing to suggest the existence of major temples.[206] In the late nineteenth century, Ulrich Stutz argued that the supposed temporal property of Germanic temples provided a background for the development of the *Eigenkirche*, proprietary churches, a Germanist reading that had its adherents before 1939. Its appeal to an archaic Germanic past was less attractive after 1945 for ideological reasons, but in any case it had never been underpinned by any evidence.[207] The transfer of property to the church thus constituted a tenurial revolution, much as Goody argued. Pagan priesthoods in the Classical world, moreover, were primarily civic offices, usually held for a short period of time, and most certainly not

---

[202] See most recently Wickham, *Framing the Early Middle Ages*, 102–15.

[203] C. Wickham, 'The Other Transition: From the Ancient World to Feudalism', *Past and Present*, 113 (1984), 3–36.

[204] For what follows, I am indebted to Penny Goodman for guidance. J. E. Stambaugh, 'The Functions of Roman Temples', in *Aufstieg und Niedergang der römischen Welt*, 2.16.1 (Berlin, 1978), 554–608, at 574–6.

[205] See M. Beard, J. North and S. Price, *Religions of Rome* (Cambridge, 1998), I, esp. 87–8, on the set-up in Roman Italy, and 340–2, on Egypt and Asia Minor. For Gaul, see P. J. Goodman, *The Roman City and its Periphery: From Rome to Gaul* (2007), 128–37.

[206] I. N. Wood, 'Pagan Religions and Superstitions East of the Rhine from the Fifth to the Ninth Century', in *After Empire. Towards an Ethnology of Europe's Barbarians*, ed. G. Ausenda (Woodbridge, 1995), 253–68, at 255–7.

[207] Stutz, *Geschichte des kirchlichen Benefizialwesens*, 89–216; curiously it was reprinted in 1961, and Mayke de Jong informs me that it was still recommended reading in Amsterdam University in 1971.

a full-time occupation.[208] The one major exception, the druids, were suppressed at the time of the conquests of Gaul and Britain. As for the Germanic world, there is no evidence for an organised priesthood.[209] There had been provision for the poor in some cities of the Roman Empire (and in Rome and Constantinople on a colossal scale), but previously it had fallen to the state or to individuals with a strong sense of civic pride, and not the temples, to address the problem.[210]

The transfer of land to God and his saints was, therefore, a major social and economic development, which frequently ran alongside the religious and spiritual change entailed by Christianisation, and not just in Anglo-Saxon England, where the question of the development of the charter, and the impact of the church on land tenure, has already attracted the attention of early medievalists.[211] Some religious historians of late Antiquity and the early Middle Ages have been fully aware of the social implications of their subject, and have rightly stressed the extent to which the lands converted to Christianity became 'a wholly sacral world'[212] – a world that might be better understood in terms of temple-building societies studied by social anthropologists than of more modern patterns of production and distribution.[213] Yet this social and economic revolution has scarcely been registered by socio-economic historians.[214] And some of those who have been aware of the scale of the change have, like Roth, seen it as a preliminary to a wider set of changes, which they call the rise of feudalism. I would suggest that the transfer of vast amounts of Western Europe in the pre-Carolingian period has been underestimated, perhaps because of the secularisations of the eighth century – and one concomitant of my argument must be that we should take those secularisations very seriously indeed. The pre-Carolingian benefaction of the church constitutes, I would argue, an important phase

---

[208] Beard, North and Price, *Religions of Rome*, I, 27–30.

[209] Wood, 'Pagan Religions and Superstitions East of the Rhine', 257–9.

[210] Wickham, *Framing the Early Middle Ages*, 72–3, 76; J.-M. Carrié, 'Les distributions alimentaires dans les cites de l'empire romain tardif', *Mélanges de l'école française de Rome: Antiquité*, 87 (1975), 995–1101.

[211] Wormald, *Bede and the Conversion of England*, summarises earlier work; Blair, *The Church in Anglo-Saxon Society*, 100–8.

[212] R. Markus, 'Between Marrou and Brown: Transformations of Late Antique Christianity', in *Transformations of Late Antiquity: Essays for Peter Brown*, ed. P. Rousseau and M. Papoutsakis (Farnham, 2009), 1–13, 11–12. C. Sotinel, 'Le don chrétien et ses retombées sur l'économie dans l'antiquité tardive', *Antiquité tardive*, 14 (2006), 105–16, plays down the economic impact of giving to the church in the late Roman period, but allows that its subsequent repercussions were considerable.

[213] While historians of early India have made comparison with early medieval Europe (see, for example, R. Thapar, *Early India from the Origins to A.D. 1300* (2002), 370–81), Western medievalists have rarely reciprocated.

[214] It is noted, but not explored, for instance, by G. Duby, *The Early Growth of the European Economy: Warriors and Peasants from the Seventh to the Twelfth Century* (1974), 37–8, 54–6.

in the social and economic history of Western Europe in its own right. It provides a key to the development of Europe as a Christian society, which is every bit as much a social and economic issue as a religious one, although its significance has been obscured by the compartmentalisation of ecclesiastical and secular history.

Transactions of the RHS 23 (2013), pp. 75–102 © Royal Historical Society 2013
doi:10.1017/S0080440113000042

EMPEROR OTTO III AND THE END OF TIME*

The Alexander Prize Essay

By Levi Roach

ABSTRACT. There has been much controversy over the role of apocalyptic thought at the court of Otto III of Germany (983–1002). This is in no small part a product of modern scholarship discussing the subject almost exclusively with reference to the so-called 'terrors of the year 1000', the result being highly polarised 'all or nothing' arguments, which run the risk of underestimating both the complexity and dynamism of eschatological expectation in this period. In contrast, the following paper argues that apocalyptic thought played an important part in politics under Otto III, but one which cannot be explained by the proximity of the first millennium alone.

Almost forty years ago Donald Bullough, in a paper read before the Society, drew attention to the importance of the *Ludus de Antichristo* for our understanding of twelfth-century society. He argued that the *Ludus* illustrates not only the role of ritual and drama in the high Middle Ages (which was the focus of his paper), but also the frequently overlooked contribution of apocalyptic thought to intellectual life of the period.[1] His point, as I take it, was that apocalyptic and prophetic literature played a key role in contemporary society and that it was modern, not medieval, sensibilities which had led to this being sidelined in discussions of such subjects as the Twelfth-Century Renaissance. Now, since Bullough's day much work has been done to redress this imbalance; nevertheless, a degree of resistance to the study of apocalypticism remains. As recently as the late 1990s, the response of a senior academic to a paper on eschatology within Carolingian court circles was outright denial: 'I cannot believe that Charlemagne had anything at all to do with eschatological matters.'[2] Less

---

* I am grateful to James Palmer for his comments and for sharing work in advance of publication. Further thanks are due to audiences at Leeds and Exeter for discussion and observations.

[1] D. Bullough, 'The Games People Played: Drama and Ritual as Propaganda in Medieval Europe', *Transactions of the Royal Historical Society*, fifth series, 24 (1974), 97–122, at 113–17.

[2] 'Ich kann nicht glauben, dass Karl der Große irgendetwas mit eschatologische[n] Dingen zu tun hatte', quoted by R. Landes, *Heaven on Earth: The Varieties of the Millennial Experience* (Oxford, 2011), 71 n. 28. This was in response to W. Brandes, '"Tempora periculosa sunt". Eschatologisches im Vorfeld der Kaiserkrönung Karls des Großen', in *Das Frankfurter*

overt, but arguably no less revealing, is Knut Görich's recent biography of Frederick Barbarossa – at or around whose court Bullough and many others, both before and since, have placed the performance of the *Ludus* – which says nothing whatsoever about eschatology.[3] The following paper seeks to challenge such reticence, building on recent work on medieval apocalypticism. Particular inspiration has come from studies of Charlemagne's reforming efforts of the eighth and ninth centuries, which argue that religious and political *correctio* were motivated in part by eschatological concerns.[4] Important from a slightly different angle is work on apocalyptic traditions in the high Middle Ages, which highlights the dynamic contribution of eschatology to movements as diverse as church reform, the crusades and the missionary efforts of the mendicant orders.[5]

Indeed, eschatology was an existential matter in the Middle Ages: it was widely believed that the world was in its sixth (and final) age and that the end might come at any point. There was nothing unorthodox about this: Augustine of Hippo taught that the world had entered its sixth and final age upon the incarnation and authorities such as Gregory the Great expressed the expectation that little if any time remained before this. That not only monks and bishops but also kings and noblemen held such beliefs should not be doubted. From its inception, the office of kingship was influenced by ecclesiastical ideals and by the Carolingian period it was understood as a form of God-given ministry (or *ministerium*), much like episcopal office.[6] Taking inspiration from the Church Fathers (in particular Augustine and Gregory), manuals were written for laymen in order to teach them in the implications of this ministry. The central message was that with power comes responsibility, since leaders will have to answer for the souls of those entrusted to them at the Day of

---

Konzil von 794. Kristallisationspunkt karolingischer Kultur, ed. R. Berndt (2 vols., Mainz, 1997), I, 49–79.

[3] K. Görich, *Friedrich Barbarossa. Eine Biographie* (Munich, 2011). On the *Ludus*, see H. Möhring, *Der Weltkaiser der Endzeit. Entstehung und Wirkung einer tausendjährigen Weissagung* (Stuttgart, 2000), 166–84; and A. A. Latowsky, *Emperor of the World: Charlemagne and the Construction of Imperial Authority, 800–1229* (Ithaca, NY, 2013), 149–60.

[4] M. Alberi, '"Like the Army of God's Camp": Political Theology and Apocalyptic Warfare at Charlemagne's Court', *Viator*, 41, 2 (2010), 1–20; J. Palmer, *Apocalypse and Authority in the Early Middle Ages* (forthcoming), ch. 5.

[5] J. Flori, *L'Islam et la fin des temps. L'interprétation prophétique des invasions musulmanes dans la chrétienté médiévale* (Paris, 2007); B. E. Whalen, *Dominion of God: Christendom and Apocalypse in the Middle Ages* (Cambridge, MA, 2009); J. Rubenstein, *Armies of Heaven: The First Crusade and the Quest for Apocalypse* (New York, 2011); M. Gabriele, *An Empire of Memory: The Legend of Charlemagne, the Franks, and Jerusalem before the First Crusade* (Oxford, 2011).

[6] M. de Jong, 'Charlemagne's Church', in *Charlemagne: Empire and Society*, ed. J. Story (Manchester, 2005), 103–35; M. E. Moore, *A Sacred Kingdom: Bishops and the Rise of Frankish Kingship, 300–850* (Washington, DC, 2011).

Judgement.[7] Rulers therefore had every reason to be concerned about the end of time and it is simply absurd to suggest that Charlemagne would not have had any interest in such matters – regardless of whether he harboured apocalyptic expectations about *anno mundi* 6000 (that is, AD 800/1), as has been suggested,[8] the one thing we can be fairly certain is that he would have given considerable thought to the Last Judgement and the fate of his soul.

To illustrate the benefits of taking eschatology seriously as a factor in medieval politics, I should like to examine the role of apocalyptic thought at the court of Otto III of Germany (983–1002). This subject has generally been subsumed into debates regarding the turning of the first millennium and the fears which some scholars claim were attendant upon this. As a consequence, opinion is highly polarised: whilst some ascribe great significance to the 'apocalyptic year 1000', seeing this as the driving force behind heightened apocalyptic expectation in Otto III's reign, others deny that such an increase in eschatological interests can be seen at all.[9] Indeed, the issue has become so fraught that Otto's most recent scholarly biographer, Gerd Althoff, avoids it altogether.[10] However, as is so often the case, it may not so much be the answers which historians

---

[7] H. H. Anton, *Fürstenspiegel und Herrscherethos in der Karolingerzeit* (Bonn, 1968); R. Stone, *Morality and Masculinity in the Carolingian Empire* (Cambridge, 2011), esp. 135–73.

[8] Brandes, 'Eschatologisches'; J. Fried, 'Papst Leo III. besucht Karl den Großen in Paderborn oder Einhards Schweigen', *Historische Zeitschrift*, 272 (2001), 281–326. On which, see J. Palmer 'Calculating Time and the End of Time in the Carolingian World, *c.* 740–820', *English Historical Review*, 126 (2011), 1307–31.

[9] From various standpoints, see J. Fried, 'Endzeiterwartung um die Jahrtausendwende', *Deutsches Archiv*, 45 (1989), 381–473, esp. 427–32; S. Freund, 'Das Jahr 1000. Ende der Welt oder Beginn eines neuen Zeitalters?', in *Der Tag X in der Geschichte. Erwartungen und Enttäuschungen seit tausend Jahren*, ed. E. Bünz, R. Gries and F. Möller (Stuttgart, 1997), 24–49 and 335–41; S. Gouguenheim, *Les fausses terreurs de l'an mil. Attente de la fin des temps ou approfondissement de la foi?* (Paris, 1999), 136–45; K. Görich, 'Das Jahr 999 und die Angst vor der Jahrtausendwende', in *Der Weltuntergang*, ed. H. Halter and M. Müller (Zurich, 1999), 31–40; B. Schneidmüller, *Jahrtausendwende. Ein Magdeburger Vortrag über Vorstellungen und Wirklichkeiten im Mittelalter* (Magdeburg, 2000); O. Ramonat, 'Otto III. – Christianisierung und Endzeiterwartung', in *Europas Mitte um 1000. Beiträge zur Geschichte, Kunst und Archäologie*, ed. A. Wieczorek and H.-M. Hinz (2 pts, Stuttgart, 2000), 792–7; M. Gabriele, 'Otto III, Charlemagne, and Pentecost A.D. 1000: A Reconsideration Using Diplomatic Evidence', in *The Year 1000: Religious and Social Response to the Turning of the First Millennium*, ed. M. Frassetto (New York, 2002), 111–32; B. Arnold, 'Eschatological Imagination and the Program of Roman Imperial and Ecclesiastical Renewal at the End of the Tenth Century', in *The Apocalyptic Year 1000: Religious Expectation and Social Change, 950–1050*, ed. R. Landes, A. Gow and D. C. Van Meter (Oxford, 2003), 271–87; H. Mayr-Harting, 'Apocalyptic Book Illustration in the Early Middle Ages', in *Apocalyptic in History and Tradition*, ed. C. Rowland and J. Barton (2003), 172–211; and H. Möhring, 'Die renovatio imperii Kaiser Ottos III. und die Antichrist-Erwartung der Zeitgenossen an der Jahrtausendwende von 1000/1001', *Archiv für Kulturgeschichte*, 93 (2011), 333–50.

[10] G. Althoff, *Otto III.* (Darmstadt, 1996).

are receiving as the questions we are asking which are wrong here. Sources from Otto III's reign say nothing explicit about the turning of the year 1000 and it is therefore impossible to establish with certainty what he and his contemporaries thought about this.[11] Nevertheless, there is ample evidence for heightened eschatological interest and expectation, as I hope to show.

In what follows, my focus shall be on events between 996 and Otto's death in 1002, with discussion framing the emperor's actions in the year 1000 within broader developments in his reign. These were, of course, the years of the famed *renovatio imperii Romanorum* (i.e. 'renewal of the empire of the Romans') and though it has long been noted that this project may have been apocalyptic in inspiration, the details have yet to be explored fully. Discussion will proceed chronologically, tracing the events of Otto's reign and the role of eschatological thought therein. The argument presented, it must be emphasised, is aggregate: any individual piece of evidence might quite reasonably be called into question; however, the cumulative impression is, I hope, persuasive.

We shall begin in 996 with Otto's first trip to Italy. Like all Saxon rulers since the time of his grandfather, Otto I, Otto III laid great store in obtaining the imperial title and began making plans for his coronation in Rome from the start of his independent reign (which seems to have begun gradually over 994–5).[12] Initially, he was held back by affairs on his eastern border, but by 996 Otto was able to proceed south. Upon arrival in Italy, he found that the pope, John XV, had passed away and arranged to have his chaplain Bruno appointed Pope Gregory V, a move which paved the way for his own imperial coronation on 21 May. Of particular interest from our present standpoint is the fact that the *Miracula S. Alexii* report that Otto wore a cloak bearing images of the Apocalypse (of John) on this occasion, which he subsequently donated to the monastery of Boniface and Alexius on the Aventine.[13] This was clearly a sumptuous item and its importance is twofold: first, it suggests that Otto began his imperial reign with eschatological considerations in mind; and secondly, it may imply an association between these and SS Boniface and Alexius.

---

[11] As H.-H. Kortüm, 'Millenniumsängste – Mythos oder Realität? Die moderne Mediävistik und das Jahr Eintausend', in *Zeit, Zeitenwechsel, Endzeit. Zeit im Wandel der Zeiten, Kulturen, Techniken und Disziplinen*, ed. G. U. Leinsle and J. Mecke (Regensburg, 2000), 171–88, rightly emphasises.

[12] T. Offergeld, *Reges pueri. Das Königtum Minderjähriger im frühen Mittelalter*, Monumenta Germaniae Historica (MGH): Schriften 50 (Hannover, 2001), 732–50.

[13] *Miracula S. Alexii*, c. 3, ed. G. H. Pertz, MGH: Scriptores 4 (Hannover, 1841), 619–20. Although the *Miracula* are in need of detailed source-critical examination, there is little reason to doubt their accuracy: not only were they written within living memory (before 1012), but embroidered cloaks were a common form of regalia at this time; see P. E. Schramm et al., *Herrschaftszeichen und Staatssymbolik. Beiträge zu ihrer Geschichte vom dritten bis zum sechzehnten Jahrhundert*, MGH: Schriften 13 (3 pts, Stuttgart, 1954–6), 578–9.

The significance of this latter point will become clearer as we proceed, but at present we should simply note that the monastery had offered refuge to Otto's friend and associate Adalbert of Prague in the later 980s and early 990s. Indeed, it was at this point that Otto first met Adalbert – an event which apparently made a deep impression on the emperor – and it may be that the Bohemian bishop introduced the newly crowned ruler to the centre.[14] However, the emperor was soon drawn back north of the Alps; Adalbert, on the other hand, who had been ordered by synodal decree to return to Prague, was only able to visit Otto briefly at Aachen before departing eastwards.

The events of the following year are particularly important. When Adalbert failed once more to establish himself at Prague he took up the mission to Prussia, where he found his martyrdom in 997. News of this reached Otto in autumn, while he was staying at Aachen once more, and his reaction was swift: he founded a monastery in honour of saint and began taking measures to promote his cult, including commissioning a *Vita* (perhaps from the pen of Bishop Notker of Liège).[15] The significance of these events lies in the nexus visible in the following years between Aachen, the memory of Charlemagne, the cult of St Adalbert and apocalyptic expectation. Indeed, not only did Otto found a monastery dedicated to Adalbert at this juncture, but he also initiated a series of changes at Aachen, the nature of which has been a matter of controversy. Thus, while Ernst-Dieter Hehl believes that the emperor intended to establish a bishopric at the site, a plan which he was prevented from realising by his early death, Ludwig Falkenstein argues that Otto's aim was simply to introduce a more 'Roman' (*stadrömisch*) form of liturgical observance and to promote the palace and its environs as an urban centre.[16] Regardless of which interpretation one favours, there can be no doubt as to Aachen's importance to the emperor; after Rome, it is

---

[14] Though K. Görich, 'Erinnerung und ihre Aktualisierung. Otto III., Aachen und die Karlstradition', in *Robert Folz (1910–1996). Mittler zwischen Frankreich und Deutschland*, ed. F. J. Felten, P. Monnet and A. Saint-Denis (Stuttgart, 2007), 97–116, at 107, suggests that Otto may have first met Adalbert in 992 (at Aachen).

[15] J. Fried, 'Gnesen – Aachen – Rom. Otto III. und der Kult des hl. Adalbert. Beobachtungen zum älteren Adalbertsleben', in *Polen und Deutschland vor 1000 Jahren. Die Berliner Tagung über den 'Akt von Gnesen'*, ed. M. Borgolte (Berlin, 2002), 235–79, esp. 254–9; Görich, 'Erinnerung', 104–9. However, see also now C. Gaspar, 'The Life of St Adalbert Bishop of Prague and Martyr', in *Saints of the Christianization Age of Central Europe (Tenth–Eleventh Centuries)*, ed. G. Klaniczay (Budapest, 2012), 77–182, at 88–93.

[16] E.-D. Hehl, 'Herrscher, Kirche und Kirchenrecht im spätottonischen Reich', in *Otto III. – Heinrich II. Eine Wende?*, ed. B. Schneidmüller and S. Weinfurter (Stuttgart, 1997), 169–203, at 186–203; *idem*, 'Aachen an der ersten Jahrtausendwende. Ein Bistumsplan Ottos III. im Zeichen Karls des Großen und Adalberts von Prag', *Geschichte im Bistum Aachen*, 6 (2001/2), 1–27; L. Falkenstein, *Otto III. und Aachen*, MGH: Studien und Texte 22 (Hannover, 1998), 91–7.

the location at which he spent the most time during his mature reign.[17] Otto's love of the palace also drew the attention of his contemporaries: the *Annals of Quedlinburg* report that it was his favourite centre after Rome and Adabold of Utrecht recalls the emperor's affection for the site.[18] Otto apparently began making plans for Aachen from the start of his independent reign and his first move to realise these came in early 997, when he secured papal permission to establish a college of cardinals at the Chapel of St Mary.[19] It was in autumn of this year, when Otto next enjoyed an extended stay at the palace, that further developments can be seen. It was at this juncture that the emperor heard of Adalbert's martyrdom and undertook to propagate the new saint's cult. It was also during this stay that Otto granted the estate of Dortmund to the chapel in a charter which opens with an *arenga* meditating on the rewards which go to those who restore churches from misfortune and neglect, perhaps reflecting the emperor's troubled state of mind. More importantly (and unusually), this grant is said to have been issued for the memory of not only Otto's parents, but also Charlemagne, which is the first time that the latter's memory is mentioned in an Ottonian diploma.[20] More extraordinary yet is a second grant in favour of the chapel issued at this point, which was likewise undertaken for the memory of Otto's parents and Charlemagne. This also opens with a lengthy *arenga*, but here the thoughts expressed are distinctly apocalyptic: Otto meditates on the fragility of life and quotes 1 Corinthians X.11 to the effect that 'we are those, upon whom the ends of the ages are come'.[21] Now, we must be careful not to make too much of this; at a literal level the charter expresses little more than the belief, shared by all medieval Christians, that the end is nigh. Nevertheless, there is an unmistakable tone of urgency. Indeed, biblical quotation is rare in Ottonian diplomata (even in *arengae*) and the specific line cited is not found in any other contemporary charter. Such deviations from standard diplomatic practice are all the more noteworthy in the light of the emperor's known penchant for drafting his own charters – it may well

---

[17] J. Fleckenstein, *Die Hofkapelle der deutschen Könige*, MGH: Schriften 16 (2 vols., Stuttgart, 1959–66), II, 141–3 and 146–7; T. Zotz, 'Die Gegenwart des Königs. Zur Herrschaftspraxis Ottos III. und Heinrichs II.', in *Otto III. – Heinrich II.*, ed. Schneidmüller and Weinfurter, 349–86, at 358–61.

[18] *Annales Quedlinburgenses*, *s.a.* 1000, ed. M. Giese, MGH: Scriptores rerum Germanicarum in usum scholarum 72 (Hannover, 2004), 513; Adalbold of Utrecht, *Vita Heinrici II imperatoris*, c. 4, ed. H. van Rij, Nederlandse historische Bronnen 3 (Amsterdam, 1983), 7–95, at 50.

[19] *Papsturkunden, 896–1046*, ed. H. Zimmermann (3 vols., Vienna, 1985–9), no. 341, with Falkenstein, *Otto III. und Aachen*, 84–111, esp. 105–8.

[20] D O III 257. Otto III's diplomas are cited according to the following conventions: D O III (with number of document) = *Die Urkunden Ottos II. und Ottos III.*, II, *Die Urkunden Otto des III.*, ed. T. Sickel, MGH: Diplomata regum et imperatorum Germaniae 2.ii (Hannover, 1893).

[21] D O III 258.

be that this document preserves elements of what Hartmut Hoffmann terms Otto's 'own dictation' (*Eigendiktat*).[22] The emperor's well-evidenced interest in Aachen makes the proposition especially tempting: if he were to have taken a hand in the formulation of any of his early charters, we should expect it to be in privileges concerning Aachen. Moreover, apocalyptic expressions are often found in documents relating to Aachen, Charlemagne and Adalbert, as we shall see, reinforcing the impression that these details were not included by chance.

Why eschatological expectations might have come to the fore at this point is difficult to ascertain. On a general level, it may be that as the year 1000 drew nigh the end of time was felt to 'loom dangerously close' (to paraphrase Johannes Fried): the Apocalypse of John famously predicted that Satan (often interpreted as Antichrist) would be bound for 1,000 years and there are indications that some took this literally to mean 1,000 years from the birth (or death) of Christ.[23] However, it may also be that Adalbert's death led Otto to consider his own mortality and the fate of his soul: having lost a close friend, it was natural for the emperor's thoughts to stray onto death and judgement. Another factor may have been events in Italy. After Otto's departure in 996, the people of Rome led by Crescentius Nomentanus had risen up and elected John Philagathos, an associate of Otto's mother Theophanu, as (anti-)pope. To make matters worse, in 997 Arduin of Ivrea, a leading north Italian magnate, killed Bishop Peter of Vercelli. As Henry Mayr-Harting notes, such events may have possessed an apocalyptic quality for contemporary observers: it was believed that Antichrist would arise in the East and John was not only Greek, but backed by the Byzantine emperor.[24] Moreover, it was expected that Antichrist's reign would be preceded by a 'falling away' (*discessio*) from the empire, something which the Roman revolt might have been felt to fulfil. Yet these are not the only biblical prophecies which might be associated with recent events. The so-called Little Apocalypse (Mark XIII, Matt. XXIV and Luke XXI) predicts that false belief will spread and love will grow cold immediately before the end of time and these rebellions might also be seen in such terms – after all, what clearer evidence could there be for love growing cold than the betrayal of John, who may have been one of

---

[22] H. Hoffmann, 'Eigendiktat in den Urkunden Ottos III. und Heinrichs II.', *Deutsches Archiv*, 44 (1988), 390–423. Note, however, that Hoffmann does not cite this diploma as an example of *Eigendiktat*.

[23] J. Fried, *Das Mittelalter. Geschichte und Kultur* (Munich, 2008), 135–63 (chapter entitled 'Die Endzeit rückt bedrohlich nahe'). See also *idem*, 'Endzeiterwartung'; and R. Landes, 'The Fear of an Apocalyptic Year 1000: Augustinian Historiography, Medieval and Modern', *Speculum*, 75 (2000), 97–145.

[24] H. Mayr-Harting, *Ottonian Book Illumination: An Historical Study* (2 vols., 1991), II, 48. On Antichrist traditions, see W. Bousset, *Der Antichrist in der Überlieferung des Judentums, des Neuen Testaments und der alten Kirche: Ein Beitrag zur Auslegung der Apocalypse* (Göttingen, 1895).

Otto's tutors?[25] To make matters more sinister, John was elected in 997, meaning that a reign of three and a half years – the length, that is, that Antichrist was expected to reign – would have taken him into the year 1000.

There are indications that contemporaries did indeed see events in such terms. Thus, the *Annals of Quedlinburg* term John and Crescentius 'ministers of Satan' at this point, a title with clear apocalyptic resonances.[26] Even more telling is the evidence of Otto's diplomata: in later privileges in favour of Vercelli, Arduin and his followers are termed heresiarchs and any who dare to oppose the bishop are said to be inspired by the devil, terms which, as Matthew Gabriele notes, associate these individuals with the false belief and diabolical machination which were expected to precede Endtime.[27] Indeed, it is uncommon for Ottonian diplomata to associate malefactors with the devil in this fashion and the source of these sentiments is probably to be sought at court.[28] This conclusion is supported by the fact that the documents in question were drafted by Leo of Vercelli, one of the emperor's chief advisers.[29] A similar, albeit more hypothetical connection with court can be postulated for the entry in the *Annals of Quedlinburg*. This work draws on the (now-lost) *Annales Hildesheimenses majores*, a contemporary set of annals kept at Hildesheim, whose bishop at the time, Bernward, enjoyed close contacts with court.[30] Gerbert of Aurillac, another leading royal adviser, may also have harboured such feelings: during earlier struggles over the archbishopric of Reims he had accused Crescentius in similarly apocalyptic terms of being a *membrum*

---

[25] G. Althoff, 'Vormundschaft, Erzieher, Lehrer – Einflüsse auf Otto III.', in *Kaiserin Theophanu. Begegnung des Ostens und Westens um die Wende des ersten Jahrtausends*, ed. A. von Euw and P. Schreiner (2 vols., Cologne, 1991), II, 277–90, at 284–6.

[26] *Annales Quedlinburgenses, s.a.* 998, 498.

[27] D O III 324, 384, 388, with Gabriele, 'Otto III', 121.

[28] H. Fichtenau, 'Rhetorische Elemente in der ottonisch-salischen Herrscherurkunde' (1960), repr. in and cited from his *Beiträge zur Mediävistik. Ausgewählte Aufsätze* (3 vols., Stuttgart, 1975–86), II, 126–56, at 133.

[29] H. Bloch, 'Beiträge zur Geschichte des Bischofs Leo von Vercelli und seiner Zeit', *Neues Archiv*, 22 (1897), 11–136, at 59–71; W. Huschner, *Transalpine Kommunikation im Mittelalter. Diplomatische, kulturelle und politische Wechselwirkungen zwischen Italien und dem nordalpinen Reich (9.–11. Jahrhundert)*, MGH: Schriften 52 (3 pts, Hannover, 2003), 267–8. While these documents are not above suspicion, they are unlikely to be outright forgeries: G. Ferraris, 'Il "cerchio magico" dei privilegi imperiali per la chiesa di Vercelli. Il diploma di Ottone III (Roma, 7 maggio 999)', in *DCCCCXCVIIII–1999. Per un millennio: da 'Trebledo' a Casalborgone*, ed. A. A. Cigna and A. A. Settia (Chiavisso, 2000), 15–48; F. Panero, 'Il consolidamento della signoria territoriale dei Vescovi di Vercelli fra XI e XII secolo', in *Vercelli nel secolo XII* (Vercelli 2005), 411–49, at 413–24.

[30] *Annales Quedlinburgenses*, 143–5; Fried, 'Gnesen – Aachen – Rom', 273–9. On Bernward, see Althoff, 'Vormundschaft', 281–4.

diaboli.[31] Hence, though there are no more than hints to work with, it would seem that the events of 997–8 inspired a degree of apocalyptic disquiet within court circles.

Such a cosmic view of these struggles may help explain the emperor's harsh response to them: upon retaking Rome in 998, Otto had John Philagathos blinded, mutilated and driven from the city; Crescentius, on the other hand, he had executed and displayed publicly. The brutality of these acts, which conform ill to the merciful approach which Ottonian rulers generally took to rebels, has long troubled historians. Gerd Althoff suggests that they are to be understood in terms of contemporary societal norms (*Spielregeln*, or 'rules of the game', as he terms them). It was, he argues, only to be expected that mercy would be offered to a rebel once and Crescentius faced harsh punishment because he had broken this rule: he had already opposed Otto during the emperor's first sojourn in Italy and thus by 998 was a 'repeat offender'. In the case of John, on the other hand, Althoff seems to suggest that he was tainted by association.[32] Though there is much to be said for this analysis, it faces at least two problems. First, it is dangerously circular: Althoff's belief that rebels could only expect pardon once derives in no small part from the treatment of Crescentius at this point. And second, it fails to explain why contemporaries were so shocked by Otto's behaviour: if the emperor were doing little more than following the established 'rules of the game', then it is hard to comprehend such dissatisfaction. In the light of these problems, David Warner has offered an alternative solution: he sees Otto's response as part of his programme of *renovatio*, designed to represent a return to Roman traditions of criminal punishment.[33] Viewing these acts in the light of the apocalyptic rhetoric seen at court opens up a further possibility: if Otto understood these struggles in cosmic terms, as a battle against evil, against Antichrist or his forerunners, then his lack of mercy would be perfectly understandable – he was not dealing with men, but 'heresiarchs' and 'ministers of Satan'.[34]

In any case, it was in 997–8 as Otto marched south to retake Rome that the group of advisers which was to characterise the rest of his reign

[31] Gerbert of Aurillac, *Acta concillii Causeiensis*, ed. G. H. Pertz, MGH: Scriptores 3 (Hannover, 1839), 691–3, at 691, with K. Görich, *Otto III. Romanus Saxonicus et Italicus. Kaiserliche Rompolitik und sächsische Historiographie* (Sigmaringen, 1993), 211–16, esp. 214–15; and P. Riché, *Gerbert d'Aurillac. Le pape de l'an mil* (Paris, 1987), 162–4. Cf. Fried, 'Endzeiterwartung', 425–6.

[32] Althoff, *Otto III.*, 101–14. See also *idem*, 'Otto III. und Heinrich II. in Konflikten', in *Otto III. – Heinrich II.*, ed. Schneidmüller and Weinfurter, 77–94, at 80–1; and *idem*, 'Vormundschaft', 286.

[33] D. Warner, 'Ideals and Action in the Reign of Otto III', *Journal of Medieval History*, 25 (1999), 1–18, at 16–18. Whether contemporaries saw these punishments as distinctively 'Roman', however, is not clear.

[34] Cf. Rubenstein, *Armies of Heaven*, 199–203.

begins to appear at court and it was at this moment that his famed *renovatio imperii Romanorum* ('renewal of the empire of the Romans') seems to have been introduced. Although opinion has shifted away from Percy E. Schramm's idealised vision of this as a conscious programme to renew the Roman Empire of antiquity, there can be no doubt that there is something distinctive about the emperor's actions in the following years.[35] Thus, soon after Otto retook Rome in April 998 his charters began to be sealed with lead bulls – rather than the wax seals preferred by his predecessors – bearing the device *renovatio imperii Romanorum*.[36] The overall appearance of Otto's diplomata also underwent changes at this point, with these documents taking on an ever more ostentatious form.[37] Indeed, though *renovatio* was probably neither as coherent nor as programmatic as Schramm imagined, Otto certainly was at pains to emphasise the imperial nature of his authority in these years and a common strand can be traced through his politics, one which repeatedly runs through Rome and Aachen. A flurry of literary patronage is also visible at this point and the resulting works praise the emperor in terms which unmistakably underline the antique nature of his *imperium*.[38] Artwork provides further evidence of an interest in Rome and empire and thus, for example, the portrait of Otto in the Munich Gospels (Munich, Bayerische Staatsbibliothek, Clm 4453) portrays the emperor receiving homage from the four constituent parts of his realm, personified as women bearing tribute: Rome, Gaul (i.e. Lotharingia), Germany and the Slavic lands.[39] That this programme owes something to the Roman rebellion of the previous year is clear: in response to threats, Otto sought to underline his claim to the city. That it followed the example of his predecessors is equally clear: since 962 every East Frankish ruler had achieved imperial status and great store seems to have

---

[35] P. E. Schramm, *Kaiser, Rom und Renovatio. Studien zur Geschichte des römischen Erneuerungsgedankens vom Ende des karolingischen Reiches bis zum Investiturstreit* (2 vols., Leipzig, 1929); on which, see T. Reuter, 'Otto III and the Historians', *History Today*, 41, 1 (1990), 21–7; Görich, *Otto III.*, 187–274; and Althoff, *Otto III.*, 114–25; as well as subsequent discussion in E. Hlawitschka, 'Kaiser Otto III., "der Jüngling, der Großes, ja sogar Unmögliches ersann". Zum Millennium der Einbeziehung Polens in den europäischen Kulturkreis', in *Vorträge und Abhandlungen aus den geisteswissenschaftlichen Bereichen*, ed. *idem* (Munich, 1999), 29–74; and J. Fried, 'Römische Erinnerung. Zu den Anfängen und frühen Wirkungen des christlichen Rommythos', in *Studien zur Geschichte des Mittelalters. Jürgen Petersohn zum 65. Geburtstag*, ed. M. Thumser, A. Wenz-Haubfleisch and P. Wiegand (Stuttgart, 2000), 1–41, at 35–41.

[36] H. Keller, 'Die Siegel und Bullen Ottos III.', in *Europas Mitte*, ed. Wieczorek and Hinz, 767–73, at 771–2.

[37] Huschner, *Transalpine Kommunikation*, 355–68. See also *Urkunden*, ed. Sickel, 387a–389b.

[38] H. Dormeier, 'Die Renovatio Imperii Romanorum und die "Außenpolitik" Ottos III. und seine Berater', in *Polen und Deutschland*, ed. Borgolte, 163–91, at 168–81.

[39] Mayr-Harting, *Book Illumination*, I, 157–78; E. Garrison, *Ottonian Imperial Art and Portraiture: The Artistic Patronage of Otto III and Henry II* (Farnham, 2012), 64–5. Cf. U. Kuder, 'Die Ottonen in der ottonischen Buchmalerei', in *Herrschaftsrepräsentation im ottonischen Sachsen*, Vorträge und Forschungen 46, ed. G. Althoff and E. Schubert (Sigmaringen, 1998), 137–234, at 193–6.

been placed in this. However, there may also have been something new and decidedly eschatological about *renovatio*. Not only could the rebellions of 996–8 be seen in apocalyptic terms, but empire, especially in its Roman guise, was intimately associated with eschatology. Since Late Antiquity, the Roman Empire had been identified with the fourth (and final) kingdom signified by the statue's feet of iron and clay in Nebuchadnezzar's dream and the restraining force mentioned in 2 Thessalonians II.6. With the *translatio imperii* from Byzantinium to the west these implications had not been lost; such teachings were preserved in authoritative works such as Jerome's biblical commentaries and later writers elaborated on the theme. The Latin renderings of Pseudo-Methodius's *Revelationes*, the earliest of which began circulating in the eight century, highlight the eschatological role of empire and Adso picked up on this in the mid-tenth century, assuring Queen Gerberga that the end is not yet at hand because the empire remains intact (in the form of the West Frankish kingdom).[40] That such knowledge was available east of the Rhine is suggested by Thietmar of Merseburg's attempts to reassure his readers that recent reverses are not evidence of Pauline *discessio*.[41]

A more direct connection between such concepts and Otto's court can be established. The evidence comes from two related manuscripts, which were originally bound together as a single codex and may have belonged to Otto's personal library: Bamberg Staatsbibliothek MSS 22 and 76.[42] These were both produced at Reichenau and contain illuminated copies of the Books of Daniel, Isaiah and the Song of Songs, along with extracts from Jerome's commentaries. As such, they testify not only to the emperor's interest in the teachings of Daniel and Isaiah, two of the most apocalyptic of Old Testament prophets, but also to his acquaintance with Jerome's teachings on these, including his famous equation of the feet of the statue of Nebuchadnezzar's dream with the Roman Empire.[43] That Otto's imperial ideals were informed by such thoughts is further suggested by Leo of Vercelli's *Versus de Gregorio et Ottone augusto* (*c.* 998), which lists Babylon and Greece amongst the nations subject to Otto. This is, of course, a play on the exegesis of Nebuchadnezzar's dream,

---

[40] Pseudo-Methodius, *Revelationes*, ed. W. J. Aerts and G. A. A. Kortekaas, Corpus Scriptorum Christianorum Orientalium 569–70 (2 vols., Leuven, 1998); Adso, *De ortu et tempore Antichristi*, ed. D. Verhelst, Corpus Christianorum: Continuatio Mediaevalis (CCCM) 45 (Turnhout, 1976).

[41] Thietmar of Merseburg, *Chronicon* VIII.6, ed. R. Holtzmann, MGH: Scriptores rerum Germincarum n.s. 9 (Hannover, 1935), 500–1, with K. Schulmeyer-Ahl, *Der Anfang vom Ende der Ottonen. Konstitutionsbedingungen historiographischer Nachrichten in der Chronik Thietmars von Merseburg* (Berlin, 2009), 174–7, esp. 174 n. 499.

[42] Mayr-Harting, *Book Illumination*, II, 31–45. However, for a note of caution, see H. Hoffmann, *Bamberger Handschriften des 10. und 11. Jahrhunderts*, MGH: Schriften 39 (Hannover, 1995), 5–34, esp. 32.

[43] Mayr-Harting, *Book Illumination*, II, 34; *idem*, 'Book Illustration', 177 n. 11.

according to which the four successive kingdoms signified by the statue were to be those of the Babylonians, Persians, Greeks and Romans.[44] In fact, this passage is very close to one in Adso's *De ortu et tempore Antichristi*, as Knut Görich notes.[45] Yet this is not the only apocalyptic passage in Leo's writings. In the *Versus de Ottone et Heinrico* (*c.* 1002) the reference to Heaven and earth changing appearance in sorrow at Otto's death may be an allusion to Christ's prediction that sun and moon will darken before the advent of the Son of Man.[46] Thus, Leo, who as we have seen had a hand in drafting apocalyptically worded royal charters, clearly appreciated the eschatological implications of Otto's programme of Roman renewal. In fact, it may be more than a coincidence that before his election to Vercelli Leo seems to have witnessed Otto's brutal retaking of Rome in 998. Further evidence for an interest in such matters in these years comes from the Bamberg Apocalypse (Bamberg Staatsbibliothek Msc.Bibl. 140), which was also produced at Reichenau, probably at the emperor's request.[47]

In any case, it is time to return to developments in Rome in 997–8. It was, as we have seen, at this point that the emperor retook the city and treated his enemies unusually harshly, a fact which seems to have occasioned unrest. According to later traditions, two of the leading ascetic figures of the day, Romuald of Ravenna and Nilus of Rossano, criticised the emperor for his actions, calling upon him to repent. Though it is difficult to sort fact from fiction in these accounts – each is designed to praise its respective saint and neither mentions the other – there is clearly a kernel of truth in the opposition they record.[48] In fact, where both accounts agree is in reporting that the emperor undertook a penitential pilgrimage to Monte Gargano in Lent of the following year (999), an event which fits within his known itinerary. Whilst this act was in part an effort to appease those (such as Romuald and Nilus) who did not approve of Otto's actions, from our perspective it is important as the first of a series of penitential undertakings on the emperor's part.[49] In this respect, Otto's

---

[44] Leo of Vercelli, *Versus de Gregorio et Ottone Augusto*, ed. K. Strecker, MGH: Poeta Latini medii aevi 5.i (Leipzig, 1937), 477–80, at 479, with Schramm, *Kaiser, Rom und Renovatio*, I, 123–4; and Mayr-Harting, *Book Illumination*, II, 50–1.

[45] Görich, *Otto III.*, 198–9.

[46] Leo of Vercelli, *Versus de Ottone et Heinrico*, ed. K. Strecker, MGH: Poeta Latini medii aevi 5.i (Leipzig, 1937), 480–3, at 481, with Bloch, 'Beiträge', 118 (citing the opinion of P. von Winterfeld).

[47] Mayr-Harting, *Book Illumination*, II, 10–24 and 215–28; *idem*, 'Book Illustration', 180–94. See also J. Fried, 'Die Endzeit fest im Griff des Positivismus? Zur Auseinandersetzung mit Sylvain Gouguenheim', *Historische Zeitschrift*, 275 (2002), 281–321, at 317–19.

[48] S. Hamilton, 'Otto III's Penance: A Case Study of Unity and Diversity in the Eleventh-Century Church', *Studies in Church History*, 32 (1996), 83–94. See also Althoff, *Otto III.*, 103–5.

[49] See S. Patzold, '*Omnis anima potestatibus sublimioribus subdita sit*. Zum Herrscherbild im Aachener Otto-Evangeliar', *Frühmittelalterliche Studien*, 35 (2001), 243–72, at 268–72.

repentance went beyond political expediency and we should do well to allow for the possibility that he genuinely felt regret and concern. Indeed, Jean-Marie Sansterre argues that these ascetic exercises were an essential part of Otto's *renovatio* and it is tempting also to associate them with the apocalyptic atmosphere at court.[50] The connection between penance and apocalypticism should be clear: the nearer the Last Judgement looms, the more urgent is the need for the remission of sin. The choice of pilgrimage site may suggest just this: Monte Gargano boasted the shrine of the Archangel Michael, who was accorded an important role in the Last Days, when he was to announce Christ's arrival and slay the dragon (sometimes identified with Antichrist), as depicted in the Bamberg Apocalypse.[51] Moreover, as noted, this was not a one-off act: shortly thereafter Otto spent further time in penitential seclusion with Franco of Worms, with whom he undertook a pilgrimage to Subiaco, where he founded a church dedicated to the Archangel and Adalbert (note once more the possible connection between Adalbert and eschatology).[52]

Yet Otto's penitential acts did not end here. Almost immediately after returning from Subiaco in late summer 999, he retired north of Rome to the abbey of Farfa, where he held a meeting with his senior advisers. The importance of this event was first noted by Schramm, who saw therein the archetypal expression of the emperor's *renovatio*: it was on this occasion, he postulated, that the extraordinary events of the following year were planned.[53] However, though the meeting itself has attracted much interest, little attention has been given to its immediate context. Indeed, our main sources for this event, two diplomata issued in favour of Farfa, have received remarkably little discussion. This is doubtless because at first glance they seem fairly mundane: petitioned by Abbot Hugh, they grant the abbey *fodrum*, annul a series of earlier transactions and confirm the abbey's liberty.[54] Nevertheless, viewed within the context of the emperor's relations with Farfa, these documents take on a much greater significance. Some background is necessary here.[55] Hugh had first become abbot of

[50] J.-M. Sansterre, 'Otton III et les saints ascètes de son temps', *Revista di storia della chiesa Italia*, 43 (1989), 377–412.

[51] C. Erdmann, *Die Entstehung des Kreuzzugsgedankens* (Stuttgart, 1935), 18; D. Callahan, 'The Cult of St Michael the Archangel and the "Terrors of the Year 1000"', in *Apocalyptic Year 1000*, ed. Landes, Gow and Van Meter, 181–204, esp. 185. Cf. Bousset, *Antichrist*, 150–4.

[52] R. Holtzmann, *Geschichte der Sächsischen Kaiserzeit (900–1024)* (Munich, 1941), 341.

[53] Schramm, *Kaiser, Rom und Renovatio*, I, 130–1.

[54] D O III 329, 331.

[55] See D. H. Schuster, 'L'abbaye de Farfa et sa restauration au XIᵉ siècle', *Revue Bénédictine*, 24 (1907), 17–35 and 374–402; H. Seibert, 'Herrscher und Mönchtum im spätottonischen Reich. Vorstellung – Funktion – Interaktion', in *Otto III. – Heinrich II.*, ed. Schneidmüller and Weinfurter, 205–66, at 254–6; S. Boynton, *Shaping a Monastic Identity: Liturgy and History at the Imperial Abbey of Farfa, 1000–1125* (Ithaca, NY, 2006), 9–11 and 110–12; and J.-M. Sansterre, '"Destructio" et "diminutio" d'une grande abbaye royale: La perception et la mémoire des

Farfa in 997, achieving the post by means of simony. As soon as Otto became aware of this, he had Hugh removed and granted the monastery to a certain Bishop Hugh (probably of Ascoli-Piceno) as a benefice. At this point, he also appointed his chaplain Herpo to oversee affairs at the centre. However, shortly thereafter Otto was prevailed upon by the monks to return the monastery to Abbot Hugh, which he agreed to do under the condition that future successions to the office be decided by free election, confirmed by the emperor.[56] Otto also confirmed Farfa's holdings and liberty, oversaw a court judgement in its favour and restored some of its lands.[57] Not long after these events, both Herpo and Bishop Hugh died unexpectedly, a turn of events which triggered a further change of heart on the emperor's part.[58] He now seems to have come to the conclusion that the placement of the abbey under the oversight of Herpo and Hugh had not only been a political mistake, but also a sin, for which the two had paid the ultimate price.

This was the situation in late September 999 when Otto held his meeting at Farfa. On this occasion, he issued a charter granting the abbey the *fodrum* due from its lands as well as annulling earlier grants which Bishop Hugh and others had undertaken; eleven days later in Rome, he issued a further diploma confirming Farfa's liberty. It is this latter document which is particularly interesting from our present standpoint. Farfa had received a confirmation of its freedom only shortly before this, so the legal nature of the transaction must have been very much secondary – it was intended to send a message. The text of the diploma contains a detailed *narratio* describing the plundering of Farfa in previous years and the roles of Bishop Hugh and Herpo therein. It then speaks of the deaths of these two figures and expresses the hope that by restoring the abbey to its former glory the emperor will be able to achieve the remedy of Herpo's soul (Bishop Hugh, however, seems to have inspired no such sympathy). This level of detail is highly unusual, but it is not the only feature which makes this privilege stand out. The document ends with a striking spiritual sanction, which threatens that any who violates its terms will have to answer alongside Otto himself (*nobiscum*) at the Day of Judgement, when Christ will come to judge the age with fire.[59] Spiritual sanctions such as this were not a standard part of Italian diplomatic and

---

crises à Farfa au Xe et dans les premières décennes du XIe siècle', in *Les élites au haut Moyen Âge. Crises et renouvellements*, ed. F. Bougard, L. Feller and R. Le Jan (Turnhout, 2006), 469–85.

[56] D O III 276.

[57] D O III 277–8, 282.

[58] Thietmar of Merseburg, *Chronicon* IV.68, 202–3; *Vita Burchardi Wormatiensis*, c. 4, ed. G. Waitz, MGH: Scriptores 4 (Hannover, 1841), 830–46, at 834. See Fleckenstein, *Hofkapelle*, II, 89 and 113–14.

[59] D O III 331.

of all Otto's charters for Farfa this is the only to bear one.[60] Even more unusual is the reference to future perpetrators facing judgement alongside the emperor – no previous Ottonian diploma contains anything like this, though the sentiment sits well with the penitential actions which Otto had undertaken in the months preceding this. Overall, it is hard not to conclude, as Hartmut Hoffmann has, that this charter was drafted by the emperor himself: Otto felt the need to confirm Farfa's liberty because he feared for the soul of his recently deceased chaplain and was concerned about the implications of Herpo's death for his own salvation.[61] Thus, this is a performative text in the sense recently outlined by Geoffrey Koziol: its issuing was not so much a legal event, as a highly political (and religious) act.[62] Indeed, it is possible that the diploma itself was read aloud and presented to Abbot Hugh on this occasion, in which case its unusual features could not have passed unnoticed.[63]

So far my argument has of necessity been largely hypothetical, but as we move into the year 1000 the evidence starts to become more solid. In this year, Otto undertook a second Lenten pilgrimage – another penitential act, it should be noted – to Gniezno in Poland. The parallels between this and the penances of the previous year, which involved pilgrimages to Monte Gargano and Subiaco, should be clear, though they have occasioned little comment.[64] It is in this context that Adalbert comes to the fore once more: the aim of this journey was to pray at the grave of the martyr, an act which Otto combined with visiting his ally Bolesław Chrobry and founding the first Polish archbishopric.[65] Otto also apparently received relics of the saint from Bolesław, though not his entire body, as may have been his hope. The timing of these events is important:

---

[60] See P. Kehr, *Die Urkunden Otto III.* (Innsbruck, 1890), 172–4; J. Studtmann, 'Die Pönformel der mittelalterlichen Urkunden', *Archiv für Urkundenforschung*, 12 (1932), 251–374, at 307–11; and M. Uhlirz, 'Rechtsfragen in den Urkunden Ottos III.', *Settimane di Studio del Centro Italiano di Studi sull'Alto Medioevo*, 2 (1956), 220–44, at 232–5.

[61] Hoffmann, 'Eigendiktat', 398–9. See also Huschner, *Transalpine Kommunikation*, 193 and 384–5.

[62] G. Koziol, *The Politics of Memory and Identity in Carolingian Royal Diplomas: The West Frankish Kingdom (840–987)* (Turnhout, 2012), esp. 17–62.

[63] Cf. H. Keller, 'Hulderweis durch Privilegien: symbolische Kommunikation innerhalb und jenseits des Textes', *Frühmittelalterliche Studien*, 38 (2004), 309–21, at 313–17.

[64] Though see L. M. Hartmann, *Geschichte Italiens im Mittelalter* (4 vols., Gotha, 1910–15), IV, 134.

[65] Amongst others, see J. Fried, 'Der hl. Adalbert und Gnesen', *Mittelrheinische Kirchengeschichte*, 50 (1998), 41–70; idem, *Otto III. und Bolesław Chrobry. Das Widmungsbild des Aachener Evangeliars, der Akt von Gnesen und das frühe polnische und ungarische Königtum*, 2nd edn (Stuttgart, 2001); G. Labuda, 'Der Akt von Gnesen vom Jahre 1000. Bericht über die Forschungsvorhaben und -ergebnisse', *Quaestiones medii aevi novae*, 5 (2000), 145–88; J. Tyszkiewicz, 'Bruno of Querfurt and the Resolutions of the Gniezno Convention of 1000. Facts and Problems', *Quaestiones medii aevi novae*, 5 (2000), 189–208; Althoff, *Otto III.*, 126–52; and the contributions to *Polen und Deutschland*, ed. Borgolte.

the emperor visited Adalbert's grave during Lent, the liturgical season of penance, then returned to Quedlinburg for Easter, before proceeding to Aachen for Pentecost. As Knut Görich observes, this itinerary suggests careful planning: Otto evidently wanted to be at Gniezno for Lent, at Quedlinburg for Easter (as was traditional) and at Aachen for Pentecost, a decision which necessitated crossing the Alps in the heart of winter (which was no mean feat in this period).[66] That this trip was conceived of as part of a conscious programme finds further support in Otto's titulature: throughout much of the journey he bears an otherwise unparalleled imperial style, *Otto tercius servus Jesu Christi et Romanorum imperator augustus secundum voluntatem Dei salvatoris nostrique liberatoris* ('Otto III servant of Jesus Christ and emperor augustus of the Romans according to the will of God, the Saviour and our Liberator'). This title, which has been the subject of much discussion, was probably modelled on papal diplomatic, emphasising the emperor's humility and apostolic aims.[67] Johannes Fried suggests that it also represents a play on the teachings of Daniel and Isaiah, copies of which the emperor may have owned, as we have seen.[68]

It is, therefore, clear that this trip was planned in advance, quite possibly at the Farfa meeting of September 999. That Aachen was the intended destination from the start is suggested by the last two diplomata issued before Otto's arrival in Gniezno. These charters, produced at Regensburg on 6 February, were issued for foundations in Aachen, indicating that the emperor was already looking towards his eventual goal. The first of these is for the community of *Marienkapelle* and includes not only a reference to the throne which had been established there by Charlemagne, but also a lengthy spiritual sanction, which reads remarkably like the one in the Farfa diploma issued a few months earlier, right down to the tell-tale reference to future malefactors facing judgement alongside Emperor Otto himself (*nobiscum*). The second, issued for the new foundation of Burtscheid, also contains a spiritual sanction and, though the wording in this case is somewhat more restrained, it too threatens perpetual malediction and anathema at the Day of Judgement.[69] Thus, once again

---

[66] Görich, 'Erinnerung', 98–9. See also W. Huschner, 'Rom – Gnesen – Quedlinburg – Aachen – Rom. Die Reise Kaiser Ottos III. im Jahre 1000', *Zeitschrift des Aachener Geschichtsvereins*, 113/14 (2011/12), 31–59; and cf. Einhard, *Vita Karoli Magni* II.6, ed. G. Waitz, MGH: Scriptores rerum Germanicarum in usum scholarum 25, 6th edn (Hannover, 1911), 9, on the logistical difficulties posed by the Alps.

[67] H. Wolfram, 'Lateinische Herrschertitel im 9. und 10. Jahrhundert', in *Intitulatio II. Lateinische Herrscher- und Fürstentitel im 9. und 10. Jahrhundert*, ed. *idem* (Vienna, 1973), 19–178, at 156–7. Note, however, that the style was routinely used only by one draftsman, 'Heribert C'.

[68] Fried, 'Hl. Adalbert', 58–69. See also Huschner, *Transalpine Kommunikation*, 375–7; and E. Eickhoff, 'Otto III. in Pereum. Konzept und Verwirklichung seiner Missionspolitik', *Archiv für Kulturgeschichte*, 83 (2001), 25–35, at 28.

[69] D O III 347–8.

we see an association between eschatology, Aachen and Charlemagne. Indeed, another diploma referring to the end of time was issued at Aachen shortly after Pentecost, further suggesting an association between such concepts.[70] Together, these documents demonstrate that the Farfa charter of 999 was not a flash in the pan: it was part of a series of documents in which Otto expresses his anxieties about sin, judgement and the end of time. They recall the emperor's grant of Tiel to the Chapel of St Mary in 997, which, as we have seen, bears an unusually apocalyptic *arenga*. They also reveal a further connection with Adalbert: not only were two issued during the journey to the saint's grave (and one at Aachen only shortly thereafter), but one was in favour of Burtscheid, whose first abbot, Gregory of Cassano, had spent time with Adalbert at the monastery of Boniface and Alexius in Rome.[71]

It is, however, Otto's own actions at Aachen in this year that are most famous. It was here, upon his return from Gniezno (via Quedlinburg), that the emperor undertook a visit to the resting place of Charlemagne. This is reported independently in three contemporaneous sources – Thietmar's *Chronicon*, Adémar of Chabannes's *Chronicon* and the *Chronicon Novaliciense* – each of which provides a slightly different version of events. Thietmar's account is the shortest, but the nearest both temporally and geographically. It reports that Otto visited Charlemagne's grave secretly at Pentecost because he had doubts as to its location; upon discovering the emperor seated upright on his throne, Otto took a gold cross from his neck as well as a piece of his clothing, but otherwise left the body undisturbed.[72] More detail is provided by the account of the Aquitanian monk Adémar, who reports that Otto, inspired by a dream in which the location of the emperor's grave was revealed to him, proceeded to have it uncovered. Here, Charlemagne was found seated on his throne, which Otto ordered to be raised up for all present to see. At this point, a canon of the church, who was known for his stature, tried on the emperor's crown, only to find it too large for him; he then compared his leg with that of the dead emperor, only to find that it too was larger than his. These actions were followed by a miracle: the presumptuous cleric's leg was broken. Clearly impressed by this, Otto had the body reburied in the right transept, where it began to be known for its many signs and miracles. The throne, however, was given to Duke Bolesław of Poland in exchange for the arm

[70] D O III 361. See Gabriele, 'Otto III', 119; and cf. Möhring, 'Renovatio imperii', 346–7.

[71] B. Hamilton, 'The Monastery of S. Alessio and the Religious and Intellectual Renaissance in Tenth-Century Rome' (1965), repr. in and cited from his *Monastic Reform, Catharism and the Crusades (900–1300)* (1979), no. III, 282–8; Huschner, *Transalpine Kommunikation*, 498–505.

[72] Thietmar of Merseburg, *Chronicon* IV.47, 184–7.

of St Adalbert.[73] While more florid, the core details of this account are much the same: there was apparently some uncertainty as to the location of Charlemagne's grave, then once discovered the Carolingian emperor was found seated and some of his accoutrements were taken (in this case his throne rather than clothing). The final report comes from the mid-eleventh-century Chronicle of Novalesa, which claims to be based on the eyewitness account of Count Palatine Otto of Lomello. According to this, Otto III entered Charlemagne's tomb with only two bishops and Count Otto. There, they found the emperor seated upright on his throne 'as if alive' (ceu vivus), untouched by the passing of time except for the fact that his fingernails had grown through his gloves and the tip of his nose had fallen off. They proceeded to say a prayer, cut the emperor's nails and replace the tip of his nose in gold before departing.[74] Once more, we see many of the same elements, albeit with different emphasis: the visit is secret (or small-scale), the emperor is found seated and mementos are taken.

The meaning of these events is not immediately clear. Some have suggested that Otto's visit was modelled on antique traditions, perhaps on Augustus's visit to the sepulchre of Alexander the Great, as recorded by Suetonius.[75] Others are inclined to be cautious about these accounts, especially where their claims regarding Charlemagne's seated burial are concerned.[76] However, the most likely explanation to date is that of Knut Görich, who sees this as an abortive attempt to establish a cult of Charlemagne. As Görich points out, all of the accounts contain elements which might be associated with the fostering of a saint's cult. Thus, it was common to visit a saint's body in the hope of finding it uncorrupted and it was normal under such circumstances to take mementos as evidence of the body's uncorrupted nature (these would become relics). The need for secrecy (however nominal) is also understandable within this context: until one knew that the body was uncorrupted (and hence that the individual was indeed a saint), one ran the risk of committing sacrilege

---

[73] Adémar of Chabannes, Chronicon III.31, ed. P. Bourgain, CCCM 129 (Turnhout, 1999), 153–4.

[74] Chronicon Novaliciense III.32, ed. G. C. Alessio (Turin, 1982), 182.

[75] H. Beumann, Die Ottonen, rev. edn (Stuttgart, 1994), 151–2; P. J. Geary, Living with the Dead in the Middle Ages (Ithaca, NY, 1994), 65; Garrison, Ottonian Imperial Art, 63. The problem here is that Suetonius's De vita Caesarum was not widely known in this period: S. J. Tibbets, 'Suetonius, De vita Caesarum', in Texts and Transmission: A Survey of the Classics, ed. L. D. Reynolds (Oxford, 1983), 399–404. Cf. H. Beumann, 'Grab und Thron Karls des Großen zu Aachen' (1967), repr. in and cited from his Wissenschaft vom Mittelalter. Ausgewählte Aufsätze (Cologne, 1972), 347–76, at 371.

[76] Beumann, 'Grab und Thron'; H. Keller, 'Die Ottonen und Karl der Große', Frühmittelalterliche Studien, 34 (2000), 112–31, at 128 n. 74. Cf. J. F. Moffitt, The Enthroned Corpse of Charlemagne: The Lord-in-Majesty Theme in Early Medieval Art and Life (Jefferson, NC, 2007), 119–25.

by defiling a Christian grave.[77] Thus, this was a further expression of the emperor's devotion to the memory of Charlemagne and it sits well with his other attempts to glorify Aachen. It is worth reflecting briefly upon the importance of Charlemagne for Otto's plans within this context. The emperor's interest in his Frankish predecessor should be seen in part as an element of his *renovatio*: Charlemagne was well on his way to achieving legendary status by this period and an interest in his memory went naturally with other efforts at imperial renewal. Otto's interest in the emperor was also consonant with his attempts to spread the cult of Adalbert (to whom a church was dedicated at Aachen) and to encourage the eastern mission: Charlemagne was remembered as the 'apostle of the Saxons' and Otto may have conceived of his own missionary endeavours as a continuation of Charlemagne's.[78] That Otto had the mission in mind when he visited Charlemagne's tomb is suggested by the choice of date: Pentecost was the moment at which the Holy Spirit had descended upon the apostles and prepared them to spread the Word. However, there may also have been an apocalyptic significance to this. Matthew XXIV.14 had predicted that Endtime would come once the Word had been preached to all the nations, a prophecy which endowed all missionary activity with eschatological implications.[79] Moreover, as Gabriele points out, by this time the memory of Charlemagne was beginning to coalesce with the legendary figure of the Last Emperor. The so-called Legend of the Last Emperor survives in many forms; first attested in the Middle East in the seventh century, it had found its way into the Latin West by the eighth. The Legend drew on the exegetical tradition associating Daniel's fourth kingdom and the restraining force of 2 Thessalonians II with the Roman Empire, elaborating on this in important fashions.[80] According to it, a Last World Emperor will reign immediately before the end of time: he will defeat Antichrist's precursors (often designated as Gog and Magog), then lay down his crown in Jerusalem, paving the way for the coming of Antichrist and the Last Judgement. As noted, Charlemagne often came to be identified with the messianic figure of the Last Emperor:

---

[77] K. Görich, 'Otto III. öffnet das Karlsgrab in Aachen. Überlegungen zu Heiligenverehrung, Heiligsprechung und Traditionsbildung', in *Herrschaftsrepräsentation im ottonischen Sachsen*, ed. Althoff and Schubert, 381–430. See further Moffitt, *Enthroned Corpse*, 125–31; A. Angenendt, 'Corpus incorruptum. Eine Leitidee der mittelalterlichen Reliquienverehrung' (1991), repr. in and cited from his *Die Gegenwart von Heiligen und Reliquien* (Münster, 2010), 109–43, esp. 122; *idem*, *Geschichte der Religiosität im Mittelalter* (Darmstadt, 1997), 691–4, esp. 692; and J. Fried, *Der Schleier der Erinnerung. Grundzüge einer historischen Memorik*, rev. edn (Munich, 2012), 166–9.

[78] Görich, 'Otto III. öffnet das Karlsgrab', 406–9; *idem*, 'Erinnerung', 101–3; Fried, 'Hl. Adalbert', 66–7.

[79] Whalen, *Dominion of God*; I. N. Wood, *The Missionary Life: Saints and the Evangelisation of Europe, 400–1050* (2001), 133–4 and 251.

[80] Gabriele, *Empire of Memory*, 107–28. See further Möhring, *Weltkaiser der Endzeit*.

as the archetypal ruler (and, after 1165, saint), it was believed that he might come again before the end of time. The accounts of Otto's visit to Charlemagne's grave seem to represent an early stage in this development: they report that the Frankish emperor was found resting, rather than dead ('almost alive', as the *Chronicon Novaliciense* puts it), ready to spring into action.[81]

Of course, to establish such a connection we must be able to demonstrate that Otto or at least those around him were aware of the Legend and in this respect there are a number of tantalising clues. The emperor's mother, Theophanu, came from the Byzantine court, where the Legend was well known (Liudprand of Cremona goes so far as to characterise such prophecies as particularly Greek[82]) and it is conceivable that she acted as a conduit for such knowledge: Theophanu would probably have been acquainted with the Legend and it is not unreasonable to presume that she might have taught her son (and possibly also husband) about this. Indeed, Jean Flori suggests that John Tzimikes, Theophanu's uncle and the reigning emperor at the time of her marriage with Otto II, modelled aspects of his rule on the Legend, in which case the queen might have identified personally with such traditions.[83] Liudprand's own writings, which preserve a version of the *Visions of Daniel* (itself a version of the Legend), as well as his activity at the Ottonian and Byzantine courts, provide a further channel whereby such ideas might have reached the *Reich*. Yet Byzantium is not the only potential source. Another is the Tiburtine Sibyl, the earliest surviving version of which comes from northern Italy and shows signs of having been redacted *c.* 1000.[84] An even more likely source is Adso's *De ortu et tempore Antichristi*, which was written for Queen Gerberga (Otto I's sister and thus Otto III's great-aunt) and enjoyed wide circulation.[85] Indeed, Alboin dedicated his redaction of this work to Otto's chancellor Heribert of Cologne, so at least one of the emperor's chief advisers seems to have been receptive to (and acquainted with) such literature.[86] Moreover, as we have seen, Leo of Vercelli's *Versus*

---

[81] Gabriele, 'Otto III', 114–22. See also *idem*, *Empire of Memory*, 120–3.

[82] Liudprand of Cremona, *Relatio de legatione Constantinopolitana*, cc. 39–41, ed. P. Chiesa, CCCM 156 (Turnhout 1998), 204–5, with W. Brandes, 'Liudprand von Cremona (legatio cap. 39–41) und eine bisher unbeachtete west-östliche Korrespondenz über die Bedeutung des Jahres 1000 a.D.', *Byzantinische Zeitschrift*, 93 (2000), 435–63, at 435–45.

[83] Flori, *L'Islam et la fin des temps*, 242–3.

[84] A. Holdenried, *The Sibyl and Her Scribes: Manuscripts and Interpretation of the Latin Sibylla Tiburtina c. 1050–1500* (Aldershot, 2006), 4–5; Möhring, *Weltkaiser der Endzeit*, 28–53.

[85] Adso, *De ortu et tempore Antichristi*, 1–3; Möhring, *Weltkaiser der Endzeit*, 144–8 and 360–8; S. MacLean, 'Reform, Queenship and the End of the World in Tenth-Century France: Adso's "Letter on the Origin and Time of the Antichrist" Reconsidered', *Revue belge de philologie et d'histoire*, 86 (2008), 645–75.

[86] Adso, *De ortu et tempore Antichristi*, 55–74, with H. Müller, 'Heribert, Kanzler Ottos III. und Erzbischof von Köln', *Rheinische Vierteljahrsblätter*, 60 (1996), 16–64, at 25–6.

de Gregorio et Ottone augusto may allude to this work, further suggesting that it was known at court. Thus, whilst it is impossible to prove beyond doubt that Otto both knew and identified with the Legend, the evidence in favour of the proposition is strong. What his aims at Pentecost 1000 were, however, remains unclear: it may be that he hoped to take on Charlemagne's mantle, as Gabriele suggests; alternatively, he may simply have wished to honour the man (or indeed saint) who he believed would come to save mankind at the end of time.[87]

It would, therefore, seem that in a number of respects these events constitute the high point of a programme which can be traced back as far as 996. The fact that this peaked precisely at the turn of the millennium inevitably raises the question of what role (if any) hopes and anxieties about the year 1000 had to play therein. Within this context, it should be emphasised from the start that sources from the *Reich* do not mention any concrete concerns about the passing of this year: they associate the end of time with Pauline *discessio* (and relate this to contemporary events), they speculate as to the eschatological role of empire and in some cases they may allude to the Legend of the Last Emperor, but at no point do they say anything about the millennium within an eschatological context. While it has been suggested that this reflects a clerical 'consensus of silence', inspired by Augustine of Hippo's anti-apocalyptic teaching, such arguments are not only dangerously circular, but presuppose a much wider dissemination of Augustinian eschatology than can be demonstrated.[88] Indeed, as Jean Flori reminds us, throughout the earlier Middle Ages many writers broke Augustine's strictures (doubtless often unconsciously) when it came to interpreting events in an eschatological light.[89] Thus when, to pick two of the most famous examples from this period, Wulfstan of York and Thietland of Einsiedeln express the belief that certain dates possess an apocalyptic quality, neither shows any sign of being concerned about reproach – quite the reverse, their awareness of the proximity of these dates seems to have driven them to write.[90] Hence, if the apocalyptic interests at Otto's court were focused entirely on the turning of the millennium, we should expect to hear rather more about

[87] Gabrielle, 'Otto III', 118–22. See also D. Callahan, 'The Problem of the "Filioque" and the Letter from the Pilgrim Monks of the Mount of Olives to Pope Leo III and Charlemagne', *Revue Bénédictine*, 102 (1992), 75–134, at 111–16; and cf. M. Ter Braak, 'Kaiser Otto III. Ideal und Praxis im Mittelalter' (1928), repr. in and cited from his *Verzameld Werk* (7 vols., Amsterdam, 1950–1), I, 401–609, at 440–2.

[88] Landes, 'Apocalyptic Year', esp. 104–10. Cf. Fried, 'Endzeit', 299–300.

[89] Flori, *L'Islam et la fin des temps*, 99–107. See similarly R. A. Markus, *Saeculum: History and Society in the Theology of St Augustine*, rev. edn (Cambridge, 1989), 162–5.

[90] *The Homilies of Wulfstan*, ed. D. Bethurum (Oxford, 1957), 134–41, at 136–7; S. R. Cartwright and K. L. Hughes, *Second Thessalonians: Two Early Medieval Apocalyptic Commentaries* (Kalamazoo, MI, 2001), 41–73, at 56.

this. Indeed, it is interesting to note that Thietland, whose monastery of Einsiedeln enjoyed close contacts with the Ottonian dynasty, anticipated the end of time coming in 1033 (that is, the millennium of the passion) rather than 1000.

On the other hand, it is clear that Otto's imperial programme reached a highpoint in the year 1000 and even those, such as Görich, who are sceptical about the degree of apocalyptic expectation at court admit that there was something special about this year. However, as Görich is at pains to emphasise, this need not be seen in apocalyptic terms; Otto's actions might have simply constituted a celebration of the thousandth anniversary of Christ's life.[91] Here is where the limitations of our sources become acute. Though we can be fairly confident that the turning of the millennium was important to the emperor, we cannot be certain what significance he ascribed to it. From our present standpoint, however, what is important to note is that the main competing interpretations need not, in fact, be mutually exclusive: it is entirely conceivable that Otto entertained the possibility that the end of time was at hand (and might come in or around the year 1000), yet also hoped that this was not the case. Indeed, there is no contradiction in seeing his actions both in eschatological terms, as preparation for a potentially imminent end, and in soteriological terms, as a celebration of Christ's salvational message. Such a mixture of hope and concern, apocalyptic expectation and concrete plans for the future is by no means unparalleled.[92] Medieval prophecy was a response to uncertainty about the future and as such less often led to the unshakable belief in a single future scenario than to efforts to weigh various interpretations.[93] Theologians and prophetic writers alike tended to hedge their bets when it came to predicting the end and it is more common to find claims to the effect that the events leading up to the Last Times have begun – that love is growing cold and heresy spreading, sometimes even that Antichrist is born or starting to make his influence felt – than that the Apocalypse itself has begun. Indeed, whilst it was widely accepted that Antichrist's reign would last three and a half years, the precise length of the period preceding this was unclear and it was possible to live an entire lifetime (or more) in the belief that this had begun.[94] Otto III may have possessed a similar perspective to that of the apocalyptic writers of the early twelfth century, many of whom believed that the events leading up to the end

[91] Görich, 'Erinnerung', 99–100. Cf. D. Barthélemy, *L'an mil de la paix de Dieu. La France chrétienne et féodale, 980–1060* (Paris, 1999), 169–72.

[92] Cf. R. E. Lerner, 'Medieval Prophecy and Religious Dissent', *Past and Present*, 72 (1976), 3–24, at 14; M. E. Reeves, *Joachim of Fiore and the Prophetic Future* (1976), 83–4.

[93] See R. W. Southern, 'Aspects of the European Tradition of Historical Writing: 3, History as Prophecy', *Transactions of the Royal Historical Society*, fifth series, 22 (1972), 159–80.

[94] A. H. Bredero, 'The Announcement of the Coming of the Antichrist and the Medieval Concept of Time', in *Prophecy and Eschatology*, ed. M. Wilks (Oxford, 1994), 3–13.

of time had begun, yet hoped that pious works might delay or even turn back this process.[95]

Appreciating that eschatological expectation coexisted with other less apocalyptic views of the future helps explain why Otto's own actions send such mixed messages. On the one hand there are, as we have seen, indications that he reckoned with an imminent end: his visit to Charlemagne's tomb, ascetic exercises and the unusual sanctions and *arengae* in his diplomata all point in this direction. Nevertheless, many of Otto's undertakings suggest the reverse: his efforts to obtain a Byzantine bride are not easy to reconcile with a conviction that the Last Times are at hand; meanwhile, the same charter sanctions which mention judgement and the end of time also include warnings for Otto's successors.[96] It would be too simplistic to suggest that the emperor's plans for the future negated his eschatological interests (or vice versa); rather, the two sat side-by-side and Otto himself may have seen little contradiction in this. As a ruler, it was less important that his actions conform to a theologically consistent plan than that he reckon with a variety of eventualities, some more apocalyptic than others. In this respect, Otto looks little different from his Byzantine counterpart, Basil II (976–1025), whose regime was influenced by apocalyptic thought, yet who was certainly not prevented from dealing with the normal demands of rule as a consequence. As Paul Magdalino neatly puts it, 'Basil II, like Otto III, did not spend all of his time rapt in expectation of the Second Coming; he spent a lot of time conducting business as usual, doing things he would have done anyway if the millennium had not been there.'[97]

The year 1000, therefore, may have provided a focus for the eschatological hopes and concerns so evident at Otto's court, but it would be too simplistic to see it as the sole cause of these. Indeed, what is perhaps most striking is the fact that the emperor's imperial plans and apocalyptic interests did not come to an abrupt halt in his final year on the throne (1001). Thus, although the unique style used during the pilgrimage to Gniezno was dropped in late 1000 and the *renovatio* bull disappeared in 1001, there are numerous indications that Otto's overall programme of renewal was maintained. In particular, a new bull was introduced to

[95] H.-W. Goetz, 'Endzeiterwartung und Endzeitvorstellung im Rahmen des Geschichtsbildes des früheren 12. Jahrhunderts' (1988), repr. in and cited from his *Vorstellungsgeschichte. Gesammelte Schriften zu Wahrnehmungen, Deutungen und Vorstellungen im Mittelalter*, ed. A. Aurast *et al.* (Bochum, 2007), 433–52. See also T. Reuter, 'Past, Present and No Future in the Twelfth-Century *Regnum Teutonicum*', in *The Perception of the Past in Twelfth-Century Europe*, ed. P. Magdalino (1992), 15–36, esp. 31–6.

[96] Schneidmüller, *Jahrtausendwende*, 33; Freund, 'Das Jahr 1000', 34; Möhring, 'Renovatio imperii', 346–7.

[97] P. Magdalino, 'The Year 1000 in Byzantium', in *Byzantium in the Year 1000*, ed. *idem* (Leiden, 2003), 233–70, at 265.

replace the old one, bearing the equally programmatic device *aurea Roma* ('Golden Rome'), while a new 'apostolic' imperial style came into use, developing ideas expressed earlier in the experimental title used during the Gniezno pilgrimage.[98] More concretely, Otto's final year was dedicated to maintaining his increasingly precarious position in Rome – *renovatio* was threatened and the emperor's response was action. Continuities can also be seen in other regards. In Hungary, Stephan was consecrated with a crown granted to him by Sylvester II and Otto, probably in 1001, and in the same year Esztergom was elevated to metropolitan status and received relics of Adalbert, developments which clearly relate to Otto's missionary efforts.[99] The emperor's concerns about sin and repentance, which as we have seen often found expression in his charters, are also visible at this point. Thus, a diploma issued for Hildesheim, which the emperor himself may have drafted, ends with a sanction threatening future malefactors with torment alongside Judas, while a grant in favour of the nunnery S. Salvatore in Pavia is said to have been issued so that the emperor might be freed from the nets of sin and merit eternal life.[100] This latter document draws specific attention to the presence of a relic of the True Cross at S. Salvatore, perhaps suggesting an association between Otto's patronage of the centre and his actions in the previous year. The True Cross, of course, was often associated with Charlemagne (in part because of his perceived role as Last Emperor). Moreover, interest in the cross (and in particular the True Cross) often went hand in hand with apocalyptic expectation, since the cross was not only the sign of Christ's sacrifice for mankind, but also the symbol of his eventual victory over Antichrist at the end of time. Indeed, the 'sign of the Son of Man', mentioned as appearing in Heaven at the Last Times (Matt. XXIV.30), had been associated with the cross since Late Antiquity.[101]

Further evidence for Otto's continuing interest in sin and repentance comes from his actions in Lent 1001, which he spent in penitential seclusion with Romuald at Pereum. On this occasion, Otto is reported not only to have encouraged some of Romuald's monks to take up the mission, but also to have promised to spend the next three years rectifying his errors before retiring to Jerusalem to live as a monk. Although Bruno of Querfurt, who records this promise, clearly has his own agenda (and is at times very critical of Otto), he was present on this occasion so his testimony

[98] Keller, 'Siegel', 772; Schramm, *Kaiser, Rom und renovatio*, I, 155–60.

[99] J. Fried, 'St. Adalbert, Ungarn und das Imperium Ottos III.', in *Die ungarische Staatsbildung und Ostmitteleuropa*, ed. F. Glatz (Budapest, 2002), 113–41.

[100] D O III 390, 415. See Hoffmann, 'Eigendiktat', 392–7; and Huschner, *Transalpine Kommunikation*, 192 and 389–92, on the former.

[101] Bousset, *Antichrist*, 154–8. See further Fried, 'Endzeiterwartung', 449–61; and D. Callahan, 'The Tau Cross in the Writings of Ademar Chabannes', in *The Year 1000*, ed. Frassetto, 63–71.

commands respect.[102] Indeed, this promise is a poignant expression of the emperor's ascetic ideals and the eschatological perspective which informed them: Jerusalem was to be the location of the Last Judgement and this promise may allude to the Legend of the Last Emperor, who was expected to lay down his crown at Golgotha.[103] Ultimately, we will never know whether Otto intended to keep this promise, but it certainly gives us an impression of his state of mind as he braced himself to travel south and face the Roman rebellion once more. In any case, he was not much longer for this world: after a brief stay in Tivoli and Rome, which ended with his retreat, Otto fell ill and died in early January 1002. His body was taken north and buried in Aachen at Easter, in an act which probably accorded with his own desires.[104]

To conclude, I should like to return to some of the broader themes touched upon at the start of this paper. There, I suggested that historians have at times been rather reticent when it comes to discussing the eschatological beliefs of their subjects and that a case-study in the reign of Otto III might illustrate the benefits of doing so. As I hope to have demonstrated, Otto's court was deeply influenced by apocalyptic thought and many of the emperor's more unusual actions cannot be understood fully without reference to this: his Lenten pilgrimages and penitential acts; the extraordinary sanctions and *arengae* in his charters; his love of Aachen and interest in empire; and, of course, his devotion to the memory (and possibly cult) of Charlemagne. Although not all of the evidence surveyed suggests acute apocalyptic angst, it certainly is indicative of a heightened interest in (and probably also expectation of) the end. Examining eschatological beliefs thus provides not only a deeper understanding Otto's reign, but also serves as an antidote to more recent studies, which have been keen to emphasise the emperor's 'normality'.[105] Otto had an interest in the end of time that clearly went beyond the

---

[102] Bruno of Querfurt, *Vita quinque fratrum eremitarum*, c. 2, ed. J. Karwasińka, Monumanta Poloniae Historica n.s. 4.iii (Warsaw, 1973), 34 and 38, with Sansterre, 'Otton III', 400–7; and Eickhoff, 'Otto III.'. On Bruno, see R. Wenskus, *Studien zur historisch-politischen Gedankenwelt Bruns von Querfurt* (Münster, 1956), esp. 95–101; and Görich, *Otto III.*, 18–51.

[103] M. Uhlirz, *Jahrbücher des Deutschen Reiches unter Otto II. und Otto III.*, II, *Otto III. 983–1002* (Berlin, 1954), 384; Wenskus, *Studien*, 100; Sansterre, 'Otton III', 404–5; Eickhoff, 'Otto III.', 33–4. Cf. L. Körntgen, *Königsherrschaft und Gottes Gnade. Zu Kontext und Funktion sakraler Vorstellungen in Historiographie und Bildzeugnissen der ottonisch-frühsalischen Zeit* (Berlin, 2001), 202–3 n. 279.

[104] Hehl, 'Kirchenrecht', 191–8.

[105] See, e.g., Althoff, *Otto III.*; and S. Waldhoff, 'Der Kaiser in der Krise? Zum Verständnis von Thietmar IV, 48', *Deutsches Archiv*, 54 (1998), 23–54. For responses, see Hlawitschka, 'Otto III.'; F.-R. Erkens, 'Mirabilia mundi. Ein kritischer Versuch über ein methodisches Problem und eine neue Deutung der Herrschaft Ottos III.', *Archiv für Kulturgeschichte*, 79 (1997), 485–98; M. Borgolte, 'Biographie ohne Subjekt, oder wie man durch quellenfixierte Arbeit Opfer des Zeitgeistes werden kann', *Göttingische Gelehrte Anzeigen*, 249 (1997), 128–41; and S.

typical: it was not every ruler who possessed copies of the Books of Daniel and Isaiah and commissioned illuminated apocalypses, nor was it every ruler who undertook extended penances and identified with the figure of the Last Emperor. Indeed, there is doubtless some truth in Johannes Fried's assertion that no emperor save perhaps Frederick II displayed such a keen interest in the Last Things.[106]

Nevertheless, viewed within a broader perspective Otto III's apocalyptic outlook also owes much to existing traditions. His interest in empire is not so different from that seen under Charlemagne, whose imperial ideals were probably also eschatologically informed.[107] Indeed, the exegetic tradition associating empire with the end of time was known throughout the earlier Middle Ages and Otto's predecessors, Otto I and Otto II, may also have been aware of this. Moreover, such interests did not disappear upon Otto's death: his successor, Henry II, possessed a cloak embroidered with cosmic images and it has been suggested that he too saw himself as 'ruler at the end of time'.[108] Later emperors were more circumspect in this regard, but the eschatological significance of empire remained a potent force. Thus when figures such as Henry IV, Frederick Barbarossa and Frederick II found themselves at odds with the papacy, this was often interpreted in apocalyptic terms.[109] Otto's more immediate contemporaries also displayed eschatological interests. In England, Wulfstan of York, a leading adviser of King Æthelred 'the Unready', famously preached that the end was nigh, while in France the response of Robert the Pious to a bout of blood rain in Aquitaine may reveal a degree of eschatological concern.[110] More generally, the Peace of God movement is suggestive of a lively interest in sin and judgement amongst the laity of France, Catalonia and the Low Countries in these years (though whether this constitutes evidence of concrete apocalyptic

Hamilton, 'Early Medieval Rulers and their Modern Biographers', *Early Medieval Europe*, 9 (2000), 247–60, at 256–60.

[106] Fried, 'Endzeiterwartung', 431.

[107] Brandes, 'Eschatologisches'; Fried, 'Papst Leo III.'; Palmer, *Apocalypse and Authority*, ch. 5.

[108] S. Weinfurter, *Heinrich II. Herrscher am Ende der Zeiten* (Regensburg, 1999), 84–92. Cf. *ibid.*, 267–8.

[109] Whalen, *Dominion of God*, 9–41, 72–99 and 166–70; K.-J. Benz, 'Eschatologisches Gedankengut bei Gregor VII.', *Archiv für Kirchengeschichte*, 97 (1986), 1–35; H.-D. Rauh, 'Eschatologie und Geschichte im 12. Jahrhundert. Antichrist-Typologie als Medium der Gegenwartskritik', in *The Use and Abuse of Eschatology in the Middle Ages*, ed. W. Verbeke, D. Verhelst and A. Welkenhuysen (Leuven, 1988), 333–58.

[110] J. T. Lionarons, *The Homiletic Writings of Archbishop Wulfstan* (Woodbridge, 2010), esp. 43–74; Andrew of Fleury, *Vita Gauzlini*, c. 68, ed. R.-H. Bautier and G. Labory (Paris, 1969), 136–8, with Fried, 'Endzeiterwartung', 381–5; Gouguenheim, *Les fausses terreurs*, 127–30; and Fried, 'Endzeit', 315–16.

expectation is unclear).[111] What stands out about Otto III, therefore, is not so much the emperor's interest eschatology *per se*, as the connections this led him to draw between Rome, the Carolingian past and the end of time. Indeed, even Frederick II, who like Otto seems to have modelled aspects of his rule on the Legend, was less interested in Rome, Aachen and Charlemagne than in crusade, Jerusalem and the Holy Land.[112]

Of course, in isolating apocalypticism for study there is a danger of exaggerating its importance. All of Otto's actions cannot be reduced to cosmic concerns regarding time and eternity and doubtless matters of a more quotidian nature were often foremost on his mind. Nevertheless, to assert that Otto's actions possess an apocalyptic quality need not (and should not) involve excluding other influences – it is simply to point out that we have not understood them fully unless we acknowledge the apocalyptic resonances which would have been so clear to Otto and his contemporaries. Here, in particular, is where the present study seeks to part ways with previous work: it sees apocalypticism as an important part of the emperor's thought-world, but not the only one – eschatology was but one ingredient in the complex mix that made up late Ottonian politics. It is for this reason that we should be cautious about attributing too much causal power to the year 1000: while Otto III's political programme came to a head at this point, other more contingent factors, such as the death of Adalbert and the Roman rebellion, also contributed decisively to his eschatological outlook. In this respect, Paul Magdalino's conclusions regarding the role of eschatological expectation in Byzantine history also hold for Western Europe in these years:

> It would certainly be a distortion to register every episode in that past as a tick or a chime in an eschatological clock. But it is equally distorting to close our ears deliberately to the eschatological echoes of worlds and actions produced in a climate of a genuine uncertainty about the future.[113]

[111] T. Head, 'The Development of the Peace of God in Aquitaine (970–1005)', *Speculum*, 74 (1999), 656–86, at 686. Cf. R. Landes, *Relics, Apocalypse, and the Deceits of History: Ademar of Chabannes, 989–1034* (Cambridge, MA, 1995), 24–49; and Gouguenheim, *Les fausses terreurs*, 177–85.

[112] H.-M. Schaller, 'Endzeit-Erwartungen und Antichrist-Vorstellungen in der Politik des 13. Jahrhunderts' (1972), repr. in and cited from his *Stauferzeit. Ausgewählte Aufsätze*, MGH: Schriften 38 (Hannover, 1993), 25–52; O. B. Rader, *Friedrich II. Der Sizilianer auf dem Kaiserthron: Eine Biographie* (Munich, 2010), 129–30, 392–5 and 445–84. See also E. Kantorowicz, *Kaiser Friedrich der Zweite* (2 vols., Düsseldorf, 1927–31), I, 9–10, 154–5, 182, 370, 388–9, 461, 565–6 and 630–2.

[113] P. Magdalino, 'The History of the Future and its Uses', in *The Making of Byzantine History: Studies dedicated to Donald M. Nicol*, ed. B. Roderick and C. Roueché (Aldershot, 1993), 3–34, at 33.

Thus, the end of time was certainly not Otto III's only preoccupation, but we do not do him justice unless we acknowledge its importance to him. Whereas some fifty years ago Josef Déer coined the famous dictum that 'Otto III is not to be understood without Byzantium',[114] we might now assert that he is not to be understood without reference to eschatology. Donald Bullough was right: the contribution of apocalyptic thought to society and politics in the Middle Ages is easy to underestimate, but we do so at our peril.

---

[114] J. Déer, 'Das Kaiserbild im Kreuz. Ein Beitrag zur politischen Theologie des früherem Mittelalters' (1955), repr. in and cited from his *Byzanz und das abendländische Herrschertum. Ausgewählte Aufsätze*, ed. P. Classen (Sigmaringen, 1977), 125–77, at 175–6, n. 272: 'Otto III. ist ohne Byzanz nicht zu verstehen'.

Transactions of the RHS 23 (2013), pp. 103–25 © Royal Historical Society 2013
doi:10.1017/S0080440113000054

OF LIVING LEGENDS AND AUTHENTIC TALES: HOW TO GET REMEMBERED IN EARLY MODERN EUROPE*

By Judith Pollmann

READ 21 SEPTEMBER 2012

ABSTRACT. Folklore experts have shown that for a legend to be remembered it is important that it is historicised. Focusing on three case-studies from early modern Germany and the Netherlands, this article explores how the historicisation of mythical narratives operated in early modern Europe, and argues that memory practices played a crucial role in the interplay between myth and history. The application of new criteria for historical evidence did not result in the decline of myths. By declaring such stories mythical, and by using the existence of memory practices as evidence for this, scholars could continue to take them seriously.

In the German city of Hamelin, there is no getting away from it. Everywhere in the old town, there are reminders of the story of the pied piper, who, on a fateful day in June 1284, played tunes so sweet that 130 enchanted children followed him outside the city gates to disappear into a mountain and never to be seen again. Yet if modern Hamelin trades heavily on its reputation as the pied piper's city, this is not such a recent phenomenon as we might imagine. Travellers' accounts tell us that, as early as the sixteenth century, references to the children and the piper could be found everywhere. People had sculpted and stained glass images of the pied piper in their homes, inscriptions on houses and public buildings referred to the tale and local people were reported to obey the ban on drumming and piping in the street through which the children were believed to have left. The event had been so momentous, travellers and chroniclers recounted, that the people in Hamelin even dated events using their own calendar, which started in the year of the children's disappearance.[1]

---

* Research for this paper was done in the context of the NWO VICI research project 'Tales of the Revolt. Memory, Oblivion and Identity in the Low Countries, 1566–1700'. I am grateful to Marten Jan Bok, Frank de Hoog, Erika Kuijpers, Marijke Meijer Drees, Johannes Müller and Ann Rigney for their help in researching and writing it.

[1] An indispensable survey and extracts of available source material to 1860 in the *Quellensammlung zur Hamelner Rattenfängersage*, ed. Hans Dobertin (Göttingen, 1970).

Although from the mid-seventeenth century there emerged sceptics who dismissed the story as a fable, far more numerous have been those who tried to find an explanation for what could *actually* have happened in this small city for such a tale to emerge. Philosopher Gottfried Wilhelm Leibniz believed the tale related to a children's crusade.[2] Other eighteenth-century scholars explained it with reference to a battle in which many Hamelin youngsters could have died, or sought links with St Vitus dances, and with natural disasters in the area. And while early modern scholars connected the tale to the migration of young Germans to Transylvania or even the New World, modern ones have suggested the children were *Ostsiedler*, migrants who had left for Bohemia or Pomerania.[3]

In his 2005 book, *In Search of the Pied Piper*, the Romanian-American scholar Radu Florescu surveys these explanations, and comes out in favour of one of them. He tells how local Hamelin historian Hans Dobbertin persuaded him that the tale originated in the move by a thirteenth-century nobleman by name of Nicholas von Spielenberg to recruit young Hamelers to settle in his family lands in Pomerania; they themselves wanted to flee their rat-infested city.[4] Yet Florescu also asks whether this knowledge really matters. Because ultimately, Florescu argues, 'the history of Count Nicholas von Spielenberg' is 'of interest only to local historians'.[5] The story would never have gained the worldwide popularity that it did, had it not been for its legendary and mythical aspects. Of course, he is quite right about this, but this article will argue that this cannot be the whole story. Because not all myths and legends have as successful and lasting a career, after all, as the pied piper story. What does it take for a myth to live on, and be remembered generation after generation? We will see that for a tale like this to have persisted and to have made it beyond the world of Hamelin, it needed not only mythical characteristics, it also needed the flavour of authenticity that is provided by historical activity and the practice of memory.

Students of myth and legend have taught us that cultures develop recurring narrative and explanatory patterns that crop up again and again when people mentally and culturally try to structure their world. The archetypes or 'motifs' which twentieth-century folklorists and

---

[2] *Ibid.*, doc. no. 96a–b, 96–9.

[3] Heinrich Spanuth, *Der Rattenfänger von Hameln. Vom Werden und Sinn einer alten Sage* (Hamelin, 1951); Bernd Ulrich Hucker, 'Die Auszug der Hämelschen Kinder aus quellenkritischer Sicht', in *Geschichten und Geschichte. Erzählforschertagung in Hameln, Oktober 1984*, ed. Norbert Humburg (Hildesheim 1985), 96–9.

[4] Radu Florescu, *In Search of the Pied Piper* (2005), 155–70; see for a critique of Dobertin's argument Werner Ueffing, 'Die Hamelner Rattenfängersage und ihr historischer Hintergrund', in *Geschichten und Geschichte*, ed. Humburg, 184–91.

[5] Florescu, *In Search of the Pied Piper*, 205.

mythologists identified appear everywhere. Familiar tales of origin and deliverance, of failure and success, of gender and generations, and of the relationships between humans and the divine, appear in new settings. Such cultural patterns structure the way we tell stories, and thus also how we remember.

But myth is not history, and until quite recently, scholars have treated the two not only as very different, but also as mutually exclusive habits of thought.[6] Historians used to think of myths as deplorable things that other people believe in, and wrongs which are for them to right. History in its modern incarnation is a way of engaging with the past that distinguishes between past and present, deploys a timeframe, follows clear habits of reasoning and is based on an assessment of available evidence. Myth, on the other hand, is usually hazy about timeframes, more often than not depends on a suspension of disbelief and approaches evidence as something that is explained by a story, rather than used to test that story's reliability. That is not just true for the supernatural stories that scholars used to insist were 'real' myths, but also for what we call 'legends', popular but unlikely tales about humans that are located in time and space.[7]

Once upon a time, scholars believed that in the *longue durée* of human development, history had replaced myth. Myth, they argued, was something that belonged to a primitive, pre-literate and pre-scientific way of life, not to the modern world. Today, scholarship has abandoned the 'myth of mythlessness', the notion that a world ruled once by myth has had to give way to a world ruled by reason.[8] Scholars from Roland Barthes to Marina Warner have pointed out that today's world actually continues to be pervaded by myth.[9] Even so, few myths can hold an epistemological monopoly; they are likely to coexist with other ways of thinking about the world, and some of those ways are historical.

Of course, distinctions between myth and history are not always clean and clear. Myths and legends can take on shapes that look, and indeed are,

[6] See e.g. Jack Goody and Ian Watt, 'The Consequences of Literacy', *Comparative Studies in Society and History*, 5 (1963), 304–45; M. I. Finley, 'Myth, Memory and History', *History and Theory*, 4 (1965), 281–302; and C. A. Tamse, 'The Political Myth', in *Some Political Mythologies. Papers Delivered to the Fifth Anglo-Dutch Historical Conference*, ed. J. S. Bromley and E. H. Kossmann (The Hague, 1975). Changing views of the relationship between history and myth are helpfully discussed in Laura Cruz and Willem Frijhoff, 'Introduction. Myth in History, History in Myth', in *Myth in History, History in Myth. Proceedings of the Third International Conference of the Society for Netherlandic History (New York: June 5–6, 2006)*, ed. Laura Cruz and Willem Frijhoff (Leiden, 2009), 1–16.

[7] Although some scholars insist that the term myth should in fact only be used to describe tales about the realm of the supernatural, modern theorists take a broader approach, see Robert A. Segal, *Myth. A Very Short Introduction* (2004).

[8] E.g. *ibid.*; Laurence Coupe, *Myth*, 2nd edn (2009), 9–15.

[9] Roland Barthes, *Mythologies suivi de Le Mythe, aujourd'hui* (Paris, 1957); Marina Warner, *Managing Monsters. Six Myths of our Time*, The Reith Lectures (1994).

quite historical, while histories often acquire mythical features. In some instances, we can follow this process fairly closely. Since 2008, a research team under my direction has been studying war memories of the Dutch Revolt in the seventeenth-century Low Countries.[10] When we surveyed the transmission of eyewitness tales about the Dutch Revolt, we found that diarists who were writing contemporaneously often expressed their fear, anger and frustration about the pointlessness of events as they unfolded. At best, they referred to them quite generically as God's punishment for a decadent society.[11] Yet, a few decades *after* the events, few of the tales which people told each other about their own war experiences were 'pointless'. Rather, war experiences had been framed in narrative formats that either helped to give some sort of providential or moral significance to the tales, or that suggested some form of control. Such stories told how villagers and townspeople had outwitted their military opponents with cunning and deceit, escapes were miraculous, sacrifices rewarded. In the process, many of these historical experiences had therefore become the stuff of legend, and had acquired mythical characteristics. Individual experiences which could not be framed in such a mythical way, such as those relating to defeat, loss and shame, were much less likely to be remembered.[12] Mythmaking, then, was an essential stage in the development of social memories of the Dutch Revolt; such myths were not the product of fading and failing memories, as some have thought, but intrinsic to the production of social memory itself.[13]

Yet we also noted something else: for such myths and legends to catch on and survive, a good story alone was not enough. These stories *continued* to thrive only when they were framed historically and/or supported by material evidence. Stories apparently need an association with a place or a date, an object or a person, to be believed, and to be transmitted,

[10] This VICI project is funded by NWO, the Netherlands Organisation for Scientific Research, and titled *Tales of the Revolt. Memory, Oblivion and Identity in the Low Countries, 1566–1700*, www.earlymodernmemory.org.

[11] Examples cited for instance in Judith Pollmann, *Catholic Identity and the Revolt of the Netherlands, 1520–1635* (Oxford, 2011), 57–9, 94–100, 113–24, 131–5, 153–8.

[12] Marianne Eekhout, 'De kogel in de kerk. Herinneringen aan het beleg van Haarlem, 1573–1630', *Holland. Historisch tijdschrift*, 43 (2011), 108–19; Erika Kuijpers, 'The Creation and Development of Social Memories of Traumatic Events. The Oudewater Massacre of 1575', in *Hurting Memories. Remembering as a Pathogenic Process in Individuals and Societies*, ed. Michael Linden and Krzysztof Rutkowski (London and Waltham, MA, 2013), 191–201; and Erika Kuijpers, 'Between Storytelling and Patriotic Scripture. The Memory Brokers of the Dutch Revolt', in *Memory before Modernity. Practices of Memory in Early Modern Europe*, ed. Erika Kuijpers *et al.* (forthcoming, 2013). On the mythologising of the siege of Leiden, Judith Pollmann, *Herdenken, herinneren, vergeten. Het beleg en ontzet van Leiden in de Gouden Eeuw*, 3 October lezing (Leiden, 2008).

[13] On mythmaking as the result of failing memories, see e.g. Adam Fox, *Oral and Literate Culture in England, 1500–1700* (Oxford, 2000), 225.

even if such stories can also be transplanted to another context when that suits the needs of the storyteller. In early modern Europe, such evidence need not necessarily be that precise – the ability to point to place in the landscape could be adduced as 'proof' for an event to have taken place there. Myths without such a supporting framework of time, space and evidence might easily be dismissed as 'fables' and old wives' tales – although that did not necessarily stop early modern antiquarians from repeating them.[14] Yet if and when a decent frame was in place, mythical tales and legends had a better chance than most of 'catching on' and of capturing the historical imagination.

Students of legends and folktales are familiar with this effect. 'Legends', as Timothy R. Tangherlini has put it,

> are best characterized as historicized narrative. The process of historicization may be likened to diachronic ecotypification [the way in which cultural practices, including narratives, will adapt to suit a new environment]. The believability of the narrative is underscored by the historicization of the account.[15]

This paper explores how such a historicisation of narrative operated in early modern Europe. Of course, the practice of history changed considerably in this period. There was growing scepticism about some myths, as we can see in the Hamelin case. Moreover, standards of evidence changed, and techniques for assessing its value and authenticity were refined and improved. But we will see that this did not necessarily endanger the survival and spread of myths and legends; quite the opposite, often it was actually modern historical and antiquarian methods and techniques that were used to strengthen, embellish and support them.

We will see that in the dynamic between myth and history an important mediating role was played by what students of memory call memory practices. The field of memory studies tells us that remembering is as much about 'practice' as about thought.[16] In Hamelin, people in the sixteenth century practised memory not only by storytelling, but also in observing the taboo on dancing in one of the streets, in the commissioning

---

[14] Daniel Woolf, *The Social Circulation of the Past. English Historical Culture, 1500–1730* (Oxford, 2003), 352–91.

[15] Timothy R. Tangherlini, '"It Happened Not Too Far From Here . . . ": A Survey of Legend Theory and Characterization', *Western Folklore*, 49 (1990), 371–90, at 379. On the concept of ecotype, see David Hopkin, 'The Ecotype, or a Modest Proposal to Reconnect Cultural and Social History', in *Exploring Cultural History. Essays in Honour of Peter Burke*, ed. Joao Paul Rubiés, Melissa Calaresu and Filippo de Vivo (Farnham, 2010), 31–54.

[16] E.g. Paul Connerton, *How Societies Remember* (Cambridge, 1989); Jeffrey K. Olick and Joyce Robbins, 'Social Memory Studies. From "Collective Memory" to the Historical Sociology of Mnemonic Practices', *Annual Review of Sociology*, 24 (1998), 105–40; general introductions to memory studies like Geoffrey Cubitt, *History and Memory* (Manchester 2007); and Astrid Erll, *Memory in Culture*, trans. Sarah Young (Basingstoke 2011), excellent as they are, have relatively little to say on pre-modern memory, but still useful is James Fentress and Chris Wickham, *Social Memory* (Oxford, 1992).

of and exhibiting of memorial inscriptions and images, and even, allegedly, by a new form of timekeeping. By doing so, they maintained a powerful presence for the story in the urban landscape; this in turn persuaded visitors and historians that there had to be 'something in it'. In that way, memory practices like those in Hamelin helped to authenticate myth, and so functioned as a mediator between mythical and historical ways of thinking about the past. I will explore this dynamic further by discussing two Dutch tales, both of which also happen to involve children, before returning to the children of Hamelin.

Baby, cat and cradle

On the night of 18–19 November 1421, the so-called St Elizabeth flood swallowed the better part of the South-Holland area that was known as the Grote Waard. Much of the land was lost for good; part of the area became a marshland area which today is called the Biesbosch. Many villages were never rebuilt and the city of Dordrecht became an island, as it still is today. Two thousand people may have died, and the event made a big enough impression for people to remember it well into the sixteenth century. In 1560, a seventy-two-year-old man named Theeus Aspersoon recalled that his father and a great-uncle who had lived to age ninety had told him about the drowning of the village of Wieldrecht.[17] Such memories were supported by material remains. An early sixteenth-century witness claimed that when sailing through the area, he had seen the vestiges of the towers of the drowned village churches sticking out over the waters.[18] We also possess a remarkable pictorial representation of the flood; sometime around 1490 people from the drowned village of Wieldrecht and their descendants commissioned an altarpiece for the altar of St Elizabeth, whose name day at that time fell on 19 November. For the outer panels they ordered two images commemorating the event. These showed not only the drowning of their village and the villagers' flight to the safety of Dordrecht, but also included a remarkable detail. On the top middle on the left altar panel we see a small cradle afloat, containing a baby and a cat (Figure 1a and b).[19] A historical account from

---

[17] Elizabeth Gottschalk, *Stormvloeden en rivieroverstromingen in Nederland / Storm Surges and River Floods in the Netherlands*, II: *1400–1600* (Assen 1975), 74. Gottschalk discusses all sources relating to the flood, including the transmission of tales about it.

[18] 'Chrysostomus Neapolitanus to Count Nugarola, *c.* 1514', in Hadrianus Junius, *Batavia* (Leiden, 1588), 182–7. The letter was first published in Martinus Dorpius, *Dialogus: in quo Venus et Cupido omnes adhibent versutias: ut Herculem animi ancipitem in suam militiam invita Virtuta perpellant. Eiusdem Thomus Aululariæ Plautinæ adiectus cum prologis ... Chrysostomi Neapolitani epistola de situ Hollandiæ viuendique Hollandorum institutis. Gerardi Nouiomagi de Zelandia epistola consimilis* ([Louvain, 1514]).

[19] Liesbeth Helmus, 'Het altaarstuk met de Sint Elisabethsvloed uit de Grote Kerk van Dordrecht. De oorspronkelijke plaats en de opdrachtgevers', *Oud-Holland*, 105 (1991), 127–39.

Figure 1a Master of the St Elizabeth Panels, *Outer Left Wing of an Altar Piece with the St Elisabeth's Flood, 18–19 November 1421*, c. 1490, SK-A-3147-A
Published with permission of the Rijksmuseum Amsterdam

1514 gives us the background story: on the waters raised by the flood, a cradle had drifted into Dordrecht, which contained a male baby who had a cat for company.[20] Floating infants are a well-known narrative motif in European folktales; in the motif-index there is a special category reserved

---

[20] 'Chrysostomus Neapolitanus to Count Nugarola', 182–3.

Figure 1b Detail of Figure 1a, showing baby, cat and cradle afloat

for 'future hero found in boat'.[21] Sometime between 1421 and 1470, a tale with a similar motif had apparently been born in Dordrecht.

This was by no means the only mythical tale to originate from the flood. By 1500, for instance, it was said that as many as seventy-two villages had been lost in the event.[22] The actual number had been much lower, yet seventy-two is a number associated in the Bible with the number of peoples at the Tower of Babel, and the number of disciples sent out by Christ among the nations in Luke 10:1. This may be the reason why the number took hold of the imagination; it was probably no accident that witness Theeus Aspersoon was reported to be seventy-two years of age. The figure was also repeated on commemorative inscriptions, like the one that appeared above a city gate in Dordrecht in 1609.

On the land and water seen here
72 parishes, as the chronicle says,
Were inundated by the force of the water
In the year 1421.[23]

---

[21] H. van de Waal, *Drie eeuwen vaderlandsche geschied-uitbeelding, 1500–1800, een iconologische studie* (2 vols., The Hague, 1952), I, 255, and II, 121.

[22] Gottschalk, *Stormvloeden*, 73, suggests it first made an appearance in the *Magnum Chronicon Belgicum* of c. 1500.

[23] See for this and a discussion of the meaning of the number Jan van Herwaarden *et al.*, *Geschiedenis van Dordrecht tot 1572* (Dordrecht and Hilversum, 1996), 162. The inscription is cited in Matthijs Balen, *Beschryvinge der stad Dordrecht, vervatende haar begin, opkomst, toeneming, en verdere stant ...* (Dordrecht, 1677), 769.

At the time the gate was built, there were already many doubts about this figure. Yet while scholars debated how many villages had actually disappeared, the inscription resolved this problem by invoking the authority of a 'chronicle' to support its claim. The figure of seventy-two has been recurring until well into the twentieth century.[24]

Other mythical elements disappeared much faster. In 1588, humanist Hadrianus Junius claimed that the flood had been the result of human intervention. A man had been so angry with his neighbours that he had made a breach in the sea dike that protected their land, thus provoking the flooding of the Grote Waard. The man was said to have suffered great remorse about the unexpected consequences of this act of spite.[25] Yet this tale did not catch on, and disappeared from view. The same happened with an earlier sixteenth-century tale, which explained the flood as the punishment for the pennypinching of the owners of the land, who had failed to pay their labourers their dues.[26] A late seventeenth-century author, who produced one of the most emotive descriptions of the flood, saw it as a providential punishment for the decadence of the area's prosperous inhabitants.[27] Even this tale made one appearance only.

However, the tale of the infant who survived the flood turned out to have a remarkable staying power. It has been suggested that it may have been someone who was associated with the tale of the cradle and the cat who insisted on the inclusion of the cradle in the altar panels in 1490; perhaps descendants of a survivor. This idea is supported by the fact that other early paintings of the flood did not include the cradle.[28] But however that may be, it seems that the tale was initially limited to a smallish circle. That the tale of the cradle survived at all, and that all accounts of the flood after 1600 were to include it, had everything to do with the intervention of a learned author. In a book that Erasmus's humanist friend, Martin Dorpius, published in 1514, he included a description of the County of Holland, allegedly written by Chrysostomos Neapolitanus and recounting the tale of a baby boy who had floated to safety with a cat in his cradle during the 1421 flood. There are indications that the author may have been using a pseudonym, and that the true author, probably the humanist Cornelis Aurelius, had all meant it as a bit of joke; nevertheless,

[24] Ruben Koman, *Bèèh ... ! Groot Dordts volksverhalenboek. Een speurtocht naar volksverhalen, bijnamen, volksgeloof, mondelinge overlevering en vertelcultuur in Dordrecht* (Bedum, 2005).

[25] Junius, *Batavia*, 249.

[26] Gottschalk, *Stormvloeden*, 73–4, discusses e.g. the version of Reinier Snoy (1477–1537), whose *De Rebus Batavicis* was published in Frankfurt, 1620.

[27] Gerrit Spaan, *Beschrijvinge der stad Rotterdam, en eenige omleggende dorpen, verdeeld in III. Boeken* (Rotterdam, 1698), 13–16.

[28] Helmus, 'Het altaarstuk'.

its humanist setting lent it a veracity that greatly helped to authenticate the story in subsequent historiography and pictorial representations.[29]

One sign of this is that the account appears to have influenced local memory culture. In 1635, an eighty-year-old Haarlem widow called Lysbeth Pieters signed an affidavit to the effect that she had often heard her grandmother tell how the latter's grandfather, Pieter van Nederveen, had miraculously floated to safety during the great flood of 1421. There was no mention of a cat in her account, but she said that the baby had worn a coral 'paternoster' necklace, with a pendant displaying a coat of arms and his name. Because of this, the boy had been recognised as a nobleman and brought up accordingly. Lysbeth made her statement at the request of a distant cousin, named Moses Jans van Nederveen, who lived in Dordrecht and who made gunpowder for a living. Moses may have been interested in the story because it would support claims to a higher social status, yet he may have also tried to stake his family's claim to the story because in Dordrecht there were other claimants around.[30] By the seventeenth century, the Dordrecht family of Roerom had apparently also started to claim a connection with the baby in the cradle. Local historian Matthijs Balen in the 1670s was the first to mention this connection and name the child in print. He included a reference to the cat, but in this version of the tale, the baby had undergone a sex change. Balen claimed that the child had been a girl, and identified her as a woman named Baete, who had eventually married a man called Jakob Roerom. Baete had been nicknamed Beatrix, 'felicitous', and it was under this name that she was from now on to be known. Through the offspring of her marriage with Jakob Roerom, Beatrix had become the great-great-grandmother of a series of elite families. Balen listed them carefully, and demonstrated the connection a second time in the genealogical tables which he included in his book. Balen allowed for other survivors and also mentioned a family who had survived the flood by clinging on to a wooden beam, yet he did not mention the Nederveen family.[31] Apparently, he knew nothing about the alternative claims of the descendants of Pieter van Nederveen. Yet however that may be, it is evident that by the seventeenth century

---

[29] As has been argued by Jan van Herwaarden, *Between Saint James and Erasmus: Studies in Late-Medieval Religious Life: Devotion and Pilgrimage in the Netherlands*, trans. Wendie Shaffer and Donald Gardner, Studies in Medieval and Reformation Thought, 97 (Leiden, 2003), 571–8; Van de Waal, *Drie eeuwen*, 255–6, was dismissive of the influence of the story, but he missed Junius's inclusion of the Colonna letter in his *Batavia*. It was published again in Petrus Scriverius, *Batavia Illustrata* (Leiden, 1609), 129ff.

[30] Noordhollands archief, Inv. 164 Notary archives Jacob van Bosvelt, 7 July 1635, fo. 172r–v. It was published in *De genealogieën van Nederveen*, ed. F. B. M. Nederveen and C. J. Nederveen (Gertruidenberg, 2006), 44–5. I am most grateful to Marten Jan Bok for bringing the existence of this document to my attention.

[31] Balen, *Beschryvinge*, 770, 1205.

the tale of the baby in the cradle had become a tale of origin. Since then, there has been a steady stream of individuals who claim descent from the rescued infant. Mostly, they mentioned Beatrix, but some also continued to maintain that the baby had been a boy. In 1885, an 'old' painting of cradle, baby and cat was sold at auction, which had been kept as evidence of a family association with Beatrix, together with a coral necklace with a gold locket that was said to have been found together with the baby.[32] It may have been an echo of the claims about the coral paternoster made by the Nederveen family, which in another version of the family history before 1800 had added details about the jewelry, and now also claimed that the baby had been accompanied by a cat.[33] In a 1698 version of the tale there was also mention of jewels which were associated with the baby.[34] Descendants of survivors continue to live to this very day. In 2007, a woman came forward in Dordrecht to tell the tale of her descent from Beatrix. Meanwhile, the Nederveen family has also been active in reappropriating the story for their family, through a local history journal, a published family genealogy and a strategic gift of a copy of their ancestor's affidavit to Dordrecht archive.[35]

Yet it was not just individual stakeholders who spread the tale. From the eighteenth century there was a trend towards broader appropriation of the story. The myth proved capable of moving in time and space. Scholars have found references to at least three other medieval and early modern Netherlandish floods in which the tale of the cradle, cat and baby reappears; the early modern stories appear to have been inspired by a version of the tale from Dordrecht.[36] The tale was included in a print of the flood made by Romeyn de Hooghe in 1675, and in an influential print which Jan Luyken made of such a tale in Groningen the baby even took centre stage (Figure 2).[37] Its appeal has not waned; the tale of a floating baby is central to the plot of a Dutch film *De Storm* from 2009, which is set during the great floods of 1953.

The story of the baby, cat and cradle was in itself modelled on an archetypal mythical tale of delivery, that of Moses. This may well explain its appearance and its attraction in fifteenth-century Dordrecht. A story

[32] J. R. W. Sinnighe, *Hollandsch sagenboek. Legenden en sagen uit Noord- en Zuid-Holland* (The Hague, 1943), 270–1.

[33] First published in the nineteenth century without much detail on provenance and date, this was republished in *De genealogieën van Nederveen*, 42–3. It appears to have been written before 1800.

[34] Spaan, *Beschrijvinghe*, 13–16.

[35] Van de Waal, *Drie eeuwen*, 258; Koman, *Groot Dordts volksverhalenboek* 109 n. 327; *De genealogieën van Nederveen*; C. Nederveen, 'Pieter, opgevist, met een kat legghende bij sigh', *Oud-Dordrecht*, 25 (2007), 26–8. This also refers to the recent tale of the descendant of Beatrix.

[36] Koman, *Groot Dordts volksverhalenboek*, 106–7; Van de Waal, *Drie eeuwen*, 255.

[37] Rijksmuseum Amsterdam, *Romeyn de Hooghe, Sint Elisabethsvloed, 1675*, RP-P-OB-76.843; and Jan Luyken, *Watersnood in Groningen in 1686*, 1698, RP-P-1896-A-19368-1562.

Figure 2 Jan Luyken, *Flood in Groningen in 1686*, 1698, RP-P-1896-A-19368–1562.
Published with permission of the Rijksmuseum Amsterdam

like this was probably shaped by the existence of an archetype about the providential rescue of floating babies, and their special mission; and that was also the reason why it stuck and survived. It had more potential than other rescue tales, in that it concerned a baby, suggested miraculous delivery and special divine favour; and this in turn also made it attractive to be associated with it. At the same time, it was essential for the long-term survival and career of the myth that it was coupled with an identifiable event and that there was supporting evidence to authenticate that event and its enormity. The flood of 1421 was only the first of a series, and at the time of their happening, these undoubtedly generated tales of their own. Yet, in the longer term, all flood stories came to be associated with the flood of 1421. This telescoping effect is quite well known among students of memory. It is significant in that it helped to reinforce an appearance of precision, which was necessary to support the absorption of memories into learned and popular historical tales. In this process, memory practices were an important catalyst; the painting and the inscription, the family tales, the jewels, have fired the interplay between myth and history, personal and public versions of the story. Oral, written and material evidence served mutually to support and reinforce one another.

In all this, the role of the cat in the story remains something of an enigma. The cat seems to have become more important for the tale when, from the late seventeenth century onwards, it was not just said to have been present, but also to have been instrumental for the rescue of the baby, by making sure that the cradle remained well-balanced.[38] In tales of other Dutch floods, the cat was also always included in tales about floating babies. The cat was first dismissed in 1808 by the poet Reyer van Someren, who explained that in his lengthy poetic account of the tale, he had 'left out the cat because it is an unpoetic being'.[39] Much more than earlier observers, Van Someren seemed to think that one might divorce the myth from the historical evidence. He did this without wanting to diminish the importance of either, because it was he himself who, in an appendix to his poem, explained and documented exactly how he had handled the historical facts. This points to a division of labour between myth and history in nineteenth-century culture, in which the role of myth was not necessarily to be historically true, but rather to lend a spiritual or psychological significance to a tale and, crucially, also to testify to its antiquity. As we will see, this had also been happening in Hamelin. Even so, its historical dimensions also remained important. In the nineteenth century, the tale of baby, cat and cradle was adopted as a typonomical explanation for the Kinderdijk (or children's dike) which people claimed owed its name to the finding of Beatrix's cradle there. Subject of fierce debate and competition, and eventually disproven with considerable solemnity, the tale of this association was to become especially popular, and is still used today to enhance Kinderdijk's status as a quintessentially Holland tourist attraction.[40]

Mythologising history

Yet if memory practices and histories can help to perpetuate and authenticate myths, early modern myth also helped to perpetuate historical memories, as we can see in another tale of deliverance. In 1685, an unknown editor was completing work on the second, extended edition of a very influential book, which is known in English as the *Martyrs' Mirror*. This scholarly Mennonite martyrology had first been published by Thieleman van Bracht two decades earlier, and was now being updated. Just as he was ready to go to press, the editor was contacted by a man who said he was a great-grandson of a woman called Anneke Jans, one of

[38] Spaan, *Beschrijvinghe*, 13–16.
[39] Reyer van Someren, *De St. Elisabethsnacht, Anno 1421. Dichtstuk in drie zangen* (Utrecht, 1841), 90; see also Van de Waal, *Drie eeuwen*, 258.
[40] Koman, *Groot Dordts volksverhalenboek*, 105–6.

the sixteenth-century martyrs who was celebrated in this book.[41] Anneke had been executed in Rotterdam on 24 January 1539. Her crime was that she rejected infant baptism, and had been rebaptised. Like many martyred heretics, Anneke had left a 'testament', in which she testified to her resolve to die for the faith.[42] It was addressed to her son Esaiah and commenced: 'Hear my son, the teachings of your mother, and open your ears to hear the speech of my mouth. Behold, today I am going the way of the prophets, apostles and martyrs, to drink the cup that they have drunk.' Soon after her death, it appeared in print as a song.[43] A prose version of the testament had been printed for the first time in 1562 in a famous collection of martyrs' testimonies called *Het offer des Heeren* or *The Sacrifice of the Lord*. It had also been included in the first edition of the *Martyrs' Mirror*. The existence of Anneke's son was thus already well known. But Anneke's great-grandson now produced new material: an extract from the court records detailing the verdict, a letter by Anneke to her son, copied in the hand of his grandfather Esaiah, and a great deal of information regarding the life of her son. The great-grandson explained that Esaiah had been a baby of fifteen months old when his mother received her death sentence. On her way to be executed, she had called upon the bystanders and asked if one of them would be prepared to look after her son. She had had a purse with some money ready for his support, which she would give to anyone who would promise to raise him as their own son. A poor baker, who already had six children to support, had stepped forward to take on this charge, and promised that he would do as she asked. She handed the child over to him 'in the name of the father, son and holy spirit', and proceeded to her martyr's death by drowning.

When the baker came home with the child, his wife was at first very angry, yet soon it emerged that God's 'blessing which he had hoped for by accepting this child' started to flow freely. The baker's business thrived, and he eventually bought himself a brewery (a big social step up for a baker) and left his children much wealth. His foster child Esaiah also became a brewer and eventually even made it to be burgomaster

---

[41] Tieleman van Braght, *Het bloedig tooneel of martelaers spiegel der Doops-gesinde of weerelose Christenen, die, om 't getuygenis van Jesus haren Salighmaker, geleden hebben, ende gedood zijn, van Christi tijd af, tot desen*, 2nd edn (Amsterdam, 1685), 48–9, and 143–4. Van Braght had died in the 1660s. We do not know who re-edited the text.

[42] Although some scholars have argued that letters like the one printed in the *Sacrifice of the Lord* were probably not genuine, precisely because they tend to include well-known narrative motifs, we are currently minded to consider them as authentic. See on this issue Gregory's introduction to *The Forgotten Writings of the Mennonite Martyrs*, ed. Brad S. Gregory, Documenta Anabaptistica Neerlandica VIII (Leiden and Boston, MA, 2002).

[43] Werner O. Packull, 'Anna Jansz of Rotterdam. A Historical Investigation of an Early Anabaptist Heroine', *Archiv für Reformationsgeschichte*, 78 (1987), 147–73; Els Kloek, 'Esaiasdr., Anneke', in *Digitaal Vrouwenlexicon van Nederland*. URL: www.historici.nl/Onderzoek/Projecten/DVN/lemmata/data/Esaiasdr (last accessed 29 May 2013).

of Rotterdam. So prominent did Esaiah become that he had acted as godfather to a daughter of the city's pensionary and later statesman Johan van Oldenbarnevelt, while Oldenbarnevelt had done the same for his son. The man who had denounced Anneke, by contrast, had come to a terrible end. As he left the place where she had been drowned, a bridge which he was crossing collapsed, and he himself died, too, by drowning. All of his family ended up in utter destitution.[44]

The tale as it was told here had a number of very satisfactory mythical elements; the baker had to overcome resistance from his wife but did the right thing and was rewarded; Anneke's son was clearly divinely favoured. The traitor, on the other hand, had not only been punished, but deservedly died the same death that she had had to endure so unjustly. This beautiful symmetry was carefully maintained in the transmission of the tale. Esaiah's grandson apparently failed to mention that Esaiah had had to leave Rotterdam in 1602 because his brewery had gone bankrupt; one of his sons had already been bankrupted in 1598.[45] Moreover, neither he nor the martyrologist wanted to spell out that, in a religious sense, the story did not quite work. No Anabaptist or Mennonite could have become burgomaster of Rotterdam. Moreover, if the Reformed city pensionary and later statesman Oldenbarnevelt was involved in the baptism of Esaiah de Lint's children, these cannot have been adults at the time, but would have been baptised as infants and in accordance with the Reformed rite, rather than that of the Mennonite successors to the Anabaptists. In a confessional, denominational sense, then, the tale was not as satisfactory as it might have been. Yet Esaiah's grandson had taken a great deal of trouble in offering precise information to enhance its authenticity. The story was supported by details about Anneke's arrest, the age of her child, the names of the breweries of the baker and Esaiah and the precise location of the collapsing bridge. And as a morality tale it was apparently so irresistible that the editor of the Mennonite *Marter's Mirror* not only thought he should include it, but also chose to have it illustrated. Like in the case of the floating cradle, it was an image by Jan Luyken that greatly enhanced the profile of the story (Figure 3).[46]

As a consequence, the tale of Anneke Jans became one of the most famous Mennonite martyrs' tales, also internationally; she inspired poems

---

[44] Van Braght, *Het bloedig tooneel*, 143–4.

[45] E. A. Engelbrecht, *De vroedschap van Rotterdam, 1572–1795*, Bronnen voor de geschiedenis van Rotterdam (Rotterdam 1973), 41–2. Esaiah was *vroedschap* from 1575 to 1602 and held office many times in the 1590s.

[46] Jan Luyken, *Anneke Jans, Condemned to Death, Hands her Son, the Later Esaias de Lind, over to a Baker, 1539*, 1698, Rijksmuseum Amsterdam RP-P-OB-44.272. Sarah Covington, 'Jan Luyken, the Martyrs Mirror and the Iconography of Suffering', *Mennonite Quarterly Review*, 85 (2011), 441–76, has argued that we should see the emotive nature of Luyken's work as an expression of a Mennonite sensibility, but I do not think this is necessary.

Figure 3 Jan Luyken, *Anneke Jans, Condemned to Death, Hands her Son, the Later Esaias de Lind, over to a Baker, 1539*, 1698, RP-P-OB-44.272
Published with permission of the Rijksmuseum Amsterdam

and a popular historical novel. She was, moreover, also appropriated both as a Rotterdam and as a Reformed heroine.[47] The De Lint family, in the meantime, continued to support their links to the story with a silver tazza, which has a later inscription suggesting that it was given to the family by Johan van Oldenbarnevelt as a *pillegift*, a gift for his godchild at the occasion of his baptism.[48] When it came to Museum Boymans van Beuningen in 1996, a press release underlined its importance with

[47] See Kloek, 'Esaiasdr., Anneke'; Adrien Bogaers, 'Het pleegkind', in idem, *Balladen en romancen* ([Amsterdam], 1846), 1–18, interestingly presented Anneke's child as a little girl, who later married the baker's son. The novel by M. van der Staal, *Anneke Jansz. Historisch verhaal uit den eersten tijd der hervorming* (Rotterdam, 1914), was last reprinted in Middelburg in 2006. 'Anneke Jans. Op 24 januari in de Schie verdronken', *Nieuwe Rotterdamsche Courant*, 22 Jan. 1939.
[48] Geeraert de Rasier, *Tazza*, before 1587, currently on loan to Museum Boymans van Beuningen, Rotterdam, Inv. No. MBZ 489. I am most grateful to Esaiah's descendant Jan de Lint who first told me about the existence of the tazza and gave me copies of some documentation.

reference to its links with Oldenbarneveld and Anneke Jans, as well as its long transmission in the De Lint family.[49] Again, we see how important it is for a memory career that the mythical and the historical claims mutually support each other, and how essential memory practices are for creating evidence; oral traditions, written tales and material culture intermingle to create a tale which benefits both from a transcendent message and historical plausibility.

Scholars as mythmakers

In this process, an interesting role is being played by learned authors, who not only play a crucial part in the authentication of myths, but also in their amplification. By collecting and listing both direct and circumstantial evidence, and by deciding which parts of a tale they choose to believe and which ones to dismiss, they do not only enable stories to grow and expand, but also to fix these new versions. An excellent example of this process we can find in the tale of the pied piper of Hamelin.

In 1654, the pastor Samuel Erich wrote a book entitled the *Exodus Hamelensis*, in which he surveyed the arguments in favour of the story of the pied piper.[50] He quoted at length from a whole series of chronicles which recounted versions of the tale, pointed to the abundant existing material evidence in the city and concluded that even though there was no written evidence for the story for the years between the thirteenth and the sixteenth centuries, both the popularity and continuity of the tale suggested that it had to be genuine. Moreover, even though he had not had the opportunity to see the council's records for themselves, other authors suggested that these also confirmed the story.

The fact that Erich wanted to write this book at all, of course, points to the existence of scepticism. A year earlier, Hamelin burgomaster Gerhard Reiche had already reported that he considered the story a 'fable'; there was no mention of it in the archives, a fourteenth-century chronicler from the city had not considered in worth mentioning and there was contradictory evidence on the location, the year in which it

[49] I thank Alexandra van Dongen, curator of Museum Boymans van Beuningen, Rotterdam, who arranged a viewing of the tazza, and made some of the information in the museum's files available to me. This included the press release announcing the transfer of the tazza to the museum on 2 Nov. 1996. That the museum did not seize the opportunity to buy the tazza in 2002 was partly because of uncertainty about the date of the inscription.

[50] Samuel Erich, *Exodus hamelensis, das ist der Hämelischer Kinder Außgang* (Hannover, 1654). I used the Dutch translation, *De uytgang der Hamelsche kinderen of de verbaasde geschiedenis van 130 burgerskinderen, dewelke in 't jaar 1282 te Hamelen, aan de Weser, in Neder-Saxen, door een gewaanden speelman uyt de stadt verleydt, en . . . in de Koppelberg verdweenen zijn.: Aan de toetssteen der waarheit beproeft*, trans. Isaac Le Long (Amsterdam, 1729).

had happened and so on.[51] Erich's attempt to rescue that story did not have the desired effect. In 1655, Hamelin senator Sebastian Spilker listed a range of the objections to Erich's book, and in 1659 the Dutch scholar Martin Schoock published a lengthy tract entitled *Fabula Hamelensis*, in which he demolished Erich's arguments in favour of the tale, which he dismissed as 'pathetic'. He cited a range of late medieval chronicles that had reported many similar stories, but which had been silent about the piper. While Schoock conceded that there might be reason to believe tales which had been transmitted from one century to the next, as long as these were in accordance with reason, this was simply not true for the story of the piper, which could boast only about 150 years of transmission and was unbelievable to boot.[52]

The dispute between Erich and Schoock turned the issue into something of an academic cause célèbre – it became a popular topic for university disputations.[53] And the sceptics seemed to have a good point. There was no evidence for the antiquity of the tale. All there was, but that was in itself remarkable, was material evidence and a whole range of sixteenth- and early seventeenth-century sources, both published and unpublished, that reported the tale. Among those reporting were some reputable intellectuals, notably Johan Weyer, best known today for his scepticism about the witch hunts, and the Jesuit scholar Athanasius Kircher, as well as the prolific Catholic propagandist Richard Verstegan. Visitors to the city itself were all told about the tale, and reported about its many representations as well as the existence of the 'Drummerfree' street. They were told that the people of Hamelin used their own calendar, which started with the year in which the children disappeared, and found evidence for that on a 1556 inscription in the New Gate, which did indeed state that the gate had been built 272 years after the disappearance of the children.[54]

It is clear that up to around 1650, the people of Hamelin were quite proud of their tale. That they could be so was apparently because they did not attach the same moral to the story that we tend to do; in the sixteenth century, this was not a salutary tale about the fate of those who refused to pay the pied piper what was his due for the destruction of the city's rats, and who had so triggered the rat catcher's terrible revenge. Rather, the piper was identified with the devil, and the tale presented as a warning to keep a close watch on one's children.[55] In that sense,

---

[51] The report from burgomaster Gerhard Reiche in *Quellensammlung*, doc. no. 69, p. 77–8.

[52] *Ibid.*, doc. no. 72, pp. 80–4; Martinus Schoock, *Fabula hamelensis sive disquisitio historica* (Groningen, 1659), 151–5.

[53] Discussed in Spanuth, *Der Rattenfänger*, 56.

[54] On the inscription *Quellensammlung*, doc. no. 10, pp. 22–3.

[55] As such, he was described in the first printed accounts in Jobus Fincelius, *Wunderzeichen* (Jena, 1555); Caspar Goltwurm Athesinus, *Wunderwerck und Wunderzeichen Buch* (Frankfurt,

it fitted well with the vogue for demonology and social disciplining that came with the Reformation, which had turned Hamelin into a Lutheran city.[56] That a text about the children was inscribed on a city gate, and that it was burgomaster Popperdieck who paid for a stained glass image of it to be put up in the local church in 1572, also suggests that in the sixteenth century it suited the local elite agenda.[57] New elements frequently appeared in the story. From the mid-sixteenth century, the sources started to mention a connection with rats; the piper had now become a rat catcher.[58] Speculation about the fate of the children similarly evolved. From around 1600, several sources suggested that the children had resurfaced in Transylvania; a century later, the New World was also mentioned.[59]

Yet in the course of the seventeenth century, as demonology went out of vogue among the educated, the tale seems to have become unpopular with the authorities. As we have seen, burgomaster Reiche and senator Spilker found the story an embarrassment, and in 1660 the church window was removed. That might, indeed, have been that. Yet what the sceptics had not really been able to explain, of course, is how the story could have become so popular in the first place. Moreover, since the tale continued to circulate in scholarly texts, some of them demonological, others relating to natural history, visitors to Hamelin and other curious scholars continued to ask after the tale. As a consequence, the rationalists of the early Enlightenment did not forget about the children of Hamelin, quite the opposite. Soon, they came to see it as their challenge to explain the existence of the tale by looking for its historical roots.[60] People who wanted to dismiss the role of the devil turned to the evidence to try and come up with a better alternative. Bits of evidence, some of them new, materialised and continued to be scrutinised. A copy of the council book had a version of the tale on the cover that was long considered credible, but no one can say when that originated. The archives of Hamelin yielded

---

1557); and Andreas Hondorff, *Promptuarium exemplorum. Historienn- und Exempelbuch aus heiliger Schrifft und vielen andern . . . Historien* (Leipzig, 1573), on which see *Quellensammlung*, doc. no. 9, pp. 21–2, doc. no. 11, pp. 23–4, and doc. no. 17, p. 29. Also in a local inscription from the mid-1550s, *Quellensammlung*, doc. no. 10, pp. 22–3.

[56] R. Po-Chia Hsia, *Social Discipline in the Reformation. Central Europe, 1550–1750* (London and New York, 1989).

[57] Ueffing, 'Die Hamelner Rattenfängersage', 186.

[58] Spanuth, *Der Rattenfänger*, 100–1.

[59] The Transylvanian link was first mentioned in print by Richard Verstegan, *A Restitution of Decayed Intelligence* (Antwerp, 1605), cited in *Quellensammlung*, doc. no. 45, pp. 58–9. Later authors cited the evidence of a chronicle from Transylvania (Siebenbürgen) that referred to local German-speakers with accents that resembled that of the Hamelin area; a New World connection was first mooted in 1701, see *Quellensammlung*, doc. no. 105, p. 103.

[60] The ongoing interest can be traced through the *Quellensammlung*. On the Enlightenment interest, see also Spanuth, *Der Rattenfänger*, 58–69.

two letters in which Jews were given permission to settle in the town, and which were dated, like the new gate, with reference to the children's disappearance. By the late nineteenth century, they were proven to be forgeries.[61]

But most importantly, scholars began to believe that the existence of mythical accretions to the story was no reason to dismiss it. In fact, the mythical characteristics confirmed them in their belief that the tale had to be transmitted orally and so had to be old. As such, and as a legend, it was included by the Grimm brothers in their collection of fairy tales, and found its way into the oeuvre of the European romantic movement. Yet, side by side with its ever-growing fame as a legend, scholars also continued to make it their business to unpack the tale and find its historical kernel.

In 1936, two of them found they had struck gold. In a fourteenth-century manuscript that was kept in the city of Lüneburg, they found an addition in a later hand, written some time between 1430 and 1450, which not only included a version of the tale, and a reference to the use of a new calendar, but also mentioned the name of an eyewitness, the daughter of one of the burgomasters, who in 1284 had apparently 'seen the children go'. Since that name could be matched with existing evidence, it may just be that this version of the tale, without rats, goes back to the fourteenth century.[62] This does not in itself do anything to answer the question of what, if anything, happened to the children from Hamelin and why. Still, for a new generation of scholars it was the impetus to go on searching, and indeed to continue using evidence that was produced centuries after the 'event', if it did happen at all, was said to have taken place. Polish phonebooks were traced for the presence of Hamelin names in Pomerania. As evidence for his theory about the noble piper, Hans Dobbertin refers to the stags on an image produced in 1592, which he believes refer to the coat of arms of this noble family (Figure 4).[63] Even Florescu, who has made it his life's work to think about legends, seems to assume that the rats must have a place in the origins of the story, simply because they emerged in it in the course of its transmission. Scholars have become the mythographers of the pied piper tale.

---

[61] *Quellensammlung*, doc. no. 5a and 5b, pp. 18–19. I am not persuaded by Dobbertin's arguments for believing them genuine. See also Ueffing, 'Die Hamelner Rattenfängersage', 187.

[62] Spanuth, *De Rattenfänger*, 91–100; *Quellensammlung*, doc. no. 4, pp. 15–18.

[63] Florescu, *In Search of the Pied Piper*, 166–7; Ueffing, 'Die Hamelner Rattenfängersage', 186.

Figure 4 The pied piper, in Augustin von Mörsperg, Reisechronik, fol. 193f, *c.* 1592
Published with the permission of the Schlossmuseum Sondershausen

Conclusion

For the defender of the Hamelin story, pastor Samuel Erich, it was self-evident that fables could not survive for long. If a story was to be believable it needed supporting detail. As he explained, a statement such as 'it is said that a certain woman has been elected pope somewhere' could easily be dismissed as a fantasy. Yet if one were to say

> In the year of our Lord 853, during the reign of emperor Lotharius the Pious, a certain woman named Joan was exercising the dignity of pope in Rome, it is immediately evident that this tale is not a fantasy but rather a truthful history, especially when witnesses agree on it.[64]

Mundane as Erich's reasoning was, he was quite right, of course, that stories are much more likely to be believed if they are firmly anchored in supporting detail. They need to be set in a time and a place, they need a 'friend of a friend' who has heard it himself and they are helped along

[64] Erich, *De uytgang der Hamelsche kinderen*, 26.

by the existence of spatial and material markers; this is how a narrative is 'historicised'. In this article, I hope to have shown how in early modern Europe such a historicisation of narrative could come about, and could be transformed into history. The agents of this process of historicisation could be manifold. Much depended on the presence of stakeholders, people like the Nederveen and Roerom families in Dordrecht, the descendants of Anneke Jans or the elite and the local historians of Hamelin. Yet the process also depended on the interplay of myth, memory and history, and the interaction of stakeholders with authoritative mediators, many of whom were scholars.

In his 2003 book on *Mythistory* Joseph Mali has argued that myth plays a larger role in the historical discipline than is usually allowed for. Writing in an intellectual history tradition, Mali sees Giambattista Vico as the godfather of the realisation that myth is fundamental to the writing of history. The cases I have discussed suggest that underlying such theoretical reflections on the relationship between myth and history, there may have been a historical practice in which historians already knew how to make myth productive.[65]

Myth and history have often been presented as subsequent phases in a linear development, but it seems that for most of Western history myths and mythical patterns of explanation have had to coexist with other ways of structuring knowledge about the past, and thus with history. The spread of literacy has undoubtedly affected the nature of that coexistence. As Carrie Benes and Adam Fox have shown for medieval Italy and early modern England respectively, in pre-modern literate societies there was much interaction between written and oral culture; written texts did as much to spread and perpetuate myths as did villagers spinning their tales.[66] But there is more at stake here than the traffic of ideas and motifs between literate and oral cultures. We have seen that when it comes to the transmission of collective memories, myth and history actually feed off one another in an even more fundamental sense. Rather than to think of myth and history as each other's opposites, as different paradigmatic *idealtypes* of engaging with the past, or as successive *phases* in the history of historical consciousness, it is more helpful to explore them as two forms of engagement with that past that are in fact closely interrelated and indeed interdependent.

Some scholars have seen this coexistence, and the blurring of history and myth which it entails, as a typically contemporary and postmodern

---

[65] Joseph Mali, *Mythistory. The Making of a Modern Historiography* (Chicago and London, 2003).
[66] Carrie Benes, *Urban Legends. Civic Identity and the Classical Past in Northern Italy, 1250–1350* (University Park, PA, 2011); Fox, *Oral and Literate Culture*, 213–58.

phenomenon.[67] I think this is unnecessary. The three tales I have explored suggest that the blurring of history and myth is not a postmodern phenomenon only; in fact, it has been common practice for at least five centuries. Does that mean, then, that this blurring is typical for the 'early modernity' of the period under discussion? Where early modernists have seen myth and history coexist, they have sometimes read this as a sign that myth was 'already' beginning to lose its sway, and increasingly needed the backup of historical evidence if it was to be taken seriously.[68] Yet the evidence I have discussed here does not really support such assumptions about a linear development away from myth and towards the use of evidence. Folklore studies suggest that to be successful mythical tales about the past have always needed the support of things in the here and now; they need references to names of places and people, to objects in the material world, to features in the landscape or days in the calendar, or testimony that is passed on orally or in writing. The study of early modern memory practices helps us to understand how such references could come into existence, how they achieved authority and how they changed over time. In early modern Europe the transmission of tales was definitely affected by the appearance of new media, new figures of authority and new notions about evidence. Yet the application of new criteria for historical evidence from the seventeenth century did not necessarily result in the decline of myths. Quite the opposite, by declaring such stories mythical, and by using the existence of memory practices as evidence of this, scholars soon found reasons to go on taking them seriously as an object of study, and of historical enquiry.

[67] Coupe, *Myth*, 15.
[68] E.g. Woolf, *The Social Circulation of the Past*, 390–1.

Transactions of the RHS 23 (2013), pp. 127–53 © Royal Historical Society 2013
doi:10.1017/S0080440113000066

THE SEMANTICS OF 'PEACE' IN EARLY MODERN ENGLAND*

By Phil Withington

READ 27 APRIL 2012 AT THE UNIVERSITY OF SHEFFIELD

ABSTRACT. This paper begins to consider the meanings of a word that was ubiquitous in early modern culture, but which has been surprisingly neglected by historians. Focusing on printed sources and taking advantage of recent advances in digital technology, it outlines the changing uses of 'peace' between 1500 and 1700 and its predominant meanings at particular moments in time. The paper suggests that while these meanings were clearly derived from Christian and civic republican sources, the political conflicts of the seventeenth century saw the term politicised, appropriated and popularised in new and unexpected ways. It also argues that the semantic confusion which often attended 'peace' – most evident, perhaps, in its capacity to legitimise and sanction violence after 1640 – stemmed from its simultaneous role as a descriptor of society and self, and of spiritual and civil life. As a result, who should define, police and enforce peace became deeply contested issues of the course of the period. In tracing the semantics of the term in this way, the article serves as a contribution to the burgeoning historical literature on the paradigmatic vocabularies of the early modern era. It also illuminates the complicated relationship between words and concepts and the importance of both in motivating and legitimising social and political action.

In May 1643 the pamphlet *Peace and Plenty Coming unto Us* outlined an intriguing proposition for its London readership. It suggested that, in order to meet some of the costs of civil war, 'all well-affected Families and Persons would forbear one meal a week, and give the value thereof ... unto the Publique-good'. Such costs, which included raising a new city regiment to fight the forces of 'antichrist' and finding supplies to meet the subsistence crisis in Ireland, reflected the origins of the proposal in the sub-committee of the London Militia Committee at the Salters' Hall on Bread Street.[1] The responsibility of the Bread Street committee was auxiliary military mobilization, and the anonymous author explained how he 'hath heard and seen somewhat said and done, for and against

---

* I would like to thank the Centre for Peace Studies at the University of Sheffield and the Royal Historical Society for the first invitation to lecture on the semantics of peace.
[1] Anon., *Peace and Plenty Comming unto Us* (1643), 1, 5.

the same Motion'.[2] His job now was to persuade Londoners to adopt the policy of a weekly fast on the assumption that 'if London begins' then 'England (except where the enemy's armies hinder) will follow her example'.[3]

The pamphlet accordingly deployed a number of arguments judged to resonate with the ordinary citizenry. It combined Old Testament and civic-republican exemplar: the pamphlet opened by invoking 2 Kings 7 and explicitly drew on the advice of 'a witty Florentine in time of famine' (possibly Machiavelli's history of Florence).[4] It also presented the 'motion' as the logical, if somewhat surprising, extension of everyday civic and familial practice. To this end, the author suggested that 'two men in every Parish went with two Books, the one with a White book and the other with a Black book', recording 'Benefactors' in one (for 'perpetual honour') and 'Malignants' in the other (for the 'infamy' of 'their Posterity').[5] More, he argued that 'This work seems to be most proper for women, especially, now when men have so many other employments.' After all, 'Have not women generally the disposing of meats and drinks in Families?' Appropriating the procedures and language of male parochial governance, he suggested that 'A few of the wisest of them here in London (joining but together unanimously, and appointing some of their sex fittest and most active in every Parish) might both ease the men of this Labour, and carry this good work through the City first, and Kingdom afterward.' These she-citizens would hence 'be honoured for it both by God and man, in all countries, and in all ages'. They would also 'give Parliament cause (as in the like case once the Dames of *Rome* did that Senate) to give them publike thanks for their love and care of the Commonwealth'.[6]

If this parochial citizenship is striking, then so, too, was the language by which the Bread Street proposal was presented to Londoners (see Figure 1). 'Peace and Plenty' was not, perhaps, an obvious epithet for weekly fasting in a time of violent conflict, nor the obvious watchword of those citizen militants who dominated the Salter's Hall committee.[7] Here, however, it was intended to describe what the proposal would help 'procure'. The word 'peace' was accordingly imbued with a number of inferences beyond the simple sense of not at war (the way we instinctively define peace today). Rather, 'this abstinence, beside the saving of our

² *Ibid.*, title-page; Anon., *Whereas the Committee for the Militia of London* (1644), 1 sheet broadside. For the political context of Salter's Hall, see Keith Lindley, *Popular Politics and Religion in Civil War London* (Aldershot, 1997), 311–12.

³ Anon., *Peace and Plenty*, 1.

⁴ *Ibid.*, 1, 3; Niccolo Machiavelli, *The Florentine Historie. Written in the Italian Tongue, by Nicholo Macchiavelli, Citizen and Secretarie of Florence. And Translated into English, by T.B. Esquire* (1595), 56.

⁵ Anon., *Peace and Plenty*, 3.

⁶ Anon., *Peace and Plenty* (1643), 7–8.

⁷ Lindley, *Popular Politics*, 314.

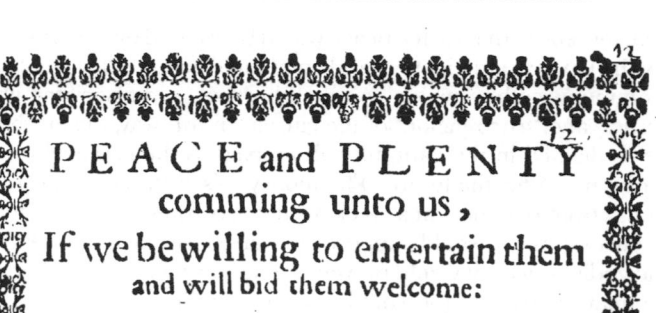

PEACE and PLENTY
comming unto us,
If we be willing to entertain them
and will bid them welcome:

Manifested in fome Obfervations upon the
Motion lately made by certaia perfons fitting
ufually at Salters-H ll in Bread-ftreet *London,*
and there imployed about raifing of new
Regiments of H o r s e and F o o t:

Viz.
That all well-affected Families and Perfons would
forbear one Meal in a Week, and give the value
thereof, for, and toward the Raifing and Maintaining of the faid Regiments.

*Written by one, who hath heard and feen fomewhat faid and
done, for and againft the fame Motion,*

And defireth that it may be more fully underftood and fur.
thered, tending (as he conceiveth) fo much
unto the Publique good.

LONDON,
Printed for *John Rothw ll,* and are to be fold at his Shop
at the figne of the Sun in *Pauls* Church yard.
May 19.   M D C X L I I I.

Figure 1 Meanings of 'peace' on a 1643 title-page
Source: Thomason/E. 102 [12], British Library.

Lives (with the Lord's blessing) will also preserve unto us our Goods,
Lands, Laws, Liberties and true Religion'. The motion rested, that is, on
a complicated and enriched sense of peace which encapsulated material,
social, political and spiritual well-being and freedom. The pamphlet

suggested, moreover, that such a peace would be secured by 'entertaining' precisely the kind of participatory and communal action – 'love and care of the commonwealth' – which was itself born of, and associated with, the 'liberties' and 'true religion' of the citizen. In this way, the attributes of peace as defined in the pamphlet also served as the practical means for securing peace for the future. The money raised through 'cheerfully abstain[ing] from one meal in a week' would accordingly provide troops 'for our own safety'; it would support the war-effort ('the only way to a good and godly peace'); it would prevent the famine which was 'otherwise so much unavoidable'; and it would ease the spiralling levels of conventional assessment, with all the discontent that extra taxation engendered.[8]

Whatever ordinary Londoners may have thought of the Bread Street motion, it was not adopted by parliament.[9] But this is not to say it is without historical interest. On the contrary, that communal abstinence in time of war could be both publicly presented in terms of 'peace' and 'plenty' and touted as an expression of civic identity more or less consistent with normal parochial and familial governance begs questions about the political culture of the time. These certainly include the ideology of the Bread Street sub-committee and its resonance, or not, with the civic consciousness of ordinary urban householders.[10] They also include the linguistic bricks and mortar out of which a pamphlet like *Peace and Plenty* was constructed. Was the author of the pamphlet usual, for example, in using the word 'peace' at once so prominently and complicatedly? Was the word's knotted web of inferences as suggested by the pamphlet normal or controversial, commonplace or partisan? How did these inferences fit within the broader semantics of peace in seventeenth-century England? Or, to put that slightly differently (and apologies to Raymond Carver): what did early moderns talk about when they talked about peace?[11]

The question is important if only because 'peace' has received so little explicit attention from historians of early modern England.[12] At first glance, this is hardly surprising. Just as for political historians the

[8] *Ibid.*, 1, 5.

[9] Anon., *At the Sub-Committee at Salters Hall* (1644).

[10] Jonathan Barry, 'Civility and Civic Culture in Early Modern England: The Meanings of Urban Freedom', in *Civil Histories: Essays Presented to Sir Keith Thomas*, ed. Peter Burke, Paul Harrison and Paul Slack (Oxford, 2000); Mark Goldie, 'The Unacknowledged Republic: Office-Holding in Early Modern England', in *The Politics of the Excluded, c. 1500–1850*, ed. Tim Harris (Basingstoke, 2001); Phil Withington, *The Politics of Commonwealth. Citizens and Freemen in Early Modern England* (Cambridge, 2005).

[11] Raymond Carver, *What We Talk about when We Talk about Love* (1989).

[12] Discussions include Steve Hindle, 'The Keeping of the Public Peace', in *The Experience of Authority in Early Modern England*, ed. Paul Griffiths, Adam Fox and Steve Hindle (Basingstoke, 1996), 213–48; Alexandra Gajda, 'Debating War and Peace in Late Elizabethan England', *Historical Journal*, 52, 4 (2009), 851–78; Gary Rivett, 'Peacemaking, Parliament, and the Politics of the Recent Past in the English Civil Wars', *Huntington Library Quarterly*, 76, 3 (2013,

seventeenth century was self-evidently an era of endemic warfare and political 'crises', so for social historians national political strife was nothing compared to the intensified 'micro-politics' of family, communal and economic life.[13] In both instances, the semantics of peace have not been an obvious interpretative priority. On closer inspection, however, the picture is more complicated. Since the 1970s, political revisionism has emphasised the consensual nature of Elizabethan and early Stuart politics, arguing for the absence of a 'radical' political agenda, or even contrary constitutional positions, which could have precipitated civil war.[14] And if the English polity accidently slipped into war in 1642, then social historians have highlighted the widespread quest for 'order' across the populace at large.[15] As Ian Archer has demonstrated, even in 1590s London the potential for social conflict was matched only by the propensity for stability.[16]

One question for this article, then, is whether the neglected language of peace can illuminate these somewhat paradoxical features of early modern politics and society. To focus on the term and its uses reflects, in turn, the burgeoning historiographical interest in contemporary language and concepts. The antecedents of this interest can be found in both the history of political thought and social history. Influential examples include Quentin Skinner's survey of how the term 'state' was adopted by political theorists and Keith Wrightson's tracing of the word 'sort' in more general contemporary discourse.[17] In both instances, ostensibly non-evaluative language accreted new meanings and concepts because of the discursive contexts in which they were used. Skinner shows how 'state', which traditionally meant 'condition' (in the sense of 'the state we are in'), was appropriated as the descriptor for the kind of abstract sovereign power eventually described by Hobbes in *Leviathan* from 1646. Wrightson demonstrates that 'sort', as an alternative for 'type' or 'kind', acquired the more specific sense of distinctive social grouping – as in

forthcoming). See also Penny Roberts, 'The Languages of Peace during the French Wars of Religion', *Cultural and Social History*, 4, 3 (2007), 297–315.

[13] Geoffrey Parker, *Global Crisis: War, Climate Change and Catastrophe in the Seventeenth Century* (New Haven, 2013); Keith Wrightson, 'The Politics of the Parish in Early Modern England', in *The Experience of Authority*, ed. Griffiths, Fox and Hindle, 10–11.

[14] For a useful overview of revisionism and post-revisionism see *The English Civil War*, ed. Richard Cust and Ann Hughes (1997).

[15] Keith Wrightson, *English Society 1580–1680* (1982).

[16] Ian W. Archer, *The Pursuit of Stability: Social Relations in Elizabethan London* (Cambridge, 1991).

[17] Quentin Skinner, 'The State', in *Political Innovation and Conceptual Change*, ed. Terence Ball, James Farr and Russell L. Hanson (Cambridge, 1989); Keith Wrightson, 'Estates, Degrees and Sorts: Changing Perceptions of Society in Tudor and Stuart England', in *Language, History and Class*, ed. Penelope Corfield (Oxford, 1991).

'better sort' or 'middling sort' – by the 1640s.[18] Both words transformed conceptually over time, in the process reconfiguring the lexicon of how people could talk and quite possibly think about their politics, their society and their relationship to both. Both words also raise the question about the relationship between concepts and language on the one hand, and institutions and practices on the other hand. How, for example, did changes in the former relate to developments in the latter? Subsequent work has expanded both the vocabularies so contextualised and, with the help of digital technology, the range and quantity of discursive contexts considered.[19] This kind of contextualised history of the English vernacular is still nascent, especially when compared to the German tradition of 'conceptual history'.[20] It is nevertheless clear that certain words – 'commonwealth' is a notable example – underwent significant changes in and contests over their meaning between the fifteenth and eighteenth centuries.[21] It is likewise clear that words which carry a particular sense today could have very different connotations 400 years earlier. An important Renaissance meaning of 'honesty', for example, was not simply sincerity and integrity but also discretion and prudence: the capacity to speak civilly rather than truthfully.[22]

As this suggests, attention to language is a powerful tool of historicism, enabling early modern culture to be recovered on its own terms. Such an approach can also tease out the ironies and paradoxes which distinguish the past from the present. Two recent examples are Alexandra Walsham's treatment of 'toleration' and Ethan Shagan's discussion of 'moderation'. Walsham notes that while in the West today 'toleration' is primarily an affirmative and idealised word 'instinctively linked with equality, liberty and democracy', in the early modern era it is best understood as a form of 'charitable hatred' – a 'casuistical stance involving a deliberate

---

[18] Keith Wrightson, 'Sorts of People in Tudor and Stuart England', in *The Middling Sort of People. Culture, Society and Politics in England, 1550–1800*, ed. Jonathan Barry and Christopher Brooks (Basingstoke, 1994).

[19] For example, see Naomi Tadmor, 'The Concept of the Household Family in Eighteenth-Century England', *Past and Present*, 151 (1996), 110–40; Andy Wood, 'The Place of Custom in Plebeian Political Culture: England, 1550–1800', *Social History*, 22 (1997), 46–60; Phil Withington, *Society in Early Modern England: The Vernacular Origins of Some Powerful Ideas* (Cambridge, 2010).

[20] Early Modern Research Group, 'Towards a Social and Cultural History of Keywords and Concepts', *History of Political Thought*, 31 (2010), 427–48

[21] David Rollison, 'Conceits and Capacities of the Vulgar Sort: The Social History of English as a Language of Politics', *Cultural and Social History*, 2, 2 (2005), 141–64; John Watts, 'Public or Plebs: The Changing Meaning of "the Commons", 1381–1549', in *Power and Identity in the Middle Ages*, ed. John Watts (Oxford, 2007); Withington, *Society in Early Modern England*, ch. 6; Early Modern Research Group, 'Commonwealth: The Social, Cultural, and Conceptual Contexts of an Early Modern Keyword', *Historical Journal*, 54, 3 (2011), 659–87.

[22] Jennifer Richards, *Rhetoric and Courtliness in Early Modern England* (Cambridge, 2003), 2.

suspension of righteous hostility and, consequently a considerable degree of moral discomfort'.[23] It was a word used not to proclaim religious freedom but as 'a weapon in religious controversy' – to 'wound, hurt, brand, stigmatize, and slur'.[24] Shagan likewise historicises the term 'moderate' in order to show that 'moderation subsumed two concepts that today are incompatible but in early modern England had not yet been differentiated'.[25] One was 'the state of equipoise': the achievement of 'order and proportion' at once internally, in terms of the self, and externally, in terms of society. The other was 'the act of restraint that produced it': the acts of government which made people and their community's moderate.[26] Shagan suggests that this semantic conflation helps explain one of the most striking paradoxes of early modern England: that the most vociferous proponents of 'moderation' tended to subscribe to the most intensive programmes of 'coercion and control'.[27] Like toleration, moderation's genealogy emerges as altogether murkier and more ambiguous than these terms' modern usage might suggest.

What follows suggests that 'peace' was a similar kind of word to toleration and moderation in important respects. As a term applicable at once to the inner life of the person, the institutions and environment constituting the wider world and the external behaviour and actions of people, peace raised important questions about the relationship between self, society, agency and governance. Could inner tranquillity always be reconciled with the rules and morality upon which social peace was based? If not, which took precedence? Likewise, just as humanists and religious writers puzzled over how to encourage people to behave moderately or tolerantly, so they wondered how to make them live in peace. In Reformation Europe the answer, more often than not, was through various kinds of force. Indeed, it was peace which legitimated the organization of political power and violence, the first systematic theory of the modern 'state' explaining

the COMMON-WEALTH, in Latin CIVITAS ... *One Person, of whose Acts a great Multitude, by Mutual Covenants one with another, have made themselves everyone the Author, to the end he may use the strength and means of them all, as he shall think expedient, for their Peace and Common Defence.*[28]

For Thomas Hobbes, the psychology of man and the endemic will to power made this 'artificial man' necessary. So, too, did the fact that

---

[23] Alexandra Walsham, *Charitable Hatred: Tolerance and Intolerance in England, 1500–1700* (Manchester, 2006), 1, 4.

[24] *Ibid.*, 5.

[25] Ethan Shagan, *The Rule of Moderation: Violence, Religion, and the Politics of Restraint in Early Modern England* (Cambridge, 2011), 8–9.

[26] *Ibid.*, 10, 9; Robert Cawdrey, *A Table Alphabetical* (1604).

[27] Shagan, *Rule of Moderation*, 9.

[28] Thomas Hobbes, *Leviathan* (1651), ed. Noel Malcolm (Oxford, 2012), 260–2.

different people had very different conceptions as to what the nature and quality of peace – whether internal or external – should be. Indeed, as the authors of *Peace and Plenty* vividly demonstrated, attaining the power to define and control peace was something for which ideologues could fight, die or at the very least go hungry.

The semantic complexities which this suggests are explored in four stages. The next sections trace the changing visibility of 'peace' in sixteenth- and seventeenth-century printed texts and survey some of what contemporaries styled its primary 'significations'. The article concludes by outlining some of the prevailing meanings and uses of the term before, during and after the mid-century civil wars.

I

How prominent a word was 'peace' in early modern printed discourse? One useful indicator of linguistic usage, a corpus large enough to be statistically significant while allowing qualitative analysis, is the Shakespearean canon. This is saturated with the term. 'Peace' appears in Shakespeare's plays an estimated 547 times, more than double the number of times 'war' is used (261 times). Although neither term approaches a word like 'God', which Shakespeare used an estimated 796 times, 'peace' also compares favourably to other words which have received especial attention from historians: for example 'state' (312 times), 'sort/s' (87 times), 'moderate' and variants (11 times), and toleration and variants (not at all).[29] A second indicator is presented by Figures 2 and 3, which simply record the number of 'hits' of 'God', 'peace' and 'war' in all searchable texts catalogued on Early English Books Online (EEBO) between 1473 and 1699. As things stand, this is the crudest method for measuring language use: by no means all texts are digitized and searchable, the search itself is prone to various kinds of error, from misrecognition to unrecognized variants, and the size of the data makes contextualisation of usage difficult.[30] The predictable ubiquity of 'God' in Figure 3 is methodologically reassuring, therefore, and lends the estimated number of appearances of 'peace' and 'war' some degree of meaning. The charts suggest that, although 'peace' appears considerably more often than 'war' in Shakespeare's plays, in the EEBO corpora 'war' was used more frequently than 'peace', at least until the 1620s. Thereafter, however, this pattern flipped, with 'peace' appearing more frequently than 'war' until the end of the century. The exception was the 1640s, when both words proliferated dramatically.

---

[29] *The Oxford Shakespeare: The Complete Works*, ed. Stanley Wells and Gary Taylor, 2nd edn (Oxford, 2005); www.opensourceshakespeare.org/concordance (consulted 6 Feb. 2013).

[30] Tim Hitchcock, 'Confronting the Digital: Or How Academic Writing Lost the Plot', *Cultural and Social History*, 10, 1 (2013), 25–45.

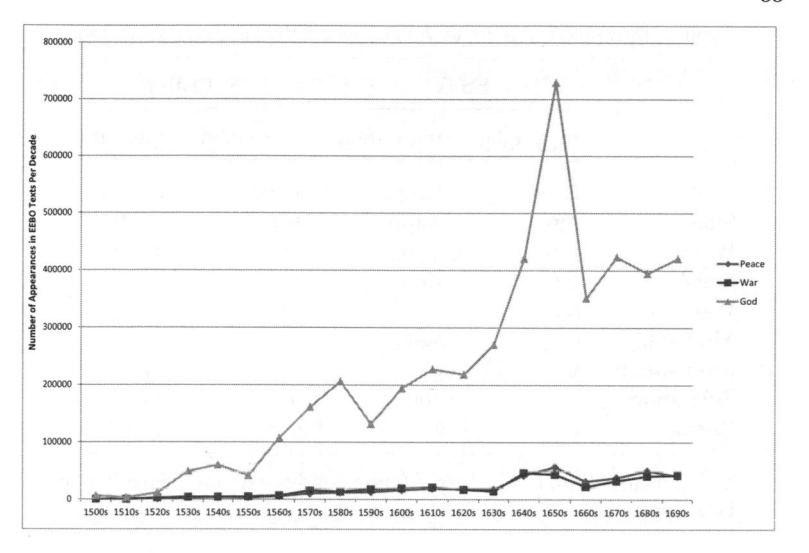

Figure 2 (Colour online) Appearances of peace, war and God in texts on EEBO, 1500–1700

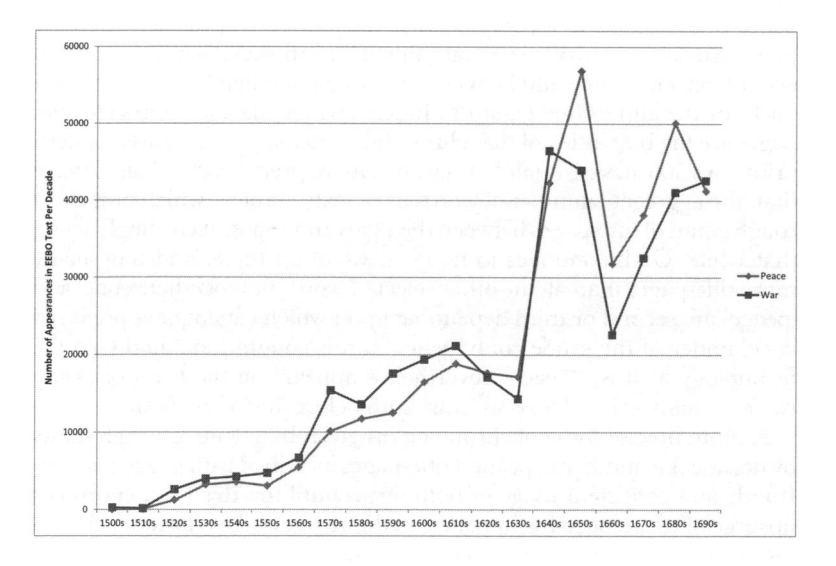

Figure 3 (Colour online) Appearances of peace and war in texts on EEBO, 1500–1700

Table 1 *Appearances of 'peace' on ESTC and EEBO title-pages, 1470–1690s*

	ESTC		EEBO	
	1473–1589	1590–1699	1473–1589	1590–1699
God	1,225	11,144	1,402	10,885
State	139	3,480	115	3,516
Peace	149	3,304	145	3,709
Sort/s	156	1,844	151	1,890
War	62	1,728	54	1,924
Moderate	0	229	2	253
Moderation	3	97	1	97
Toleration	0	209	0	254
Tolerate	*0*	*1*	*0*	*3*

Source: http://estc.bl.uk; http://eebo.chadwyck.com (consulted 6 Feb. 2013).

A third means of measurement focuses on surviving title-pages catalogued on EEBO and the English Short Title Catalogue (ESTC). This method rests on the assumption that the typography and wording of title-pages was an important component of the publishing process.[31] Because title-pages at once invoked textual content and appealed to potential read-ers and buyers, words and images were not chosen lightly or even, neces-sarily, by the author (see Figure 1). Indeed, when taken in aggregate title-pages are the best index of that elusive but valuable quarry: early modern print consciousness. Certainly, they are a more precise indication of usage than the aggregate number of words in all texts. Table 1, which provides a rough count of title-pages between the 1470s and 1690s, accordingly shows that while 'God' continues to be (as it were) up there, adorning many more title-pages than all the other selected words put together, 'state' and 'peace' are second or third depending upon which catalogue is preferred (a reminder of the crude contingency of this counting method with the technology as it is). 'Peace' nevertheless appears on the front of nearly twice as many printed texts as 'war' both before and after 1600.

A more precise sense of chronology is given by Figure 4, which shows by decade the number of printed title-pages inscribed with peace and war. It indicates consistent usage of both terms until the 1630s; an enormous upsurge of use, especially for peace, in the 1640s; and a relative decline in use by the 1660s, although peace continues to appear considerably more often on title-pages than it did before 1641. This is, of course, a period in

---

[31] Withington, *Society in Early Modern England*, 9–10, 79–80.

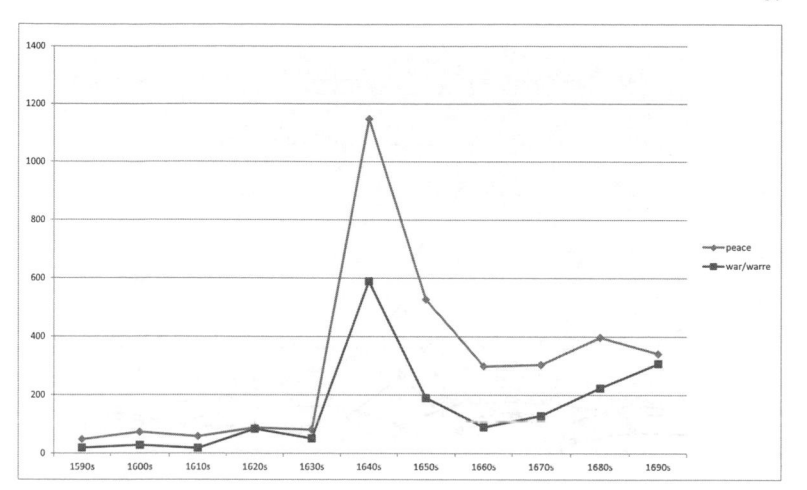

Figure 4 (Colour online) 'Peace' and 'war' on printed title-pages, 1590s to 1690s

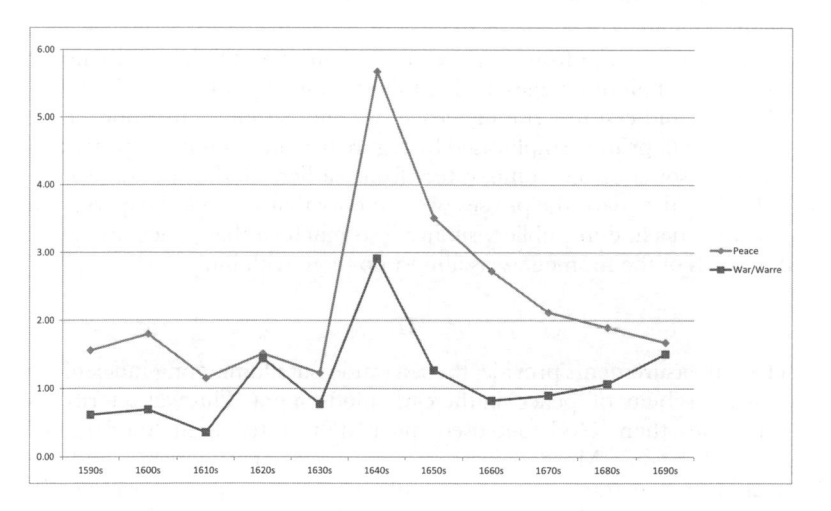

Figure 5 (Colour online) 'Peace' and 'war' on printed title-pages (%), 1590s to 1690s

which the number of all printed texts increases exponentially. Figure 5, which gives the number of 'peace' and 'war' title-pages as a percentage of all printed title-pages catalogued on the ESTC, demonstrates that the

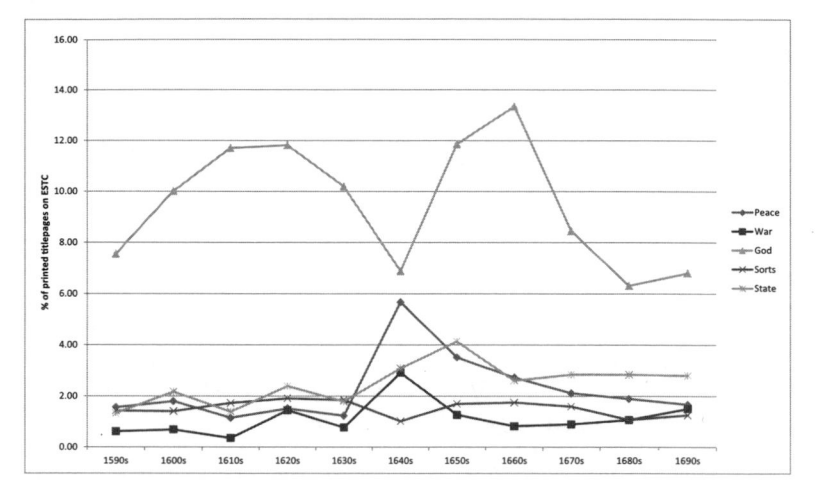

Figure 6 (Colour online) 'Peace' and 'war' compared with some keywords (%), 1590s to 1690s

rise of 'peace' and 'war' was not merely a function of this more general trend. The aggregate rise in the use of peace in the 1640s makes for a percentage increase from just over 1 per cent of all title-pages to almost 6 per cent of all title-pages, falling to just under 3 per cent by the 1660s. That the mid-century rise of 'peace' was not simply a function of the expansion in print is emphasised by Figure 6, which compares peace and war with some of the comparators from earlier: God, state and sort/s. Indeed, in the 1640s the presses were so busy that even God experienced a relative decline in public visibility – so much so that peace, as one of the words of the moment, was almost up there with him.

II

These measurements provide, then, a crude but illuminating index of the relative visibility of 'peace' in the early modern era. This was a term less ubiquitous than 'God' but used much more often than 'moderation' and 'toleration'. More prominent than 'war' on title-pages and the Shakespearean stage, the seventeenth century saw 'peace' overtake its antonym in printed text more generally. Most striking, perhaps, is that with the outbreak of civil war 'peace' became especially prominent, appearing more often than 'state' and almost as much as 'God'. All of which suggests that the print-reading English-speaking public of the sixteenth and seventeenth centuries talked and thought a lot about peace.

What did they mean when they did so? Three kinds of Renaissance text can be used to exemplify the rich and complicated semantic fields which peace delineated long before the interventions of Hobbes and the Bread Street committee. Such texts include vernacular translations of influential medieval treatises, 'Englished' for the first time in the sixteenth and seventeenth centuries; versions of the more accessible autodidactic literature which increasingly characterised the reading proclivities of early modern men and women; and performative genres which popularised and re-presented 'learned' language and ideas for wider audiences: for example, through the theatre. Each of these textual types – translations, self-helps, performances – was integral to making classical and medieval ideas available to new, vernacular and more socially extensive audiences. At the same time, the very development of these genres also distinguished early modern culture from what had gone before.

To take the Renaissance translations: peace was an organizing paradigm of two medieval treatises deeply implicated in the English Reformation, but which linked the concept to two contrasting discursive traditions. In the first instance, the Spanish humanist Juan Luis Vives dedicated his Latin edition of St Augustine of Hippo's *The City of God* to Henry VIII in 1522. In return, Henry congratulated Vives on bringing Augustine 'from darkness to light' and restoring him 'to his ancient integrity, for all posterity', and entrusted him with the tutorship of his daughter, Mary.[32] For Augustine and perhaps Henry in the 1520s, the 'peace of all things lies in the tranquillity of order; and order is the disposition of equal and unequal things in such a way as to give to each its proper place'.[33] This imperative applied to the body and soul, whether 'rational' (human) or 'irrational' (animal), as well as relations between people – in their households, their cities and with God. In theorising peace as a 'universal' imperative, however, Augustine made two important distinctions: between pagan and Christian peace; and between earthly and heavenly peace.[34] Thus, while ancient philosophers like Cicero believed ultimate peace, or the 'Supreme Good', to exist 'in the here and now' and through 'their own efforts', for Christians 'the earthly city' was merely a prelude to 'the Heavenly City' and 'the enjoyment of eternal peace'.[35] Christians valued 'earthly peace' and the political institutions which guaranteed it, especially if these institutions embraced 'Christian precepts' and enabled the church to do 'her work effectively'.[36] But ultimate redemption was 'the peace of the Heavenly City': a 'perfectly

---

[32] Cited in J. H., *Saint Augustine of the Citie of God with the learned comments of Jo. Lodovicus Vives* (1610), preface. Subsequent references are from Augustine, *The City of God against the Pagans* ed. R. W. Dyson (Cambridge, 1998).

[33] Augustine, *City of God*, 938.

[34] *Ibid.*

[35] *Ibid.*, 919, 940.

[36] *Ibid.*, xxvii.

ordered and perfectly harmonious fellowship in the enjoyment of God, and of one another in God'.[37]

This was not the moral of *The Defence of Peace* by Marsilius of Padua, which was 'translated out of the Latin into English' by William Marshall thirteen years later, in 1535, in order to justify Henrician imperial power against 'the proud bishops of Rome'.[38] Whereas Augustine's peace was the foundation stone of ecclesiastical authority, and 'the city is ordered to religion rather than the other way round', Marsilius reclaimed peace as the embodiment of civil society as derived from classical exempla.[39] Peace, or what he also styled 'tranquillity', 'will then be that good condition of a city or realm, in which each of its parts is enabled perfectly to perform the operations appropriate to it according to reason and the way it has been established'.[40] It followed that 'intranquillity will be that bad condition of a city or realm (just like the sickness of an animal) in which all or some of its parts are prevented from performing the operations appropriate to them'.[41] For Marsilius, not only was law-making – by which tranquillity was established and defended – the preserve of the prevailing part of the civic community as customarily established.[42] It was 'the avarice, desire for power and deceitfulness of the human interpreters of Christ's religion' which was most likely to disturb the peace of the city or realm.[43] A weak response to this scenario (Marsilius was commenting on the fourteenth-century papacy) was the exclusion of priests from temporal power. A strong response, developed in the second half of his book and adopted by Marshall for Henry VIII, was that the 'supreme civic legislator rightfully has all power over spirituals'.[44]

An Augustinian conception of peace accorded with Henrician kingship before the break with Rome; its treatment by Marsilius was much more conducive to Tudor *imperium* thereafter. Viewed in these terms, it is unsurprising that while *Defender of the Peace* was available in the vernacular from 1535, *City of God* remained untranslated until 1610 (remarkably late for such an important text). This Reformatory hedging of peace in classical and civil discourse was replicated in two texts with much greater communicative potential than works of political theory, translated or otherwise. Sir Thomas Elyot's Latin–English dictionary, published

[37] *Ibid.*, 938.

[38] Marsilius of Padua, *The Defence of Peace: Lately Translated out of Laten into Englyshe with the Kings Most Gracious Privilege* (1535). Subsequent references are from Marsilius of Padua, *The Defender of the Peace*, ed. and trans. Annabel Brett (Cambridge, 2005). See also Shelley Lockwood, 'Marsilius of Padua and the Case for Royal Ecclesiastical Supremacy', in *Transactions of the Royal Historical Society*, sixth ser., 1 (1991), 89–119.

[39] Marsilius, *Defender*, xxii.

[40] *Ibid.*, 13.

[41] *Ibid.*

[42] *Ibid.*, xxii–iii.

[43] *Ibid.*, xxviii.

[44] *Ibid.*, xxxi.

in 1538, marked at once the beginning of the English lexicographical tradition; an early example of Renaissance autodidactism (it was designed to teach yourself Latin); and a crucial moment in the development of the printed vernacular.[45] 'Peace' appeared throughout the dictionary, though never with religious inferences. Instead, Elyot translated the Latin *pax* as 'peace, a quiet liberty' and used 'peace' to translate a host of terms associated either with diplomacy and the opposite of war, or with civil governance (both of self and society).[46] Especially significant in this respect was his gloss on '*Irenarches, & irenarcha*' as 'he which is in authority to see peace kept in a country or city, which among us may be called a Justice of the Peace'.

This was significant if only because, for the 100 or so years after the publication of Marsilius and Elyot, it was on handbooks explaining how to be a justice of the peace that English readers of printed texts were most likely to have encountered the word 'peace'. Moreover, in William Lambarde's bestselling version of the genre, which explicitly invoked *Eirenarcha* to depict *the Office of the Justices of Peace* and was reprinted twelve times between 1582 and 1620, readers would also have found the single most coherent and accessible 'signification of this word Peace'.[47] In contrast to Elyot's pithy 'quiet liberty', Lambarde explained that 'Of the Latin word *Pax*, the Normans framed their *Paix*, and we (out of that) our *Peace*, the which hath sundry significations both in Holy Scripture of God, and in the laws of our Country.'[48] Lambarde explained that peace was both inward and outward. Echoing Augustine, he noted that 'Good inward peace' involved 'Peace with God' and 'Peace of Conscience, for that our Consciences (by faith in Christ) at Peace, both with God and itself'. 'Evil inward peace' was, in contrast, a 'mundane peace'

---

[45] Thomas Elyot, *The dictionary of Syr Thomas Eliot Knyght* (1538); Richard Foster Jones, *The Triumph of the English Language* (Oxford, 1953).

[46] To give some examples: 'Caduceato' was an 'ambassador ... sent for peace, or to take a truce'; 'Conciliare affinitatem, uel pacem' was 'to make alliance or peace'; 'Dicere leges' was 'to appoint laws or conditions of peace'; 'Indutiae' was 'truce, or peace for a certain time'; 'Inire foedus, to make a league or treaty of peace'; 'Conventa pax, peace, accorded'; and so on. Likewise '*ST*' translated as 'a voice of him that commands silence, as we say in English, bush, what we wold have one to hold his peace' and 'Quiescas, uel quiesce, Hold thy peace, Leave.' Peace translated 'Quin taces? Wilt not thou hold thy peace?; Tacemodo, de{us} respiciet nos aliquis, peace now, some god will have pity on us'; 'Reticeo, cui, ticère, to hold ones peace, to speak no word, to keep secret, to say nothing'; 'Segrega sermonem, taedet, Hold thy peace, I am weary, or it irks me to hear thee'; '*Tacitus*, he that holds his peace, and is secrete.' And '*Bat*, is a word that is spoken to one, when we will have him speak no more, as peace or hush.' This sense of enforced quiet or voluntary silence merged with 'peace' as a referent for terms associated with political authority. 'Conticeo, ticui, ceere' were 'to hold my peace with another'. Just as 'Conventus maximus, may be taken for a parliament', so 'Minores conventus' was the 'sessions of the peace'. 'Perpaco' was 'to set all things in peace'.

[47] William Lambarde, *Eirenarcha: Or Of the Office of the Iustices of Peace* (1599).

[48] *Ibid.*, 5.

amounting to nothing more than 'carnal security': an earthly tranquillity derived not from God but other material, corporeal or philosophical sources.[49] Lambarde also explained there were two kinds of 'outward peace'. One was 'opposed (or set) against all manner of striving and contention, whether it be in countenance, gesture, word, or work'; 'the other is only an abstinence from actual force, and offer of violence, and is rather contrary to arms and war'.[50]

Echoing Marsilius, Lambarde accordingly observed that while 'the Law of our Realm likewise uses the word peace diversely, but yet so, as it is altogether occupied about these outward Peaces': 'the law of God (which is the only true Philosophy) respects the mind and conscience, although the laws of men do look but to the body, hands, and weapons'.[51] Budding magistrates instead learned to conceptualise their peace in three ways: as 'Protection or Defence'; as 'Rights, Privileges, and Liberties'; and as 'a withholding (or abstinence) from . . . injurious force and violence'.[52] They were also told that:

> Justices of the Peace were not ordained (as some have thought) to the end to reduce the people to an universal amity (or agreement of minds) which is indeed a Thing rather to be wished for, then to be hoped after: Neither is it any part of their office, to forbid lawful suits and controversies.[53]

Lambarde's literary successor, Michael Dalton, concurred, though with the caveat that he could 'see not why Justices of the Peace should be restrained from preventing and repressing such other offences, misbehaviours, and deceits, as may break the amity, quiet, and good government of the people'; that the concept of peace should also incorporate the notion of 'Good Behaviour'.[54]

C. 1600, therefore, English magistrates were provided with a complicated conception of outward civil peace which ranged from active 'defence', to the assertion of 'liberties', to restraint from and punishment of 'violence': peace which had civic as well as simply judicial connotations. These 'peaces' were defined in relation to religious peace, by which was meant the social organization and provision of faith and the condition of the soul and conscience (whether 'good' or 'evil'). It also segued into diplomatic peace, involving the absence of war between sovereign bodies and the diplomatic processes used to achieve it.

A similar set of 'significations' can be found in the works of Lambarde's contemporary, Shakespeare. We have already seen that Shakespeare used the term readily (547 times compared to 261 uses of war). Although

[49] *Ibid.*, 5.
[50] *Ibid.*, 5–6.
[51] *Ibid.*, 6.
[52] *Ibid.*, 6–7.
[53] *Ibid.*, 7.
[54] Michael Dalton, *The Countrey Justice* (1619), 7.

Table 2 *Types of 'peace' in Shakespeare's Coriolanus and King John*

	Coriolanus	King John
Civil peace *including general designations; 'office';* *public and self-governance*	24	16
Religious peace *including church; conscience; soul*	0	4
Diplomatic peace *including 'not-war'; diplomacy*	13	15

'peace' appears at least once in most if not all of the plays, there are four plays in which the word is used 30 times or over, acquiring, it could be argued, a degree of paradigmatic power. These 'peace plays' were *Henry IV 2*, *Henry VI 1*, *Coriolanus* and *King John*; plays, that is, about societies in conflict and at war. Table 2 accordingly shows that, like readers of Elyot's dictionary, audiences of the Roman *Coriolanus* or the Anglo-Norman *King John* would have been bombarded with uses of peace with civil and diplomatic inferences.

Religious connotations, in contrast, were all but absent from the stage. Putting that slightly differently, insofar as the semantics of peace were concerned, these Elizabethan and Jacobean audiences were children of Padua rather than Hippo.

III

These contemporary significations suggest that a defining feature of the word 'peace' was its connective power: its use, that is, to describe and idealise at once the inner self (whether earthly or spiritual), the external world (civil and religious), the quality of relationships (between individuals, households, associations or states) and the establishment and maintenance of all of the above. This connectivity is not always apparent in the historiography, with historians tending to focus on peace within a particular semantic field – and so historical sub-discipline – rather than explore its centrality to several.[55] Even as sophisticated a historian as John Bossy nevertheless corrals 'peace' to describe a particular 'moral tradition' informed by what he terms three 'items': 'the notion or practical instinct that to be a Christian means to love your neighbour, and in particular your enemy'; the urgent need for such 'peacemaking' in periods of accentuated 'enmity' (such as the Reformation); and the 'historical' or 'archaic' role

[55] For one aspect of judicial peace, see Hindle, 'The Keeping of the Public Peace', 213–48; for religious discourse see Roberts, 'The Languages of Peace', 297–315; for diplomacy see Gajda, 'Debating War and Peace', 851–78, and Rivett, 'Peacemaking'.

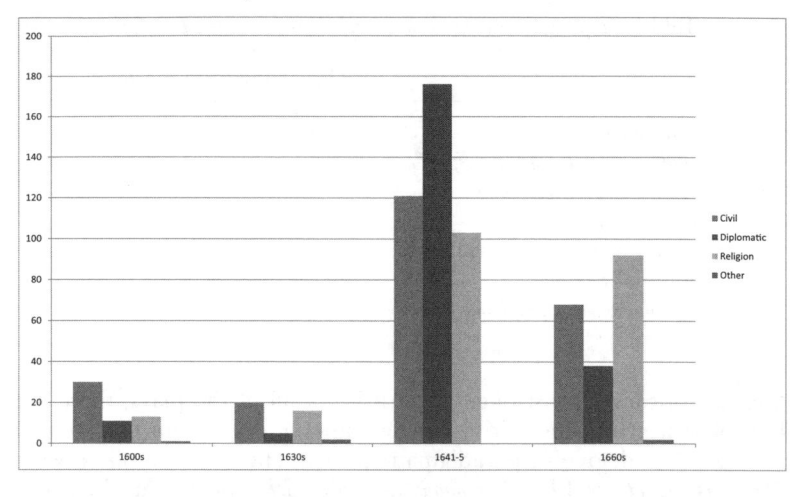

Figure 7 (Colour online) Civil, diplomatic and religious uses of peace on printed title-pages, 1600s, 1630s, 1641–5, 1660s

of the church in facilitating peace.[56] Bossy takes this Christian tradition, which he labels 'peace', to have been 'rather deeply embedded in the consciousness of the populations of the time of Reformation' and wonders 'what happened to it thereafter'.[57] His answer is that it was eventually eroded by 'the current of civility' and 'civil society'. As he puts it: 'Invented, for our purposes, by the Renaissance, precipitated by the wars of religion, civil society must be the real terminus of the moral tradition, insofar as it has one.'[58] Yet even as cursory an analysis as the one above has shown that just as semantically 'peace' in the Reformation was not limited to a single 'moral tradition', so diachronically it was a rising rather than declining term. At the very least, 'civil' and 'Christian' connotations of 'peace' remained concurrent throughout the sixteenth and seventeenth centuries. Other meanings and uses of the term only complicate Bossy's story further.

There is no space here to tell an alternative, let alone comprehensive, story of early modern peace. It is possible, however, to take the word's civil, religious and diplomatic significations as a historicised framework for tracing relative changes in meaning and usage before, during, and after the civil wars. Figure 7 accordingly compares the appearance of civil, diplomatic and religious significations on printed title-pages at four

[56] John Bossy, *Peace in the Post-Reformation* (Cambridge, 1998), 2.
[57] *Ibid.*
[58] *Ibid.*, 99–100.

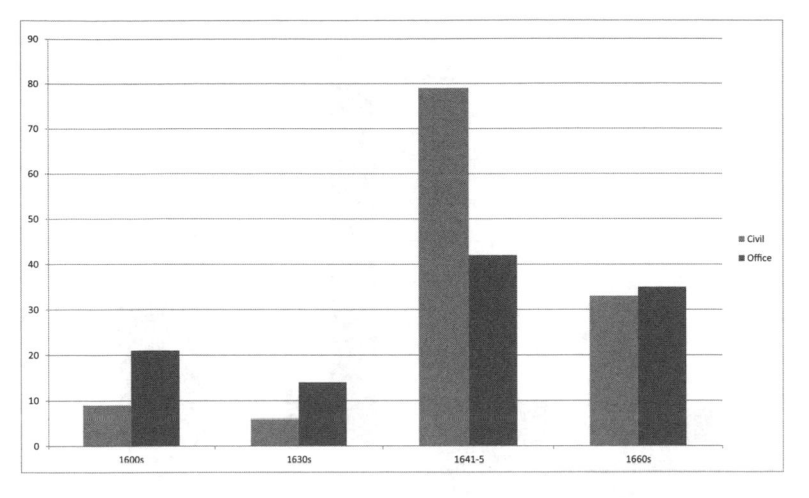

Figure 8 (Colour online) Civil peace on printed title-pages: general and office, 1600s, 1630s, 1641–5, 1660s

intervals during the seventeenth century. These are the 1600s, the first decade of Stuart rule in England; the 1630s, when Charles I ruled without parliament; 1641–5, coinciding with the first civil war; and the 1660s, the decade following the Restoration of the Stuart monarchy. The chart nicely illustrates the proliferation of all significations of peace in the first half of the 1640s, especially diplomatic inferences which followed from the peace negotiations which accompanied war. It also depicts a longer-term trend. At the beginning of the seventeenth century, printed significations of civil peace appeared far more often than diplomatic or religious significations. By the 1660s, the opposite was the case. This was not so much because people had stopped talking about the civil semantics of peace; far from it. Rather, it was because there was now even more printed discourse about religious peace.

Two final charts give a more detailed picture of this change in emphasis. Figure 8 divides uses of civil peace into its two predominant types: as a general evocation of quiet liberties, in which the term was often coupled in phrases like 'laws, liberties, and peace', 'public peace', 'peace and safety', 'peace and freedom' and 'settled peace'; and as a specific referent to institutions and offices authorised to keep and defend the peace (most obviously justices of the peace). While it was officers of the peace who dominated title-pages until the 1630s, in the early 1640s this tendency was dramatically reversed, with notions of liberties and freedoms increasingly signalled. In the 1660s, there was almost parity between the two senses of the term. Somewhat more ambiguously, Figure 9 shows the changing

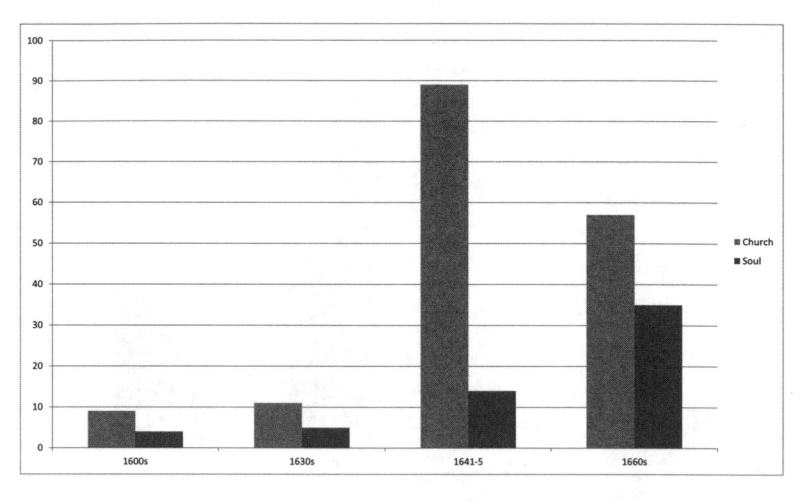

Figure 9 (Colour online) Religious peace on printed title-pages: church and soul, 1600s, 1630s, 1641–5, 1660s

number of references to the 'outward' church on the one hand – its organisation, constitution, liturgy, form and so on – and the 'inward' soul and its synonyms on the other hand. (The data is ambiguous because for many commentators the one implied the other; this chart describes only *explicit* references to, and concern with, peace of conscience or mind). With that caveat in mind it can nevertheless be seen that while in the early 1640s religious evocations of peace most often referred to external forms, by the 1660s discourse about conscience had significantly increased.

There are at least three striking features of this (albeit extremely schematic and exploratory) survey of the texts introduced by 'peace' on their title-pages. One is the multi-edged nature of civil peace. Social historians have tended to understand 'peace' simply as the restraint or amelioration of conflict within communities: 'the resolution of social conflict, the keeping of the public peace'.[59] However, during the middle of the seventeenth century the more assertive and civic connotations of 'defence' and 'liberties' invoked by 'peace' – and recognized by magistrates – became more prominent.[60] In the political circumstances of the 1640s, that is, justices empowered to 'keep of the peace' were also encouraged to become (in the language of Marsilius) 'defenders

---

[59] Hindle, 'The Keeping of the Public Peace', 213.
[60] Richard Cust, 'Reading for Magistracy: The Mental World of Sir John Newdigate', in *The Monarchical Republic of Early Modern England. Essays in Response to Patrick Collinson*, ed. John F. McDiarmid (Aldershot, 2007).

of the peace'. As a result, peace became not merely the justification for magistracy and governance but also a politicised slogan of war. The second, more obvious point is that whether or not Bossy's 'moral tradition' really did decline over the course of the seventeenth century, religious significations of the term in general, and notions of inner tranquillity and conscience in particular, clearly increased in prominence; might be said, indeed, to have been a consequence of the mid-century troubles. Certainly, peace as a term of religious enunciation remained very much in the discursive mix of 'civil society'. More obvious still is that, insofar as the semantics of peace were concerned, the revolutionary era was extremely significant. This was true not so much because it saw the invention of new meanings for the term – the significations of peace were well established by 1600. Rather, it was the intensity and mutability of how peace was used which was different. As one exasperated commentator (typically) declared in 1643: *Will and Law, Reason and Religion, Treasons and Rebellion, Peace and War, Payments and Punishments, People and Parliament, Are Words of Wonder to Weak and Wise Men, and by Them Malignants Deceive the Multitude.*[61]

IV

Telling a coherent story in an era of such semantic flux and conflict is a hazardous interpretative exercise. By way of conclusion, I would never-theless like to suggest a narrative of peace between the 1630s and 1660s which at least begins to make sense of the patterns revealed by the data and the significations available to contemporaries. This narrative is based on a sequence of key appropriations of the word: while there were always concurrent and conflicting claims on peace, at particular moments certain claims were more emphatic, or at least visible, than others. Told in these terms the story involves a transition from 'peace and unity' in the 1630s to 'peace and truth' in the 1640s to 'peace and conscience' by the 1660s.

Notions of civil, religious and diplomatic peace were integral to the kingship of the early Stuarts. James I cultivated the epithet of 'peacemaker' at home and in Europe and both he and his son were drawn to the conflation of unity, order, hierarchy, beauty and peace promised by episcopacy. The poet Robert Aylett knew which buttons to press in his 1622 poem, *Peace with her Four Guarders*. The guarders of peace were 'concord', 'chastity', 'constancy', courtesy' and 'gravity' – virtues embodied in bishop and king. As Aylett explained to John Williams, bishop of Lincoln:

> Thou great Peace-keeper, whom the greatest King / That our great God of Peace did ever bring / To rule these Western Isles, in happy Peace, / For Honour, Arts, and Piety's

---

[61] Anon., *Will and Law, Reason and Religion, Treasons and Rebellion, Peace and War, Payments and Punishments, People and Parliament, Are Words of Wonder to Weak and Wise Men, and by Them Malignants Deceive the Multitude* (1643).

increase, / Thou, whom this Mighty Monarch doth intrust, / With his Great Seal, as Prudent, Faithful, Just. / God to thy outward bliss, add inward Peace, / That Goodness with the Greatness may increase.[62]

After James's death in 1625, Aylett became a close ally of William Laud, a dominant figure in the Caroline regime, and he remained a loyal lieutenant of the archbishop throughout the 'Personal Rule'. The centrality of peace to Caroline (and Laudian) ideology was nicely expressed in a royal proclamation for the 'Establishment of the Peace and Quiet of the Church of England' as early as 1626.[63] This announced the king's 'utter dislike of all those, who to show the subtlty of their wits, or to please their own humours, or vent their own passions, do ... stir up or move any new Opinions, not only contrary, but differing from the Sound and Orthodox grounds of the true Religion'. In contrast, the 'Divine Providence put into his hands as shall be ... for the repressing and severe punishing of the insolencies of such, as out of any sinister respects, or disaffection of Government, shall dare either in Church or State, to disturb or disquiet the Peace thereof.' Such 'disquiet' which disturbed the peace included most forms of discursive activity, whether 'writing, preaching, printing, conferences, or otherwise'. In Augustinian fashion, the king accordingly corralled all 'his reverend Archbishops and Bishops [civil magistrates] speedily to reclaim and repress all such spirits, as shall in the least degree attempt to violate this bond of peace'. The king's offices of peace were accordingly aligned against 'unquiet and restless spirits' who 'to express their rash and undutiful insolencies, shall wilfully break that Circle of Order, which without apparent danger to Church and State, may not be broken'. Faced with such a threat, 'his Majesty shall and will proceed against all such offences ... with that severity ... they deserve, so that by the exemplary punishment of some few ... all others may be warned'.[64]

In Caroline ideology, then, 'outward peace' conflated divine power, monarchical will and civil and religious institutions into a 'circle of order'; it precluded not only the usual acts of violence but also public discourse *per se*; it criminalised attempts at religious peace (both inward and outward) outwith the strictures and structures of the established church; and it also raised questions about the 'quiet liberties' which subjects enjoyed semi-autonomously of their monarch. This vision of peace was shattered by the so-called Bishops' Wars of 1639 and 1640, which led directly to the Short and Long parliaments and the chance to redress grievances. Given the Caroline aversion to discursive noise,

---

[62] Robert Aylett, *Peace with her Four Garders* (1622), sig. A3r.
[63] *By the King. A Proclamation for the Establishing of the Peace and Quiet of the Church of England* (1626), two sheets.
[64] *Ibid.*

the sudden outpouring of 'opinion' – in declarations, speeches, petitions, news-books, sermons, pamphlets, treatises, ballads, dialogues, tracts, and the rest – must have been cacophonic.[65] Indeed, a begging speech by Charles to the corporation of Oxford in 1643, subsequently published, suggests just how closely Charles had aligned his inner peace with the outward 'circle of order', and the psychological damage its disintegration was causing:

> We lose Our Royalty [and the] benefit of Our Exchequer revenues ... We lose Our Strength in the loss of Our Subjects (the strength of Kings) and We lose that which is more precious to us than all things else, Our peace and quiet of mind, never free from cogitations of Our people's injuries and Our own sufferings.[66]

The speech also shows how discursively marginalised the royalist conception of 'peace' had become; because what is most striking about the intense discourse of peace in the early 1640s was how parliamentarian polemicists successfully appropriated civil and religious significations of the term as a justification – epithet even – for war.

They did this in at least three ways. First, an active and intrinsically civic conception of peace was presented, alongside notions of liberties, laws, freedoms and estates, as a fundamental attribute of the subject. This peace was now in grave jeopardy and had to be defended, with force if necessary. From the very outset, parliamentary declarations explained that they 'do hold themselves bound in Conscience to raise forces for the preservation of the peace of the kingdom and protection of the subjects in their Persons and Estates [for] the publique good which they will always prefer before their own lives and fortunes'.[67] It was precisely in this spirit that tracts like *Peace and Plenty* could be written. Second, the king's recruitment of Cavaliers and other military malcontents (as characterised by parliamentary propaganda) threatened, in a very real and tangible way, these 'quiet liberties'. In such circumstances, militarisation became an extension of legitimate civic responsibilities and participation. The anonymous author of *The Kingdom's Case*, who 'prays and studies the peace of the kingdom', asked 'whether the king's subjects may not by the laws of this kingdom ... oppose quell and vanquish ... the five or ten thousand or more persons who aggregate and assemble themselves

---

[65] See for example David Zaret, *Origins of Democratic Culture: Printing, Petitions and the Public Sphere in Early Modern England* (Princeton, 2000); Jason Peacey, *Politicians and Pamphleteers: Propaganda during the English Civil Wars and Interregnum* (Aldershot, 2004); Michael J. Braddick, *God's Fury, England's Fire. A New History of the English Civil Wars* (2008).

[66] *His Majesties Speech Spoken to the Mayor, Aldermen, and Commonaltie of the Citie of Oxford, and to the High Sheriffes of the Counties of Oxford and Berks, with Divers Justices of Peace in the Said Counties, at a Generall Summons* (1643), 5.

[67] *The Kings Maiesties Intention concerning the Setting up of his Standard, and Levying of Warre against both Houses of Parliament* (1642), 6.

together, in a warlike manner under the name of the king'.[68] It was a leading question. Their assembly 'is a breach of the peace, and that in the highest degree; now every man may take up arms, to preserve the Peace, nay ought, if otherwise it cannot be preserved'. More, their assembly was 'Rebellion' and 'High Treason': 'If the assemblers to pull down Enclosures were adjudged Traitors, much more these Rebels assembled to pull down ... our Religion, Law and Liberties.'[69] Third, because of the political dependency of the king on Catholics and other 'Evil Counsellors', the Protestant church – and so outward peace with God – remained in mortal danger. This warranted forceful defence. However, the providential turn of events also meant that the church need not simply be protected but also, finally and properly, reformed. Thus Richard Bernard could write

> To the Watchful Eyes in this our State, the worthy Justice, Imprisoners of Malefactors, and Preservers of Peace; that peace is wished which pass all understanding, with the zeal of God, in due execution of Justice against the enemies of Christ, and our country.[70]

The semantics of this position, which was monopolised by parliamentary propagandists, were nicely outlined by John Saltmarsh, who became chaplain to Thomas Fairfax and the New Model Army and (like most parliamentary writers) was a self-confessed lover of 'true peace and liberty'. In 1643, Saltmarsh explained: 'That which I now conceive to be the only Interest of our Reformation, is not a Pacification but a Peace, for a Pacification is a more proper and safe notion for foreign states than our own.'[71] The usual diplomatic process, 'the accommodating of a difference, and a meeting of several principles, and a resolving to agree with one another, without any further incorporation, but cannot be intrinsic nor natural enough for us of the same kingdom'. This was because even 'as our new and holy fundamentals call over purest and soundest peace ... there will break forth any fresh and mutual contending'. It followed that 'there must needs be more security in that peace where all possibility of resistance is taken away'; this could only be achieved through war.[72] In the same year, John Norton lamented at once the prevalence and the power of these arguments. Also claiming to be a *Lover of Truth and Peace*, he bemoaned 'Salamander Spirits' who 'will admit of nought that sounds of peace, but cry down all accommodation,

---

[68] *The Kingdomes Case, or, The Question Resolved whether the Kings Subjects of this Realm of England May or Ought to Ayd and Assist Each Other in Repressing the Persons now Assembled together under the Name of the Kings Army* (1643).

[69] *Ibid.*, 2–3.

[70] Richard Bernard, *An Epistle Directed to All Iustices of Peace in England and Wales* (1642), sig. A2r.

[71] John Saltmarsh, *A Peace but no Pacification, or, An Answer to that New Designe of the Oath of Pacification and Accomodation Lately Printed* (1643), sig. B3r.

[72] *Ibid.*, sig. B3r–v.

unless their own prodigious fancies (conditions worse than war) may be the ingredients'.[73] He complained that 'I cannot meet with any two of them that concur in the same particular, only this far they agree in the general, that is for the maintenance of the Protestant Religion, and the Laws of the Land.' He wondered how this belief in law and religion could be consistent with war. And he saved his especial scorn for those who 'seeking to varnish over their bloodthirsty desires with a pretended inclination to peace, say, they refuse it not, so it may be accompanied with truth. Tis well said, I wish it were as truly meant. He must be a man of very easy credulity that can assent to credit it.'[74]

Disingenuous or not, this conception of peace made for a powerful military ideology. As early as 1642 that quintessential Cavalier, Prince Rupert, advised his uncle, 'Consider the composition of our Enemies, they fight for Conscience, Liberty and Law, though misinterpreted, and there is none but knows what power and charm that bears over him that doth make use of it.'[75] Misinterpreted or not, it was nevertheless out of this ideology that a third conception of peace, as worrying to Presbyterians as it was to Episcopalians, emerged. It centred on the liberty of each person to find inward religious peace – peace of conscience – however and with whomsoever one pleased. The first half of the 1640s saw the publication of some of the key works which identified 'peace and truth' with 'liberty of conscience'.[76] As is well known, parliamentary victory in 1645 inaugurated not so much the true reformation of the national church (for which most mainstream Puritans initially fought) as the devolution of 'inward peace', or quiet liberty, into separate 'sects' and 'societies'. Following the abolition of monarchy in 1649, protecting this liberty became an imperative of the Commonwealth governments and was one of the main reasons why politicians like Oliver Cromwell were unable to dispense with the New Model Army. For many, however, the military enforcement of liberty of conscience contravened civil peace and liberties, and this tension between civil and religious peace and also inward and outward peace proved fatal for the revolutionary regime after the death of Cromwell in 1658. The return of the monarchy in 1660 not only robbed the dispersed churches, like the Quakers, of their military enforcers; it inaugurated a systematic reaction against liberty of conscience based on unitary and hierarchical principles reminiscent of the 1630s. Accordingly, the establishment of outward religious peace at the

---

[73] John Norton, *The Miseries of War* (1643), 2.

[74] *Ibid.*, 2, 5.

[75] Prince Rupert, *A Speech, Spoken by Prince Robert* (1642), sig. A3r.

[76] Henry Robinson, *Liberty of Conscience: Or The Sole Means to Obtaine Peace and Truth* (1643); Roger Williams, *The Bloudy Tenent, of Persecution, for Cause of Conscience, Discussed, in a Conference betweene Truth and Peace* (1644).

Restoration was based on the exclusion of so-called nonconformists and dissenters from the national church and the persecution of unauthorised congregations and churches – 'conventicles' – by justices of the peace. In this way, liberty of 'inward peace' was configured as antithetical to 'outward peace' (both religious and civil); and it was because Quakers relentlessly contested this configuration both in print and in practice that they emerge as by far the most voluble proponents of 'peace' in the 1660s (when 19 per cent of printed texts with peace in the title can be attributed to Quakers).

This radical conception of inward peace entailed, on the one hand, a personal relationship with God that was unmediated by scripture or ritual. On the other hand, it required the autonomous association or 'society' of likeminded souls in silent and communal worship. George Bishop explained in 1663 that 'Every Man must come to his proper state, and know how it is with him, because Every Man must account to God; and before his Judgment all must stand.'[77] And as Humphrey Smith wrote in 1662, 'Peace' was integral to this state.[78] This was true externally: 'Friends, this is a time of quietness and stillness, or a time for you so to be, and there hath been a large time of gathering; and for convincing, and now the Lord is proving and trying them that are gathered.'[79] It was also true internally:

> In peace my lines are read my words are heard my mind is known my language understood my love received ... what shall I say I am with, here or in the midst of all the innocent lambs by the virtue of the power and invisible spirit which ruleth all in all? And in silence with you could I long rest.[80]

V

Early moderns talked about a lot when they talked about peace. This was as true for 'this word's sundry significations' as it was for the variety of ideologies into which it, or rather they, became appropriated over the course of the seventeenth century. The resulting semantics were messy and political and make for a word significantly more complex and powerful than has been allowed by those religious, political, and social historians who have concentrated on only one aspect of its meaning and usage. This points, in turn, to the connective power of the term: over the course of the sixteenth and seventeenth centuries, peace drew the self and society, church and state and human and

[77] George Bishop, *A Little Treatise concerning Things Indifferent, in Relation unto Worship* (1663), 21.

[78] Humphrey Smith, *To the Meek and Open Hearted Lambes, and Flock of Heaven, in Meekness of Love, with Greetings of Peace from the Seat of Infinite Mercy* (1662).

[79] *Ibid.*, 5.

[80] *Ibid.*, 4.

corporate bodies into potentially pathological juxtaposition. It also enabled Laudians and parliamentarians, Presbyterians and Quakers, and indeed Hobbes and the Bread Street Committee, to use the same language to mean different and conflicting things. These semantics must have been especially confusing for justices of the peace, whose monopoly of peace charged them not only with resolving and punishing conflict within the community but also defending the community from external threats and asserting and protecting perceived rights and liberties. Many if not all of these tensions and vagaries were apparent as early as the 1530s: it is not difficult to discern the ghosts of Augustine and Marsilius in seventeenth-century discourse. Cumulatively, however, this semantics swelled, mutated, changed, politicised and was used to different intents and purposes across the social spectrum. As a consequence, peace underwent a sustained process of displacement and atomization: from the grand 'circle' of Caroline monarchy in the 1630s to the more intimate spaces of personal spirituality by the 1660s. While Marsilius would no doubt have appreciated the semantic confusion faced by justices of the peace, the Quaker imperative of inner and unmediated spiritual tranquillity may have proved more baffling.

The approach to the word taken here begs more questions than it answers. How did the printed uses and appropriations so traced sit alongside quotidian practices and conversations? Can the schematic dots that have been painted be joined by more systematic and contextualised analyses? What other words, and other semantic fields, were used and invoked alongside peace? What is clear is that, like toleration or moderation, there was much more to peace than meets the modern eye. As the philologist Adam Littleton noted in 1669, 'The charming name of Peace itself is now become an Alarm, and entertained by most as unwelcome news; and they, that bring any tidings to it, looked upon as Enemies, and ill-affected.' Littleton acknowledged that 'The reason of this 'tis a hard matter to find out.'[81] It remains, nevertheless, a paradox worth exploring.

[81] Adam Littleton, *The Churches Peace Asserted upon a Civil Account* (1669), sig. Ar–v.

Transactions of the RHS 23 (2013), pp. 155–73 © Royal Historical Society 2013
doi:10.1017/S0080440113000078

WHAT IS PAIN? A HISTORY
THE PROTHERO LECTURE *

By Joanna Bourke

READ 4 JULY 2012

ABSTRACT. What is pain? This article argues that it is useful to think of pain as a 'kind of event' or a way of being-in-the-world. Pain-events are unstable; they are historically constituted and reconstituted in relation to language systems, social and environmental interactions and bodily comportment. The historical question becomes: how has pain been *done* and what ideological work do acts of being-in-pain seek to achieve? By what mechanisms do these types of events change? Who decides the content of any particular, historically specific and geographically situated ontology?

Pain does not emerge naturally from physiological processes, but in negotiation with social worlds. It is surprisingly difficult, however, to define what is meant when people use that word 'pain'. The English noun 'pain' encompasses a host of phenomena that are incommensurate. 'Pain' is a label that adheres to scraped knees, headaches, phantom limbs and kidney stones. It is assigned to heart attacks and heartaches. The adjective 'painful' is so broad that it can be applied to a toothache as easily as to a boil, a burst appendix and a birth. Pain can be inflicted by knives or hula-hoops (as in the 1959 mini-epidemic of children diagnosed with 'hula-hoop syndrome' caused by 'excessive hooping').[1]

Furthermore, even a cursory examination of the historical record uncovers a headache-inducing range of theological, scientific, medical and philosophical definitions of pain. In 1882, Friedrich Nietzsche famously declared that 'I have given a name to my pain'; it was called 'dog'. For him, pain was 'just as faithful, just as obtrusive and shameless, just as entertaining, just as clever as any other dog, and I can scold it and vent my bad mood on it, as others do with their dogs, servants, and wives'.[2] It was an apt analogy, even if rather insulting to non-figurative dogs, servants and wives. However, if pain was a dog,

---

* I am very grateful to The Wellcome Trust for supporting this research.
[1] Zafar H. Zaidi, 'Hula-Hoop Syndrome', *Canadian Medical Association Journal*, 80 (1959), 715–16.
[2] Friedrich Nietzsche, *The Gay Science*, trans. Walter Kaufmann (New York, 1974; 1st publ. 1882,), 249–50.

it was a beast of gargantuan proportions. Nietzsche was adopting a functionalist definition: his pain-Dog was defined by its function in the great philosopher's life. Such ways of conceptualising pain have proliferated. For centuries, theologians have assumed that pain was a kind of chastising communiqué from a Higher Being; nineteenth-century evolutionists contended that it was a mechanism to protect the organism from harm; and many clinicians from the late nineteenth century onwards have drained pain of any intrinsic meaning altogether, making it little more than a sign or symptom of something else (a dis-ease). With brain imaging technologies from the late twentieth century, the subjective person-in-pain could be eradicated altogether, with pain morphing into little more than 'an altered brain state in which functional connections are modified, with components of degenerative aspects'.[3]

Still others have diced pain using different scalpels. In innumerable ways, philosophers and scientists have sought to pare pain back to its bare skin and bones. Was pain the reaction of filaments and animal spirits to noxious stimuli, as René Descartes and his disciples believed in the seventeenth century and beyond?[4] Was it caused by 'too great irritability' or 'a want of sufficient irritability', as the author of *Asthenology* (1801) claimed?[5] Or was it more correct to say that pain was a sensation in the sense that it 'has a threshold, is localised and referred to a stimulus'?[6] In the 1830s, Sir Charles Bell in England and Francois Magendie in France focused on the biological nature of pain in the context of the motor and sensory functions of the dorsal (Bell) and ventral (Magendie) roots of the spinal cord. Johannes Müller, Richard Bright, Maximiliary Von Frey and A. Goldschneider fixed attention on the nerves, disagreeing fiercely about whether specificity theory (the body has a separate sensory system for perceiving pain) or pattern theory (the receptors for pain are shared with other senses such as touch) best described the physiology of pain.[7] In 1976–7, the International Association for the Study of Pain (IASP) attempted to tame Nietzsche's beast by calling together a diverse group of pain specialists (including experts in neurology, neurosurgery, psychiatry,

---

[3] Silvia Camparesi, Barbara Bottalico and Giovanni Zamboni, 'Can We Finally "See" Pain? Brain Imaging Techniques and Implications for the Law', *Journal of Consciousness Studies*, 18, 9–10 (2011), 257–8.

[4] René Descartes, 'Meditations on First Philosophy', trans. Elizabeth S. Haldane and G. R. T. Ross, ed. Enrique Chávez-Arvizo, *Descartes: Key Philosophical Writings* (Ware, 1997; 1st publ. 1641), 183, and René Descartes, *Traité de l'homme* (Paris, 1664), 27.

[5] Christian Augustis Struve, *Asthenology: Or, the Art of Preserving Feeble Life; and of Supporting the Constitution under the Influence of Incurable Diseases*, trans. William Johnston (1801), 423.

[6] E. Guttmann and W. Mayor-Gross, 'The Psychology of Pain', *The Lancet*, 20 Feb. 1943, 225.

[7] For summaries, see Ronald Melzack and Patrick D. Wall, 'Pain Mechanisms: A New Theory', *Science*, 150, 3699 (1965), 971–9, and Roselynne Rey, *The History of Pain*, trans. Louise Elliott Wallace (Cambridge, MA, 1995).

psychology, neurophysiology, dentistry and anaesthesia) to adjudicate definitively on the question 'what is pain?' Their definition is now the most cited one in the field of pain studies. The IASP concluded that pain is 'an unpleasant sensory and emotional experience associated with actual or potential tissue damage, or described in terms of such damage'. This definition emerged directly from the invention in 1965 of the Gate Control Theory of Pain, which introduced the idea of a 'gating mechanism' in the dorsal horns of the spinal cord that allowed the perception of pain to be modified. Crucially, the Gate Control Theory and, consequently, the IASP's definition insist that sensory, cognitive and affective processes influence people's experience of pain. As such, the definition is remarkably flexible and it opens the door to social, psychological and physiological explorations. This does make it very useful indeed to the historian.

However, as historians have consistently argued, it is extremely problematic to overlay a late twentieth- and early twenty-first-century understanding of pain on to earlier periods. Equally troubling, adopting the IASP's definition would have meant taking a particular position on that long-standing, thorny debate about what some have dubbed the 'myth of two pains',[8] that is, emotional versus bodily pain. Although the IASP's definition may seem to side with those who seek to undermine the distinction between the emotional and the physiological, in fact it does nothing of the kind. It simply states that both are valid 'pains' (if a person described her emotional pain in terms of tissue damage, it is allowed to be called 'painful'). The Cartesian distinction between mind and body (and it may be noted that Descartes himself was not a fully signed-up Cartesian)[9] is alive-and-well and does a vast amount of ideological work for physicians, psychiatrists, psychologists, the pharmaceutical industry and chronic pain patients today.

One useful starting point in beginning to define what is meant by the word 'pain' can be found in the musings of a prominent Victorian physician, Dr Peter Mere Latham. Latham had been born in London in the year of the French Revolution and died eighty-six years later. He was one of the most renowned physicians in London, working at the Middlesex Hospital and then St Batholomew's, and (like his father) was appointed Physician Extraordinary to the Sovereign. Portraits show him bedecked in robes, with a magisterial forehead, penetrating gaze and self-assured smile. Given that his everyday routines were frequently shattered by attacks of asthma, he clearly had thought a great deal about suffering.

---

[8] For the best discussion, see David B. Morris, *The Culture of Pain* (Berkeley, 1991), 9.

[9] For a discussion, see Jan Frans Van Dijkhuizen, 'Partakers of Pain: Religious Meanings of Pain in Early Modern England', in *The Sense of Suffering. Constructions of Physical Pain in Early Modern Culture*, ed. Van Dijkhuizen and Karl A. E. Enenkel (Leiden, 2009), 189–219.

What is most striking about Latham, however, are his thoughts on bodily pain, published between the 1830s and the early 1860s. He also wanted to know the answer to that simple question: what is pain? Latham recognised that pain assumed many guises. 'There is a Pain which barely disturbs the complacency of a child', he noted, and 'a pain which is too much for the strength of a giant'. Are these two kinds of pain actually the same, differing only 'in degree'? Could it really be the case that 'the smallest Pain contain[s] all that essentially belongs to the greatest, as the minutest atoms of matter have separately the same properties of their largest aggregates', he asked? In everyday language, dramatically different experiences of pain are spoken of using one word – 'pain'. But if we 'suppose ourselves at the bed-side and within hearing, when Pain raises its cry of importunate reality', the likenesses of painful experiences are exposed as nothing more than a linguistic deceit. The 'things of life and feeling' – that is, each person's unique encounter with suffering – are 'different from all things in the world besides'.[10]

So, how did Latham seek to define pain? The correct response to anyone who asks 'what is Pain?', he rather grumpily contended, was simply to state that 'he knew himself perfectly well what it was' and he 'could not know it the better for any words in which it would be defined'. Hammering home the point, Latham insisted that 'Things which all men know infallibly by their own perceptive experience, cannot be made plainer by words. Therefore, let Pain be spoken of simply as Pain.'[11]

Latham's definition of pain – pain is what is spoken about as 'Pain' – is one that many historians, anthropologists, sociologists and even clinicians espouse. Anyone claiming to be 'in pain', *is* in pain; if a person describes her experiences as 'painful', they are. For the purposes of historical analysis, so long as someone says that they are suffering, that claim is accepted. In Latham's words, 'The fact of pain being suffered at all must always be taken on the patient's own shewing [*sic*].' Of course, like Latham, we might admit that 'there is such a thing as shamming Pain',[12] but that does not alter our primary definition.

This approach to pain has been highly productive. It is well suited to the way many historians conduct their research. It is profoundly respectful towards the ways peoples in the past have created and recreated their lives, and it remains courteously neutral about the veracity of any specific claim. It allows for multitude, even conflicting, characterisations of suffering. Crucially, the definition enables historians to problematise and historicise every component of pain-talk. It insists that 'pain' is constructed by a host

[10] P. M. Latham, 'General Remarks on the Practice of Medicine', *British Medical Journal* (28 June 1862), 677.
[11] *Ibid.*
[12] *Ibid.*

of discourses, including theological, clinical and psychological ones. Done badly, it can lead to literary practices that assume that 'pain' can be 'read' transparently from various texts; done well, however, this approach to pain encourages subtle, deconstructive analyses of past experiences and behaviours.

However, the definition comes up against a major limitation. The clue to the problem lies in the fact that whenever Latham wrote about 'pain', he capitalised it: for Latham, pain was Pain. In other words, there is an assumption that pain is an 'it', an identifiable thing or concept. To be fair, Latham recognised this problem. He was not convinced that 'pain' was an 'it', excusing himself on the grounds that his reifying (although he would not have used that word) of 'Pain' was driven by pragmatic observations. As he observed, 'No man, wise or foolish, ever suffered Pain, who did not invest it with a *quasi* materialism.' In the throes of physical anguish, even the most rational philosopher finds himself 'outreasoned by his feelings'. 'I have known many a philosopher', Latham continued, 'take to rating and chiding *his Pain*, as if it were an entity or quiddity of itself.' Therefore, 'for practical purposes, we must often let people think and speak of things as they seem to be, and not as they are, making a compromise between philosophy and common sense. We must let them speak so of Pain. There is no help for it.'

Ignoring Latham's condescending tone, his basic point is a legitimate one. Sufferers of pain are entitled to say 'I don't know what *you* mean by pain, but *I* know "it" when I feel "it"', and then go on to describe their pain as though it were an independent entity within their body ('I have a pain in my tooth') or an entity that attacks from the outside (as in: pain is a weapon that stabs, a fire that burns, an animal that bites). But, for the historian, there are many dangers involved in referring to pain as though it were an entity. The chief one is that it risks giving 'pain' an independent life. The ease with which we can slip into making this error can be illustrated by turning to Elaine Scarry's influential book *The Body in Pain* (1985). Scarry argues that pain is outside of language, absolutely private and untransmittable. Indeed, in her most often-quoted statement, Scarry goes even further, insisting that 'Physical pain does not simply resist language but actively destroys it, bringing about an immediate reversion to a state anterior to language, to the sounds and cries a human being makes before language is learned.'[13] This is an extreme version of reification. As literary scholar Geoffrey Galt Harpham rightly observes, such an argument

> treats as an immediate and monochrome physical experience, a baseline of reality, what is in fact a combination of sensations, dispositions, cultural circumstances, and

[13] Elaine Scarry, *The Body in Pain. The Making and Unmaking of the World* (New York, 1985), 4–5.

explanations, a phenomenon involving body, mind, and culture. She has, in other words, misconceived the character of pain precisely by giving it a character, by treating it as a fact – a brute fact, the first and final fact – rather than as an interpretation.[14]

In other words, Scarry has fallen into the trap of treating metaphoric ways of conceiving of suffering (pain bites and stabs; it dominates and subdues; it is monstrous) as descriptions of an actual entity. Of course, metaphorically, pain is routinely treated as an independent entity within a person, as in statements such as 'he has a pain *in* his shoulder', 'the pain *went away*, and 'bleeding will *get rid of* the pain' but, for Scarry, these metaphors are literalised.[15] 'Pain', rather than a person-in-pain, is given agency. This is an ontological fallacy.

How can pain be conceived of non-ontologically? It is helpful to begin from the premise that pain is not an object; it is a *type of event*. Pain is a *way* of being-in-the-world. Pain-events are unstable; they are historically constituted and reconstituted in relation to language systems, social and environmental interactions and bodily comportment.

What is meant by saying that pain is an event? By designating pain as a 'type of event' (I will discuss what I mean by '*type of* event' shortly), I mean that it is one of those recurring activities that we regularly experience and witness that participates in the constitution of our sense of self and other. Events are not entities or mental objects; they are ways of being-in-the-world. An event is designated 'pain' if it is identified as such by the person claiming that kind of consciousness. Being-in-pain requires an individual to give significance to this particular 'type of' being. This word 'significance' is not being used in the sense of 'importance' (a pain can be a momentary pin-prick) but in the sense of 'recognised' (a stomach*ache* rather than the gurgling of the stomach before lunch). It is never neutral or impersonal. In other words, a pain-event possesses what philosopher Paul Ricoeur called a 'mineness'.[16] A pain-event always belongs to the individual's life; it is a part of her life story. In this way, the person becomes or makes herself into a person-in-pain through the process of naming.

An individual has to name pain – she has to identify it as a distinctive action – for it to be labelled a pain-event. But how do people know what to name as pain? If the words we use for sensations are private or subjective, then how do we know how to identify them? How do people give the label 'pain' to one subjective sensation and not another?

[14] Geoffrey Galt Harpham, 'Elaine Scarry and the Dream of Pain', *Salmagundi*, 130/131 (2001), 208.

[15] For an extensive discussion of metaphor and pain, see my article 'Pain: Metaphor, Body, and Culture in Anglo-American Societies between the Eighteenth and Twentieth Centuries', *Rethinking History* (forthcoming, 2014).

[16] Paul Ricoeur, *Oneself as Another*, trans. Kathleen Blamey (Chicago, 1992), 132.

In recent years, scholars exploring the senses have turned to the ideas of the philosopher Ludwig Wittgenstein for stimulation. In *Philosophical Investigations*, Wittgenstein turned his mind to the question of whether there can be such a thing as a private language. How do 'words *refer* to sensations', he asked? Like Latham, he acknowledged that people routinely talk about their sensations. As Wittgenstein put it 'don't we talk about sensations every day, and give them names', so why the fuss? Simply put, he continued, the problem is 'how is the connection between the name and the thing set up? This question is the same as: how does a human being learn the meaning of the names of sensations? – of the word "pain" for example.' Wittgenstein modestly suggested 'one possibility', that is, 'words are connected with the primitive, the natural expressions of the sensations and are used in their place. A child has hurt himself and he cries; and then adults talk to him and teach him exclamations and, later, sentences. They teach the child new pain-behaviour.' He imagined an interlocutor interrupting him with the question, 'So you are saying that the word "pain" really means crying?' 'On the contrary', Wittgenstein continued, 'the verbal expression of pain replaces crying and does not describe it.'[17]

Imagine, he mused, a world in which there were no outward expressions of sensations – where, for instance, nobody cried or grimaced. In such a world, how could a person know he was in pain? This man could scrawl an 'S' in his diary each time he experienced a particular sensation. But how would he know that it was the same sensation he was experiencing each time? And how would other people know what 'S' stood for? This diarist would have no criterion for knowing when he was experiencing 'S' and when 'T'. To have any meaning, Wittgenstein concluded, words for feeling-states like pain must be inter-subjective and able, therefore, to be learned. In other words, the naming of a 'pain-event' can never be wholly private. Although pain is generally regarded as a subjective phenomenon – it possesses a 'mine-ness', to use Ricoeur's term – 'naming' occurs in public realms.

Wittgenstein clearly enjoyed imagining other worlds. On another occasion, he invented a world in which everyone possessed a box, which contained a beetle. No one was able to peer into anyone else's box, however. Because people only knew what the beetle was by looking into their private box, it was entirely plausible that each person believed that 'beetle' referred to a complete different entity. Indeed, the 'beetle in the box' might change regularly. The box might even be empty. But if everyone believed that they possessed a 'beetle in a box', then the word 'beetle' was useful in communication. In terms of language, in other

[17] Ludwig Wittgenstein, *Philosophical Investigations*, trans. G. E. M. Anscombe (Oxford, 1953), 89.

words, the 'actual content' of the box does not matter. What is important is the role of the 'beetle in the box' in terms of public experiences.

Now substitute the word 'pain' for 'beetle': it does not matter that I have no direct access to your subjective consciousness, so long as we have a shared language to discuss our various 'pains'. For my purposes, this 'beetle in the box' analogy is not perfect – after all, my pain is not 'in' my body (although we often speak as though it is) in the same way that a beetle is 'in' a box – but Wittgenstein's language-game draws attention to an approach to pain that can be very productive for historians. As Wittgenstein succinctly put it, 'mental language is rendered significant not by virtue of its capacity to reveal, mark, or describe mental states, but by its function in social interaction'.[18] For historians, it is important to interrogate the *different* language games that people residing in the foreign kingdom of the past have played, in order to enable us to make educated guesses about the diverse and distinctive ways people have packaged their 'beetle in the box' or pain in their lived-bodies.

My approach to pain also states that pain is a '*type of* event'. In other words, it is useful to think of pain-events in adverbial terms. Philosopher Guy Douglas has an interesting way of explaining this point. He points out that there is a difference, for example, in saying 'I feel a sharp knife' and 'I feel a sharp pain.' In the first instance, the knife is what linguists call an 'alien accusative' (that is, the knife refers to the object of the sentence) while, in the second instance, pain is a 'connate accusative' (it qualifies the verb 'to feel' rather than being a sensory object in itself). In the first sentence, we are 'describing a knife *apart from* the way it feels, while in saying that *pain is sharp* we are describing the feeling', that is, a sensation similar to being injured by a sharp object. In other words, in saying 'I feel a sharp pain', we are qualifying a verb rather than a noun.[19]

The other way of expressing this is by saying that pain describes the *way* we experience something, not *what* is experienced. For example, we say that a tooth is aching, but the ache is not actually the property of the tooth but is our way of experiencing or perceiving the tooth. As Douglas put it, 'sensory qualities are a property of the way we perceive the object rather than the object itself'. Pain is 'not the thing or object that one is feeling, it is what it is like to feel the thing or object'. Crucially, pain is not an intrinsic quality of raw sensation; it is a way of perceiving an experience.[20] Pains are modes of perceptions: pains are not the injury or noxious stimuli itself but the way we evaluate the injury or stimuli. Pain is a way-of-being in the world or a way of naming an event.

[18] *Ibid.*, 188.
[19] Guy Douglas, 'Why Pains Are Not Mental Objects', *Philosophical Studies*, 91, 2 (1998), 127–48.
[20] *Ibid.*, 127–48.

The historical question, then, becomes: how has pain been *done* and what ideological work do acts of being-in-pain seek to achieve? By what mechanisms do these types of events change? As a type of event, pain is an activity. People do pain in different ways. There is no decontextual pain-event: so-called 'noxious stimuli' may excite a shriek of distress (corporal punishment) or squeal of delight (masochism); there is no necessary and proportionate connection between the intensity of tissue damage and the amount of suffering experienced since phenomena as different as battle enthusiasm, work satisfaction, spousal relationships and the colour of the analgesic-pill can determine the degree of pain felt; and people have no difficulty using the same word 'pain' to refer to a flu injection and an ocular migraine.

Although each individual is initiated into cultures of pain from birth, being-in-pain is far from static or monochrome, which is why it requires a history. People can – and regularly do – challenge dominant happenings of pain. Indeed, the creative originality with which some people-in-pain draw on and transform language games, environmental exchanges and bodily performances (or gestures) of suffering is striking. Of course, the most dominant 'doing' of pain is to objectify it as an entity – giving it independence outside the person doing the pain. It becomes important to ask, therefore, who decides the *content* of any particular, historically specific and geographically situated ontology? What is excluded in these power-acts?

As historians, it is therefore possible both to let 'people think and speak of things as they seem to be', as Latham expressed it (that is, conceiving of pain as an 'it' or an entity to be listened to, obeyed or fought) and to acknowledge that ways of being-in-pain involve a series of agents, all of whom are immersed in complex relationships with other bodies, environments and linguistic processes. It would be disingenuous to suggest that Latham would wholly agree with this interpretation, but he seemed to be gesturing towards such a position when he shrewdly remarked that

> Pain, itself a thing of life, can only be tested by its effects upon life, and the function of life. And whether it be small or great (so to speak), or of whatever degree, it is to its affect upon life and the functions of life that we must look.[21]

In other words, pain is always a 'being-in-pain', and can only be understood in relation to the way it disrupts and alarms, authenticates and cultivates, the 'states of being' of real people in the world.

There are a number of advantages to adopting an events-based approach to pain in history. The first one is that we do not have to jettison Latham's main insight that 'Things which all men know infallibly by their own perceptive experience, cannot be made plainer by words.

[21] Latham, 'General Remarks', 677.

Therefore, let Pain be spoken of simply as Pain.' In other words, pain is what people in the past said was painful. We are not required to privilege one, historically specific meaning of pain over any other. Defining pain as a 'type of event' remains neutral about the 'truth value' of any philosophical or scientific definition. Instead, it asks: what does the scientific *content* of any particular, historically specific and geographically situated scientific ontology tell us about the way philosophers, scientists and physicians have sought to classify pain-events. As historians of science have reiterated time and again, scientific practice itself is social action. We invent, rather than discover, pain. Pain-as-event enables us to avoid reifying pain in terms of a single incarnation.

If the first advantage in thinking about pain as a 'type of event' is that it is historically flexible, the second advantage is that it is historically complex. People perceive pain through the prism of the entirety of their lived experiences, including their sensual physiologies, emotional states, cognitive beliefs and relational standing in various communities. As a consequence, the definition is sceptical of any pain-account that claims that pain is simply a sensual response to noxious stimuli or – to put it in the language used earlier – that Nietzsche's pain-Dog only *reacts* to the world rather than *responds* to it (which many philosophers believed was what distinguished animals from humans).[22] As mentioned earlier, the most famous conceptualisation of 'pain-as-ensation' was that of Descartes. According to him, pain occurred when fast-moving particles of fire rushed up a nerve fibre in the foot towards the brain, activating animal spirits which then travelled back down the nerves, causing the foot to move away from the flame. In this model, the body was a mechanism that worked 'just as, pulling on one end of a cord, one simultaneously rings a bell which hangs at the opposite end'.[23] Although nociceptive impulses and endorphins were subsequently substituted for filaments and animal spirit, Descartes's basic, mechanistic model of pain-as-sensation has dominated both scientific and 'folk' beliefs about pain into the mid-twentieth century.

Claims that pain is simply a sensual or physiological response to noxious stimuli cannot account for the way that people in the world experience what they call pain. The model of pain-as-sensation implies that a person 'feels' a noxious stimuli, *after which* affective, cognitive and motivational processes 'kick in' – responding and interpreting the happening. However, these things occur in dynamic interaction.

Conceiving of pain as a 'type of event' allows us to disentangle pain-situations from pain-experiences. This is not to deny that a person dying of the plague is likely to have an excruciating headache. But many aches and

---

[22] For a discussion, see my book *What It Means To Be Human: Reflections from 1791 to the Present* (2011).

[23] Descartes, 'Meditations on First Philosophy', 183, and Descartes, *Traité de l'homme*, 27.

pains are not caused by bodily damage. People can suffer, yet be lesion-free, as in many chronic pain states. They can be in pain, yet not possess the limb that is 'feeling pained', as in phantom limb sensations. They can be in situations that self-evidentially warn of agony, yet be calm. As Edmund Burke noted, Italian theological and astrologer Tommaso Campanella, who was tortured on the rack, 'could so abstract his attention from any suffering of his body, that he was able to endure the rack itself without much pain'. As Burke correctly concluded, 'our minds and bodies are so closely and intimately connected, that one is incapable of pain or pleasure without the other'.[24] Being-in-pain is multifaceted: attitudes, motivations, belief systems and cognition all contribute to making or signifying the event.

Another way of making this point is to argue that pain only exists in the act of evaluating it. Not all 'acts' are 'events'. Indeed, some acts (having a limb blown off in combat, to take one example) may not be designated pain-events by the person affected. A particularly stark example of this can be seen in the context of the Second World War. Lieutenant Colonel Henry K. Beecher, who served in combat zones on the Venafro and Cassino fronts, was struck by the fact that many severely wounded men did not complain of pain. Medical officers found that there was no necessary correlation between the size and depth of any specific wound and men's expressions of suffering. Beecher decided to explore this paradox systematically, questioning 215 seriously wounded men. To his surprise, three-quarters did not report experiencing significant pain. One third claimed to be feeling no pain at all, while another quarter said they were experiencing only slight pain. Remarkably, three-quarters of all seriously wounded men did not even ask for pain relief, despite the fact that being asked the question would have served as a reminder that relief was available. What was happening? Perhaps, Beecher speculated, men who had been wounded were simply less sensitive generally. But this explanation failed to account for the fact that 'a badly wounded patient who says he is having no wound pain will protest as vigorously as a normal individual at an inept venipuncture'. Instead, Beecher found, there must be a difference between wounds caused in civilian contexts (a car accident, for example) and those caused during combat. Perhaps the strong emotions aroused in combat were responsible for the absence of acute pain. Pain might also be alleviated by the fact that wartime wounding would release a soldier 'from an exceedingly dangerous environment, one filled with fatigue, discomfort, anxiety, fear and real danger of death, and gives him a ticket to the safely of the hospital. His troubles are about over, or he thinks they are.' This was in

---

[24] Edmund Burke, *The Works of the Right Hon. Edmund Burke, with a Biographical and Critical Introduction by Henry Rogers*, I (1837), 60.

contrast to civilian accidents, which only heralded in 'the beginning of disaster'.[25]

This is not to deny the importance of the sensory nature of pain – pain is 'what hurts'. However, it is to insist that, by itself, the sensation approach is much too narrow. The 'sensations' definition simply does not help explain the vast number of different sensations that we place under that single label 'pain' (a headache and a heartache). It also cannot help interpret the lives of people who have been lobotomised – an operation performed on people with intractable pain from 1943. These patients could still claim to be in pain (and could discriminate between different degrees of noxiousness) yet were completely uninterested and unconcerned about the sensation.[26] The event of being-in-pain is evaluative. It stands in relation to the individual in an adverbial sense: pain is 'not the thing or object that one is feeling, it is what it is like to feel the thing or object'.[27] Pain may be rendered significant because it is unpleasant but there is no phenomenological state that is in and of itself 'painful', as any zealous saint or keen sadomasochistic practitioner can attest.

The event-ness of pain also draws attention to the fact that different emotional reactions adhere to pain-events. Depending on the presence of other objects and people, pain-events can elicit distress (face-to-face with a torturer), fear or panic (crashing through the car window), anticipation or surprise (the moments after a heart attack). They can also elicit pride (gout in the eighteenth century), relief (self-cutters) or joy (childbirth).

This can be illustrated by looking at the way Joseph Townend wrote about pain in the middle of the nineteenth century. For this impoverished manual labourer, pain was an event that adhered to some acts and not others. It was not mentioned, for example, when he wrote about the lingering deaths of four of his siblings (his father simply exclaimed, 'Bless the Lord, there's *another safe* landed!'). Nor did he evoke pain when he described extreme hunger or working (from the age of seven) seventeen-hour shifts in the carding room of a Lancashire cotton mill. Rather, Townend only summon the spectre of pain in the context of a severe burn he suffered as a child, which resulted in his entire right arm being

---

[25] Lt. Col. Henry K. Beecher, 'Pain in Men Wounded in Battle', *Annals of Surgery*, 123, 1 (1946), 96–105.

[26] Walter Freeman and James W. Watts, *Psychosurgery. In the Treatment of Mental Disoerders and Intractable Pain*, 2nd edn (Oxford, 1950), 550; J. W. Watts and Walter Freeman, 'Psychosurgery for the Relief of Unbearable Pain', *Journal of the International College of Surgeons*, 9 (1945), 679; Everett G. Grantham and R. Glen Spurling, 'Selective Lobotomy in the Treatment of Intractable Pain', *Annals of Surgery*, 137, 5 (1953), 602; W. Tracey Haverfield and Christian Keedy, 'Neurosurgical Procedures for the Relief of Intractable Pain', *Southern Medical Journal*, 42, 12 (1949), 1077; Mical Raz, 'The Painless Brain Lobotomy, Psychiatry, and the Treatment of Chronic Pain and Terminal Illness', *Perspectives in Biology and Medicine*, 52, 4 (2009), 560.

[27] Douglas, 'Why Pains Are Not Mental Objects', 127–48.

fused to his side. Even in this context, the process of hurting was a positive one: as he declared, 'heaven must recompense our pains'.

For Townend, painful happenings constituted his place both in *this* world and the next. In his narration, the most important event in his entire life occurred when he trudged all the way to the Manchester Infirmary to have his arm cut free. The surgeon gruffly warned: 'Now, young man, I tell you, if when you feel the knife, you should jerk, or even stir – you will do it at the hazard of your life.' Anaesthetics like chloroform would not be invented for another twenty-three years and no analgesic (like whiskey or laudanum) was offered. 'All was still', Townend recalled, when 'with a forcible thrust, through went the knife, as near the pit of the arm as possible, and close to my side . . . the progress of the instrument I distinctly heard'. The pain was 'most exquisite'. As the 'smoking wound' was being dressed and bound, Townend was left to reflect on 'my past neglect and wickedness in resisting the Holy Spirit'. He thought of the Methodist chapel, attendance at which he had neglected. He 'wept bitterly': saying his 'mind [was] fully made up to be entirely the Lord's when I should return home'.

For Townend, bodily agony was a gift inflicted by a loving, heavenly Father. But he was equally clear that the function of pain was to teach him submission not only to hierarchies of power in the next life, but also in *this* one. Townend had only praise for his surgeon but when he attempted to thank him by shaking his hand – obviously, using his left hand – the surgeon shouted at him: 'Do you offer a gentleman your left hand?', then he grasped Townend's right arm and dragged him off the bed: 'Immediately my leg and foot were covered with blood; and on the web [of skin] being loosed, I saw that it was turned black: and my poor side was drenched in blood, and smoked almost like a kiln.' Another doctor observed that his wound was inflamed, forcing Townend to admit that he had 'partaken rather freely of port wine'. The doctor was 'very much grieved; and [so] he suddenly jerked up my shoulder, which made me sweat with pain, and it cracked like the firing of a pistol'. Townend's only comment on this act of the doctor whom he called 'easy, kind, careful and communicative' was 'So much for wine.' Pain was a legitimate punishment for socially insulting a 'gentleman' and partaking in alcoholic beverages.[28]

Pain performed two acts for Townend: it drew him into the exulted embrace of God's family while reminding him of his lowly status in the family of Man. His being-in-pain was a world away from later, secular beings, in which pain was no longer conceived of as an entity that had to be passively endured or embraced. Rather, it was an 'enemy' to be

[28] Rev. Joseph Townend, *Autobiography of the Rev. Joseph Townsend: With Reminiscences of his Missionary Labours in Australia*, 2nd edn (1869), 16–18.

fought and ultimately defeated. In the words of the anonymous author of 'The Function of Physical Pain' (1871), now that pain had been 'made optional' by anaesthetics, it 'necessitates a complete revisal [*sic*] of the theories of the purposes of bodily pain hitherto held by moralists'.[29] When the pharmaceutical possibility of eradicating acute pain was limited, endurance could be valorised as a virtue: the introduction of effective relief (at least for the kinds of pain that plagued the young Townend's life) made passive endurance perverse rather than praiseworthy. Stripped of its mysticism and its history in foundational theological texts, pain became an evil in itself, unequally distributed (afflicting the saintly as carelessly as the sinner) and serving, at most, a rather limited diagnostic function.

In other words, people in the past interpreted their pains not as contained (in the Wittgensteinian sense of 'the beetle in the box'), isolated, individual bodies, but in interaction with other bodies and social environments. Cognition also mattered. It made a difference whether the person-in-pain conceived of the event as being inflicted by an infuriated deity, due to imbalance in the ebb and flow of humours, an inevitable punishment for a lifetime of 'bad habits', or the result of an invasion by a germ.[30] The body is never pure soma: it is configured in social, cognitive and metaphorical worlds.

This discussion anticipates the third advantage to conceptualising pain as a 'type of event': there is no such thing as a private pain-event. I have already discussed this aspect from a Wittgensteinian point of view, but here I mean something less philosophical and more historical. From the moment of birth, infants were initiated into cultures of pain. What these infants in the 1760s learned about the cognitive, affective and sensory meanings arising from the interface between their interior bodies and the external world was very different to what their counterparts in the 1960s learned. In the humoral physiology of the eighteenth century, for example, bodies consisted of four fluids – phlegm, black bile, yellow bile and blood. Linked to these humours were personality types (sanguine and melancholic). There were also three kinds of spirits, which acted on the humours: the natural, the vital and the animal. In this model – unlike the biomedical one that was dominant until the 1960s – distinctions between bodies, minds and souls were not clear-cut. Pain was the result of disequilibrium or imbalance. Illness was the result of disrupted relationships as much as disrupted physiologies. As a result, humoural

---

[29] 'The Function of Physical Pain: Anæsthetics', *Westminster Review*, 40, 1 (1871), 198–200 and 205.

[30] For an extensive discussion, see my article 'Pain: Metaphor, Body, and Culture in Anglo-American Societies between the Eighteenth and Twentieth Centuries'.

theory provided rich figurative languages of ebbs and flows. For example, take John Hervey's 1731 description of his sister's suffering. She was

> choked with phlegm, tormented with a constant cough, perpetual sickness at her stomach, most acute pains in her limbs, hysterical fits, knotted swellings about her neck and in her joints, and all sorts of disorders, consequent to a vitiated viscid [*sic*] blood, which, too glutinous and weak to perform its proper circulation, stops at every narrow passage in its progress, causes exquisite pains in all the little, irritated, distended vessels of the body, produces tumours in those that stretch most easily, and keeps the stomach and bowels constantly clogged, griped, and labouring, by the perspirable matter reverting there for want of force to make its due secretions and evacuate itself through its natural channels in the habit and the pores of the skin.[31]

Pain in this account was a blockage of natural flows. It pervaded all parts of the body, and not just particular organs. This was a world away from the body-in-pain of nineteenth-century biomedicine or twenty-first-century neurology. Physiological models of the body draw attention to certain things and not others, fundamentally affecting what is *noticed* – and given meaning – and what is regarded as incidental. The physiological body is constituted by the figurative languages that bring the body into the world. Figurative languages 'disclose' our being-in-the-world.[32]

Once taught what constituted a pain-event, messages communicated though language, facial expressions and gestures helped inform people-in-pain how they ought to respond. There was a rich corpus of texts explicitly instructing people how they *ought to* behave when in pain. These 'comportment manuals' or prescriptive pain-texts changed from the explicitly hagiographical ones of the eighteenth and nineteenth centuries to the more psychologically infused texts of more recent decades. More subtle instructions were given through gesture. There is a vast literature documenting the different 'gestural styles' in pain-instructions.[33]

These communicative acts were normative. They did not simply document the various ways people-in-pain responded to their affliction: they contained veiled instructions on how people *should* act. People-in-pain sought to conform to these instructions for numerous reasons. Correctly adhering to highly esteemed scripts might increase a person's confidence in an affirmative posthumous existence. Pain-performances might be important in order to protect the witnesses, rather than the sufferer herself. This was what was being conveyed in Rachel Betts's memoir of 1834. Betts was described as suffering 'excruciating pain', after which she observed her sister weeping. Betts was mortified, admitting

---

[31] John Hervey, 'An Account of my Own Constitution and Illness, with Some Rules for the Preservation of Health; for the Use of my Children', in his *Some Materials Towards Memoirs of the Reign of King George II*, III, ed. Romney Sedgwick (1931; 1st publ. 1731), 971.

[32] *Ibid.*

[33] For a discussion, see my *Stories of Pain: From Prayer to Painkillers* (Oxford, forthcoming, 2014).

that 'I cannot help expressing how great my pain is' since 'it seems a relief' to vent it. However, she added, 'I do not wish to distress you.' A short time later, when her mother asked her if she 'continued easier', Betts simply replied, 'Quite easy.'[34] Sufferers might also seek to conform for non-reflexive reasons (this might be especially true of those figurative ways of speaking about pain that were internalised from infancy or were deeply embedded in language).

In this way, pain can be seen as a learned exegesis. As influential pain-psychologist Ronald Melzack discovered in the 1970s, Scottish terriers who had been raised in isolation from birth and protected from all normal environmental stimuli, including painful ones, proved unable of identifying and responding 'normally' to a flame or pinpricks when exposed to it in maturity.[35] They simply hadn't 'learned' what it meant to be-in-pain.

Of course, we do not need dogs (whether they belong to the scientist Melzack or the philosopher Nietzsche) to show us that pain is social action. Human bodies in pain are profoundly connected and communicative. Not surprisingly, the social norms expected in the expression of pain differed according to the gender, class, occupation and age of the person-in-pain. They have changed dramatically over time as people-in-pain creatively perform pain.

As a public 'type of event', being-in-pain was always political. Both chronic and acute beings-in-pain could be the *result of* economic deprivation (hazardous working conditions, lack of medical insurance, the failure of physicians and pharmacists in poor areas to stock the most effective analgesics) as well as the *cause of* destitution. The politics of gender also adhered to pain-events: the exquisite sensitivity required of upper-class men in the salons of Edinburgh in the late eighteenth century can be contrasted to the burly hardiness of American frontiersmen. In Martin Pernick's insightful book *A Calculus of Suffering. Pain, Professionalism, and Anesthesia in Nineteenth Century America* (1985), he correctly maps out the way that American physicians ranked different people's sensitivity to painful stimuli: in that great Chain of Feeling, certain people (distinguished by class, gender, 'race', religion, occupation and so on) were relatively insensitive.[36] What he does not explore is the contradictory assumptions behind the Chain of Feeling. For instance, in nineteenth- and much of the twentieth-century discourse, non-European peoples and workers could be denigrated as possessing lesser bodies: their position at the lower echelons of the great Chain of Feeling was due to their physiological

---

[34] Rachel Betts, *Memoir of the Last Illness and Death of Rachel Betts* (1834), 22.

[35] Ronald Melzack, 'The Perception of Pain', in *Physiological Psychology*, ed. Richard F. Thompson (San Francisco, 1971), 223.

[36] Martin S. Pernick, *A Calculus of Suffering. Pain, Professionalism, and Anesthesia in Nineteenth Century America* (New York, 1985).

insensibility. However, often in the same text, they could also be designated as inferior on precisely the opposite grounds: *excessive* or 'exaggerated' sensitivity. The alleged insensitivity of non-Europeans, immigrants and workers was proof of their rudimentary nervous systems and thus humble status, yet the profound sensitivity of these same people was also proffered as evidence of their inferiority (they lacked strength of will).[37] The fact that *both* beliefs could be held simultaneously was responsible for the appalling high levels of underestimation of the bodily pains of certain groups of patients. Indeed, it took until the late twentieth century for the routine underestimation of the pain of African-Americans, immigrants, women and the poor to be deemed scandalous in the medical literature.[38] Interestingly, this vast debate was conducted almost solely in terms of the under-*medicalisation* of pain – a significant indicator about the ideological labour being performed in clinical pain-narratives.

The instability of pain-events as refracted through social interactions can also be illustrated by exploring the dramatic *shifts* in the Chain on Feeling. It was not only a contradictory hierarchy; it was also volatile over time. One illustration of this can be seen in medical discussions about the sentience of infants, which shifted from an emphasis on the exquisite sensitivity of infants in the eighteenth century to almost total insensibility to pain from the 1870s and then back again to acute sensitivity from the 1980s. The exquisite sensitivity of infants to painful stimuli was at the heart of eighteenth-century debates within the professionalisation of pediatrics – indeed, it helped perform the work of professionalisation. In the 1780s, Michael Underwood (the first obstetrician to be appointed to the Royal College of Physicians in London and the physician most responsible for establishing paediatrics as a discipline in its own right) argued that the chief reason that very young children had been neglected by the medical profession was because they lacked the capacity 'to give account' of their pain. As a result, their care had been entrusted to 'old women and nurses'. It was time that this changed, he insisted. After all, infants displayed their aches and pains 'plainly and sufficiently' on their faces. 'Every distemper', he continued, had 'a language of its own' and it was 'the business of a physician to be acquainted with it'.[39] In Pye Henry Chavasse's textbook *Advice to a Mother on the Management of her Children, and on the Treatment on [sic] the Moment of Some of their More Pressing Illnesses and Accidents*, he further reflected on the 'sympathy ... in the nervous system' between different parts of the infant's body. When we consider 'how susceptible the young are to pain', he observed, 'no surprise can be

---

[37] For an extended discussion, see my 'Pain Sensitivity: An Unnatural History from 1800 to 1965', *Journal of Medical Humanities* (forthcoming, 2013).

[38] This is addressed in great detail in my *Stories of Pain*.

[39] Michael Underwood, *A Treatise on the Diseases of Children, with Directions for the Management of Infants from the Birth; especially Such as Are Brought up by Hand* (1784), 4.

felt at the immense disturbance and the consequent suffering and danger frequently experienced by children while cutting their *first* set of teeth'.[40]

The exquisite sensitivity of infants to painful stimuli was disrupted from the 1870s in particular. Experimental embryology, in particular, was drawing conclusions about the biology of sentience. The work of Paul Emil Flechsig was especially important. Flechsig had systematically examined sections of the brain of foetuses, newborn infants and older infants, showing that nerve fibres developed at different rates. At Flechsig's 1894 address at the University of Leipzig (published the following year as *Gehirn und Seele*), he argued that

> The structures at the base of the brain, for the most part, and the cerebellum were found to be myelinated before birth; whereas in the newborn infant the cerebrum only exhibited isolated regions of myelination around the primary fissures – namely, the central, calcarine, and the Sylvian; these are the regions of the primary projection centres of movement and of the special senses. The remainder of the cortex is not myelinated, and constitutes the association centres as yet unprepared for function. Upon anatomical grounds, therefore, it may be postulated that a child at birth may have a simple sensation.[41]

In other words, at birth, infants were not fully 'wired'.

This pain-work was much more than a rhetorical or scientific exercise: it justified giving children as old as ten inadequate pain relief – or withholding it altogether. As the author of *Modern Surgical Technique* (1938) claimed, 'no anesthetic is required' when carrying out even major operations (such as amputations and heart operations) on young infants. Indeed, 'a sucker consisting of a sponge dipped in some sugar water will often suffice to calm the baby'.[42] As late as the 1970s, over half of children aged between four and eight years who had undergone major surgery – including amputations – in American hospitals received *no* medication for pain.[43] Dismissive attitudes towards the sensual worlds of infants and young children only changed significantly from the 1980s – not coincidentally in the contexts of contestations of the acute-pain model by women and ethnic minorities as well as debates within pro- and anti-abortion movements.

Finally, the social also adheres to the physiological body itself. This is the fourth advantage of conceiving of pain as a 'way of naming an event'. The act of 'naming' influences bodily responses. Anthropologist William

---

[40] Pye Henry Chavasse, *Advice to a Mother on the Management of her Children, and on the Treatment on [sic] the Moment of Some of their More Pressing Illnesses and Accidents*, 9th edn (Philadelphia, 1868), 70.

[41] Paul Flechsig's lecture, summarized by Frederick W. Mott, 'Cerebral Development and Function', *British Medical Journal*, 1, 3145 (1921), 529.

[42] Max Thorek, *Modern Surgical Technique*, III (Philadelphia, 1938), 2012.

[43] Joann [sic] M. Eland and Jane E. Anderson's chapter in *Pain. A Sourcebook for Nurses and Other Health Professionals*, ed. Ada Jacox (Boston, MA, 1977), 453–76.

Reddy has called this 'emotives'.[44] Language does things to bodies. It acts upon them. This is another way of saying that the body-in-pain is not simply an entity awaiting social inscription (as in Wittgenstein's 'the beetle in the box' analogue or as implied in the 'body as text' metaphor) but is an active agent in both creating pain-events and, in turn, being created by them. The repeated recitation of particular way of naming a pain, for example, can affect the physiological body. Figurative languages can inform an individual's autonomic arousal, cardio-vascular responses and sensorimotor actions. Or, put in the language of the very different, humoural physiology, metaphors can affect whether blood freezes or gushes through the irritated, distended vessels of the body; they direct the ebb and flow of phlegm, black bile and yellow bile. Naming can instruct bodies how to respond. This concept of 'retrojection', or the means by which ways of naming pain are mapped back into the flesh, is important for any historian of the body. When a series of figurative languages or concepts for pain are repeated time and again from infancy, they become internalised and infused literally within the individual's body.[45] Through retrojection, sufferers 'infuse the imagery of cultural metaphors' into their bodies, thus, feeling 'the power of discourse within'.[46]

To conclude: sentience is socialised. It is a state of being, constituted within complex, temporal worlds. Pain is a type of event that involves sensation, cognition, affect and motivational aspects. Meanings, history, learning and expectations all influence ways of being-in-pain. As a type of event, pain is always meaningful to the person experiencing it. There is no pain-entity independent of the way it impinges on people's being-in-the-world. People often speak as though they 'have' a pain – and the contrasting ways they 'have' it is important in mapping changes over time – but the body-in-pain is a lived event. As a historically unstable practice, pain-events are constituted and reconstituted in relation to other practices, including language systems, social and environmental interactions and bodily comportment. Contestations to this ideological work is important. As Latham reminded his readers in the 1860s, the 'things of life and feeling' – that is, each person's *unique* encounter with suffering – are 'different from all things in the world besides'.[47]

[44] William M. Reddy, *The Navigation of Feeling: A Framework for the History of Emotions* (New York, 2001).

[45] I develop this argument in 'Pain: Metaphor, Body, and Culture in Anglo-American Society between the Eighteenth and Twentieth Centuries'.

[46] Michael Kimmel, 'Properties of Cultural Embodiment: Lessons from the Anthropology of the Body', in *Body, Language, and Mind*, II: *Sociocultural Stuatedness*, ed. Rosleyn M. Frank, René Dirven, Tom Ziemke, and Enriquè Bernárdez (New York, 2008), 99 and 101.

[47] Latham, 'General Remarks', 677.

Transactions of the RHS 23 (2013), pp. 175–201 © Royal Historical Society 2013
doi:10.1017/S008044011300008X

A ROOM WITH A VIEW: VISUALISING THE SEASIDE, *c.* 1750–1914*

By Peter Borsay

READ 3 NOVEMBER 2011 AT THE UNIVERSITY OF GLAMORGAN

ABSTRACT. The expansion in consumption that marked the British economy in the eighteenth and nineteenth centuries was based not only on a growth in material goods, but also of experientially and culturally rich products such as leisure and tourism. Underpinning the latter of these, and of key importance in the rise of the seaside resort, was the process of visualisation. The 'tourist gaze' became a commodity in its own right, geared around environmental and social subjects, and facilitated by a transformation in the content and reproductive potential of visual culture and an engineering of resorts to deliver views.

In one of the houses perched on the cliff ... we resided, during our pleasant stay at Tenby ... so near as to be almost part of the dwelling is the OLD SQUARE TOWER [Belmont Tower, see Figures 1 and 7] – one of the seaward defences of the town. Hence there is a wide-spread and very beautiful view: immediately underneath, at the foot of that huge rock, the firm sand extends to St. Catherine's Isle, seen to great advantage from this point, in combination with Castle Hill. Immediately fronting us is Caldy Island ... From the higher rooms of the house, or from the summit of the tower, a fine view is obtained of Giltar Point, and, further off, 'Proud Giltar', one of the most picturesque of all the sea cliffs of the district; while in the extreme distance is seen the land that encircles Carmarthen Bay, and, on clear days, Lundy Island and the coast of Devonshire. It is difficult, indeed, to find anywhere a prospect at once so extensive, and so beautiful, as that we obtain from this house ... From this tower, gentle reader, we have watched (as you may, and, we hope, will), at all hours of the day, the thousand things that make a sea-side dwelling a supreme delight ... The sands were alive always. When the tide was full in the contrast between the foam, and cliffs up which it dashed, was a glorious sight for the artist; and, when the tide turned, it seemed as if its halt was stayed by the horizon. Beneath, upon the hard sands, were troops of laughing children, tripping ladies ... and gentlemen with telescopes, or opera-glasses, phaetons and horses, 'promenading'. The sands are alive with company.[1]

In this account of a visit to Victorian Tenby, Mr and Mrs Hall make clear the importance of the view from their lodgings. The mixture of

---

* This is my part of a presentation, jointly delivered with Dr Louise Miskell, on 'Visualizing the Resort: Pictorial Representations of Tourists and their Destinations c. 1750–1914'. I am grateful for the comments and observations made by my colleague and those in the audience.

[1] Mr and Mrs S. C. Hall, *Tenby: History, Antiquities, Scenery, Traditions, and Customs* (Tenby, [1860]), 46–50.

Figure 1 (Colour online) Belmont Tower with Caldey Island (left) and St Margaret's Island and Giltar Point (right) in the distance, 2012. Taken from the Imperial Hotel, the site of the Halls's accommodation (Belmont House) while in Tenby (Peter Borsay)

environmental and human elements, the detailed identification of places, the calculated shifts from foreground to background, the liberal sprinkling of aesthetic judgements, all suggest a carefully calculated analysis of a scene that for them is freighted with meaning. The view, spontaneous and 'natural' as it may appear, is as carefully crafted an object as any luxury item of material culture. And, as we know today, there is a real market value to the visual. In a resort hotel, a room with a view will cost more than one without, a property facing the sea more than one hidden in a side street. When and why did views come to have a value? From what did their value derive, and how was it achieved? How important was the process of visualisation to the development of the seaside resort? To answer these questions a range of approaches is necessary. The first part of this paper will examine consumerism, the rise of tourism and the seaside resort, and the role of the 'tourist gaze'; the second part the seaside and visual culture; and the third and fourth parts the two types of visualisation present at the seaside, environmental and social. In these final sections, Tenby in West Wales will be taken as a case-study (see

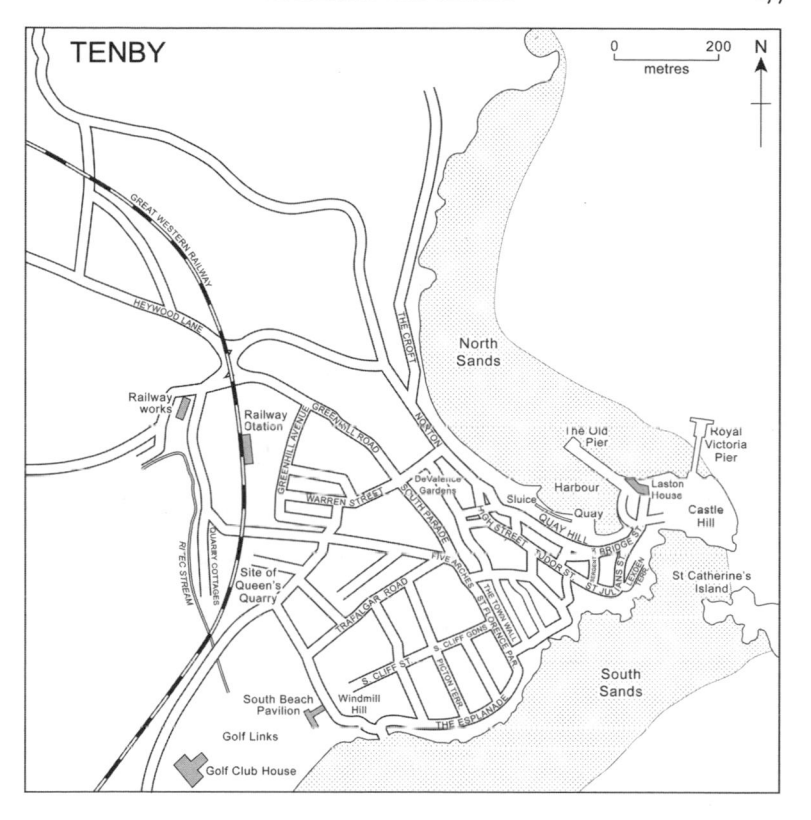

Figure 2 Map of Tenby, *c.* 1940 (Peter Borsay and Antony Smith)

Figures 2 and 3).[2] Sea bathing may already have been underway there as early as the 1760s, though serious investment in the resort's infrastructure seems to have taken place from the early nineteenth century. In these early years, Tenby was a highly fashionable watering place. The coming of the railways in the 1860s widened the social profile of its clientele, though up

[2] The research on Tenby was undertaken as part of a project on 'Resorts and Ports: Swansea, Tenby and Aberystwyth, 1750–1914', funded by the Board of Celtic Studies. I should like to thank the Board; my co-directors of the project Louise Miskell and Owen Roberts; and Kate Sullivan, the research assistant on the project, who undertook bibliographic work and collected primary material. I am grateful for the considerable assistance I have received from the staff of the National Library of Wales, and from Mark Lewis, collection manager, and Sue Baldwin, the honorary librarian, at Tenby Museum, and for permission from the Museum to reproduce Figures 4, 5, 7, 10, 11 and 12.

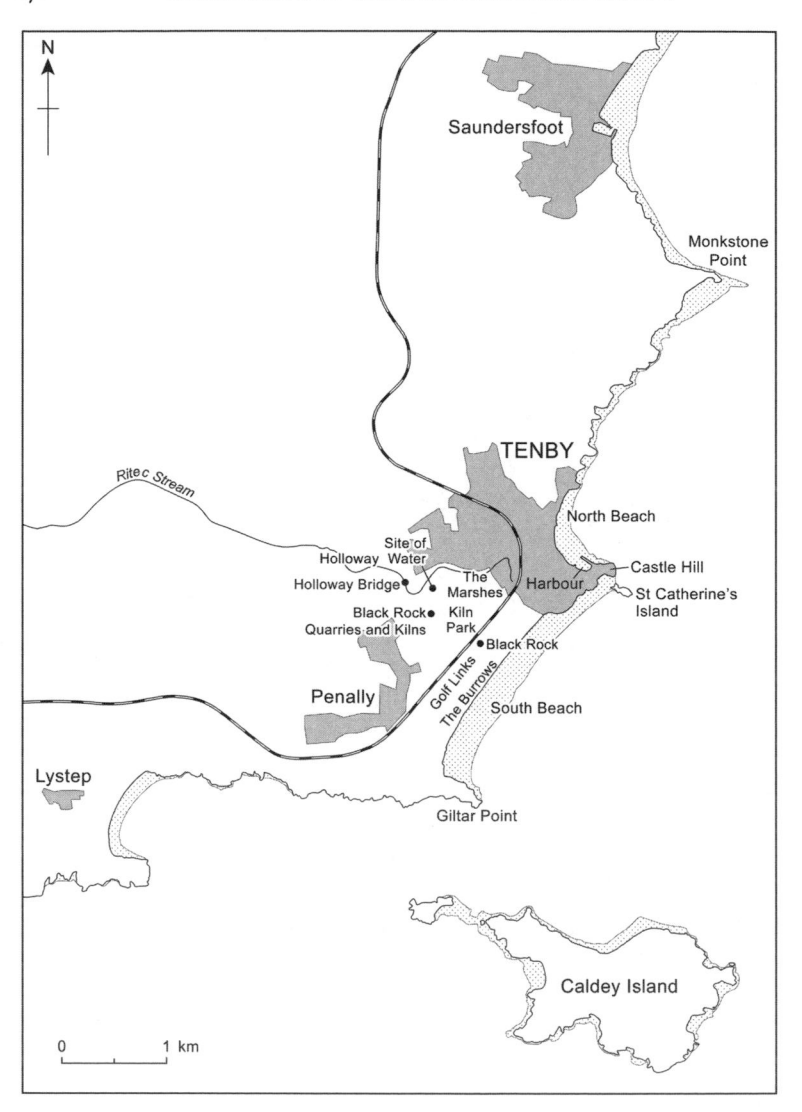

Figure 3 Map of Tenby and surrounding area, 2010 (Peter Borsay and Antony Smith)

until the First World War it continued to sell itself as an exclusive resort and service what was probably a predominantly middle-class clientele.[3]

Tourism, the seaside and the tourist gaze

Though it may now seem over-dramatic to talk, as some historians have, of the 'birth of a consumer society', and of a 'consumer revolution' in eighteenth-century Britain[4] – ignoring important elements of economic change in the medieval and early modern eras – it is clear that the period witnessed a gear change in the nature of the consumer economy. Maxine Berg has referred to a 'reconfiguration of consumption from needs to desires', and of a 'product revolution', in which the objects of consumption were 'the material products of enlightenment and modernity, of fashion and global commerce'.[5] What characterised these new products was the balance of their cultural as opposed to their utilitarian content. Most of their value derived not so much from what they did in practical terms as from their psychological impact in delivering culturally mediated experiences; for example, aesthetic goods like politeness and beauty, or social goods like fashion and status. Growing personal disposable income was the engine driving change. It was this that provided the surplus wealth that could be invested in luxury and semi-luxury products. One social group particularly identified with the expansion in disposable income is the burgeoning middling order, who, as John Styles has argued, 'shared an aspiration to a genteel way of life that found much of its expression in owning, using and displaying the right goods. It was they, above all, who sustained that growing multitude of manufactures producing the high design objects that comprised the essential props of gentility.'[6] In this new world of goods, historians have tended to place the emphasis upon items of material culture such as fine chinaware, metalwork, furniture and dress. However, non-material forms of cultural expression were just as much economic products and objects of luxury expenditure as material goods. In particular, high-status commercialised leisure – which often provided the context in which luxury materials goods could be displayed – was expanding rapidly in the eighteenth century, with the growth of assemblies, theatre, concerts, book shops, clubs and various sports. Much of this was based in towns, and the century also witnessed

---

[3] J. Tipton, *Fair and Fashionable Tenby: Two Hundred Years as a Seaside Resort* (Tenby, 1987); P. Borsay, 'From Port to Resort: Tenby and Narratives of Transition, 1760–1914', in *Resorts and Ports: European Seaside Towns since 1700*, ed. P. Borsay and J. K. Walton (Bristol, 2011), 86–95.

[4] N. McKendrick, J. Brewer and J. H. Plumb, *The Birth of a Consumer Society: The Commercialization of Eighteenth-Century England* (1983).

[5] M. Berg, *Luxury and Pleasure in Eighteenth-Century Britain* (Oxford, 2007), 6, 11.

[6] M. Snodin and J. Styles, *Design and the Decorative Arts: Georgian Britain 1714–1837* (2004), 32.

the rise and development of a category of urban settlements – spas and seaside resorts – specialising in the provision of leisure and health.[7]

The modern spa, offering commercialised medical water treatment to well-off society, first emerged in Britain in the later Tudor and early Stuart period. Growth would seem to have halted during the Civil War years, before the later seventeenth and early eighteenth centuries see the proliferation of new springs and consolidation of existing ones. Health remained an important function of these settlements but it became clear that the provision of leisure services was an increasingly important part of their business. It was during this period that Bath and Tunbridge Wells developed into the principal fashionable resorts in Britain.[8] The leading spa in the north of England was Scarborough. There, the spa house was located on the beach beneath the cliffs. At some point – certainly by 1735 when John Setterington's 'Perspective Draught of the Ancient Town, Castle, Harbour and Spaw of Scarborough' shows naked swimmers and a bathing machine adjacent to the spa – the town also became home to sea bathing.[9] This heralded the emergence of a new and highly innovative form of watering place, with no real historical precedent, the seaside resort. Despite Scarborough's early incursion into the field the first concentration of resorts developed in the south-east, particularly on the Sussex and Kent coasts, responding to the market demand generated by London, a metropolis of half a million people by 1700, and almost a million by 1800. During the later eighteenth and early nineteenth centuries, the net began to spread much wider, embracing the coasts of the south-west of England, Wales and East Anglia.[10]

Many of these later resorts were located in remote parts of the coastline, requiring an extensive journey to access them for visitors coming from the populous London, south-east and midlands of England. It was not uncommon to incorporate resorts in the itineraries of those undertaking tours around Britain. Recreational travel or tourism developed on a significant scale from the later seventeenth century. The most prestigious and expensive form of this was the Grand Tour, involving an extended

---

[7] P. Borsay, *The English Urban Renaissance: Culture and Society in the Provincial Town, 1660–1770* (Oxford, 1989).

[8] P. Hembry, *The English Spa, 1560–1815: A Social History* (1990).

[9] A. Brodie, 'Scarborough in the 1730s – Spa, Sea and Sex', *Journal of Tourism History*, 4 (2012), 125–53.

[10] J. K. Walton, *The English Seaside Resort: A Social History 1750–1914* (Leicester, 1983); J. F. Travis, *The Rise of the Devon Seaside Resorts 1750–1900* (Exeter, 1993); A. Brodie and G. Winter, *England's Seaside Resorts* (Swindon, 2007); P. Borsay, 'Health and Leisure Resorts 1700–1840', in *The Cambridge Urban History of Britain*, II: *1540–1840*, ed. P. Clark (Cambridge, 2000), 775–803; P. Borsay, 'Le développement des villes balnéaires dans l'Angleterre géorgienne', in *Les villes Balnéaires d'Europe occidentale du XVIIIe siècle à nos jours*, ed. Y. Perret-Gentil, A. Lottin and J.-P. Poussin (Paris, 2008), 13–34.

visit to continental Europe, with key destinations Paris and Rome, and by the later eighteenth century a route which incorporated the Alps. Less investigated by historians, but widely undertaken by the better off, was the British tour. This was not just a scaled-down, less-expensive and less time-consuming version of the European tour. Getting to know the various parts of Britain was considered an important part of the education of elite men and women, and travellers were expected to keep an account of what they observed. This helped structure perceptions in a way that influenced observations at the time and later in a process that stimulated and cumulatively refined the mind of the observer.[11]

The personal diaries composed during these tours were sometimes accompanied by drawings, and, together with the growing guide literature to service the market in travel, are among the earliest manifestation of what John Urry has called the 'tourist gaze', a way of looking

> directed to features of landscape and townscape which separate them off from everyday experience . . . [there is] a much greater sensitivity to visual elements . . . than is normally found in everyday life. People linger over such a gaze which is then normally visually objectified or captured through postcards, films, models and so on. These enable the gaze to be endlessly reproduced and recaptured.[12]

Visualisation is at the core of this experience and seaside resorts were saturated with visually stimulating phenomena. Two types of visualisation are at work here: environmental and social. Resorts encouraged an acute engagement with the natural and built environment through consumption of 'views' of sea, beach, sky, cliffs, rocks, greenery, boats, piers, pavilions, hotels and such like. Resorts also developed rich audience-orientated entertainments, such as beach theatre and shows. But visitors themselves were also part of the social theatre, engaging in intensive observation of each other and themselves – what Peter De Bola writing about the clientele of Vauxhall Gardens has called 'autovoyeurism' – in a context that encouraged high levels of personal and group performance and display.[13]

The tourist gaze, in its environmental or social form, was at the heart of resort life, and developed as an economic good in its own right. The seaside view had a value and was as much a part of the consumer revolution as material goods. It also spawned an expanding visual culture of drawings, paintings and photographs that was fundamental to the process of visualisation.

---

[11] E. Moir, *The Discovery of Britain: The English Tourists 1540–1840* (1964); I. Ousby, *The Englishman's England: Taste, Travel and the Rise of Tourism* (Cambridge, 1990).

[12] J. Urry, *The Tourist Gaze: Leisure and Travel in Contemporary Societies* (1990), 3.

[13] P. De Bola, *Painting, Landscape and Architecture in Eighteenth-Century Britain* (Stanford, 2003), 79.

The seaside and the visual

Visual culture, the creation and consumption of representations of people and landscape, underwent major changes during the course of the eighteenth and nineteenth centuries that impacted on the process of visualisation itself. First, there was an aesthetic shift towards the incorporation, alongside portraiture and history painting, of landscape, topography and natural forms, and with it the picturesque and sublime, into the body of high-status art. It was a process reflected in the kudos attached to the works of the seventeenth-century French artist Claude Lorraine, in the growing importance of landscape elements in the work of native painters like Richard Wilson, John Constable and Joseph Mallord William Turner and in the rise of landscape gardening as a form of art. Second, there was the development of illustrative material which focused on social and political observation and commentary, sometimes deploying humour and techniques not associated with 'high' art, reflected in the satirical work of figures like William Hogarth and Thomas Rowlandson, and later in *Punch* cartoons and in postcards. Third, there was the accelerating technological developments in printmaking, the so-called 'industrialisation of art', which meant that visual images could be reproduced many times, individually and in books and magazines, permitting competitive pricing and widespread dissemination both socially and geographically. Fourth, there was the introduction of photography from the 1840s, and roll film and 'pocket' cameras from the 1880s, with the potential this provided for the accurate, instantaneously produced, endlessly reproduced images by professionals and amateurs.[14]

These developments in the forms and commodification of visual culture ran parallel with the rise and maturation of the seaside resort. Indeed, the two fed off each other. With the new significance given to 'nature', the sea and coastline – which previously had been perceived in negative terms, a dangerous place only to be visited out of economic necessity, a location to avoid rather than seek out – provided artists with a huge, largely unexplored, and inherently dramatic landscape resource to investigate the picturesque and sublime.[15] At the same time the beach and promenade also offered rich pickings for artists engaged in depicting humans and their social interaction. The result was, as Christiana Payne has shown, a

[14] These developments can be traced in *The History of British Art 1600–1780*, ed. D. Bindman (2008); M. Rosenthal, *British Landscape Painting* (1982); T. Williamson, *Polite Landscapes: Gardens and Society in Eighteenth-Century England* (Stroud, 1995); R. T. Godfrey, *Printmaking in Britain: A General History from its Beginnings to the Present Day* (Oxford, 1978); H. and A. Gernsheim, *A Concise History of Photography* (1971); G. Clarke, *The Photograph* (Oxford, 1997).

[15] A. Corbin, *The Lure of the Sea: The Discovery of the Seaside in the Western World* (Cambridge, 1994).

surge of interest in painting sea and coastline. Resorts and their vicinities became an important focus of attention for major and minor artists, many of whom specialised in coastal views and visited particular resorts on a regular basis to gather material to supply a growing market.[16] Some artists resided (permanently or for a portion of each year) in popular resorts to service this market, such as Anthony Vandyke Copley Fielding (1787–1855), Richard Henry Nibbs (1816–93), W. J. Leathem (*fl.*1840–55) and W. E. Bates (1812–72) in Brighton and Hove.[17] As early as 1800, it could be claimed that 'what gives the schools, at Brighton, a decided advantage, is, the number of capital masters in music, drawing, painting, dancing, &c. &c. who are settled in the town'.[18] By the later part of the nineteenth century, artists' colonies were emerging in some of the smaller, remoter and more 'untouched' coastal settlements, such as Walberswick in Suffolk and Newlyn and St Ives in Cornwall.[19] Accessing the paintings to view and/or purchase was important if the new visual culture was to impact on visitors' sensibilities. Many resorts contained stationers and booksellers where paintings and prints could be purchased.[20] In about 1800, the London printseller John Wallis sent his son to the up-and-coming exclusive resort of Sidmouth in South Devon to open a sea-front shop selling topographical material.[21] In 1851, a group of Brighton artists formed the Brighton and Hove Fine Art Society, and used space in the Royal Pavilion (acquired by the Brighton town commissioners from the crown estate in the previous year for £53,000) to mount an annual exhibition. Money from the entrance fee was directed to purchase paintings by local artists, including Nibbs and Leathem, which were used to form the basis of a permanent town collection. Additional display space was provided in 1873, when a new Museum, Art Gallery and Library was opened in the converted Dome (former royal stables, also acquired from the crown estate), which contained one of the first purpose-built municipal picture galleries in the country. Within the first decade it attracted 800,000 visitors.[22]

---

[16] C. Payne, *Where the Sea Meets the Land: Artists on the Coast in Nineteenth-Century Britain* (Bristol, 2007); D. B. Brown, S. Skinner and I. Warrell, *Coasting: Turner and Bonnington on the Shores of the Channel* (Nottingham, 2008).

[17] C. Hemming, *British Painters of the Coast and Sea: A History and Gazetteer* (1988), 109–11.

[18] F. G. Fisher, *Brighton New Guide: Or, a Description of Brighthlemston, and the Adjacent Country,* 4th edn ([1800]), 37.

[19] J. Mattingly, *Cornwall and the Coast: Mousehole and Newlyn* (Chichester, 2009), 133–46; D. Tovey, *St Ives Art Pre-1890* (Tewkesbury, 2008); T. Cross, *The Shining Sands: Artists in Newlyn and St Ives 1880–1930* (Tiverton, 1999).

[20] S. Berry, *Georgian Brighton* (Chichester, 2005), 140.

[21] G. Holmes, *Sidmouth: A History* (Sidmouth, 1987), 50–1.

[22] www.bbc.co.uk/arts/yourpaintings/galleries/collections/brighton-and-hove-museums-and-art-galleries-166/foreword (last accessed 1 June 2013); N. Antram and

Figure 4 (Colour online) Tenby harbour showing studio (centre) of Charles Smith Allen, cantilevered off the upper floor of the Bath House (Tenby Museum)

Photography was custom built to meet the needs of resorts and their clientele. In the period before the First World War, eight different professional photographers have been identified operating out of permanent or seasonal studios in Tenby. This excludes individual peripatetic photographers and large-scale businesses like that of Francis Frith making an occasional visit to collect material. The most important early resident practitioner in Tenby was Charles Smith Allen (1831–97), a native of Rugely in Staffordshire attracted, like several of the town's photographers, by the business opportunities (see Figure 4).[23] As with Tenby, Worthing and its local area supported a corpus of professional photographers, who from the 1870s were producing single view *cartes de visite*, albums and stereoscopic cards of the resort. In neighbouring Brighton everything would have been on a grander scale; a directory of 1886 lists thirty-two photographers working in the town.[24] Photography,

R. Morrice, *Brighton and Hove* (New Haven and London, 2008), 44–7; J. G. Bishop, *The Brighton Pavilion and Its Royal Associations*, 5th edn (Brighton, 1884), 95–102, 116–17, 131–9.

[23] *Tenby in Camera: A History of Photography and Tenby Photographers* (Tenby, 2002), 1–11.

[24] G. Godden, *Collecting Picture Postcards* (Chichester, 1996), 14–20; *Robinson's Popular Brighton Directory* (Brighton, 1886), 500.

once cards without the pre-paid printed stamp (1894), of a larger size (1899) and with full-sided images (1902) were permitted, greatly added to the appeal of the postcard. Its 'golden age' has been dated 1902–18 and it became the form of resort communication *par excellence*, with its ideal combination of the visual image and brief textual message.[25] Not that the photographic in any way forced out the handcrafted image on cards, with the prolific Alfred Quinton (1853–1934) producing his popular picturesque views, primarily for the Kent firm of J. R. Salmon, and the rise of the comic seaside postcard.[26] Photography also widened the range of options in guide literature, which by the late nineteenth century was expanding enormously, both in terms of volume and variety. Illustrative material had of course long been included in topographical works. This is a reminder both of the fact that written text was frequently used to create visual images for readers, and therefore was critical to the visualisation process, and of the way visual images regularly interacted with printed text in a way which modified the meaning of both.

Environmental visualisation

Visitors went to the seaside to immerse themselves in the environment. They could do this by physical activities, such as bathing and walking, but above all engagement with the environment was a visual exercise. The grandest form of this was the panoramic view, such as that described by the Halls, with its elevated perspective, broad sweep, carefully modulated sense of foreground and background and rich mixture of elements. For those visiting Tenby, this began with their first sight of the town and its setting, a rite of passage, primed by the guidebooks, engendering a frisson of excitement as travellers were made aware that they had entered a visually rich space in which they expected to be stimulated by, and for their part to be highly receptive to, the scenes before them. Philip Gosse recorded how in 1854 'our eyes were enchanted by the noble view that ... burst upon us, of the harbour of Tenby, the Bay of Caermarthen, and the North Cliffe', echoing the sentiments of a tourist of almost a century earlier who commended how 'on the rising of a Hill, the Prospect of the Channel opens ... very Beautifull, the worms head on one side, a most bold headland, & the Rocks off Tenby with Caldy Island make Carmarthen or Burrey Bay'.[27] What added to the impact of the prospect on approaching the town was the contrast with the countryside on the

[25] E. J. Evans and J. Richards, *A Social History of Britain in Postcards 1870–1930* (1980), 1–5, 125–46.

[26] C. W. Hill, *Picture Postcards* (Princes Risborough, 1987), 4–14; Godden, *Collecting Picture Postcards*.

[27] P. H. Gosse, *Tenby: A Seaside Holiday* (1856), 9; National Library of Wales (NLW) MS 147C (Journal of a tour in Wales, 1767–8), fo. 27.

road from Carmarthen, described as 'very ugly', 'none of its striking bold features', the 'whole road is uninteresting'.[28] In the 1830s, Charles Norris complained that the recently constructed new road into Tenby, 'excavated at enormous expense', failed to afford 'the traveller a single glimpse of the fine expanse of Carmarthen Bay, the rocky promontories ... and beautiful crescent-like swell of the Peninsular of Tenby ... this ill-contrived approach exhibits it as a town of very common place pretensions'.[29] His anxieties were unfounded, as later accounts of those entering the town demonstrate, but his comments show how important the first sighting of the town was felt to be in setting up expectations.

Once settled in the town the visitor could enjoy the spectacular views from the elevated natural platform on which Tenby sat, instructed by one of the many accounts in the guide literature. Early on, Gosse provides extensive panoramic descriptions from the garden of his lodgings overlooking Castle Beach, and from the summit of the adjacent St Catherine's Island; later, he adds an account of the view from the Croft and North Cliff.[30] The early panoramas share some of the elements of the Halls' account of six years later, taken from a similar location. This reflects a process by which certain views and viewpoints, by repetition in the guide literature and visual representations, become iconicised. The more a particular view is described, celebrated and circulated, the more embedded it becomes in the visual imagination of the resort and its visitors. Fred Gray has argued that 'postcards were particularly significant in establishing and developing the image of a place, helping determine the essential resort sites and sights'.[31] Gosse's later panorama parallels a series of paintings of the view of the town from North Cliff, beginning with W. Golding's oil of 1799 (see Figure 5), followed by J. Storer's view of 1810, Edmund 'Waterfall' (so-called because of his fondness for depicting water features) Gill's oil of 1843 and A. R. Quinton's postcard illustration of the early twentieth century.

Alongside the panoramic perspective are accounts of particular landscape elements such as rocks, cliffs, caverns, trees and of course the sea. Some of these descriptions adopt a language imbued with drama. Later eighteenth-century accounts of Tenby refer to the 'caverns of immense magnitude' at the bottom of the Castle Hill, and the 'large dens or fissures ... made in many places [in St Catherine's rock] by the persevering percussion of the Ocean'.[32] Gosse's detailed depictions of

---

[28] NLW MS 147C, fo. 27; NLW Deposits 6685C (Journal of a tour in Wales, 1831), fo. 25.

[29] NLW MS 1347B (Letter addressed by Charles Norris to the burgesses and inhabitants of Tenby, 9 July 1831), fo. 75.

[30] Gosse, *Tenby*, 12–16, 289–91.

[31] F. Gray, *Designing the Seaside: Architecture, Society and Nature* (2006), 85.

[32] 'Tour through South Wales and Some of the Adjacent English Counties', in *The British Tourist's Companion, or Traveller's Pocket Companion*, V, ed. W. Mavor (1798), 155; NLW, Deposits

Figure 5 (Colour online) Tenby from the North Cliff, W. Golding, oil painting, 1799 (Tenby Museum)

the cliff formations at Monkstone Point and especially Giltar Point – 'a truly magnificent precipice of grey limestone nearly two hundred feet high, with the strata perpendicular' – echo those of travellers to many resorts, particularly ones located on rocky coastlines, such as Lynton and Ilfracombe, the latter presenting to the Rev John Swete in 1789 'a scene extremely romantic, of wild mishapen rocks, towering to the skies'.[33]

Gosse draws explicit parallels between the natural landscape at Giltar and Lydstep and the medieval abbey and castle that he had recently been visiting at Lamphey and Pembroke; 'the stratification is absolutely perpendicular ... taking the appearance at every turn of enormous towers, castles and abbeys ... Probably the associations of yesterday's excursion had something to do with all this ... but how grander was the masonry of nature than anything we saw yesterday!'[34] The perception of a resort would be filtered through a single visual imagination, in which human and natural forms would be fused together, even if the latter was taken to have priority. Undoubtedly one of Tenby's primary assets, though in other respects this might be seen as a distinct disadvantage, was its

18943B (Narrative of a tour through Wales by an anonymous English gentleman, late eighteenth/early nineteenth centuries), fo. 20.

[33] Gosse, *Tenby*, 50, 123–9; P. J. Hunt, *Devon's Age of Elegance* ([Exeter], 1984), 24.

[34] Gosse, *Tenby*, 126–7.

rich and decaying historic fabric, which included a castle and extensive fortifications, evocatively depicted in Charles Norris's *Etchings of Tenby* (1812). All three of Wales's earliest resorts, Aberystwyth, Swansea and Tenby, were medieval towns and possessed ruinated castles that appealed to the gothic taste of visitors. Many resorts contained, within their boundaries or immediate vicinities, a built heritage to whose presence and appearance tourists could be alerted. The *Pictorial Guide to Yarmouth* (1860) drew attention to the considerable surviving pieces of the medieval fortifications and religious fabric, while in 1850 it was claimed of Whitby that 'irregular terraces . . . give to this part [the east side] of the town, an exceedingly romantic appearance . . . the effect being further increased by the venerable church of St. Mary and the time worn ruins of the Abbey, which crown the summit'.[35] However, it would be wrong to give the impression that visualising the built human environment was simply about antiquities. Modernity was also celebrated, in guides and postcards, with good reason since resorts were important sites of architectural innovation and cutting-edge engineering in areas such as church building, residential terraces, sea defences, promenades, piers, hotels and winter gardens. Moreover, during the interwar years, the seaside became an important site of modernist architecture, literature and art.[36]

Resorts had long been receptive to new tastes and fashions. Much of this goes back to the invention of the picturesque in the eighteenth century. For our purposes, the key figure is William Gilpin, and the location not the sea but the limestone gorge of the lower Wye Valley. Gilpin was not the inventor of the idea of the picturesque, whose origins date back at least to the early eighteenth century and the development of landscape gardening in Britain.[37] However, his *Observation on the River Wye*, compiled during a tour in 1770 but not published until 1783 – it had gone into five editions before 1800, and spawned a glut of similar guides – was to prove critical in codifying and popularising the idea.[38] He opens his text by claiming that 'the following little work proposes a new object of pursuit; that of examining the face of a country *by the rules of picturesque beauty* . . . not the offspring of theory, but . . . taken immediately from the scenes of nature as they arise'. In non-emotive practical language, he described how 'the most perfect river-views . . . are composed of four grand parts: the

[35] *Pictorial Guide to Yarmouth*, 9th edn (Great Yarmouth, [1860]), 22–7, 45–54, 114–22; *The Guide to Whitby and the Neighbourhood* (Whitby, 1850), 3.

[36] *Modernism on Sea: Art and Culture at the British Seaside*, ed. L. Feigel and A. Harris (Witney, 2009).

[37] J. D. Hunt, *The Picturesque Garden in Europe* (2002), 1–89; M. Andrews, *The Search for the Picturesque: Landscape Aesthetics and Tourism in Britain, 1700–1800* (Aldershot, 1989).

[38] *An Oxford Companion to the Romantic Age: British Culture 1776–1832*, ed. I. McCalman (Oxford, 2001), 523–4; J. Mitchell, *The Wye Tour and its Artists* (Woonton Almeley, 2010), 1–40.

area, which is the river itself; the two *side-screens*, which are the opposite banks, and lead the perspective; and the *front-screen*, which points out the winding of the river'. He goes on to describe how variation is built into this framework, in particular by the introduction of 'ornaments', which he lists under four heads '*ground, wood, rocks,* and *buildings*', each of which he describes in detail.[39] Gilpin provided the ordinary tourist, not steeped in high theory and possessing limited technical abilities, with a toolkit for how to observe the environment and, for those so inclined, to capture a representation of it. It was this approach, transferred to the highly receptive environment of the sea shore, which underpinned the construction and commodification of the coastal 'view'. Significantly, Gosse, on his rail journey to Tenby in the 1860s, observed from his carriage window 'the rocky cliffs of Chepstow; the grand isolated masses which rise from the edge of the rails, alternately hiding and revealing the picturesque Wye'.[40] Accounts of seaside views in diaries and guidebooks are peppered with references to the 'picturesque' and allied aesthetic sentiments such as the 'romantic' and the 'sublime'. Tenby was declared a 'situation . . . more romantic and interesting that that of either Aberystwid or Swansea' (1803), said to contain 'fragments of singular and most picturesque architecture' (1832) and to be a place where 'picturesque rocks fringed the bay on either side' (1863).[41] In a similar vein, the 'view' from the Cobb at Lyme Regis was said to be 'uncommonly fine and romantic . . . The whole of this scenery was an intermixture of the Picturesque and Romantic' (1794).[42] For some tourists, painting and drawing were holiday pastimes, but the artist's perspective was one all visitors were encouraged to adopt, as, for example, when a Tenby guide of 1863 suggested that the 'grandeur and sublimity' of the scene on a wind-swept 'walk to Proud Giltar . . . can never be forgotten, and would form a most magnificent storm subject for the canvass of Backhuysen' (the seventeenth-century Dutch marine painter).[43] Such comments were of course geared to a knowledgeable and aspiring clientele, but we should be wary of dismissing the concept and aesthetic of the 'view' as entirely an elite commodity. The notion of the picturesque might have been developed as a pastime of the well off, but the importance of pictorial views in railway posters and popular

[39] W. Gilpin, *Observations on the River Wye, and Several Parts of South Wales, &c. Relative Chiefly to Picturesque Beauty*, intro. R. Humphreys (2005), 17, 25–6.

[40] Gosse, *Tenby*, 3. The Severn Tunnel was opened in 1886, obviating the need to travel along the Wye valley to access South Wales.

[41] B. H. Malkin, *The Scenery, Biography and Antiquities of South Wales* (1807), 535; NLW MS 1347B, fo. 75; W. Freeman, *My Summer Holiday: Being a Tourist's Jottings about Tenby* (1863), 12–17.

[42] Hunt, *Devon's Age of Elegance*, 42.

[43] *Allen's Guide to Tenby*, ed. F. P. Gwynne (Tenby, [c. 1868]), 124; see also B. H. Becker, *Holiday Haunts by Cliffside and Riverside* (1884), 1–2.

postcards (including many produced by artists despite the existence of photography), and the choice of groups of workers, such as those from Swindon's GWR works, of scenic if small resorts like Tenby and St Ives for their annual holiday, suggests a deeper permeation of the idea.[44]

Obtaining a view depends upon tourists accessing a viewpoint or platform from which to observe the scene before them. One characteristic of a successful resort was the possession of a landscape naturally sculpted to provide effective observation points. The situation of Tenby upon a large rock projecting into the sea, connected to which was the smaller Castle Hill from which could be obtained a 360 degree panoramic perspective, and the further presence of lofty cliffs in close proximity, gave the town considerable advantages as a location in this respect. However, what was critical in realising this natural potential was the way that Tenby and other resorts were engineered to maximise their visual assets. Traditionally, the architecture of coastal settlements had eschewed exposure to the sea, huddling in thoroughfares and narrow lanes away from the water's edge (as, for example, at Brighton), or literally turning its back on the sea (as in the waterside rows of cottages at Fowey and Appledore). The last thing on the mind of those dwelling on the coast was a room with a view. This configuration of the built environment was to be reversed with the rise of the seaside resort and the picturesque. Seafront locations were now treated as premium real estate and their role as viewing boxes exploited. Where possible the multi-dwelling multi-storey classical terrace pioneered in London, with its extensive array of perfectly proportioned windows, and the crescent developed in Bath specifically to capture views of the surrounding countryside, was imported. The 'earliest unified architectural composition among Brighton's terraces ... and the earliest demonstration of a sympathy with the sea' was the Royal Crescent (1799–1802, see Figure 6). The idea was copied by many smaller resorts like Teignmouth (Den Crescent 1826), Hayling (Norfolk Crescent c. 1825), Ilfracombe (Hillsborough Terrace c. 1835), and has its parallels in Tenby with the Croft (1830s) and Lexden Terrace (1843, see Figure 7).[45]

During the first half of the nineteenth century, Tenby's rocky circumference became lined with tall residential and hotel accommodation enjoying extensive sea views. However, the south-western portion of the promontory on which the town was situated remained largely unbuilt upon. With the arrival of the railway in the 1860s, this extensive area was opened up for development, its premier feature

[44] B. Cole and R. Durack, *Railway Posters 1923–1947* (1992); R. Matheson, *Trip: The Annual Holiday of GWR's Swindon Workers* (Stroud, 2006), 48–70.

[45] Antram and Morrice, *Brighton and Hove*, 132–3; B. Cherry and N. Pevsner, *Devon*, 2nd edn (1989), 505–6, 799; T. Lloyd, J. Orbach and R. Scourfield, *Pembrokeshire* (New Haven and London, 2004), 480, 483.

Figure 6 (Colour online) The Royal Crescent (built 1799–1802) Brighton, 2012 (Peter Borsay)

Figure 7 (Colour online) South Sands, Tenby, from St Catherine's Island. Lexden Terrace is far right, Belmont Tower far left (Tenby Museum)

Figure 8 (Colour online) The Esplanade, Tenby, 2010 (Peter Borsay)

being the Esplanade (see Figure 8), a promenade with tall lodging houses and hotels, and a spectacular prospect across to Caldey Island, Giltar Point and beyond. The value of a room with a view was well understood by developers, proprietors and visitors. When the new project was being considered, one guidebook could write of 'magnificent sites for building purposes along the South Cliff [which] might be profitably converted into terraces of stately residence ... this beautiful spot ... having a sea view of unsurpassed extent and beauty'.[46] Building to capture a view was very much in the mind of John Nash and his client Sir Uvedale Price, like Gilpin one of the key oracles of the picturesque movement, when they built the triangular Castle House (1791–4) perched on the foreshore at Aberystwyth, with one room skewed to catch a view of the dramatic rocky prominence of Constitution Hill and the coast beyond.[47] Less exalted holidaymakers were equally conscious that part of what they were purchasing when choosing a place of residence was the prospect from their window. The adverts for seaside hotels that sandwich the text in many guides are replete with references to sea views; for example one

---

[46] *Allen's Guide to Tenby*, p. 12; Brodie and Winter, *England's Seaside Resorts*, 16–19, 68–78.
[47] T. Lloyd, J. Orbach and R. Scourfield, *Carmarthenshire and Ceredigion* (New Haven and London, 2006), 412.

guide of 1896 contained notices for the Barmouth Hotel, 'most pleasantly situated overlooking the Estuary of the Mawddach . . . [which] commands extensive views of the far-famed Cader Range', the Royal Castle, Lynton, which 'commands uninterrupted views of the Valleys of the East and West Lynn, the Welsh Coast, and the far-famed Valley of Rocks', the Ilfracombe Hotel, 'the PRINCIPAL and ONLY HOTEL facing the sea' and Skelmerdale House, Folkestone, 'ABSOLUTELY facing the sea'.[48] One guest of the White Lion Hotel in Tenby in 1831 observed that 'we have a sea view, which none of the Coburg [*sic*] rooms enjoy, or at least if at all but a slight peep', which sits oddly with a nineteenth-century trade card for the Cobourg which 'humbly solicits and hopes that from the Sea Prospects it commands . . . it will merit a continuance of public support'.[49] *Caveat Emptor*!

Engineering a resort to deliver views went beyond provision of residential accommodation. The Croft and the Esplanade at Tenby were also public promenades. The genesis of this type of space can be found in the fashionable walks constructed in spas and county towns from the seventeenth century, where even from this early stage a prospect of the countryside was considered an important asset.[50] When compared with inland watering places, resorts started with some considerable advantages. There was the presence of the beach as a walking area, and of structures, such as quays, jetties, piers and sea defences, which though built to protect the town and service its commerce, were also excellent vantage points, adjacent to or projecting into the sea, which could easily be appropriated and adapted to the purposes of polite perambulation. The sinuous Cobb at Lyme Regis is among the most celebrated examples, not least because of its appearance as a promenade in Jane Austen's *Persuasion* (1818), but it was commonplace for resorts to integrate structures of this type into the leisure facilities available. At Tenby, the earliest bath house of the 1780s was located in a converted chapel on the stone pier which formed part of the harbour, while the elegant new bath house of 1810 lay close by, and included 'bed-rooms . . . for invalids and a handsome Coffee-room . . . commanding a delightful view of the harbour, shipping, &c.' (see Figure 9).[51] In 1834, it was claimed that 'the Cobb [at Lyme], as a promenade, is allowed to be unrivalled, excepting by the chain-pier at Brighton'. Piers, plunging deep into the sea, came to characterise the viewing potential of seaside architecture, and their numbers proliferated as they became a hallmark building for any aspiring resort.[52] Tenby never

[48] *Black's Guide to South Wales*, 9th edn (1896), adverts, 9, 36, 45, 67.
[49] NLW, Deposits 6685C, fo. 25; Tenby Museum (TM), TD/Hotels and Tourism.
[50] Borsay, *English Urban Renaissance*, 162–72, 350–4.
[51] TM, TEM/SE/36–36b, indenture 1782 between mayor etc. of Tenby and John Jones; *Carmarthen Journal*, 28 July 1810.
[52] G. Roberts, *The History and Antiquities of the Borough of Lyme Regis and Charmouth* (1834), 246; K. Lindley, *Seaside Architecture* (1973), 33–56.

Figure 9 (Colour online) The Bath House (1810), Tenby, 2010 (Peter Borsay)

quite made a full-blown pier, though there were plans in the 1890s to build one which got as far as a prospectus, conjectural drawing and the claim that 'the pier thus built out from a promontory between two beautiful Bays, cannot fail to become a popular Promenade from which the most charming views of any coast scenery in the United Kingdom will be obtained.' In the end the town had to settle for a much less impressive pier-cum-landing-stage (the Royal Victoria Pier), first opened in 1897 (see Figure 10), which nonetheless proved a popular location for fishing and a measure of promenading.[53] Both the built and conjectural piers projected from the Castle Hill (see Figure 11), described in 1864 as

> a bold promontory of rock ... surrounded by the sea at high water, with the exception of a narrow neck by which it is connected with the mainland. Its grassy slopes, well kept pathways, and seats for the accommodation of visitors, together with the picturesque ruins of the summit, and rugged cliffs at its base, unite their attractions to form a promenade which we are not aware any other watering-place excels.

---

[53] NLW, MS 4821, Prospectus for Tenby Pier and Promenade Ltd; Tipton, *Fair and Fashionable Tenby*, 33–4; TM, N42, book of newspaper cuttings *c.* 1892–1902.

Figure 10 (Colour online) The opening of Royal Victoria Pier in 1897, Tenby (Tenby Museum)

Figure 11 (Colour online) Castle Hill, Tenby, before the construction of Jubilee Bandstand in 1897 (Tenby Museum)

In 1908, it was considered the 'favourite promenade' of Tenby, enabling 'visitors to combine sea breezes and a fine seascape to perfection'.[54] On a clear day, it is possible from the walks on Castle Hill to catch a sight, across the Bristol Channel, of the lofty cliffs of the North Devon coast. Cut precipitously into one of these as early as 1817 was the vertiginous North Walk, 'considered one of finest cliff walks in England'. This connected Lynton to the primeval looking Valley of Rocks, guarded over by Castle Rock, 'which rears its perpendicular peak hundreds of feet above the blue waters of the Bristol Channel, the view from the summit being magnificent'. Fortunately for visitors, 'steps of rock cut in a winding path make it easily accessible'.[55] Landscaping natural features in this way to provide a viewing platform was part and parcel of resort engineering, as was the provision of sea front promenades (frequently as part of a wider project of sea defences), costly and controversial as this may be with curmudgeonly rate payers.[56] Promenades and piers, and the views which they shaped, were simply an essential part of a resort's infrastructure.

Social visualisation

Promenades were of course about more than just viewing the natural landscape; they were also – and for many holiday makers this may be as if not more important than the wonders of nature – for ogling each other. Social visualisation, though less explicitly addressed than environmental visualisation in the guide literature, was just as structured and rule-driven. Much of the coding and practice here was formulated on the promenades of later Stuart and Georgian towns, which were constructed as spaces of intensive display and observation.[57] The purpose of these walks was to provide highly public spaces in which to show off, social network, acquire status and pursue sexual and marital partners. There is little reason to believe that the Victorian seaside promenades served fundamentally different functions, though patterns of behaviour and observation would have been modified to meet the practices and aspirations of the widening class profile of visitors. One space which had no direct antecedent in the Georgian spa was the beach. Judging by visual and written accounts, a more informal regime may have operated and have been one of the

---

[54] *A Guide to Tenby and Its Neighbourhood*, ed. R. Mason, 5th edn (1864), 29; *South Wales and Wye District of Monmouthshire* (1908), p. 142.

[55] *Seaside Watering Places* (1900–1), 350; W. H. Turner, *Picnic: An Illustrated Guide to Ilfracombe and North Devon* (Bristol, 1890), 76; P. Keane and B. Pearce, *Valley of Rocks Lynton* (Oxford, 1993), 13.

[56] Walton, *English Seaside Resort*, 117, 129–30, 139–41, 146–7, 152, 154.

[57] P. Borsay, 'Walks and Promenades in London and Provincial England in the Long Eighteenth Century', in *La promenade au tournant des XVIIIe et XIXe siècles (Belgique-France-Anglettere)*, ed. C. Loir and L. Turcot (Brussels, 2011), 79–95.

attractions of the seaside resort over the spa. The Halls' account of the beach at Tenby, occupied by 'troops of laughing children, tripping ladies . . . and gentlemen with telescopes', or Gosse's description of the way the 'sands are seen to advantage. The gay dresses and many-hued parasols of the ladies are dotting them over by scores; little boys and girls are scampering hither and thither, picking up shells and sea-weeds, throwing pebbles into the sea', suggests something more relaxed, both in terms of behaviour and visualisation, than the promenade.[58] The 'phenomenal success' of William Powell Frith's almost anarchic depiction of Ramsgate Sands (1854) points to the extent to which such a perception of the beach had embedded itself in the visual imagination.[59]

It is tempting to see the beach as the carnivalesque counterpart to the orderly promenade. This was reinforced by the presence on the sands of a variety of entertainers such as *Punch and Judy* men, minstrels and pierrots. Yet ways of looking were regulated on the beach as elsewhere. Before the twentieth century and the arrival of the cult of the sun, the problem was not exposed bodies on the beach but in the water. The bathing machine, still being widely used in the early twentieth century, was invented in part to conceal female bathers from the gaze of male voyeurs. In Tenby, as in many Victorian resorts, rules existed governing bathing practices. A guide of the 1860s reported that 'bathing from the rocks or beach, instead of a machine, is not permitted during the day; persons who commit the impropriety, outrage the laws of decency, infringe the By-laws of the town, and may be punished for the offence'. Those who wished to bathe from the rocks or beach had to do so at the extremities of the town's sands, and only between 8 pm and 8 am, while 'those who prefer a deep sea swim may hire a boat for the purpose, but must, in that case, row seawards to the distance of two hundred yards from any of the promenades or beaches'.[60] Formal attempts to control visual practices seem to have been a relatively recent innovation. In 1800, it was reported in *The Observer* that 'the indecency of numerous naked men bathing in the sea close to the ladies' bathing machines, and under the windows of the principal houses at most of the watering places, has long been complained of, but in general has not been . . . redressed', and one contributor to a family diary kept of a visit to Ramsgate in 1828 recorded 'directly after breakfast we sallied down to the beach which was crowded with males & females to see one another bathe'.[61] In all likelihood, the regulations introduced simply added to the sexual frisson already surrounding the

[58] Gosse, *Tenby*, 12.

[59] Payne, *Where the Sea Meets the Land*, 86–7.

[60] *Allen's Guide to Tenby*, pp. 4–5.

[61] J. Whyman, *The Early Kentish Seaside (1736–1840): Selected Documents* (Gloucester, 1985), 183, 387.

beach and encouraged male (and female) display and voyeurism, the latter satirised – but also to a degree celebrated – in sketches by artists like Thomas Rowlandson, and in early postcards.[62] Moreover, by the early twentieth century it is clear that regulation was breaking down. In 1912, a Tenby bathing machine proprietor complained 'it is really disgraceful to see adults on the beach in an almost nude state when I am renting the machines to them at such a small cost', while five years later the deputy town clerk of Aberystwyth, in response to an enquiry from the town clerk at Tenby, admitted that 'our last Bathing Byelaws were made in 1884 and are now to a very great extent obsolete'.[63] Not that we should assume that visual practices became any less structured. Perception of the body, as much as that of the landscape, depends upon culturally determined 'criteria and conventions'.[64]

The visitors did not confine the process of social visualisation to themselves; they also drew the indigenous population into their field of vision. One tourist in the late eighteenth century recorded how in the environs of Tenby 'I embraced the opportunity . . . of mingling familiarly among the lower classes of the people; and was of course repeatedly delighted with that simplicity of manners, that happiness in poverty, which appears so conspicuously among the poor Welch people.'[65] A guide of the 1860s advocated using the newly established rail line at Tenby to take an excursion into the countryside, 'the peasantry and native are invariably civil to strangers . . . It is by such methods only that strangers meet with the peasantry whose peculiarities of dialect are correctly and amusingly noticed in Purnell's "Englishery of Pembrokeshire".'[66] The local population were being observed in much the same way as a piece of landscape or an old building, something that adds to the quaintness and pictorial quality of the scene. In 1863, one account of a holiday in Tenby refers to a shrimper, 'often a Welsh girl, with her flannel dress tucked up above her knees, wading through the flood and pushing her net before her' as 'a picturesque sight'.[67] There is evidence here of the growing Victorian interest in a mixture of rural primitivism and social realism, in which peasant workers are observed as a survival of a pre-industrial, pre-urban world. In the case of coastal settlements, the place of the peasantry

[62] Gray, *Designing the Seaside*, 147–61.

[63] TM, TEM/SE/35, letter from J. E. Rogers to the council, 22 July 1912; TEM/SE/35, letter from the deputy town clerk of Aberystwyth to G. Lort Stokes, 26 Nov. 1917.

[64] J. Berger, *Ways of Seeing* (1972), 47.

[65] W. Matthews, *The Miscellaneous Companions: Being a Shorter Tour of Observation and Sentiment through a Part of South Wales* (Bath, 1786), 186.

[66] *Allen's Guide to Tenby*, 135.

[67] Freeman, *My Summer Holiday*, p. 49.

is taken by fisherfolk.[68] The choice by a number of painters to form 'colonies' in small fishing towns and villages, such as Newlyn and St Ives, reflects these trends. The decline of the indigenous fishing fleet in Tenby in the early nineteenth century might have ruled the town out for such treatment, were it not for the fleet's revival in the later part of the century. The fishermen and their families crowded into the small cottages and narrow lanes around the harbour, and they and their boats became a favourite subject for photographers, in particular Charles Smith Allen whose studio overlooked the harbour (see Figure 4).[69] One particular subject of attention was the Llangwm fisherwoman (see Figure 12). Hailing from a small fishing village on the Daugleddau waterway inland of Milford Haven, she sold her wares in Tenby. Dressed in traditional Welsh costume, and carrying her distinctive creel of oysters, she was painted (1880) by William Powell Frith and captured by Allen and many other photographers, as well as earning a description in the guidebooks:

> The Langwm fisherwomen are natives of a village of that name … and are of a race peculiar to that place. They dredge for oysters … first tying their petticoats round their legs so as to resemble Turkish trousers, and afterwards carry the oysters in a 'creel', as shown in the illustration, to market, bringing some of them to Tenby … The Langwm people universally inter-marry, and thus the peculiarities of their race are perpetuated.[70]

This is an account shot through with ambivalence. The 'authenticity' and primitive virtues of these hard-working women are extolled. But the references to orientalism, race and inter-marriage suggest a form of social visualisation, derived from contemporary notions of imperialism and social Darwinism, that challenged the genetic credentials of the fisherwomen and their community.

Conclusion

The expansion in consumption that marked the British economy in the eighteenth and nineteenth centuries was based not only on a growth in the range and volume of material goods, but also of less tangible, experientially and culturally rich goods such as leisure and tourism. Underpinning the latter of these, and of key importance in the rise of the seaside resort, was the process of visualisation, with a transformation of what John Berger has called 'ways of seeing'.[71] The 'tourist gaze',

---

[68] L. Lambourne, *Victorian Painting* (2004), 326–47; Payne, *Where the Sea Meets the Land*, 171–99.

[69] A. H. Galvin, *Sea of Change: 19th Century Maritime Activity in S. E. Pembrokeshire* (Coventry, 2002), 53–91; Borsay, 'From Port to Resort', 97–8; R. Worsley, *Prince of Places: A Pictorial and Social History of Tenby Featuring the Work of Pioneer Photographer Charles Smith Allen* (Haverfordwest, 1979).

[70] *A Guide to Tenby and its Neighbourhood*, ed. Mason, 144.

[71] Berger, *Ways of Seeing*.

Figure 12 (Colour online) Langwm fisherwoman, photographed by Charles Allen Smith (1831–97) (Tenby Museum)

and with it the room with a view, became a commodity in its own right. Changes in material culture were of course required to facilitate alterations in perception. Visual culture had a material dimension, which underwent transformations in content and reproductive potential, and the built environment of resorts had to be 'engineered' to deliver views.

However, it is valuable, at least as a heuristic device, to recognise that the visual experience was a commodity in its own right; otherwise the holidaymaker would be content to make do with a room without a view. Two types of visual experience have been suggested in this paper, environmental and social. The one built on a surge of interest in the natural world, and on new ways of perceiving and capturing this, such as the picturesque; the other drew on continuing and changing patterns of social interaction. Throughout the paper there have been allusions to the deeper meaning and function of the visual experience at the seaside, and much more could be said about this in areas such as the gothic experience, religious sentiments, popular science, status and class relations, family life, national identities and empire. At the most basic level, it would be helpful to analyse the relationship between large-scale industrialisation and urbanisation, the rise of seaside resort, and new 'ways of seeing'. Because resorts were invariably also sites of commerce and industry, and some resorts became large towns in their own right, the relationship was far more complex and entangled than might at first seem.[72] For the purposes of this paper, however, the key point has been to establish that the visual mattered, and that a room with a view – as every hotelier understood – had a value. In 1909, the aggrieved proprietor of 4 Esplanade at Tenby complained to the council that having generously 'handed over' land in front of his property to the town, 'there are [now] 5 deck chairs placed within the limits of the land ... which I consider obstruct the view from my lower windows & I shall be much obliged if you will give orders for their removal'.[73]

[72] *Resorts and Ports*, ed. Borsay and Walton.
[73] TM, TEM/SE/35, letter from W. Warton (?) to Tenby council, ? 1909.

Transactions of the RHS 23 (2013), pp. 203–21 © Royal Historical Society 2013
doi:10.1017/S0080440113000091

SAFETY FIRST: THE SECURITY OF BRITONS IN INDIA, 1946–1947

By Ian Talbot

READ 19 OCTOBER 2012 AT THE UNIVERSITY OF SOUTHAMPTON

ABSTRACT. A month into his viceroyalty, Lord Mountbatten took time out from sounding Indian political opinion about independence to discuss the future security of British residents with his provincial governors. By this stage, the concerns stemmed from fears of a general breakdown in law and order and Hindu–Muslim conflict rather than nationalist assault. Detailed plans were developed for a sea-borne evacuation. In the event, the only Britons who were evacuated were those airlifted from Srinagar in November 1947 as they were in the path of an invasion of the disputed Kashmir territory by Pakhtun tribesmen from Pakistan. Despite numerous articles on the British departure from India and the aftermath of Partition, little has been written about either the airlift or the broader strategic planning for European evacuation. The paper will focus on this neglected corner of the history of the transfer of power. It argues that while anti-British sentiment declined from a peak around the time of the Indian National Army trials, of 1945–6, the memories of the wartime chaotic flight from Burma and Malaya and the irreparable damage this had done to British prestige in Asia coloured the safety first approach adopted in 1947.

It all ended in cheers. The British granted India independence on 15 August 1947 amidst tumultuous crowds in New Delhi.[1] The former Viceroy Mountbatten recorded that

> never (had) such crowds been seen within the memory of anyone . . . Apart from the usual cries of '*Jai Hind*' (Victory to India) and '*Mahatma Gandhi ki jai*' (Victory to Mahatma Gandhi) a surprising number shouted out 'Mountbatten ki jai' (Victory to Mountbatten) and '*Lady Mountbatten ki jai*' (Victory to Lady Mountbatten) and more than once '*Pandit Mountbatten ki jai*'.[2]

The British were similarly feted in Calcutta. James Murray who ran a family business in Old Court House Street Calcutta selling clocks, thermometers, marine and surveying instruments recalled that 'Trains

---

[1] Critics of Mountbatten have juxtaposed these scenes with the grisly murders in the Punjab at the same time. See S. Wolpert, *Shameful Flight: The Last Years of the British in India* (New York, 2006).

[2] These extracts from Mountbatten's *Report on the Last Viceroyalty* are cited in H. V. Hodson, *The Great Divide: Britain – India – Pakistan* (1969), 390–1.

were stopped at stations and everybody turned out onto the platforms. European and Indian alike, and there was hand-shaking and arms flung round our shoulders. In the streets it was the same, massive crowds everywhere and we were stopped and the same enthusiastic embracing and comments exchanged.'[3] Less than eighteen months earlier, hostile crowds in New Delhi had marred the Victory celebrations and Europeans had been the victims of random assaults.

A month into his viceroyalty, Mountbatten took time out from sounding Indian political opinion to discuss the security of British residents with his provincial governors. By this stage, the concerns stemmed from fears of a general breakdown in law and order and Hindu–Muslim conflict rather than nationalist assault. Detailed plans were developed for a sea-borne evacuation. In the event, the only Britons who were evacuated were those airlifted from Srinagar in November 1947 as they were in the path of an invasion of Pakhtun tribesmen from Pakistan. Despite the detailed examination of the British departure and its aftermath, little has been written about either the Kashmir airlift episode, or the broader strategic planning for European evacuation. The paper will focus on this neglected corner of the history of the transfer of power. Before doing so, it will briefly look at the threats to the security of Britons in 1945–6. The anxieties these aroused, however, can only be fully appreciated in the light of events in wartime Burma and Malaya, just three years earlier.

The legacy of Britain's wartime Asian imperial crisis

Until the human tragedy of the 1947 Partition of India, the mass exodus of Britons and Indians from wartime Burma was the most traumatic flight in modern South Asian history.[4] Thousands perished as they attempted to cross the rain-drenched mountain passes into Assam. In all, as many as 80,000 people may have died from malnutrition and disease.[5] The scenes at Myitkyina airport including the bundling of the portly Governor Dorman-Smith onto one of the last flights out of North Burma were as harrowing, although not as publicised, as the US Operation Frequent Wind in Saigon in April 1975. Thousands of 'women and children were stranded without food, water or medical supplies'.[6]

With the closing of the North Burma airports, the fate of refugees worsened. One British evacuee who escaped on foot across the hills

---

[3] James Murray, 'Box Wallah', *Indo-British Review: A Journal of History*, 25th Anniversary Number 1993, 'To Independence and Beyond', 123.

[4] See Hugh Tinker, 'The Indian Exodus from Burma 1942', *Journal of South East Asia Studies*, 6, 1 (1975), 1–22.

[5] Christopher Bayly and Tim Harper, *Forgotten Armies: The Fall of British Asia, 1841–1945* (2004), 167.

[6] *Ibid.*, 182.

reported that the conditions were worse than any he had experienced in the Mesopotamia Campaign during the First World War. He arrived in Calcutta in rags.[7] Claims that there was an easier 'white' overland route as opposed to the 'black' route which claimed so many Indian lives laid bare the racism at the heart of the Asian Empire. It had been displayed earlier at Rangoon when Indians had been denied berths so Britons could flee.[8] While Indians died in vastly greater numbers, 'last-ditcher' Britons also faced horrendous jungle and mountain treks into northern Assam. Women and children perished en route. The Assam planters who assisted the arriving refugees were shocked to see Britons arriving emaciated and in rags.

The earlier flight of Britons in the Malay Peninsula to Singapore, while marginally less harrowing, had also been a chaotic and undignified scramble; stories of Japanese atrocities at the fall of Hong Kong added to the panic. Again, racial hierarchies were cruelly exposed in the commandeering of boats and other available transport. From Perak to Singapore, a sorry spectacle was witnessed of an empire literally in retreat. As one British evacuee from Penang recorded, the manner of the British withdrawal was 'a thing which I am sure will never be forgotten or forgiven'.[9] Singapore brought no safe haven as the 'impregnable' fortress surrendered to the Japanese on 15 February 1942. Last-minute flight often sealed the fate of Britons whose boats were sunk by Japanese dive bombers. Survivors faced a period of harrowing internment in remote areas.

British prestige never recovered in Burma or Malaya from its Asian Dunkirk. Chaotic flight which revealed the racist imperial underbelly was more damaging than military defeat and even the fall of Singapore. Both on humanitarian grounds and because of the need to maintain prestige in the wider world, London could not countenance a chaotic repetition at the time of the handover of power in India, especially as this was occurring in peacetime. The response was the attempt to assess the risk facing British civilians and the drafting of detailed contingency plans for evacuation. While uncertainties arising from communal conflict persisted in April 1947, the general political situation was much less menacing than it had been just eighteen months earlier.

Anti-imperial disturbances: November 1945 – March 1946

The attempt to prosecute those army officers and men who had been captured in Singapore and subsequently joined the Japanese-sponsored

[7] *Ibid.*, 182.
[8] *Ibid.*, 168.
[9] Cited in *ibid.*, 120.

Indian National Army (INA) provided the catalyst for widespread disturbances from November 1945 to February 1946. A final wave of protests was unleashed when the British attempted to restore prestige and 'rally' loyal soldiers against the 'deserters' with the Victory Day celebrations in New Delhi. The four months of disturbances were marked both by Hindu–Muslim cooperation and increasing attacks on British civilians as well as symbols of state authority. Congress grew uneasy as the protests spiralled out of control and enabled the Communist Party to renew its challenge for the leadership of anti-colonial struggle in India.

The cycle began with the protests arising from the announcement of the guilty verdict in 5/7 charges which had been brought against Captain Abdul Rashid of the 14th Punjab regiment. Calcutta which had a long revolutionary tradition and was the political base of the INA founder Subhas Chandra Bose was at the heart of violent protests on Abdul Rashid Day (12 February). Clashes between British troops and protestors resulted in eight deaths and over ninety injuries. Protestors attacked US Army lorries injuring three soldiers. US troops were confined to the barracks in which they had been based during the war against Japan after these episodes. Congress members joined arms with the Muslim League Prime Minister Hussain Shaheed Suhrawardhy and Communists in a mile long procession which paraded through Dalhousie Square on 13 February.[10] A couple of weeks later, thousands of students went on strike in Lahore in protest at the seven years' sentence imposed on another INA officer, Captain Burhanuddin. The governor's car was stoned on the Mall and its windscreen smashed and the Union Jack torn from the bonnet.[11]

The Royal Indian Navy (RIN) Mutiny in Bombay harbour was accompanied by a wave of strikes in the city led by the Communist Party. The British repression on 23 February according to the Communist Party mouthpiece *People's Age* was the most 'notorious' and 'murderous' since the 1919 Amritsar massacre; 270 people were killed and some 2,000 wounded.[12] Given the RIN Mutiny's immense repercussions, relatively little has been written about it.[13] The mutiny began with a strike on the vessel *Talwar* which was more about local grievances than nationalist demands. The strike spread to twenty other ships in the harbour and to twelve shore establishments. Ships in the harbour flew the Indian flag rather than the Union Jack. Gunfire was exchanged for seven hours between the ratings and British military personnel, but by far the greatest

[10] See *Statesman* (Calcutta), 12 and 13 Feb. 1946.

[11] See *Hindustan Times* (Delhi), 28 Feb. 1946.

[12] See the *Peoples'Age*, editorial 3 Mar. 1946, entitled, 'In the Name of Our Dead'. This extract is contained in *Towards Freedom: Documents on the Movement for Independence in India 1946*, ed. Sumit Sarkar, I (New Delhi, 2009), 65.

[13] The exceptions are S. Banerjee, *The RIN Strike* (New Delhi, 1981); B. C. Dutt, *Mutiny of the Innocents* (Bombay, 1971).

violence accompanied the strike in Bombay in support of the ratings. There was widespread looting, strikes by textile workers and the burning of trams, buses and post offices. The Congress and Muslim League sent out peace brigades to try to restore order.[14] The ratings decided to surrender their arms after the mediation of the Congress deputy president, the pugnacious Sardar Vallabhbhai Patel.

There were nationwide protests in sympathy with the RIN ratings. Worryingly for the colonial authorities, some of these were directed against British civilians. The Sind police superintendent reported for example that, in Karachi, 'Hoolganism by students and loafers had increased hourly.' He went on to say that 'Traffic was obstructed, Europeans, Anglo-Indians and government buildings stoned and people attacked and forcibly deprived of their hats and ties which were burnt on the spot.'[15] The latter type of incident was designed to humiliate British residents. It was recorded more widely at the time of the protests against the Victory Day Celebrations in New Delhi.

Daybreak in Delhi on 7 March revealed that the wooden victory arches had been torn down and Queen Victoria's statue was vandalised. Shortly afterwards, a fire had to be extinguished in the town hall which had been similarly attacked at the height of the 1942 Quit India movement disturbances in New Delhi.[16] The worst clashes between protestors and the police occurred in Chandni Chowk and in front of the Red Fort. Crowds were only dispersed after repeated firings and use of tear-gas. The procession route was free from violence, but the bystanders were heckling rather than cheering. The officer in charge of the Regimental Colour Party reported the hostile reception accorded to the Indian troops as they marched pass the commercial centre of Connaught Place. 'In Connaught Place . . . the shouting was so loud to deaden the band and our step. Such cries as "Thrown down our Colours", "You people are *'be-iman'"* *(without honour)* whilst serving the army *"Jai Hind"* and *"Inquilab Zindabad"* *(Long Live Revolution)* were heard.'[17] The participating soldiers 'looked terribly depressed'.[18] Protestors vented their anger at British passers-by as well. 'Crowds which collected on main roads and crossings, challenged and

[14] Telephone message E. A. Simms to Intelligence Bureau, 23 Feb. 1946, in *Towards Freedom*, ed. Sarkar, 83.

[15] Report by Supt. Police Sind K. R. Eates on RIN Strike and Reactions, 5/14/46 Home Poll NAI, in *Towards Freedom*, ed. Sarkar, 94.

[16] Note by chief commissioner Delhi, 8 Mar. 1946, 6?13/46 special branch chief commissioners officer Delhi, 1946; Department of Delhi Archives in *Towards Freedom*, ed. Sarkar, 134.

[17] Report by Captain Wyllie Carrick, officer in charge regimental colour parties to War Department GOI, 9 Mar. 1946, file 6/13/46, Special Branch Commissioner's Office Delhi, 1946, Department of Delhi Archives, in *Towards Freedom*, ed. Sarkar, 139.

[18] *Hindustan Times* (Delhi), 8 Mar. 1946.

insulted men in English dress', the deputy director of Central Intelligence noted in his report. 'Their hats and neckties were taken off . . . a Bishop passing near the Fountain was stopped, his hat taken off and his coat burnt. The mob also chased Europeans who happened to go that way and threw stones on their vehicles.'[19]

It is hardly possible to conceive a greater contrast with the Independence Day celebrations. What had happened in the ensuing months? Why had violence and hostility given way to mutual celebration? How much had the change resulted from British policy and how much did it owe to the Congress leadership? We will attempt to answer these questions in the next section.

A different war dance

The late colonial period was marked by rapid constitutional development, a convergence of Congress and British interests and intensifying communal conflict. The politics of anti-imperial protest were increasingly replaced by those of Hindu–Muslim conflict. The INA disturbances dispelled any lingering thoughts of reinforcing the Raj. Instead, attention turned to what would now be termed an imperial 'exit strategy'. The Attlee administration's 'new imperialism' put good relations with independent India's future rulers at the heart of this. Archibald Wavell's inability to provide any prospect other than an 'ignominious scuttle' cost him the viceroyalty and it was left to Victoria's great-grandson, Lord Mountbatten, to bring down the curtain on the Raj. Mountbatten would only agree to take on the role of viceroy if a deadline was announced for the British transfer of power in India. The impending British departure improved relations with Congress, but it also raised the stakes in the struggle over Pakistan. The Muslim League's success in the elections held in India's provinces early in 1946 strengthened its hand and made the formation of a separate Muslim state a real possibility.[20] This increased tensions and violence in its future North Indian heartland of Bengal and Punjab. The new mood was seen in that Britons could move unmolested in areas torn apart by Muslim–Hindu rioting. 'The start of a street fight was delayed to allow my wife to cross the road', one British newspaper editor recalled with bemusement.[21]

---

[19] G. Ahmed, deputy director Central Intelligence Delhi, 13 Mar. 1946, file 5/2.46, Home Political Department GOI, in *Towards Freedom*, ed. Sarkar, 141.

[20] On the Muslim League breakthrough in the previously Unionist dominated Punjab which Jinnah had termed the 'corner-stone of Pakistan', see D. Gilmartin, *Empire and Islam: Punjab and the Making of Pakistan* (Berkeley, 1988); I. Talbot, *Punjab and the Raj, 1849–1947* (New Delhi, 1988).

[21] Yasmin Khan, *The Great Partition: The Making of India and Pakistan* (New Haven and London, 2007), 28.

Communal conflict only claimed a handful of British victims who were unlucky enough to be in the wrong place at the wrong time. Public responses revealed, however, that the contingency planning for mass evacuation in the event of a major collapse of order had not been an exaggerated response to the catastrophes arising from the uncoordinated British evacuation in Burma and Mayala in 1942.

British deaths prompted questions in parliament, which generated extensive correspondence between the Commonwealth Relations Office, the Delhi High Commission and the Indian authorities. Hence, while we know nothing of the circumstances of the countless Indians who were the victims of the 'August madness' attacks on the crowded refugee railway trains, it is possible to piece together the last journey of Medcalf, a British civil engineer who was murdered while travelling by train in East Punjab, as he travelled from Pakistan to take up a new posting in Calcutta.[22]

The most celebrated British victims were Lt Colonel Dykes and his wife who died in the ransacking of St Joseph's mission in Baramulla as the first phase of the Kashmir dispute unfolded in November 1947 with the incursion of Pakhtun tribesman from Pakistan. These events became front page news in Britain.[23] The 'hard-bitten' Fleet Street journalist Sydney Smith broke the story as a personal account following his capture by tribesmen and incarceration in the hospital ward along with the survivors of the initial assault. Nehru sensing that the episode fixed Pakistan in international eyes as the aggressor in Kashmir visited the town which lay some thirty-five miles from Srinagar, four days after its capture by Indian troops. He memorably remarked of the devastation at St Joseph's mission that 'nothing was left intact except the flowers'.[24] Margaret Bourke-White, the celebrated American photographer for *Life* magazine and recorder of the partition violence further publicised the Baramulla episode following her visit to the Mission.[25] The events, which tapped into fears of the violation of white women and tribal savagery deep in the imperial British psyche, inspired second-rate novels by the future author of 'The Darling Buds of May', H. E. Bates, and the former *Observer* Indian news correspondent Alan Moorehead.[26] The Academy award nominee producer and screen play writer Anthony Havelock-Allan even talked of a movie.

[22] Office High Commission New Delhi to Commonwealth Relations Office London, 20 Nov. 1947, L/P&J/7/12442 IOR.

[23] *Daily Express* (London), 10 Nov. 1947.

[24] Andrew Whitehead, *A Mission in Kashmir* (New Delhi, 2007), 180.

[25] Margaret Bourke-White, *Halfway to Freedom: A Report on the New India in the Words and Photographs of Margaret Bourke-White* (New York, 1949).

[26] The novel by H. E. Bates was titled, *The Scarlet Sword* and was published in London by Joseph in 1950. Alan Moorehead's book, was entitled, *The Rage of the Vulture* (1948).

Tom Dykes, like a number of British officers, had stayed on after independence to oversee the reorganisation of the divided Indian Army, in his case the Sikh Regiment as it moved its headquarters from Nowshera in Pakistan to the Indian garrison town of Ambala. Ironically, these troops were to be the first to be airlifted into Kashmir to drive back the tribal invaders. Serving British officers had been shifted from Kashmir as tensions rose in the state in the aftermath of India's independence. Tom had returned to be with his wife, Biddie, who had recently given birth in the well-appointed Baramulla mission hospital. Like many British officers, Dykes had happy memories of Kashmir arising from houseboat holidays on the bewitchingly beautiful Dal Lake. His eldest son had been born at the same hospital just five years earlier. Their happy valley became a valley of death. When the tribesmen literally smashed their way into the hospital, Tom Dykes was shot. He suffered a lingering death. His wife's partly clothed body was discovered in a nearby well. The Dykes are buried alongside three other victims in the orchard graveyard on the far side of the convent.[27] Their three sons, including the two week old James, survived and were later evacuated to England.

The mission compound had attracted the tribesmen because of its prominent position on the Jhelum Valley Road. It provided opportunities for loot, as had earlier the Anglican church, club and Nedou's hotel at the hill resort of Gulmarg, where the raiders even stripped the coverings off the garden umbrellas. At Buniyar, they looted the bungalow belonging to Ronald Davis, head of the World Wide Evangelist Crusade.[28] By the time that his remains were discovered, dumped by the bank of the Jhelum River, an airlift had been organised to evacuate those British residents who wished to leave Kashmir. As we shall in the next section, contingency planning had been made for British evacuation throughout the subcontinent at the time of independence. It was, however, only in Kashmir that it had to be implemented.

Britons and independence

Surveying the community

Attlee's announcement that power would be transferred to Indian hands by the end of June 1948 prompted Lord Listowel, the secretary of state, to order an enquiry into the size and distribution of the European population.[29] Figures were obtained from the governors' secretaries, the chief commissioner of Delhi and the British residents in the Princely

---

[27] For details, see Whitehead, *A Mission in Kashmir*.
[28] For details, see J. S. H. Shattock, HC Delhi to H. A. F. Rumbold, Commonwealth Relations Office, 3 Dec. 1947, L/P&S/13/1850 IOR.
[29] This meant British nationals, not 'foreign' nationals, nor Anglo-Indians.

States. Listowel dutifully reported to the India and Burma Cabinet Committee that there were around 80,000 Britons resident in the subcontinent. Almost a quarter of these lived in Bengal. Women and children comprised a high proportion of this population, accounting for around 50,000 persons. Two elements of the report rang alarm bells in London. First, the admission that the figures 'were only a rough estimate' and secondly, that about a fifth of the British residents lived in places where 'they would be particularly exposed to danger in the event of serious disturbances'.[30] This resulted in the drawing up of contingency evacuation plans.

Mountbatten discussed at length the movement of civilians at a meeting with the provincial governors held on 15 April 1947, less than a month into his viceroyalty. It provides fascinating insights into official perceptions of the Britons in India at the end of the Raj and their likely response to independence. The governors revealed the highly differentiated characteristics of the British community which continued after independence. The Punjab governor, Sir Evan Jenkins, who was in the midst of increasingly serious communal disturbances, provided the most downbeat assessment. If all went well, he maintained, the 2,500 or so Britons would be safe, 'but they were in fact already in some danger and that was liable to increase'. His advice was to reduce the number as soon as possible. Whilst he admitted that he had not yet sounded out European opinion, he felt that the time might come when the government would be faced with a really serious commitment and people 'might have to be moved under great strain in a great hurry', even if serious disturbances did not occur before June 1948:

> After that date, whatever happened, the Punjab was likely to be equivalent to a foreign country and the only authority which would be capable of getting people out would be the FO working through the HC. No one would suppose that evacuation in these circumstances would be very easy or free from danger. Therefore it was for consideration whether, on some future date, it might not be necessary to compel people to evacuate through the issue of an ordinance.[31]

Jenkins had some support from his Bengal counterparts, although the need was recognised to 'keep commerce going' in Calcutta and to not shock the various British associations in the province by suggesting anything along the lines of Jenkins's compulsory evacuation. Governor Burrows had more concerns about the 6,000 or so Britons living in 'outlying areas' than the 14,000 in Calcutta. The latter might have to be brought into the city if conditions deteriorated. The 5,000–6,000 officials and their families would in any case leave after independence.

---

[30] Secretary of state, memo European civilians in India, 18 Feb. 1947, India and Burma Cabinet Committee, MB1/D228, University of Southampton.

[31] Governors' Conference, 15 Apr. 1947, MB1/D229, University of Southampton.

In Burrows's view, no 'purposeful' attack on Britons was anticipated, but, 'if there were shortages of food Europeans and rich Indians would be a general target'.[32] The possibility of Communists organising agitations in Bengal's tea plantations was also noted, especially in the light of the planters' lack of progress in improving labour conditions.

The governor of neighbouring Bihar, Sir Hugh Dow, also expressed concerns regarding the maintenance of law and order until June 1948 given the fact that the police in his province were 'entirely unreliable'. There were only some fifty European officials. Dow, whose greatest administrative achievements had been in Sindh, believed that a large number of missionaries would doubtless stay. Most Britons, around 2,000 including their families were engaged in industrial enterprises. Dow somewhat cynically remarked that 'So long as he (a businessman) was making money and all was quiet', he would not consider leaving, 'but a very quick change might be expected in his attitude once there was an interference with law and order on a wide scale.'[33]

Sir Andrew Clow, who had served in India since 1914 and had informed Mountbatten that leaving would be a wrench, confirmed that by far the largest number of Europeans in Assam were planters.[34] More of them had their wives with them than ever before. They were mostly living in one of the least tense areas of the Province and the majority he thought intended to stay on. The missionaries would nearly all stay. The retired residents always talked of going home but never did so.

The situation was very different in Orissa with its tiny British population of just 132 people. Its Indian governor, Sir Chandulal Trivedi, optimistically reported that he did not anticipate any communal conflict or breakdown in law and order. Sir Frederick Bourne gave a similar report with respect to the Central Provinces. He believed most of the small population of a few hundred Britons would stay. Sir Francis Mudie, whose sympathies for the Muslim League were later to earn him the governorship of the Pakistan Punjab, reported that there were very few Britons in Sind outside Karachi. There had been no talk of Europeans leaving except in the services. His ministry would be horrified at the thought of the European business community leaving.[35]

The erudite Sir Olaf Caroe, whose position was threatened by Congress claims of his partiality for the Muslim League, confirmed that the majority of Englishmen in the North-West Frontier Province were missionaries, bankers, officials and their wives. The situation in his opinion 'was very shaky' but might improve. He pointed out first that whatever happened

[32] Ibid.
[33] Ibid.
[34] See Khan, The Great Partition, 89.
[35] Governors' Conference, 15 Apr. 1947, MB1/D229, University of Southampton.

in Punjab would have a major impact on the Frontier and secondly that
when considering evacuation, it should be remembered that this 'was the
province furthest from the sea'.[36]

Madras, because it was removed from the communal conflicts of North
India, was not seen as presenting a problem by its governor, Sir Archibald
Nye. He divided the British population into four main categories – officials
of whom the majority would leave before June 1948; missionaries who
would nearly all stay; businessmen of whom the majority would stay.
Out of a total of 5,000 he thought 4,000 would remain. Francis Wylie, a
former political adviser to the viceroy and now the governor of the United
Provinces, followed suit. He believed that missionaries and the majority
of businessmen would remain, while officials and most of the commercial
community of Cawnpore would depart.

British evacuation

Mountbatten had called the conference because he was already
apprehensive not just about the security situation, but the practical issues
of coping with a large migration of Britons from India. The latter concerns
were prompted by the British government and were in keeping with its
need to dispel any sense of chaos and lack of control in the winding up of
the Indian Empire. There was to be no repetition of the wartime chaos
in Burma and Malaya. The shipping issue revealed in fact how difficult
it was for the outgoing rulers to coordinate policy matters when they
no longer retained control of all the levers of power. This was because
a Plan A for movement of Europeans had to be considered alongside
a worst case Plan B scenario situation of emergency evacuation. The
latter contingency involved military movements of civilians to a holding
transit camp in Bombay. Plan B had been originally conceived before the
creation of the Indian-led interim government. Its existence raised the
spectre that further planning and execution would have to have the 'prior
knowledge and agreement' of Baldev Singh, the defence member of the
interim government.[37]

The shipping issue had surfaced because of concerns in London early
in 1947 that civilian morale in India might be affected by lack of passenger
berths. The increased demand was attributed to the growing communal
disturbances in the Punjab and British residents' anxieties about the
impact on access to hill stations such as Simla in the forthcoming hot
season.[38] Extra ships were made available, but the British cabinet in return
wanted assurances that there would be a planned shipping operation over

---

[36] *Ibid.*
[37] Auchinleck to Abell, 2 Apr. 1947, MB1/D228, University of Southampton.
[38] Secretary of state to viceroy telegram, 20 Mar. 1947, MB1/D228, University of
Southampton.

the next fourteen months. It suggested that Mountbatten in discussion with the governors, but not significantly the members of the interim government, should consider its coordination. If necessary, he was granted permission to reintroduce the wartime controls on passage.[39]

Mountbatten had responded that the projected civilian requirement of passages from India up to the end of June 1947 was in fact only slightly higher at 12,294 than had been the figure for the corresponding months of 1937 and 1938. He had also confirmed that the services requirement stood at over 10,000.[40] Most importantly, he had maintained that the military contingency plan (the Movement Control Board) would only operate openly in conditions of widespread disorder and confusion.[41] Mountbatten shortly afterwards agreed to the provision of reports on each ship sailing for England showing the number of empty berths and the reasons for them. This followed irritation in London that extra ships had been diverted from other purposes, but had not in the event been required as a result of the cancellation of some 900 passenger requirements.[42]

The ensuing discussion in New Delhi resulted in a proposal for a Civil Passages Control Plan to minimise the effects of speculative bookings and late cancellations. This involved a system of registration at the provincial level overseen by the governors who would draw up priorities. They would allocate passages under a monthly quota system based on the decisions of a Central Committee overseen by the viceroy.[43] It would assess the demands on berths and allocate passages bearing in mind the provincial proportions of European residents. This cumbersome machinery was never implemented as the rush of events following the decision to advance the date of independence terminated concerns about the logistics of civilian passages. It was only after independence, at the outset of conflict in Kashmir, that a large-scale movement of European residents took place.

Evacuation of British residents from Kashmir

The narrative of the evacuation of British residents from the state of Jammu and Kashmir awaits its historian. Indian writers have focused on the destruction at Baramulla and the heroism of the first military martyrs in the long Kashmir struggle. The sadistic killing of the pro-Indian activist Maqbool Sherwani inspired a slender novel by the left-leaning author

[39] *Ibid.*

[40] Viceroy to secretary of state telegram, 27 Mar. 1947, MB1/D228, University of Southampton.

[41] *Ibid.*

[42] Secretary of state to viceroy telegram, 4 Apr. 1947, MB1/D228, University of Southampton.

[43] Note by Christie, 3 Apr. 1947, MB1/228, University of Southampton.

Mulk Raj Anand.[44] The airlifting of British residents sits uncomfortably with such accounts, as it seems a throw-back to an imperial past. The episode is in fact historically significant because of the light it throws on the impact of the presence of British civil servants and army officers on developments in Kashmir. It is thus about far more than the evacuation of cantankerous British citizens from the beleaguered city of Srinagar.

Kashmir's future was unresolved at independence. Its ruler had not joined either India or Pakistan. The autocratic Hari Singh had been troubled for some time by democratic movements led by Sheikh Abdullah, the self-styled 'lion of Kashmir'. The logic of the two nation theory assigned Kashmir to Pakistan, but this had little appeal for a Hindu ruler. He also feared that accession to India would strengthen the hand of Abdullah who was a close ally of Nehru whose support for Kashmir's inclusion in India is well known. It linked family ties with the belief that an Indian Kashmir would be 'a powerful lever for secular sentiment' in a country whose birth had been scarred by communal massacres.

The incursion of around 7,000 armed 'tribal invaders' on 22 October marked the first of a series of attempts by Pakistan to use proxy forces militarily to wrench Kashmir into its grasp.[45] The extent to which British officers in the Pakistan Army were aware of the operation is one of a number of disputes surrounding the events.[46] In all probability, the use of tribal proxies was a means to keep British staff officers out of the loop. The policy placed European residents in the path of the ill-disciplined tribal irregular forces.

There was a constant exchange of telegrams between the High Commissions in India and Pakistan and the Commonwealth Relations Office in London as tensions grew in Kashmir. Pakistan blockaded supplies of fuel in order to put pressure on its vacillating ruler Hari Singh who still harboured thoughts that an independent Kashmir could be the 'Switzerland of the East'. By the beginning of October, tension had increased to the extent that a military officer, Major W. P. Cranston, delegated to the British High Commission in New Delhi was sent to Srinagar to plan the voluntary evacuation of British citizens. From the first week of October, Cranston made frequent journeys between India and Pakistan to discuss transport arrangements for the movement of British civilians. His peregrinations led some people to believe that he was in fact working for British intelligence.[47] Cranston met mainly with the British officials and servicemen who had stayed on in Pakistan, including

---

[44] Mulk Raj Anand, *Death of a Hero: Epitaph for Maqbool Sherwani* (Delhi, 1968).

[45] See P. Swami, *India, Pakistan and the Secret Jihad: The Covert War in Kashmir, 1947–2004* (New York, 2007).

[46] For a discussion, see Whitehead, *A Mission in Kashmir*, 59–60.

[47] *Ibid.*, 142.

General Douglas Gracey and Sir Francis Mudie, the governor of the West Punjab. The latter on 16 October promised Cranston transport and security along the main Srinagar–Baramulla–Domal–Kohala–Murree road route. Gracey had also promised to help British evacuation 'in any way he possibly could', but had more circumspectly said he needed authorisation from the central Pakistan government.[48]

Cranston reported to New Delhi that the bulk of the British citizens, which numbered around 200, were now living in Srinagar, the capital of the Princely State. A Miss Nancy Hotz, 'who had driven an ambulance at the time of the London Blitz', had collected the names of those who wished to leave. Hotz, together with a retired Punjab engineer, Mr Betterton, and Sir Alan Henderson, a Calcutta high court judge, were to play leading roles in the later evacuation. This was also assisted by William Nedou, the Swiss proprietor of Nedou's hotel Srinagar who transported evacuees to the aerodrome, eight miles out of the city, and provided free accommodation for those Britons who could not access their bank accounts.[49] Some residents, Cranston noted, were trying to leave by car, but were handicapped by the severe petrol shortage as a result of the government of Pakistan's blockade. He reckoned that at least 170 buses were standing idle because they had run out of fuel.[50]

Cranston struggled to persuade Britons to leave their homes in Kashmir. A hint of frustration can be discerned in his report that 'the people were rather out of touch with reality and did not realize the seriousness of the general situation in India nor the danger for possible disturbances in Kashmir'.[51] Despite a more imminent Japanese threat, some Britons had been reluctant to abandon their homes in Burma and Malaya in 1942. On 22 October, Cranston returned with further ammunition in the form of an official warning from Sir Laurence Grafftey-Smith, the UK high commissioner in Pakistan, that residents should take advantage of the arrangements to leave Kashmir, 'as it might not be possible ... later to protect them in case of serious disorders'.[52] Even after the tribal invasion, some residents cavilled at the necessity for evacuation, especially if it meant that they had to leave their pets behind.

Thursday 23 October had been earmarked for a road evacuation, but these plans 'were upset' when Sheikh Abdullah informed Cranston that the Jhelum Valley Road down to Rawalpindi was under fire. Armed tribesmen who had crossed over from Pakistan territory in military trucks

[48] Report by Major W. P. Cranston, 18 Oct. 1947, L/P&S/13/1850 IOR.

[49] W. P. Cranston, report on situation in Kashmir and movement of British civilian residents from Kashmir in Oct./Nov. 1947, 27 Nov. 1947, L/P&S/13/1850 IOR.

[50] *Ibid.*

[51] Report by Major W.P. Cranston, 18 Oct. 1947, L/P&S/13/1850 IOR.

[52] UK high commissioner Pakistan to secretary of state Commonwealth Relations, 18 Oct. 1947, L/P&S/13/1850 IOR.

had seized Muzaffarabad and Domal the day before and were advancing east on Kohala.[53] Cranston now began a hectic air shuttle between Srinagar, Delhi and Lahore. The initial plan was to evacuate residents via the 9,000 feet high Banihal Pass to Jammu and thence to Sialkot. When this passage over the 'blizzard' pass was deemed too risky for a large convoy, the only remaining option was air evacuation using the two RAF Dakota squadrons that could be moved to Rawalpindi from their Mauripur (Karachi) base. Just a matter of weeks earlier, the Air Ministry in London had discussed the withdrawal of the transport squadrons on 'account of manpower shortage' and economic 'crisis in the UK'. This had alarmed Mountbatten as he thought that his York aircraft would also be withdrawn. 'I need hardly remind you', he wrote to Ismay on 9 October, 'that the York may well be the only means by which we could evacuate our families in extreme necessity, though I sincerely hope that will not arise.'[54] In the event, the Air Ministry had decided to delay reviewing the situation until 1 December, meaning that the Dakotas were still available.

The British airlift was acutely sensitive as it was arranged on the cusp of Kashmir's accession to India and with its state forces retreating before the Pakistan supported Pakhtun tribesmen. The British government authorised the action, although Attlee underlined his concern that 'the 2 RAF transport squadrons now in India and Pakistan should not be used to assist either Dominion, in any way in connection with disturbances in Kashmir'.[55] In the subcontinent, authorisation was given by senior British officials now in the service of the two states, including Sir Hugh Walmsley, the air marshal, and by the supreme commander-in-chief, the soon to be departed Sir Claude Auchinleck. In all the meetings and telephone conversations which Cranston records, only one senior South Asian official is named, V. P. Menon, in his capacity as secretary of the states ministry.[56] He informed the acting British high commissioner in New Delhi that it would be 'prudent to arrange early removal by air of those persons who wish to leave'.[57]

Cranston flew from Delhi to Srinagar on 27 October, the day that the Maharaja's signature of the instrument of accession was accepted in New Delhi. The specially chartered plane also carried Mehr Chand Mahajan, the prime minister of Kashmir, V. P. Menon and Sheikh Abdullah, who was to make the transition from political prisoner to chief minister in five

[53] Defence Committee meeting, 25 Oct. 1947, MB1/D42/9, University of Southampton.
[54] Mountbatten to Ismay, 9 Oct. 1947, MB1D279, University of Southampton.
[55] Ministry of Defence London to UK High Commission Delhi top secret cypher telegram, 27 Oct. 1947, L/P&S/13/1850 IOR.
[56] Report by W. P. Cranston, 27 Nov. 1947, L/P&S//13/1850 IOR.
[57] Indian High Commission to Commonwealth Relations Office telegram, 27 Oct. 1947, L/P&S/13/1850 IOR.

weeks. Whilst he was making the final arrangements for the evacuation from Srinagar, Cranston was handed a letter by Mr J. E. Thompson, a retired army officer who now managed a timber company in Baramulla. This was the last communication from Lt-Colonel Dykes, asking for transport for his family to Srinagar. Thompson found his way to the mission hospital, but Kashmir Army headquarters refused permission to send a lorry when state troops were already in retreat from the town.[58]

The fall of the state capital Srinagar was only averted by the airlifting of India's first Sikh battalion after Hari Singh acceded to India.[59] Mountbatten justified their induction as necessary to prevent the 'pillaging' of Srinagar and the massacre 'of the couple of hundred British citizens in Kashmir'.[60] He advised the Indian Defence Committee which he chaired to go for the recapture of Baramulla, 'regardless of casualties'.[61] It was, however, a number of days before the tide of battle turned. The limited landing facilities at Srinagar slowed the reinforcing of Indian troops. The Royal Indian Air Force was desperately short of planes and pilots. Just four of the ten transport aircraft in its No. 12 squadron were 'serviceable'.[62] Troops were airlifted in modified civilian planes flown by British, Australian and American pilots. They sometimes had space for less than twenty servicemen and their equipment. If Pakistan troops had been committed at this moment as Jinnah intended, the Kashmir Valley might have been lost to India. Gracey and Mudie rowed over the phone, when the Pakistan commander-in-chief refused to order deployment without first consulting Auchinleck, the supreme commander in New Delhi.[63] It was to be another six months before Gracey ordered deployment, by which time Pakistan troops were needed to cling on to gains in Poonch, rather than 'liberate' the Valley.

The tribesmen's advance up the Kashmir Valley slowed as they spent time ransacking Baramulla. The town of orchards became a site of desolation. The looting bought the Indian forces precious time. As it was, the Afridis advanced to within a few miles of Srinagar and its aerodrome. Kashmir's capital bore the appearance of a frontline city. Its electricity was cut off following the destruction of the Mahura power plant. War correspondents and pilots congregated in the bar at Nedou's, while Sikh officers commandeered its map displays as they tried to plan

[58] W. P. Cranston, 27 Nov. 1947. Note on Colonel and Mrs D. & T Dykes, L/P&S/13/1850 IOR.

[59] There is great controversy as to whether the accession document was signed before the first troops were airlifted.

[60] Governor-general's personal report, 7 Nov. 1947, L/PO/6/123 IOR.

[61] Defence Committee meeting, 4 Nov. 1947, MB1/D43/4, University of Southampton.

[62] Sir Thomas Elmhirst to Mountbatten, 9 Oct. 1947, MB1 D279, University of Southampton.

[63] Whitehead, A Mission in Kashmir, 119.

troop deployments. The booze did not run out, but guests had to eat by candlelight and faced food shortages. 'We never thought we would be in the siege of Srinagar', one British resident, Gwen Burton, wrote home.[64] On 6 November, the tribesmen got to within five miles of the city. This was the extent of their advance, before a rapid retreat back along the Jhelum Valley Road. Within two days, Baramulla was 'recaptured' by the Indian troops. By the 12th, with the fall of Uri, the whole of the Kashmir Valley was in Indian hands as the tribesmen fled pell-mell towards Muzaffarabad, the present-day capital of Pakistan Azad Kashmir.

Following a reconnaissance of the restricted landing facilities, two RAF planes landed in Srinagar on 28 October. They brought over 1,000 gallons of petrol for the road transport which was being organised to take some of the British residents to Sialkot and then Lahore via the Banihal Pass. The first road convoy of five cars flying the Union Jack arrived safely in Lahore on 3 November, the second one containing the redoubtable Miss Hotz some five days later.[65] The final road convoy of three cars departed on 11 November. Just four days earlier, six trucks with two tanks and armoured cars in escort brought the eighty-nine Baramulla mission evacuees to Pakistan. They included a number of nuns and Anglo-Indians, the journalist Sydney Smith who had broken the news of the attack and the three Dykes boys.[66] Sir George Cunningham, the governor of the Pakistan North-West Frontier Province, had made the security arrangements. Ironically given the earlier events, the greatest danger was attack by Indian planes on what to all intents and purposes would have appeared a military convoy.

The British airlift began in earnest on Wednesday 29 October when ten sorties were made. By its completion, 136 persons along with 23,253 lbs of luggage had been safely transported to the Dakotas' base at Chaklala in Pakistan.[67] Wisps of smoke could be seen rising from the surrounding villages as the planes banked out of Srinagar. There were fears that the tribesmen might down a plane or permanently damage the runway. An advance party got to within a mile of the aerodrome perimeter. The journalists Margaret Patton from *Herald Tribune* and Eric Britter from *The Times* had arranged seats on the first flight. When they reached the airfield and saw the newly arrived Indian spitfires and civilian transports, they realised the possibility for a major scoop and after interviewing pilots

[64] *Ibid.*, 150.
[65] UK High Commission Pakistan to Commonwealth Relations Office telegram, 8 Nov. 1947, L/P&S/13/1850 IOR.
[66] Pakistan High Commission to the Indian High Commission telegram, 8 Nov. 1947, L/P&S/13/1850 IOR.
[67] Indian High Commission Delhi to Commonwealth Relations Office telegram, 30 Oct. 1947, L/P&S/13/1850 IOR.

and crewmen returned to Nedou's.[68] The following day, a further three aircraft flew into Srinagar bringing another thousand gallons of petrol. The chaotic conditions prevailing around Srinagar meant that only ten Britons could be airlifted to safety. This left another sixty or so awaiting evacuation.[69]

Cranston shuttled back to New Delhi on 2 November. Following discussions with Auchinleck, the high commissioner and the air commodore, the government of India agreed to the evacuation of the remaining British residents on the civil airlines that were operating between Srinagar and Delhi. Cranston returned on 6 November to Srinagar with the unpopular news that passengers would have to pay their fares. The Indian authorities did, however, provide an armed escort to the aerodrome. On the initiative of the British deputy quartermaster general, Indian Army trucks which had transported supplies to the front returned to New Delhi carrying the luggage and in some instances the pets of the residents. Cranston returned on 17 November from Srinagar on the last evacuee flight. 'This left', Cranston's report concluded, seventy-seven British people in Srinagar and thirty-one outside, the latter almost entirely missionaries who declared that they did not wish to leave Kashmir this winter; some would remain in Kashmir permanently and some would leave for England and other countries in the spring if conditions permitted.'[70]

Conclusion

Concerns for the safety of British citizens in India prompted elaborate plans for their evacuation at the time of independence. In the event, the replacement of anti-European sentiment by communal conflict meant that large-scale evacuation was not required. This paper argues that the planning needs to be understood not just in terms of humanitarian concerns, but a desire to avoid a repetition of the loss of imperial prestige arising from the chaotic evacuation of Burma and Malaya in 1942.

Independence with Partition did not as was hoped solve 'Hindu'–'Muslim' conflict in the subcontinent. Instead, it internationalised it. The conflict focused on the fate of the Princely State of Jammu and Kashmir which alongside its strategic value symbolised different visions of the nation building enterprise in post-colonial South Asia. The British residents of the state found themselves in the path of the first 'proxy war' launched by Pakistan. Their successful evacuation depended in part

---

[68] Whitehead, *A Mission in Kashmir*, 151.

[69] Indian High Commission to Commonwealth Relations Office telegram, 30 Oct. 1947, L/P&S/13/1850 IOR.

[70] W. P. Cranston report, 27 Nov. 1947, L/P&S/13/1850 IOR.

on the activism of civilian volunteers which was a legacy from the war years. The cooperation of the British High Commissions in India and Pakistan also helped. Most important, however, was their direct access to the shortly to be wound up supreme military headquarters in New Delhi. RAF planes were able to make repeated authorised sorties from Pakistan into Indian air space. They landed at an aerodrome whose primitive runaway and maintenance facilities were stretched to the limit by the need to rush India reinforcements from their bases in Amritsar and Ambala. In the event, the fledgling Pakistan Air Force was unable to take advantage of these chaotic circumstances.

The presence of British military commanders not only smoothed the airlifting of residents but also prevented further escalation of the military conflict between two members of the Commonwealth. Attlee's anxieties about the need for an even-handed British approach, however, continually resurfaced, as in the ensuing decades, Kashmir troubled both South Asian and wider Commonwealth relations.

Transactions of the RHS 23 (2013), pp. 223–45 © Royal Historical Society 2013
doi:10.1017/S0080440113000108

THE 'TROPICAL DOMINIONS': THE APPEAL OF DOMINION STATUS IN THE DECOLONISATION OF INDIA, PAKISTAN AND CEYLON

By Harshan Kumarasingham

READ 19 OCTOBER 2012 AT THE UNIVERSITY OF SOUTHAMPTON

ABSTRACT. The paper examines the reasons that India, Pakistan and Ceylon chose to become Dominions within the Commonwealth instead of becoming republics on independence as many expected. Each of these South Asian states had different motives that compelled them to take on a form of government more associated in areas where the British had settled in significant numbers. The 'Tropical Dominions' differed from the settler cases and tested this vague British concept. The British and South Asians had to compromise their wishes in order to satisfy their wants. India is characterised here as the 'Expedient Dominion', Pakistan the 'Siege Dominion' and Ceylon the 'Imitation Dominion'. This paper focuses on the years immediately prior to independence to understand the various objectives of the South Asian elites that negotiated with the British for their sovereignty and how they varied from each other and from the Dominion ideal.

Introduction

Few today, including those who work on the subcontinent, recollect that India, Pakistan and Sri Lanka did not become republics the day British rule ended. Even distinguished scholars of Empire like Perry Anderson and A. G. Hopkins have made the common assumption that India naturally became a republic upon independence on 15 August 1947.[1] Instead, all three of these South Asian states began their independent life as Realms within the British Commonwealth and mirrored the style and institutions of the Dominions of Canada, Australia, South Africa and New Zealand. Though their sovereignty was in no way impaired by this seemingly ambiguous position they all held the British sovereign as their head of state who was represented in each capital by a governor-general appointed on the advice of the local prime minister. India, Pakistan and Ceylon were Realms from 1947 to 1950, 1947 to 1956 and 1948 to 1972 respectively. So many of the great events that shaped

[1] Perry Anderson, 'After Nehru', *London Review of Books*, 34, 15 (2 Aug. 2012), 21; and A. G. Hopkins, 'Rethinking Decolonization', *Past and Present*, 200 (Aug. 2008), 212 n. 8.

their country's destiny occurred during these regnal years that would shape how democracy operated. Prior to gaining power, the new leaders of these independent states had all negotiated their interpretation of freedom through the rubric of Dominionhood. This meant that rather than advocate 'pure' severance from Britain and rejection of cooperation, the elite South Asian leaders knew pragmatically that in order to gain their objectives it was wiser to parley with the British using the Dominion model. The British also presumed that by allowing the emergence of these new Dominions they could exercise influence without having to maintain expensive and increasingly unpalatable direct rule. Rather than focus on the independence movements and the partition of India this paper focuses on the South Asian political elites and their interaction with the British in the years immediately prior to independence to understand why this region, not part of the 'kith and kin' Dominion pantheon, decided to become Dominions and not break away from Crown and Commonwealth as their rhetoric sometimes pointed. Rather than looking at what benefit Britain gained from persuading these territories to become Dominions[2] this paper examines what benefits the South Asian elites perceived they would gain. Instead of taking the view that these Asian states 'unexpectedly joined the Commonwealth',[3] this paper attempts to explain the immediate pre-independence appeal of starting national liberation as a Dominion and the reasoning of keeping the Commonwealth connection. Most Indian politicians for instance saw Dominion status as a temporary step to placate the British before establishing a republic while keeping many useful executive instruments from the viceroyalty; Pakistani leaders saw it as a safety mechanism to prevent Indian hegemony in the region and as support against the spectre of wholesale Indian occupation; while the Ceylonese elite, by persuasively demonstrating how similar they were to the 'traditional' Dominions and their outward fealty to British interests, shrewdly used Dominionhood to achieve independence earlier than some expected. All were unsure how this essentially British constitutional monarchical system, developed over centuries, would work in the very different contexts of India, Pakistan and Ceylon. It quickly became apparent, at the very least, that the king's South Asian Dominions would be very different from his settler Dominions.

---

[2] A very good article that discusses the defence benefits to Britain and the Commonwealth of India and Pakistan being Dominions can be found in Anita Inder Singh, 'Imperial Defence and the Transfer of Power in India, 1946–1947', *International Historical Review*, 4, 4 (Nov. 1982), 568–88.

[3] Wm Roger Louis and Ronald Robinson, 'The Imperialism of Decolonization', *Journal of Imperial and Commonwealth History*, 22, 3 (1994), 466.

Decolonisation and dominionisation

The foundation of New Delhi was meant to be one of the great moments in the history of Britain's imperial mission. The architectural audacity of Lutyens's and Baker's imperial metropolis was consciously planned to inspire paternalistic awe over the inhabitants and demonstrate the permanence of Britain's Indian Empire. This colossal imperial project had its foundation stone laid by George V during his 1911 Durbar visit. However, for all its magnificence and palatial self-importance it had nonetheless for many a sense of imperial ambiguity when inaugurated in 1931. As Morris observed, the new capital of British India

> was not altogether sure what it was to commemorate. It was too late for arrogance, too soon for regrets, and one could not be sure whether these structures were intended to be the halls of an eternal dominion, or . . . Indians themselves sitting in graceful succession upon these thrones of power.[4]

Georges Clemenceau observing the construction of the viceroy's residence in 1920, a palace once complete would be larger than his own country's Versailles, exclaimed that New Delhi 'will be the finest ruin of them all'.[5] One of the ambitions of building New Delhi was for the Indians to feel more part of the imperial family and increase its resemblance in convention and status to the other Realms. Less noticed today are four tall columns between Baker's huge secretariats each showing respectively the emblems of Canada, Australia, South Africa and New Zealand, which were opened by representatives of each country in February 1931. Their presence and construction was meant to demonstrate that India would be a brother Dominion – though the enormous inscription on the walls of the secretariats facing the columns was unlikely to inspire fraternal feeling from the Indian people – *'Liberty Does Not Descend To A People. A People Must Raise Themselves To Liberty. It Is A Blessing That Must Be Earned Before It Can Be Enjoyed.'* The Indian subcontinent[6] had always occupied pride of place in the British Empire. Well before independence, India, though not one of the 'kith and kin' Dominions, had achieved certain prerogatives that demonstrated limited equivalence with the settler cases. Due to its contribution to the war effort, India was represented at the Paris Peace Conference and in the imperial war cabinet (the first non-white members) by the maharajah of Bikaner (who was India's signatory of the Treaty of Versailles) and Sir S. P. Sinha (who in 1919 became the first Indian to be raised to the British peerage and was a member of judicial committee of the privy council).[7]

---

[4] Jan Morris, *Farewell the Trumpets: An Imperial Retreat* (1998), 374.

[5] Robert Grant Irving, *Indian Summer: Lutyens, Baker and Imperial Delhi* (1981), 355.

[6] Ceylon was not part of the Indian Empire and governed separately from India as a Crown Colony since 1802.

[7] See Hugh Purcell, *Makers of the Modern World: Maharajah of Bikaner: India* (2010).

What dominionhood actually is and was is still debated, but at the very least it meant politically *de facto* indigenous rule within the Commonwealth and a readiness to accept common linkages with Britain and the other Dominions including, above all, the Crown. For the settler Dominions the monarchy was the sacred centre of the imperial family and they saw themselves as the close and loyal family elders.[8] The abstract and nebulous conception of being a Realm and Dominion suited the chaotic situation that Britain and its South Asian possessions found themselves in the 1940s when actions and decisions were needed rapidly, with little time or ability to deliberate on the merits of such an approach. For the South Asian states, being Dominions had very different meanings from their settler cousins in Canada, Australia, South Africa and New Zealand. In many ways, the South Asian cases illustrate even more Darwin's assessment on how the settler Dominions worked prior to the Second World War – 'Like "responsible government", Dominionhood was unsystematic and "conventional", fashioned as much by the local requirements of Dominion politicians as by policy-makers in London.'[9] Darwin in his latest work on the British Empire ascribes three further forms of British connection that bound the Dominions. First having a sense of 'Britannic identity among Canadians, Australians, New Zealanders and the English in South Africa' where the Empire was a 'shared enterprise' run by a 'white ethnic commonwealth'. Secondly was a sense of 'mutual dependence' in financial, commercial and geopolitical matters that made 'separation unattractive, even dangerous'. Finally was the 'mystic allegiance to the faraway British Crown', which ultimately legitimised their connection, and any thought of breaking this imperial link would 'unravel the fabric of political unity'.[10] The 'Tropical Dominions' would either have issues with or could not satisfy all three of these British connections.

For many in Britain (and in the Dominions themselves) being a Dominion did not mean independence. The ambiguity of what a Dominion meant was in many ways intentional. This meant the concept could contain both the openly rebellious case of Ireland and the openly loyal case of New Zealand. Ireland barely concealed its disdain for any British connections and saw the British king as no more important to Irish affairs than the 'Mikado of Japan'. New Zealand on the other hand was ultra loyal and their prime minister, William Ferguson Massey, assured

---

[8] See Philip Murphy, *Monarchy and the End of Empire: The House of Windsor, the British Government and the Postwar Commonwealth* (Oxford, forthcoming).

[9] John Darwin, 'A Third British Empire? The Dominion Idea in Imperial Politics', in *The Oxford History of the British Empire*, IV: *The Twentieth Century*, ed. Judith M. Brown and Wm Roger Louis (Oxford, 1999), 77.

[10] John Darwin, *Unfinished Empire: The Global Expansion of Britain* (2012), 202.

his people that though their country had been admitted to the Paris Peace Conference the 'dangerous' theory circulating that New Zealand was an independent nation separate of Britain was completely wrong and New Zealand's devotion to the king-emperor irrevocable.[11] Lloyd George himself told the House of Commons in 1921 that it was 'difficult and dangerous to give a definition' as to what Dominion status meant.[12] The moderate constitutionalist elites in South Asia sought Dominion status for their region as the logical way to gain political autonomy without overly antagonising the imperial power. The Imperial Conference of 1926 (where once again India joined Britain and the Dominions and was represented by the maharaja of Burdwan) formulated the Balfour Declaration, which resulted in the Statute of Westminster Act 1931. The Statute of Westminster described the Dominions. 'They are autonomous Communities within the British Empire, equal in status, in no way subordinate one to another in any aspect of their domestic or external affairs, though united by a common allegiance to the Crown, and freely associated as members of the British Commonwealth of Nations.' Though it explicitly did not apply to India, it naturally captured the attention of moderate local leaders who wished to retain British connections, but operate in the higher status of a Dominion within the Empire. As Marshall argues, the 'presence of representatives of India would have been a daily inescapable reminder that there was no hard and fast distinction between the self-governing fraternity and the other elements in the Empire'.[13] While from the Indian perspective their presence amongst the self-governing Dominions gave hope that they would soon join the ranks of this small influential group within the Empire. For the traditional elites of Congress, whose political aspirations were 'overwhelmingly legalistic', the full status of being a Dominion alongside Canada and Australia appealed greatly.[14] They themselves through the 1925 Commonwealth of India Bill (which the British Labour party helped draft) and the 1928 Nehru Report all basically advocated the Dominion model for India. They accepted continuation of the Crown in India, but sought internal autonomy. However, the possibility of an Indian Dominion in the 1930s was hamstrung by a combination of British reluctance to accept Indian constitutional parity with the settler Dominions and the feeling among younger Indian nationalists that Dominion status was not enough and

---

[11] See Harshan Kumarasingham, *Onward with Executive Power: Lessons from New Zealand 1947–57* (Wellington, 2010), 12.

[12] K. C. Wheare, *The Constitutional Structure of the Commonwealth* (Oxford, 1960), 10.

[13] Peter Marshall, 'The Balfour Formula and the Evolution of the Commonwealth', *The Round Table: The Commonwealth Journal of International Affairs*, 90, 361 (2001), 545.

[14] C. A. Bayly, *Recovering Liberties: Indian Thought in the Age of Liberalism and Empire* (Cambridge, 2012), 329–30.

degrading.[15] The intensity of opposition to even the restrictive devolution of power to Indians that the Government of India Act 1935 produced from 'Die-hards' like Winston Churchill showed the limitations of hoping the Dominion model would be applied to the subcontinent.[16] Ironically, by the time British governments did come around to offering Dominion status for *all* of India in the 1940s it was too late to entice the Congress leadership. Congress had become by then less a club of anglophile moderates content to confine their strategy for greater autonomy within the Empire to legal arguments to a mass organisation fired by the genius of Gandhi for a revival of Indian civilisation through civil disobedience and disavowal of gradualist passivity to British overlordship. Nehru in an article written for a French periodical in 1936 spoke of the impossibility of India becoming a Dominion and even predicted the disintegration of inter-Dominion cooperation. Nehru reasoned that 'racial ill-treatment and a policy of exclusion of Indians' meant an Indian Dominion unconscionable. Interestingly, rather than stressing India's reluctance to be a Dominion he stressed that the most important reason was that Britain and the Dominions themselves would not tolerate India's economic independence.

> India, by virtue of her size, population and potential wealth, is by far the most important member of the British Empire. So long as the rest of the empire exploits her, she remains on the imperial fringe. But a free India in the British group of nations would inevitably tend to become the centre of gravity of that group, Delhi might challenge London as the nerve-centre of the empire. The position would become intolerable for England as well as the white dominions. They would prefer to have India outside their group, an independent but friendly country, rather than to be boss of their own household.[17]

It was in this context that the most liberal approaches to India from British cabinet ministers like the 1942 Cripps Mission offer of Dominion status after the completion of war in exchange for Indian cooperation in the war effort was too late – as Gandhi himself famously said it was like receiving a 'post-dated cheque' from a failing bank. The Indians could also see that with Churchill still prime minister nothing was likely to be achieved in their direction.[18] Labour's assumption of office in

---

[15] See W. David McIntyre, *The Britannic Vision: Historians and the Making of the British Commonwealth of Nations, 1907–48* (2009), 194–216.

[16] For more information on the interwar years regarding India and Britain, see Andrew Muldoon, *Empire, Politics and the Creation of the 1935 India Act* (2009); D. A. Low, *Britain and Indian Nationalism: The Imprint of Ambiguity 1929–1942* (Cambridge, 2002); and R. J. Moore, *The Crisis of Indian Unity, 1917–1940* (Oxford, 1974); and N. C. Fleming, 'Diehard Conservatism, Mass Democracy, and Indian Constitutional Reform, *c.* 1918–1935', *Parliamentary History*, 32, 2 (2013), 337–60.

[17] Jawaharlal Nehru, 'India and the World', *Vendredi*, Paris, 6 Jan. 1936, in *The Oxford India Nehru*, ed. Uma Iyengar (New Delhi, 2008), 482.

[18] See Peter Clarke, *The Cripps Version: The Life of Sir Stafford Cripps 1889–1952* (2003).

1945 signalled more positive reactions from Downing Street, but from India there was still suspicion at British intentions while the new cabinet were worried not just whether India would accept Dominion status, but more so if they could hold India for much longer without the whole region disintegrating into violent anarchy. With disorder and increasingly depressive and resigned reports from the viceroys about the dire situation, the cabinet saw the futility of further imposition of British rule. On the other hand, the cabinet did not want 'an inglorious end to our long association with India' and believed that public opinion, parliament, the king, the Empire–Commonwealth and the world would view any withdrawal that did not salvage a constitutional settlement as 'a policy of scuttle unworthy of a great power'.[19]

There was also the temptation across party lines that the Dominions and Commonwealth in the post-war world would give and promote British power on the international scene since they envisaged that British leadership would still carry across the former Empire. As Hopkins argues, the British gambled on the 'possibility of a bonus if the readvertised Commonwealth could be transformed into a multiracial organisation that would march in step, yet still be led by white officers'.[20] Mazower demonstrates that Field Marshal Smuts and other theorists of the British Empire thought that the Commonwealth, though 'respectful of sovereignty', would not only 'acknowledge the primacy of great powers', which in Smuts's thinking meant the settler states, but also potentially preserve colonialism by arguing the morality of Western civilizational values after the defeat of fascism. The Commonwealth was seen as an opportunity to justify and legitimise British power in the new world order.[21] Though the extent of Smuts's views had restricted reach, the idea was widely held that the Commonwealth would accentuate British stature in the world after the war had diminished its economic and military strength. Rather than die as a concept after 1945, it 'was expected that the dominions would continue to function as satellites, even without direct political control' and help in 'reviving the old empire'.[22] What Smuts and other imperial ideologues were less confident about was whether non-settler possessions could rise to such expectations and even more pertinent was whether they would be willing to play such a role. Even without ruling them South Asia was still the most prominent part of the strategy to preserve British standing. Senior members of the Attlee

[19] '"India: Constitutional Position": Cabinet Conclusions (Confidential Annex)', 10 Dec. 1946, in *The Labour Government and the End of Empire 1945–1951, Part I High Policy and Administration, British Documents on the End of Empire (BDEE)*, ed. Ronald Hyam (1992), 31–2.

[20] Hopkins, 'Rethinking Decolonization', 217.

[21] Mark Mazower, *No Enchanted Place: The End of Empire and the Ideological Origins of the United Nations* (Princeton, 2009), 20–38, 189.

[22] Hopkins, 'Rethinking Decolonization', 218.

administration held the view that making Dominions in South Asia could hold the region for Britain and disguise any loss of prestige, which outright secession implied. Ernest Bevin while foreign secretary, for instance, pleaded with the colonial secretary to avoid the word 'independence' if at all possible in a letter as late as May 1947 to the Ceylonese leader D. S. Senanayake: 'I do not like the repetition of the word 'independence' the whole time. There is quite a different meaning attached to this by the Eastern people from ours.'[23] In the end, the letter excluded any mention of independence and instead allowed 'fully responsible status within the British Commonwealth' to obfuscate the Ceylonese.[24]

Before South Asian decolonisation in 1947–8 the term Dominion generally applied to the traditional cases of Canada (the Dominion of Newfoundland joined the Canadian Federation in 1949), Australia, New Zealand and to an extent South Africa. Together under the imperial Crown they shared common British subjecthood and nationality – an issue of heated discussion after independence of whether this extended to the conspicuously non-British South Asian Dominions.[25] The settler cases were seen to be especially bound by the 'British Embrace' and formed the 'British World' in terms of complementary cultural and political identities until well into the 1950s and 1960s.[26] This formed the distinction between the 'empire of settlement and the tropical empire'. The 'lordly' word Dominion meant these settler partners had higher status and though distinct from each other were collectively 'keyed into imperial Britain by ties of kinship, trade, defence and cultural aspirations' that made them '*dominionative*' – a sensation that lingered well into the post-war era.[27] Outside of the Dominion elect was Ireland, which due to its historically strained relationship with Britain has been described as the 'Captive Dominion'[28] – a term that shows the ambivalence the Dominion label had west of the Irish Sea. In the pre-1947 period, Belich has recently used the term 'Adopted Dominions' to describe the close relationships and influence Britain had in parts of Latin America, especially Argentina in the nineteenth century, where though there was not formal political control there was little doubt as to their place in the 'Anglo-World'

[23] Bevin to Creech Jones, 20 May 1947, CAB 118/29, in *The Labour Government and the End of Empire, BDEE*, ed. Hyam, 71–2.

[24] Creech Jones to Bevin, 23 May 1947, CAB 118/29, in *The Labour Government and the End of Empire, BDEE*, ed. Hyam, 74.

[25] See Sarah Ansari, 'Subjects or Citizens? India, Pakistan and the 1948 British Nationality Act', *Journal of Imperial and Commonwealth History*, 41, 2 (2013), 285–312.

[26] See, for example, Stuart Ward, *Australia and the British Embrace: The Demise of the Imperial Ideal* (Melbourne, 2001).

[27] Jim Davidson, 'De-Dominionisation Revisited', *Australian Journal of Politics and History*, 51, 1 (2005), 108–9.

[28] Donal Lowry, 'The Captive Dominion: Imperial Realities behind Irish Diplomacy, 1922–49', *Irish Historical Studies*, 36, 142 (Nov. 2008), 202–26.

orbit.[29] Dominionism could have been also applied to parts of Africa in the more traditional meaning, such as in Rhodesia.[30] However, the South Asian cases stood apart and were internally distinctive. They achieved independence and sovereignty before any other non-white case, but nonetheless chose to accept Dominion status and with it formal allegiance to the Crown for a variety of reasons, which will be discussed below. D. S. Senanayake used the term 'Tropical Dominions' to describe the Asian candidates for independence.[31] 'Tropical Dominions' gives a flavour to their difference and the occasionally inclement conditions in South Asia for this vague British conception. The Australian-born Oxford-based constitutional scholar K. C. Wheare contemplated in a February 1948 BBC broadcast how the new Asian Dominions would operate. Wheare candidly admitted that he never thought any of them would become Dominions believing they would prefer the republican path. Unlike the settler countries where the people 'are almost a hundred per cent of British stock' most other states in the Empire–Commonwealth did not have such demographics and should instead see Britain not as the 'mother-country', but the 'mother-in-law' country. The Asian cases were more unique again since on independence they immediately in terms of population outnumbered all the other Dominions put together.

> Perhaps we shall find that India, Pakistan and Ceylon not to mention other communities in the British Empire though they are not daughter nations have come to regard themselves as adopted daughter nations, having been brought up in the family, we might say, and having been treated like the others, and reared at last to adult status, they may be ready to say: we are members of the family by adoption and we're glad to take the name Dominion. Well, it may prove to be so. But it's not as simple as that.[32]

Indeed, it would not be as simple as that and the experiment of Asian daughters left their settler cousins anxious and their 'mother-in-law' (perhaps step-mother would be more accurate) wondering whether the new additions would keep together or break up the family.

---

[29] James Belich, *Replenishing the Earth: The Settle Revolution and the Rise of the Anglo-World, 1783–1939* (Oxford, 2009).

[30] Donal Lowry, 'Rhodesia: The Lost Dominion', in *Settlers and Expatriates: Britons over the Seas*, ed. Robert Bickers, Oxford History of the British Empire Companion Series (Oxford, 2010).

[31] D. S. Senanayake to George Hall, 16 Aug. 1945, CO 54/986/6/2, 113, in *Sri Lanka, Part II Towards Independence 1945–1948, British Documents on the End of Empire, Series B, Volume 2*, ed. K. M. de Silva (1997), 40.

[32] Text of a BBC broadcast on 9 Feb. 1948 by Professor K. C. Wheare, concerning the new constitutional position of British Dominions, D132, Papers of Earl Mountbatten of Burma: official papers as last viceroy and first governor general of India, 1947–8, University of Southampton (henceforth Mountbatten Papers).

India – the expedient dominion

Months before independence, the Constituent Assembly passed a resolution on 22 January 1947 with the objective that India must become an 'Independent Sovereign Republic'.[33] The resolution put the Indian leaders symbolically against the concept of the Crown's continuance that Dominion status held axiomatic. The resolution seemed to have quelled any thought that India would be anything other than a republic. The Crown appeared an insuperable barrier to inclusion in the Commonwealth. Nehru and the Congress elite instead looked to the French Revolution with its symbolic humiliation of the Crown and the forging of a fraternal republic. Nehru told Indian parliamentarians in 1946 that he looked 'back to that mighty revolution which took place over 150 years ago and that 'Constituent Assembly' that had met in comparable radical circumstances'.[34] Austin in his seminal account of the foundations of the Indian constitution compared it to the context of Philadelphia in 1787 where the American colonialists purposively rejected the British monarchy and Westminster system in drawing up the institutions of their republic.[35] Nehru wished to be the Indian Washington not its Walpole – or so it seemed. The settler Dominions were not as romantic in their symbolism or precedence for the Indian nationalists. As argued above, theirs was a path of gradualism with conspicuous cultural and political links to Britain, which was unlikely to stir the blood of Gandhian followers aiming for indigenous *swaraj*. Though the Dominions operated with political independence, the nominal but emblematic retention of the Crown as enshrined in Dominion status could only seem unpalatable to India's leaders in-waiting. The Crown had no place in the 'national philosophy of India' and the thought that it could has been described as 'absurd' and 'beneath contempt'.[36] However, for all the rhetorical remonstrance against the Crown, pragmatic considerations reopened the issue almost as soon as they were thought settled and the mixed messages began.[37] The arrival of Lord Mountbatten, just weeks after the resolution, as the new viceroy with specific instructions from Attlee

[33] 'Objectives Resolution', in Shiva Rao, *The Framing of India's Constitution: A Study* (Bombay, 1968), 121–2.

[34] Nehru's speech to the Constituent Assembly, 13 Dec. 1946, cited in Subhash C. Kashyap, *Jawaharlal Nehru and the Constitution* (New Delhi, 1982), 78.

[35] Granville Austin, *The Indian Constitution: Cornerstone of a Nation* (Oxford, 1966).

[36] Bhikhu Parekh, 'The Constitution as a Statement of Indian Identity', in *Politics and Ethics of the Indian Constitution*, ed. Rajeev Bhargava (New Delhi, 2009), 46–7.

[37] Harshan Kumarasingham, *A Political Legacy of the British Empire: Power and the Parliamentary System in Post-Colonial India and Sri Lanka* (2013), 25–45.

to deliver independence, but maintain British influence in India,[38] was to have considerable effect on Indian political opinion – particularly on Nehru. The Indian leaders realised that in order to achieve independence quickly they would need to cooperate. The British also knew that only with compromise could they simultaneously save face and save their influence in the subcontinent. Aside from getting independence quickly, the Congress leadership realised that even with the withdrawal of the Muslim League and acknowledgement of partition there were still many parts of British India that were reluctant to accept Congress leadership. Nehru and Mountbatten discussed what seemed a constitutional impasse on one of their first meetings in March 1947. Mountbatten noted the following from his interview:

> Nehru said that he did not consider it possible, with the forces which were at work, that India could remain within the Commonwealth. But basically, he said, they did not want to break any threads ... (I feel that they are beginning to see that they cannot go out of the Commonwealth; but they cannot afford to say that they will stay in; they are groping for a formula). Nehru gave a direct implication that they wanted to stay in; but a categorical statement that they intended to go out.[39]

For the Indians and the British, a critical point was what being a Dominion meant. Unlike the traditional settler states, India was not willing to shroud its independence under the carapace of the Crown, but they did see that Dominionism offered a 'fast-track' for political freedom. Attlee, who had been Dominions secretary in the war cabinet, faced the predicament of appeasing the Indian nationalists who wanted their freedom unfettered by Dominion status and his critics at home who argued that Dominion status did not mean independence, but self-government within the Commonwealth. Winston Churchill, now leader of the opposition, debated with Attlee the meaning of independence and Dominionism when they wrote to each other over the title of the Indian Independence Bill in July 1947.

> Dominion Status is not the same as Independence, although it may be freely used to establish independence. It is not true that a community is independent when its Ministers have in fact taken the Oath of Allegiance to The King ... The correct title would be ... 'The Indian Dominions Bill'. I should however be quite willing to support if it were called 'The India Bill 1947' or 'The India Self-Government Bill'.

Attlee did not change the title, though he considered it, and refuted Churchill's interpretation

---

[38] Attlee to Mountbatten, 18 Mar. 1947, in *Constitutional Relations between Britain and India: The Transfer of Power 1942–47* (henceforth *TOP*), IX: *The Fixing of a Time Limit 4 November 1946 – 22 March 1947*, ed. Nicholas Mansergh (1980), 972–4.

[39] Interview between Mountbatten and Nehru, 24 Mar. 1947 in *TOP*, X: *The Mountbatten Viceroyalty Formulation of a Plan 22 March – 30 May 1947*, ed. Nicholas Mansergh (1981), 11–13.

I do not agree with the point which you make. Dominion Prime Ministers constantly stress the point that they are independent states within the British Commonwealth. They bear allegiance to The King who is The King of all the Dominions. The insistence on independence does not touch the point of allegiance, but emphasizes the complete freedom of every member of the Commonwealth from control by any other member. I think this is the most valuable counter to demands for independence outside the Commonwealth as it shows that this demand can be satisfied within it. This is, in fact, the meaning of Dominion Status.[40]

Despite Attlee's explanation, the Labour government hoped, like Churchill, that Dominion status would in fact cement interdependence and British use of India's vast military and physical potential, especially in the Cold War climate when resources were stretched. Lord Wavell, as viceroy, and the cabinet acknowledged in July 1946 that India had 'an almost inexhaustible supply of manpower' and could produce 'almost as many soldiers as the Commonwealth could maintain'. As Inder Singh argues, defence was critical to both Conservative and Labour in their motives in keeping in India in the Commonwealth.[41]

From the Indian perspective, defence and the Commonwealth relationship was also a serious topic. In New Delhi, the new viceroy was busy at work to convince the Indian leaders that Dominion status did mean independence and furthermore India would earn advantages from ignoring the symbolic temptation of ditching the king and erecting a republic. Why would the Indians do this after their freedom struggle and quest to rid all vestiges of imperialism, which the king and Dominion status represented? The Congress leadership wanted power and it wanted it quickly. It also wanted the armoury of British rule, both militarily and politically, to be transferred to the new independent state. Mountbatten quite craftily was able to paint a convincing portrait to the Congress hierarchy on why they should become a Dominion. Krishna Menon, who claimed authorship of the famous January 1947 resolution for an 'Independent Sovereign Republic', had an interview with Mountbatten in April 1947. Menon inadvertently brought up the issue by asking the viceroy whether British officers could stay on after the transfer of power. Mountbatten replied that 'no British officer worth his salt would willingly resign his commission to become an adventurer in the Indian Services' since by India becoming a republic all officers would no longer hold the 'King's Commission' and would not tolerate working for a 'Foreign Power'. Field Marshal Auchinleck as commander-in-chief of the Indian Army had already indicated to the viceroy days earlier that 'British officers could not serve in any India that was neither under the Crown nor a British

[40] Churchill to Attlee, 1 July 1947, and Attlee to Churchill, 4 July 1947, CHUR 2/43 B, Sir Winston Churchill Papers, Churchill College, University of Cambridge.

[41] Anita Inder Singh, 'Keeping India in the Commonwealth: British Political and Military Aims, 1947–1949', *Journal of Contemporary History*, 20, 3 (July 1985), 472.

Dominion, since the oath of allegiance taken by the officers was to the King.'[42] Menon, seeing the point, stated that the term 'Independent Sovereign Republic' was a mistake and he 'regretted choosing such drastic terminology' as its author. The viceroy then proceeded to provide Nehru's confidante with three pieces of advice on how things could be amended so that British officers and other benefits could remain while Indian nationalism assuaged. First, the Constituent Assembly should delay implementation of the republican resolution for five years and then put it to a plebiscite. This would allow the Indian leaders to 'openly give the reason that this was to enable British officers to remain to assist in the gradual hand-over throughout the Army'. Secondly, that India should 'avoid the expression "Dominion Status" and use terms like "Free Nation of the Commonwealth" or "Free India" or, as he himself [Menon] put it, "Union of India"'. Finally, on 'no account must they renounce the link with the Crown' if they wanted British officers and British goodwill. Menon considered this very sensible advice, but indicated the difficulty of keeping the Crown since for 'purely political warfare motives Congress had been attacking the Crown as a symbol of oppression'. The impresario in Mountbatten, when asked for his opinion, stated that he 'was one of those sentimental fools' in favour of the link before starkly reminding Menon that in regard to keeping the Crown and the Congress happy was 'his headache' and that Menon 'could not have his cake and eat it'. Mountbatten also ventured that everyone in India bar the Congress were in favour of Dominion status. Menon, at least viewed from the official record, then made the collusive suggestion that unless the viceroy himself should 'take the first step and approach us [Congress] nothing will be done'. Mountbatten testily retorted to this offer

> Then nothing will be done, because it is entirely your loss, and I am not going to allow any sentimental reasons to make me pull your chestnuts out of the fire. If you do not take the first step, you will have a rotten army; you will lose the benefits of the Commonwealth; and you will save the other nations of the Commonwealth the expense, anxiety and responsibility of your defence.

Menon, seeing how the conversation was turning, dangled the prospect that if the 'British were voluntarily to give us now Dominion Status, well ahead of June 1948, we should be so grateful that not a voice would be heard' against keeping the Crown and Commonwealth connection. Mountbatten indicated his assent to the idea, which he had very clearly planted.[43] The viceroy even thought that Nehru and Congress's adamant position that no foreign power should have defence facilities on Indian

---

[42] Interview between Mountbatten and Auchinleck, 5 Apr. 1947, in *TOP*, x, ed. Mansergh, 134.

[43] Interview between Mountbatten and Krishna Menon, 17 Apr. 1947, in *TOP*, x, ed. Mansergh, 310–13.

territory did not extend to Commonwealth powers, but meant the United States, a view which the cabinet concurred with.[44] Nehru and Menon were able to use the advantages of Dominion status to mitigate the natural protestations of Congress republicans. Dominion status would be an expedient step and the royal link disguised to bring independence closer and with it the promised republic.

Rivalry between these successor states also played a critical role in both Pakistan and India becoming Dominions. The British had appealed to both sides' vanity by saying if one became a Dominion the other would face at least some disadvantage. Mountbatten had originally envisaged at least three Dominions coming from British India: Hindustan, Pakistan and the States. India was warned that it could be 'a separate foreign State' surrounded by Commonwealth Realms, which aside from Pakistan could have included Bengal and the princely states of Hyderabad, Kashmir, Travancore and Mysore as all these states had indicated this preference to the viceroy.[45] The idea that British India would be further divided after partition and on top of that these areas having continued links with the Crown naturally troubled Congress. Agreeing to be a Dominion not only appeased any thought India would be negatively effected, but also in regard to the other presumptive Dominions meant New Delhi could claim to have inherited the British Raj's powers of paramountcy over the princely states and hold them within the union – though the princely states themselves disputed this interpretation, believing that their treaty obligations to the centre ended with British rule.[46] Dominion status offered independent India a convenient ruse to maintain the colonial *status quo* of suzerainty of these semi-autonomous states, especially after Mountbatten promised that their princely prerogatives would be retained.[47] Dominion status offered the Congress leaders a method whereby they would be bequeathed almost the full powers of the Raj over the states and the compromise of keeping the Crown and Commonwealth appeared worth the charge of hypocrisy. The issue of Dominion status perhaps exemplifies Chatterjee's assessment that many Indian scholars, at least in an earlier period, tried to avoid 'the problematical and contradictory aspect's of Nehru's personality'.[48] The independent Dominion of India showed the gap between emotion and expedience, but arguably this was natural in the tumultuous context.

[44] Minutes of the India and Burma Committee, 28 May 1947, in *TOP*, X, ed. Mansergh, 1019–20.
[45] See Ian Copland, *The Princes of India in the Endgame of Empire* (Cambridge, 1997).
[46] Kumarasingham, *A Political Legacy of the British Empire*, 92–101.
[47] Barbara N. Ramusack, *The Indian Princes and their States* (Cambridge, 2004), 272–3.
[48] Partha Chatterjee, *A Possible India: Essays in Criticism* (New Delhi, 1997), 23.

For figures like Mountbatten and senior Indian bureaucrats, who had been admitted into the hallowed sanctum of the Indian Civil Service, like V. P. Menon and Sir Tej Bahadur Sapru, Dominion status offered an opportunity to maintain the traditions of the laws and conventions of Britain they so admired, but the same status could also be sold as an idea to the Congress leadership as a transitional period that gave political independence before the republic could be formed. The anglophile civil servants hoped the Dominion would last much longer than Congress envisaged. The ever-present V. P. Menon even hoped 'a Ruling Prince will be selected as Governor-General' of the Indian Dominion when Mountbatten left.[49] Nehru, on the other hand, saw the substantial power and flexibility traditional Dominion prime ministers wielded and saw how he could use them for the untraditional context of India to create the 'Indian Version of First Among Equals' that could mould Indian democracy.[50] Nehru therefore was swift to demand, once Dominion status had been agreed, that he should be treated as a Dominion prime minister even before the formal hand over of power. Nehru told the viceroy in May 1947 'very vehemently' that the Indian interim government 'should be treated by Convention as a Dominion Government' since it would have 'a great psychological effect' and said if this was not granted he would resign. To sweeten acceptance of Nehru's view, he told the viceroy he was 'prepared to give the Governor-General over-riding powers' in certain areas such as dealing with Pakistan and the protection of minorities once the Dominion of India was inaugurated.[51] However, though Nehru did become a *de facto* Dominion prime minister before August 1947 Mountbatten's plan to be a 'super-Governor-General' of both Dominions was scuppered by the wishes of the other Dominion.

Pakistan – the siege dominion

If independent India's decision to become a Dominion was partly to do with securing British officers and securing control over demanded territories, these reasons were even more pronounced in the Dominion of Pakistan. Jinnah was swift, when he knew Pakistan was to be more than an idea, that he had to persuade British personnel in India to stay to ensure continuity in the military and civil service. The Muslim League leader understood that India, or Hindustan as he stubbornly referred to it since he believed that the state ruled from Delhi had no exclusivity to that evocative name, would most probably take the lion's share of British India's assets. Critically, the renowned Indian Army of almost half

[49] Menon to Mountbatten, 27 Sept. 1948, F38, Mountbatten Papers.

[50] Kumarasingham, *A Political Legacy of the British Empire*, 46–89.

[51] Interview between Mountbatten, Nehru and Sardar Patel, 17 May 1947, in *TOP*, X, ed. Mansergh, 870–1.

a million soldiers and commanded by an overwhelmingly British officer corps would need to be 'cut and pasted into new national formations', even though only seven of the twenty-three infantry regiments in the pre-partition era were exclusively based on sectarian lines.[52] Congress and the Muslim League predicted rightly that over the division of the subcontinent they would become 'Dominions in Dispute'. A view that was shared by the British chiefs of staff 'who displayed little faith in the idea of a new Commonwealth as their civilian counterparts. They referred to the new Dominions as "temporary", as questionable allies on the basis of the unwritten rules of Commonwealth co-operation for defence' at least.[53] Despite the British defence chiefs' doubts and prognosis, Pakistan saw merit in Dominion status precisely because it offered the military support from the Commonwealth Realms, which as a state born into conflict and depravation was greatly desired.[54]

Though the Empire–Commonwealth had usually avoided statuary or treaty requirements in terms of military obligations to each other, the convention was that they would support each member's defence needs in times of crisis. The Dominions Office during this time and after argued that officials and ministers should stress that one of the justifications that should attract Commonwealth members was 'co-operation, to the extent desired and approved by each Government, in the military defence of common interests'.[55] Commonwealth diplomats in all three states were the core representatives in the region. They enjoyed easy access to ministers and officials and, especially British diplomats, had considerable influence on local politics that other foreign diplomats lacked in the region.[56] Though beyond the remit of this article, it was understandable that Pakistani Prime Minister Liaquat Ali Khan sought Commonwealth arbitration over Kashmir and appealed in 1950–1 for peace-keeping troops from the other Dominions to solve this ever-present dispute 'within the family' of the Commonwealth where no Dominion had ever gone to war with another. Though this convention would soon be broken in South Asia, the prime ministers of India and Pakistan did establish a month after independence the Military Evacuation Organisation to try and manage the logistical and social chaos that revolved around the massive refugee

[52] Yasmin Khan, *The Great Partition: The Making of India and Pakistan* (New Haven, 2008), 113–17.

[53] R. J. Moore, *Making the New Commonwealth* (Oxford, 1987), 18.

[54] A. Martin Wainwright, *Inheritance of Empire: Britain, India and the Balance of Power in Asia, 1938–55* (Westport, 1994), 61–7.

[55] 'The Commonwealth Relationship', Feb. 1949, DO 121/72, The National Archives (henceforth TNA).

[56] Lorna Lloyd, *Diplomacy with a Difference: The Commonwealth Office of High Commissioner 1880–2006* (Leiden, 2007), 127–38; Louis and Robinson, 'The Imperialism of Decolonization', 473; and Kumarasingham, *A Political Legacy of the British Empire*, 114–70.

crisis and created protocols so the 'troops of the other dominion could enter its territory to rescue and protect its "own" refugees'.[57]

For Pakistan, this was a massive appeal and reflected the predominant focus on military over democratic infrastructure.[58] As Liaquat candidly told the viceroy in April 1947, 'there is no doubt that Pakistan wants to remain a dominion, we want to have your officers'.[59] The Muslim League leaders during this tense time before the handover were buoyed, and the Congress leaders simultaneously apprehensive, by Mountbatten's prediction that with British, Commonwealth and American help 'places like Karachi would become big naval and air bases within the British Commonwealth' and Pakistan would 'in no while have armed forces superior to those of Hindustan'.[60] Mountbatten's ploy of encouraging Dominion status through a combination of fear and necessity was working even though his entreaties to both parties were factually dubious and lacked firm commitments from the British government. However, his promotion of the idea that if both sides took Dominion status then independence could be brought closer was real. This strategy, also known as the 'V.P. Menon Plan' after the Indian mandarin, offered the transfer of power as an 'interim measure on Dominion status basis' meant that the sting could be drawn from the pan-Indian nationalists and instead inspire goodwill between the United Kingdom and the new Dominions. Predicting that the division of India would take 'not less that 4 or 5 years to frame their Constitutions', the latent status of being a Dominion would recede into the background as urgent problems of administration and development took centre stage so allowing the link with the Crown to endure in the background. Menon speculated that 'having realised the importance and usefulness of the presence of a Governor-General appointed by His Majesty, both the parts of India may see the benefit of retaining that link with Great Britain'.[61]

Unlike India, Mountbatten's tactics with Pakistan was to tell them that it was by no means certain that they would be accepted as a Dominion to try and wrest further agreements from Jinnah. However, as Attlee disclosed to the prime ministers of Canada, Australia, New Zealand and South Africa, Jinnah had 'threatened to appeal over the Viceroy's head to the "people of the Commonwealth" and argued that no part of

[57] Joya Chatterji, 'South Asian Histories of Citizenship, 1946–1970', Historical Journal, 55, 4 (Dec. 2012), 1058.

[58] See Ayesha Jalal, The State of Martial Rule: The Origins of Pakistan's Political Economy of Defence (Cambridge, 1990).

[59] Interview between Mountbatten and Liaquat, 11 Apr. 1947, in TOP, x, ed. Mansergh, 201.

[60] Interview between Mountbatten and Baldev Singh, 22 Apr. 1947, and interview between Mountbatten and Krishna Menon, 22 Apr. 1947, in TOP, x, ed. Mansergh, 370–4.

[61] Minutes by Ismay and Mountbatten, 25–8 Apr. 1947, in TOP, x, ed. Mansergh, 437–40.

the Commonwealth could be forcibly extruded against its will'.[62] The Commonwealth Dominions were seen to have some precedents, which the rival Indian Dominions could draw upon. The constitutional advisor to the Constituent Assembly, B. N. Rau, suggested in June 1947 that India and Pakistan should emulate the 1944 Canberra Pact between the Dominions of Australia and New Zealand, which established protocols and procedures regarding defence, trade and other areas of cooperation. Rau believed it 'might be a good thing if the two dominions contemplated in India could be induced, from the start, to enter into a similar agreement and set up machinery for collaboration in matters of joint concern'.[63] This idealistic plan did not eventuate and though both Dominions sought and received considerable cooperation from their Australasian counterparts Pakistan broke tradition by not commemorating ANZAC Day 'because of the Muslim connection with Turkey'.[64]

Aside from the military aspects, Pakistan was in dire need for further support in almost every sense. Talbot argues convincingly that '[f]ew states have sprung into existence with as many material disadvantages, institutional weaknesses and uncertain national loyalty'.[65] Jinnah relied not only on the British for senior defence personnel, all three heads of the Pakistan Defence Services were British, but also for the Civil Service and key leadership roles. Jinnah for example purposefully had Britons as governors with wide prerogative powers in four of the five provinces – the exception being Sindh where the Quiad-i-Azam (Father of the Nation) intended to control himself effectively. The proposed territories that would form the Dominion of Pakistan ostensibly linked by religion gave the state a famously 'moth-eaten' look with the Bengali province separated from the designated capital Karachi by over a 1,000 miles of Hindustan. Jinnah knew that the context and circumstances demanded strong leadership to keep this divided and fragile state together and restore order after the bloody legacies of partition – his was a Dominion under siege. This unquestioned leader of the Muslim League took an unexpected route to achieve these tall aims.

Unlike India, which had ideologically committed to a republican model and tolerated the Dominion transition for pragmatic purposes the Pakistani leadership, though not overt monarchists, decided to utilise the provisions of vice-regal rule for their own intentions. Mountbatten had hoped, as did many in British India and Britain itself, that he would become governor-general of both Dominions. Jinnah punctured

[62] Attlee to King, Chifley, Fraser and Smuts, 23 May 1947, in in *TOP*, X, ed. Mansergh, 973.

[63] Note for Mountbatten by Sir B. N. Rau, 12 June 1947, D131, Mountbatten Papers.

[64] Note of meeting, 6 Aug. 1947, D316, Mountbatten Papers.

[65] Ian Talbot, *Pakistan: A Modern History*, 3rd edn (2008), 123.

Mountbatten's vanity by denying him the further accolade of presiding over two Dominions by taking the job in Karachi himself. Jinnah decided to take on the position as the king's representative and was to be one the most unique governors-general in the history of the Commonwealth. What made Jinnah different from his Dominion colleagues is that he existed unquestionably as the supreme political authority in Pakistan and not as a ceremonial figurehead. Jinnah candidly told the crestfallen Mountbatten that the only way 'he could sell the idea of all these British high officials to the inhabitants of Pakistan would be if he himself became the Governor-General'. Mountbatten in disbelief recorded of Jinnah;

> He is suffering from megalomania in its worst form for when I pointed out to him that if he went as a Constitutional Governor-General his powers would be restricted but as Prime Minister he really could run Pakistan, he made no bones about the fact that his Prime Minister would do what he said. 'In my position it is I who will give the advice and others will act on it.'[66]

The Muslim League leader resisted the fear that if Mountbatten did not become governor-general of both Dominions 'Pakistan would be likely to get less than their fair share of all-India assets.' Mountbatten's staff in turn alarmingly considered Jinnah as the king's representative 'could be a "Hitler" and take no notice' of the conventions of his vice-regal office.[67] Jinnah believed he would have more influence vis-à-vis Mountbatten if he too were his equal as a governor-general. Jinnah would prove his comment above correct and completely redefined the ideals of what a Dominion governor-general would be. As a *Dawn* editorial noted in July 1947, whatever the

> constitutional powers of the Governor-General of a Dominion may nominally be, in Quaid-i-Azam's case no legal or formal limitations can apply. His people will not be content to have him as merely the titular head of the Government, they would wish him to be their friend, philosopher, guide and ruler, irrespective of what the constitution of a Dominion of the British Commonwealth may contain.[68]

The governor-general designate of Pakistan then showed how he intended to rule by taking his active position as the inaugural president of the Constituent Assembly, which was also the parliament of Pakistan, and held this critical role concurrently with his vice-regal office until his death in September 1948. Jinnah had seen the powers available to successive viceroys and intended to exercise all the powers formally vested in the king's representative and to project the full prestige of the office over

---

[66] Viceroy's Personal Report, 4 July 1947, in *TOP*, XI: *The Mountbatten Viceroyalty: Announcement and Reception of the 3 June Plan 31 May – 7 July 1947*, ed. Nicholas Mansergh (1982), 898–9.

[67] Note by Erskine Crum, 3 July 1947, in *Quaid-i-Azam Mohammad Ali Jinnah Papers*, III: *On the Threshold of Pakistan 1 July – 25 July 1947*, ed. Z. H. Zaidi (Islamabad, 1996), 804–5.

[68] *Dawn*, 12 July 1947.

not only his future country men and women, but also over the British themselves. Jinnah's enthusiasm for British links went only so far. To Mountbatten's hope that the Dominion of Pakistan would include the Union Jack in the upper canton of the new flag, the governor-general designate replied 'he had been unable to find one single supporter' for the idea.[69]

Ceylon – the imitation Dominion

The Ceylonese inter-communal elite purposively projected themselves as being different from British India and articulated a message at odds with the Indian National Congress and the Muslim League. Ceylon, of course, had always been governed separately from British India as a Crown Colony and revelled in its status as a 'model colony' that was envied across the Empire for its peace and prosperity.[70] Repudiating the non-cooperation methods of Gandhi and the steely brinkmanship of Jinnah, the Ceylonese preferred to advocate their cause through the gradualist and non-violent strategy of showing that unlike their northern neighbours they openly wanted to be a Dominion in the traditional mould of the settler cases. The Soulbury Commission's 1945 report, which advocated the British Westminster parliamentary model for the island, explained some of the reasons behind its decision:

> It must be borne in mind that a number of the political leaders of Ceylon have been educated in England and have absorbed British political ideas. When they demand responsible government, they mean government on the British parliamentary model and are apt to resent any deviation from it as 'derogatory to their status as fellow citizens of the British Commonwealth of Nations and as conceding something less than they consider their due'. To put it more colloquially, what is good enough for the British people is good enough for them.[71]

The key members of the Ceylonese political elite would not have disagreed with a word of the above. Whereas the Pakistanis and especially the Indians needed to be convinced by the British of the virtues of Dominionhood, the Ceylonese had to convince the British they were ready for Dominion status and self-government. The Ceylonese strategy was therefore to demonstrate their loyalty to Britain and the Commonwealth and to contrast its constitutionalist non-violent methods with the unruly ways of their larger Asian neighbours.[72] Sir Oliver

---

[69] Interview between Mountbatten and Jinnah, 24 June 1947, D315, Mountbatten Papers.

[70] See K. M. De Silva, *A History of Sri Lanka*, Special Sri Lanka edn (Colombo, 2005), 570–89.

[71] [Soulbury Report] Colonial Office, *Ceylon: Report of the Commission on the Constitution*, Cmd 6677 (1945), 110.

[72] For a more in-depth comparison between the decolonisation in Sri Lanka and India, see Harshan Kumarasingham, *A Political Legacy of the British Empire*, and 'The Jewel in 'East,

Goonetilleke, a leading member of the local elite, without irony publicly pronounced that the world should 'think of Ceylon as a little bit of England' and enthused that 'Ceylon will rival Australia as the first Dominion to rally to the side of the Mother Country.'[73] During the independence negotiations in July 1947, when the Indian leaders were accepting Bagehot's[74] 'efficient' parts of the British constitution, but discarding or hiding the 'dignified' ceremonial aspects of Dominion status the Ceylonese delegation in London was requesting that their new Dominion be labelled the 'Kingdom of Ceylon', which even those who wanted Asian Dominions at Whitehall thought 'quite inappropriate'.[75]

In further contrast to the 1942 'Quit India' campaign the Ceylonese leadership under D. S. Senanayake openly sided with the British and its allies during the Second World War and in a clever gambit offered the continued use of its strategically valuable bases in Trincomalee, Colombo and Katunayake to the Royal Navy and Royal Air Force after independence, pointing out the added value of the bases in the wake of British withdrawal from the Indian mainland.[76] The war had sharpened British assessments of the Empire's defensive strategy and Ceylon had been a key territory in this world conflict.[77] Senanayake was arguing for traditional Dominion status as the best tactic for securing independence, which some in the Colonial Office and cabinet thought premature. The anglophile indigenous elite could point to many marketing ploys: the island had a long history of responsible government including being the first colony to achieve universal suffrage in 1931, it had high living and education standards, a productive economy, no public disturbances and, as yet, no communal discord that threatened the unity of the future state. These factors added with the post-war geopolitical situation, Ceylonese eagerness to join the Dominion club and the riotous context in British India forced the British to reconsider their reluctance. Senanayake wrote to the colonial secretary, George Hall, in August 1945 explaining as he saw it the desirability and worthiness of giving Ceylon Dominion status it deserved despite not being able to offer 'a rebel general – the experience of South Africa and Burma seems to suggest that it would be easier if we could'.

yet Has its Flaws": The Deceptive Tranquility Surrounding Sri Lankan Independence, *Heidelberg Papers in South Asian and Comparative Politics*, Working Paper no. 72 (June 2013).

[73] James Manor, *The Expedient Utopian: Bandaranaike and Ceylon* (Cambridge, 1989), 199.

[74] Kumarasingham, *A Political Legacy of the British Empire*, 1–24.

[75] Minute by K. O. Roberts-Wray, 14 July 1947, CO 537/2226, 1, in *Sri Lanka, Part II, BDEE*, ed. De Silva, 318.

[76] 'Ceylon: Constitution: Draft Agreements Precedent to Self-Government: Defence', 1947, CO 537/2217, TNA.

[77] Ashley Jackson, 'The Empire/Commonwealth and the Second World War', *The Round Table: The Commonwealth Journal of International Affairs*, 100, 412 (2011), 65–78.

> There has been no rebellion in Ceylon, no non-cooperation movement and no fifth-column: we were among the peoples who gave full collaboration while Britain was hard-pressed. Ireland obtained Dominion status; Indian has been promised it; Burma is being offered full self-government within the Commonwealth; but Ceylon gets none of these.

Senanayake then continued by astutely showing the advantages Britain would gain from giving Ceylon the status it craved. He was 'ready to pledge' to London that any independence deal would have 'defence as an integral part of an agreement for Dominion status'. The Ceylonese leader boldly promised the secretary of state

> of a friendly people and a friendly Government, another Dominion, on the sea and air routes to Australia and New Zealand. It would assure Great Britain of naval and air bases that would dominate the Indian Ocean ... It will indeed do more. It will add to the powers of the British Commonwealth of Nations. [A Ceylonese Dominion would] show the dependent peoples all over the Empire that your professions are not mere professions, and that it is possible for a people which, a hundred years ago, was almost completely lacking in educational facilities and was compelled to live on a very low standard of life [could] achieve the status of a Dominion within the British Commonwealth of Nations.[78]

It is hard to imagine Nehru or Jinnah writing such a letter, but Senanayake was no less successful in his aim than they were. Senanayake's enthusiasm was by no means shared by all the Ceylonese politicians, but this made his appeal for Dominion status that much more persuasive. Lord Soulbury, head of the commission that was sent to Ceylon, wrote to the colonial secretary, with Senanayake's knowledge, that there were younger, more radical and socialist Ceylonese nationalists that not only thought Dominion status was a 'sham independence', but also would align their republican agenda with the expulsion of British personnel from the island's bases. Soulbury and Senanayake shrewdly calculated that the risk of waiting for communal and political questions to be answered was outweighed by the risk of a handover to uncooperative leaders on the island where the Communists were by far the best-organised political force and offered a credible alternative.[79] If, Soulbury continued, the elderly Senanayake, despite similar undertakings in India, was unable to get Dominion status due to the 'non possumus of H.M.G.' he could well lose control of the legislature and Ceylon could transform from a loyal friend of Britain and the Crown to being more akin to Ireland. Soulbury, a former minister in the Chamberlain Cabinet thought, surprisingly as events later proved, that many 'of the Ceylonese resemble the Irish in temperament and intelligence and like the Irish they have long memories.

---

[78] Senanayake to Hall, 16 Aug. 1945, CO 54/986/6/2, 113, in *Sri Lanka, Part II, BDEE*, ed. De Silva, 40–2.
[79] Nira Wickramasinghe, 'Sri Lanka's Independence: Shadows over a Colonial Graft', in *Routledge Handbook of South Asian Politics: India, Pakistan, Bangladesh, Sri Lanka, and Nepal*, ed. Paul R. Brass (2010), 46–7.

It would be a tragedy to repeat in Ceylon any of the colossal mistakes we have made in Ireland.'[80] Patrick Gordon Walker as a minister in the Commonwealth Relations Office echoed this view in early 1948 when Britain did agree that Dominion status was warranted and reasoned that since 'Senanayake is in the genuine tradition of Dominion Prime Ministers' they had made the right choice. 'It is hardly too much to say that if we treat then strictly as a Dominion, they will behave very like a loyal colony: whereas if we treat them as a Colony we many end in driving them out of the Commonwealth.'[81] The Ceylonese ploy of imitation had worked, but whether it would last was another matter.

Conclusion

India has been described as the 'Lost Dominion'[82] in regard to the possibilities after the First World War. The jewel in the crown of the Empire was predicted to have become the Dominion diamond of the Commonwealth when the concept was in vogue. India can be more accurately described as a late Dominion since it did, like Pakistan and Ceylon, become one after independence. The 'Tropical Dominions' showed a very different trajectory to Dominionhood than the traditional settler cases bound by 'kith and kin'. Aside from the obvious point of them being non-British, these South Asian cases also became Dominions for very different reasons from the white self-governing members. Rather than examining Britain's interests in securing their inclusion as Realms in the Commonwealth, this paper examined the reasons that drove the South Asian elites towards what would at first seem an unlikely option. A combination of strategy, security and especially usefulness, but rarely sentiment, guided their objectives to become Dominions. The story of their attainment of Dominionhood reveals a significant chapter in the decolonisation of South Asia and shows how principles gave way to practicalities in order to achieve the ultimate goal: independence.

---

[80] Soulbury to Hall, 5 Oct. 1945, CO 54/986/6/3, 174 in *Sri Lanka, Part II, BDEE*, ed. De Silva, 110–13.

[81] Patrick Gordon Walker, 'Report on Ceylon', 17 Mar. 1948, CAB 129/26, in *Sri Lanka, Part II, BDEE*, ed. De Silva, 365.

[82] McIntyre, *The Britannic Vision*, 209–16.

ROYAL HISTORICAL SOCIETY
REPORT OF COUNCIL
SESSION 2012–2013

Officers and Council

- At the Anniversary Meeting on 23 November 2012 the Officers of the Society were re-elected.
- The President retiring under By-law XVI was Professor C D H Jones and the President-elect in his place was Professor P Mandler, BA, MA, PhD.
- The Vice-Presidents retiring under By-law XVII were Professor M C Finn and Professor P Mandler. Professor R A Burns, BA, MA, DPhil and Professor A M Walsham, BA, MA, PhD were elected in their place.
- The Officer retiring under By-law XVIII was:
  Professor A R Burns, Literary Director. Dr E Griffin, BA, MA, PhD was elected to replace him;
- The Members of Council retiring under By-law XX were Professor S Barton, Professor J M Cornwall and Professor C Whatley. Professor J S Henderson, BA, MA, PhD, Professor M J Stoyle, BA, DPhil and Professor P Summerfield, BA, MA, DPhil were elected in their place.
- The Society's administrative staff consists of Dr Sue Carr, Executive Secretary and Mrs Melanie Ransom, Administrative Secretary. Dr Jane Gerson replaced Melanie Ransom during maternity leave.
- Kingston Smith were re-appointed auditors for the year 2012–2013 under By-law XXXIX.
- Brewin Dolphin Securities were re-appointed to manage the Society's investment funds.

Activities of the Society during the year

The Royal Historical Society is the only representative organisation that can speak for professional historians in the UK. Our aim is to defend, promote and advance historical scholarship. We do this in two main ways. First, the 'outward facing' functions of the Society include disseminating and running campaigns on issues that affect historical research and education. Second, we aim to foster and develop historical scholarship within the academy through activities that include a programme of research grants, fellowships and conference support. Our publications and lecture programme remain at the heart of our activities, but we are also developing other ways of communicating with our Fellows and Members and with the wider historical community.

In 2012–13, we began a programme to improve our communications. Our aims are to raise the profile of the Society, make our activities better known and appreciated both within the profession and outside it, and develop a stronger relationship with our Fellows and Members. To this end, we are in the process of introducing a new integrated database and website and are overhauling our administrative procedures. We are delighted that Dr Jane Gerson has joined our administrative team as the Society's first Research and Communications Officer. Dr Gerson has responsibility both for overseeing the implementation of the new software systems and also for developing, in conjunction with our Honorary Director of Communications, a communications strategy. For the first time, the RHS now has a Twitter feed (@RoyalHistSoc) and a Facebook page. The new website, which we hope to launch in 2014, will have a fresher, cleaner look, will be continually updated, easier to navigate and will include, for the first time, the ability to pay subscriptions and apply for grants online. The new system will make it easier for Fellows and Members to interact with the Society. It will also be a resource for information about the profession and the work of the Society. The Executive Secretary, Dr Sue Carr, and the Administrative Secretary, Mrs Melanie Ransom, continue to provide first class support for the Society, and it is our aim that the new database and website should preserve and enhance the important relationships that the Society has with its membership and with the wider public.

The Society's work is carried out largely through committees. Reports from each are below. Two of the committees exist to co-ordinate the Society's policy and advocacy in relation to research and education. The other five committees deal with aspects of the Society's internal activities, including the awarding of research grants to postgraduate research students and overseeing the Society's publications, which include the Camden series of edited texts, the *Studies in History* series of monographs by new authors, the *Bibliography of British and Irish History (BBIH)* and *Transactions*.

The last year has been a very busy one in terms of our policy work. As detailed below in the report from the Chair of the Education Policy Committee, the Society has been heavily involved in negotiations over the Coalition government's proposed new national curriculum for History, and also proposed changes to GCSEs and A Levels. The Chair of the Research Policy Committee reports below on the work we have done in relation to the implications of Open Access publishing for the financial infrastructure of research funding, for the viability of journal publishing on the current model and, above all, for the careers of young as well as established scholars.

The Society's aim of representing the interests of all parts of the historical profession has been advanced through collaboration with other bodies. Indeed, we believe that without such collaboration, the interests of the discipline cannot be properly defended. We have worked closely with the Historical Association over the issue of the government's proposed A-Level reforms, with the British Academy, with other learned societies (through the Arts and Humanities User Group), and with history journal editors over 'Open Access' and with History Lab Plus to offer skills and networking sessions to early career historians. The Society continues to work closely with the IHR and its Director, Professor Miles Taylor, and with representatives of university History departments through History UK. Termly meetings of representatives of the Society, the IHR, the HA, and History UK have been held at the IHR. The Honorary Secretary participated in the interviews for Postgraduate Fellowships at the IHR in June 2013, including the Society's Centenary and Marshall Fellowships. Collaboration with TNA and the IHR also continues in the form of the Gerald Aylmer seminar. We hope to build on these collaborations with other historical organisations in the coming years.

Two of the Society's meetings were held outside London, at the University of Southampton on 19 October 2012 and the University of Leicester on 27 March 2013. At Southampton, Professor Ian Talbot led a series of papers under the theme 'The Independence of South Asia and its Aftermath'. At Leicester, the Society sponsored a symposium on 'Croatia and Europe' and the President chaired a plenary session. At both institutions Council members held meetings with academic and research staff and postgraduate research students in the Departments of History.

Council and the Officers record their warm gratitude to the Society's excellent administrative staff: the Executive Secretary, Sue Carr and the Administrative Secretary, Melanie Ransom. We thank them both for their expert and dedicated work on the Society's many activities.

RESEARCH POLICY COMMITTEE, 2012–13

The Research Policy Committee continued to coordinate and advise on the Society's relations with all the main bodies related to research funding and policy.

Open Access Publishing

Much of the committee's work this year was devoted to alerting policy-making bodies to the potentially disastrous implications for History and the humanities in general of a headlong rush to implement the Finch Report. The Society made representations to the following bodies: the Dept for Business, Innovation and Skills; a House of Lords Science and Technology Committee Inquiry into the Implementation of Open Access; a House of Commons BIS Committee Inquiry; RCUK and HEFCE. An important meeting was held in conjunction with the Wellcome Trust to consider Open Access licensing for the humanities and social sciences. After RCUK published its policy in May 2013, the President wrote to all Fellows and Members to advise them of the implications and of the Society's intention to monitor the effects so that we can respond fully and appropriately to the review that RCUK have planned for 2014. HEFCE policy for REF 2020 is still in draft form; the Society responded to the July 2013 consultation and will keep fellows and members informed.

REF 2014

The Society responded to a call for further nominations to the History REF panel and was pleased to see that nearly all of our nominees were invited to join.

Early Career Researchers

Arising from our cooperation with History Lab Plus, the forum for postdoctoral researchers hosted by the IHR, a survey was conducted asking ECRs in History about their experiences and expectations of the academic job market.

Over 200 people replied, expressing a range of concerns, which a small working party was set up to try to address. The survey revealed that relatively small and inexpensive improvements in practice by employers could make a substantial difference to the life and work of an ECR. A Code of Good Practice has been drafted and will be publicised during the academic year 2013–14.

Research Councils

The AHRC Strategic Plan 2013–18 made a welcome commitment to sustain responsive-mode funding, as had been urged by Society and other learned societies at meetings held in 2012. It also recognised the importance of funding postgraduate research, although there were no signs of any improvement on the Delivery Plan 2011–15 allocation of 'around one-third' of its budget to PG research grants, which is a reduction on previous levels of about 40%. Stand-alone MA degrees will no longer be funded, although the Strategic Plan states that BGP2 intends to enable institutions to fund MAs that will lead on to doctoral work.

The Society joined other History societies at a meeting convened by the Economic History Association, attended by representatives of the AHRC and the ESRC, in December 2012. The main item of discussion was open access policy. The Society will also, as usual, be represented at the annual AHRC meeting with subject associations in September 2013, where a new vehicle for engagement with the academic community, the AHRC Commons, will be one of the main items on the agenda.

The National Archive

We are pleased to report that a History student has been appointed as the postgraduate representative to the TNA Advisory Group.

Gender Equality

The RHS welcomes the initiative by the Equality Challenge Unit to publish a Charter for Gender Equality in the humanities and social sciences, an equivalent to the Athena SWAN Charter for STEM subjects. We have responded to their survey of learned societies, plan to carry out some research of our own and will follow the progress of the proposed Charter, which is planned for 2014.

Research Policy Forum

The new Society website (to be launched early in 2014) will create a forum for research policy issues so that all fellows and members can be more easily kept informed about this fast-moving landscape.

The Committee has continued to benefit from the contributions of its co-opted members: Valerie Johnson, from TNA; Emily Robinson of History Lab Plus; Anish Vanaik, as the Marshall Fellow (2012–13); and Prof. Andrew Thompson (from February 2013). We record our thanks to them and to all the other committee members for their work.

EDUCATION POLICY COMMITTEE, 2012–13

The Education Policy Committee considers all aspects of History in education from schools to postgraduate level, and continues to gain valuable input from its co-opted members, Dr Andrew Foster (representing the Historical Association), Dr Jason Peacey (History UK), Mr Peter D'Sena (HEA Subject Lead for History) and Dr Michael Maddison (Ofsted National Adviser for History). This year we added an early career researcher, Dr Emily Robinson (History Lab Plus) to the Committee, and from November we will also benefit from advice on issues relating to History in the schools from Dr Michael Fordham, senior teaching associate at the University of Cambridge Faculty of Education, who brings both valuable recent classroom experience as head of History at Cottenham Village College, and his curriculum expertise as a co-editor of *Teaching History*.

As last year, government proposals to reform the school curriculum dominated the committee's deliberations, with the processes of change accelerating and requiring extremely rapid and yet often complex and detailed responses. During the course of 2012–13, the Society made several extensive submissions to a series of official consultations: twice on the National Curriculum; once on the abortive English Baccalaureate Certificate proposals; twice on GCSE reform (one to the DfE and one to OfQual) once the EBC had been abandoned; once on A-level assessment practices; and once on A-level reform more generally to the Joint Council on Qualifications. Our most important submissions were made available on the Society website. Throughout the year we worked very closely with the Historical Association, sharing ideas and discussing practicalities in the classroom before making our submissions, and this both enabled us to make more effective responses and reinforced the excellent working relationship between the two organizations which has developed in recent years.

One of the challenges of the year was the fact that all three key stages of the school curriculum were in flux at the same time, leaving those engaged in the discussion without fixed points of reference. Moreover, not only was consultation unsatisfactorily limited in the early stages of the process, but even when consultation took place in the later part of the year much of it was sought on a confidential basis, limiting opportunities to seek out views from other interested parties, or to 'join the dots' between consultations involving different parties. In part for these reasons one aim of the Society in its interventions was to try to ensure that the outcomes created a coherent pathway for the study of History in schools, both leading to HE and also delivering an enduring legacy of historical awareness and engagement with the past – not just of Britain but of the wider world, and not just of political history but of past human life in all its multifaceted interest – to those pupils choosing to end their study of the subject at an earlier stage. We were also concerned about the practicalities of implementation for our colleagues teaching in schools, given the particular challenges that any significant alteration to the History curriculum can pose in terms of acquiring new subject knowledge.

Of the various processes mentioned above, the most controversial was the reform of the National Curriculum for History. The publication of the draft Curriculum generated considerable (and sometimes unhelpfully heated) public debate. The Society made its own contributions to this discussion, with the President issuing a joint statement with representatives of History UK, the Historical Association and the British

Academy in response to the first draft issued by the DfE at the start of the year, and the Vice-President (Education) speaking at the Westminster Education Forum. The Committee shared the widespread concern that the initial draft was overly Anglo-centric and overloaded in terms of prescribed (and often age-inappropriate and historiographically dated) content, as well as taking insufficient account of the needs of younger children first encountering History. Following the consultation the DfE surprised many of its critics by engaging in an extensive revision of the proposals in which the Society took an important role, with the Vice-President (Education) attending two roundtables hosted by the Secretary of State and being invited to work in a smaller group on revisions to the draft in the light of these meetings and the consultation exercise. The extensively revised curriculum which emerged from this process was widely welcomed as an improvement on the initial proposal. It retained the strong emphasis on English history taught in broadly chronological sequence that lay at core of the first draft, but now with a more appropriate division between those elements taught at primary and secondary schools at 1066 rather than 1707, thus ensuring that some pre-modern history was delivered in secondary schools (reinforced by an injunction to revisit the pre-1066 period at some point), while a counterbalancing element of more recent history was allocated to the primary curriculum. This has the additional benefit of ensuring that many excellent teaching resources and collaborations with the heritage sector that have developed in recent years for primary schools will not be rendered redundant. Equally welcome was a stronger (though some might argue still insufficient) emphasis on important themes in non-British history in both the primary and secondary curriculum. The new Curriculum, to be introduced from 2014, will not be imposed on academies, but will be very important particularly in the primary sector none the less: it is therefore very pleasing to record the part the Society has played in helping fashion a curriculum which is now widely seen as practicable and in places potentially exciting in the opportunities it creates for imaginative teaching, even among some of those most alarmed by the initial proposals.

One reason why many did not anticipate that the DfE would revise its proposals so extensively was that it had already very publically abandoned the proposals for the English Baccalaureate Certificate announced earlier in the year. This decision was welcome to the Society, which had argued strongly against aspects of the proposals in its submission to the consultation. Some features of the EBC scheme were still prominent in the proposals later announced for the overhaul of GCSE. Here there was much to welcome in the case of the History GCSE, long felt by many to be the weakest aspect of current provision. In particular the Society welcomed an explicit commitment to prevent students concentrating exclusively on the history of the recent past, a more appropriate approach to engagement with source material, and the explicit inclusion of the study of the history of the locality among the criteria to guide the Awarding Bodies in the development of new curricula. Less welcome was a decision to insist on external examination as the only means of assessment, accompanied by a proposal that the accepted importance of independent research both to the historian and as an especially valuable transferable skill would be acknowledged, but only in an unassessed but still compulsory individual project. In our submission to the consultation the Society argued strongly that independent study should retain a place within the assessed content, and for other changes to the assessment criteria. As in the case of the Curriculum, the Society was invited to consultation meetings at the DfE, and the Vice-President was once more asked to join a small expert advisory group advising on the revision of the draft in the light of the consultations undertaken. As this report is written, the DfE has postponed the implementation of the new specifications to 2016 rather than 2015, and the final version of the History specifications has yet to be approved by ministers. It is therefore too soon to report on the success or otherwise of the representations the Society has made, but those closely involved in the process are optimistic that the end result will represent an improvement on the current specification, and it has once again been encouraging to see the Society's opinion both solicited and having an influence on the shaping of this key qualification.

Turning finally to A-level reform, the Society monitored the ongoing implementation of the reforms discussed in the report for 2011–12. Here our chief concerns have been with the new arrangements being set in place for the ongoing supervision of A-level provision entrusted to the Russell Group universities (but which we are keen to see include representation from a much wider constituency), and with the consequences of the decision that AS level will no longer contribute directly to A2. The difficulties involved in imposing rapid change in A level alongside those already described seem to have encouraged a gradualist approach to change, and initially at least, it is likely that curriculum specifications will not be significantly affected. However, it is clear that for some years university admissions tutors will face a difficult task when confronted not just by 'reformed' A-levels in facilitating subjects, but 'unreformed' A-levels in others, and a divergence in practice between England, Wales, and Northern Ireland. We will continue to consult with other interested parties and intervene in discussions where we believe it appropriate over coming months.

The committee continues to monitor closely the uptake of History GCSE and A-Level, principally through its annual meeting with representatives of the examination boards for England and Wales, which was held again this year. The uncertainties of the situation in which examination boards found themselves as commercial rivals in the context of the reforms inevitably made some issues more sensitive than they have been in the past, but we none the less benefited greatly from our consultation with them, which revealed a reassuring picture of a subject still in good health in the schools, with the 'English Baccalaureate' helping consolidate the strong position of History as a core academic subject. The various processes of reform described above have also served to increase both our formal and informal contact with individual examination boards, where we make our subject expertise available on a non-exclusive basis to any that seek it out. Such contacts proved extremely valuable in crystallising some key issues for consideration in our responses to the various DfE consultations.

Our final contribution to ongoing discussions of History in the schools was our contribution to a panel convened by the Royal Statistical Society to advise them in developing a proposal for embedding statistical methods in teaching across a wide range of subjects including History. In our contribution to the discussions which fed into the report (Roger Porkess, *A World Full of Data: Statistics Opportunities across A-level Subjects*, 2013), we welcomed the opportunity to recognise the potential for good statistical method to inform historical work at A-level with all the additional benefits for numeracy and transferable skills that would bring with it, while remaining sceptical of the desirability of any attempt to make such method a compulsory element in historical education.

Looking ahead to the coming year, the Committee is conscious of the need to engage especially vigorously with History in HE after a year so taken up with Schools issues. The future of Masters courses in the context of the new undergraduate fees regime remains a subject of concern, as do the repercussions of the lifting of caps on the recruitment of high achieving A-level students for departmental recruitment at undergraduate level. Hard and comprehensive as opposed to anecdotal evidence has been slow to surface, although it is clear that the 2012 admissions round was more testing than usual for many departments as others swallowed up much larger numbers than in the past. The 2013 figures, where the sheer novelty of the position will be less significant a factor than in 2012 resulting, one presumes, in fewer instances of sheer miscalculation, will repay close study. The effects on UK Border Agency policy on the recruitment of overseas students, and of changes in policy on the training of teachers in the HE sector, are two further subjects to which we intend to direct our attention in 2013–14.

GENERAL PURPOSES COMMITTEE, 2012–13

The remit of this committee ranges across many activities of the Society. It receives suggestions from Fellows and Council for paper-givers and makes recommendations to Council on the Card of Session, taking into account the need for a balanced programme in terms of chronological and geographical spread. In addition to the regular sessions held at UCL and outside London, it is also responsible for the Prothero Lecture, the Colin Matthew Lecture and the Gerald Aylmer Seminar.

After discussion with the Literary Directors, the General Purposes Committee committed itself to deciding the Card of Session for two years ahead. Giving invited speakers more time to prepare, it was thought, would help ensure a high standard of papers for both delivery and subsequent publication.

The programme of lectures and visits for 2013 was confirmed, including visits to the University of Leicester in April and Bath Spa University in October. Proposals for 2014 and 2015 have been discussed and speakers invited. Regional symposia and visits to the University of East Anglia and the University of Huddersfield will take place in 2014. The Committee continues to review the purpose and success of both lectures and visits, and to consider ways of increasing their reach, for example through podcasting and repeat lectures. The Committee was pleased to receive several proposals for regional symposia, and would like to encourage more departments to make such proposals. The 2013 Gerald Aylmer Seminar was held in February on 'Why Material Culture?' and discussions with TNA and the IHR for the 2014 seminar are under way.

The Committee is also responsible for the appointment of assessors for the Society's prizes, and receives their reports and proposals for award winners. It regularly reviews the terms and conditions of the awards. From 2014 the Rees Davies Prize will be re-configured as a prize for the best dissertation submitted as part of a postgraduate master's degree.

The Society is extremely grateful to members of Council for their hard work in reading entries and selecting the prize winners. Attracting entries for the Alexander Prize and the Rees Davies Prize continues to be problematic.

This year the Committee has also considered broader administrative and developmental issues aimed at raising the Society's profile within the academic community. Several initiatives have resulted from the questionnaire circulated to the membership. Work on the website and on the database of Fellows and Members, past and present, has continued.

Consideration was also given to the establishment of a prize for Public History. It is hoped that this initiative, which emerged from an approach from the Public History Seminar of the Institute of Historical Research, will lead to the announcement of a new prize for an exhibition, television or radio series or programme, with nominations from the broader historical community.

Meetings of the Society

At the ordinary meetings of the Society the following papers were read:

Prothero Lecture: 'Pain: A History of Sensation', Professor Joanna Bourke (4 July 2012)

'On the experience of change in early modern Europe' Professor Judith Pollman (21 September 2012)

At the Anniversary Meeting on 23 November 2012, the President, Professor Colin Jones delivered his final address on 'French Crossings IV: Vagaries of Passion and Power in the Enlightenment'.

'Andres Bello and the Challenges of Spanish American Liberalism', Professor James Dunkerley (8 February 2013)

'Producing Material Culture for Global Markets: Craftspeople of Eighteenth and Twenty-first Century India', Professor Maxine Berg (10 May 2013)

The Colin Matthew Memorial Lecture for the Public Understanding of History was given on Wednesday 7 November 2012 by Professor Justin Champion 'Why the Enlightenment still matters today'. These lectures continue to be given in memory of the late Professor Colin Matthew, a former Literary Director and Vice-President of the Society.

Prizes

The Society's annual prizes were awarded as follows:

The Alexander Prize for 2012 attracted eleven entries and was awarded to Jasper Heinzen for his article, 'Transnational Affinities and Invented Traditions: The Napoleonic Wars in British and Hanoverian Memory, 1815–1915', *English Historical Review*, vol. 127, no. 529 (2012).

The judges' citation read:

This impressively researched and imaginatively conceived article sheds important new light on how cultural memory of the Napoleonic Wars evolved between 1815 and 1915 and its role in the formation of transnational affinities in Britain and Germany. Consistently comparative in character, the article breaks free of the nationalist paradigms within which previous scholarship has been constrained to offer original insights about the complex cultural entanglements and tensions that comprised the Anglo-German relationship in the century preceding the outbreak of the First World War. It advances our understanding of how nostalgia, amnesia and the invention of tradition operated and engages fruitfully with influential claims about their place in the making of modern nationalist ideologies. It has considerable resonance for scholars working in other periods.

The judges nominated a proxime accessit:

Mark Williams (University of Leicester) for his article 'Between King, Faith and Reason: Father Peter Talbot (SJ) and Catholic Royalist Thought in Exile', *English Historical Review*, 127: 528 (2012).

The David Berry Prize for an article on Scottish history for 2012 attracted two entries and was awarded to Sarah Tebbit (University of Cambridge) for her essay 'Papal pronouncements on legitimate lordship and the formulation of nationhood in early fourteenth-century Scottish writings'

The judges' citation read:

'Papal pronouncements on legitimate lordship and the formulation of nationhood in early fourteenth-century Scottish writings' is a highly original contribution to a central - and otherwise well-trodden - area of medieval Scottish historiography. With precision, sophistication and persuasiveness, Dr Tebbit sets out a series of precedents which informed first Scottish pleadings at the papal curia around 1301 and then, indirectly, the celebrated Declaration of Arbroath of 1320. She shows how formulae employed by Pope Innocent IV in the bull *Ad apostolicae* (1245) when framing the deposition of the Hohenstaufen Emperor Frederick II resurfaced in the way the Scottish canonists of the early fourteenth century depicted the offences of Edward I. Interestingly Sicily – which Frederick wished to incorporate within the Empire - was a papal fief: a telling parallel with the Scottish situation. Moreover, there were also echoes in the Scots pleadings of the case made by Neapolitan lawyers against Charles of Anjou's rule in southern Italy in the second half of the thirteenth century. Dr Tebbitt's work serves to remind Scottish historians that the Declaration of Arbroath was not only an appeal to the emotions, but was also – and more importantly - grounded in the juridical concepts apparent in the Scottish pleadings of 1301. In this way Dr Tebbitt's article takes onto a new level discussion of the rhetorical universe from which the Declaration of Arbroath emerged. The judges admired the author's formidable technical grasp of Romano-canonical jurisprudence. The range of sources deployed was also particularly impressive. The author's subtle analysis of a range of demanding Latin texts is supported throughout by a working knowledge of scholarship in German and Italian, in addition to the current secondary literature in Scottish historiography. Dr Tebbitt brings to the attention of Scottish medievalists a range of materials with which they might otherwise have been unfamiliar. Above all her article is a welcome re-integration of major themes in Scottish history within the mainstream of European history.

The Whitfield Book Prize for a first book on British history attracted thirty-eight entries. The prize for 2012 was awarded to:

Ben Griffin for *The Politics of Gender in Victorian Britain. Masculinity, Political Culture and the Struggle for Women's Rights* (Cambridge University Press, 2012).

The judges' citation read:

Ben Griffin's beautifully clear and crystalline monograph makes an important contribution both to Victorian political history and to gender studies. He argues that the fortunes of the women's movement in parliament can only properly be understood by considering the notions of masculinity articulated by the legislators themselves. By showing the degree to which individual allegiances often shifted, he shows the inappropriateness of simplistic pro-suffrage/anti-suffrage, pro-feminist/anti-feminist categories. The book combines statistical data with some wonderfully executed individual vignettes revealing some very curious species of anxious masculinities. It moves deftly between politics, gender studies, social history, and the history of the law.

The judges nominated a proxime accessit:

Richard Huzzey (University of Liverpool) for *Freedom Burning: Anti-slavery and Empire in Victorian Britain* (Cornell University Press, 2012).

The Gladstone Book Prize for a first book on non-British history attracted seventeen entries.

The Prize for 2012 was awarded to:

Joel Isaac (Christ's College, Cambridge) for *Working Knowledge: Making the Human Sciences from Parsons to Kuhn* (Harvard University Press, 2012).

The judges' citation read:

Joel Isaac's *Working Knowledge* is a truly impressive and original book. Tackling some of the most important epistemological controversies of the twentieth century by focusing on academic work undertaken in between the established disciplines at Harvard, Isaac systematically deconstructs a widely accepted teleological narrative, replacing a more conventional and disembodied story of texts and theses by one with the people and contexts put back. The methodology is both sophisticated and convincing. The book is well written and despite the complexity of the subject matter accessible to the non-specialist reader. It will be of interest also to historians who might not otherwise concern themselves with this particular chapter of intellectual history, not least because the story it tells is itself one about history in practice.

The Society's Rees Davies Essay Prize for the best article based on a conference paper delivered by a recipient of a Royal Historical Society travel grant

The Prize for 2012 was awarded to:

Mark Hailwood (University of Cambridge) for 'The Honest Tradesman's Honour': Occupational and Social Identity in Seventeenth-Century England'.

The judges' citation read:

This elegant essay explores the social identity of seventeenth-century tradesmen through their varying representation in ballads. Although the tension between the hard working tradesman and the prodigal gentleman suggests a growing social confidence, nevertheless the marketplace is shown to be as much a threat as an opportunity given the fragility of credit relationships, while the tradesman's patriarchal authority was likewise insecure. It is a fascinating piece at the intersection of class, gender, and occupational identities.

In order to recognise the high quality of work now being produced at undergraduate level in the form of third-year dissertations, the Society continued, in association with *History Today* magazine, to award an annual prize for the best undergraduate dissertation. Departments are asked to nominate annually their best dissertation and a joint committee of the Society and *History Today* select in the autumn the national prizewinner from among these nominations. The prize also recognizes the Society's close relations with *History Today* and the important role the magazine has played in disseminating scholarly research to a wider audience. Thirty-one submissions were made.

The Prize for 2012 was awarded to:

Frederick Smith (University of Warwick) for his essay 'Discerning cheese from Chalke: Louvainist Propaganda and recusant identity in 1560s England'.
An article by the prize-winner presenting his research will appear in *History Today* in 2014.

The German History Society, in association with the Society, agrees to award a prize to the winner of an essay competition. The essay, on any aspect of German history, including the history of German-speaking people both within and beyond Europe, was open to any postgraduate registered for a degree in a university in either the United Kingdom or the Republic of Ireland. No prizewinner was announced in 2012.

The Frampton and Beazley Prizes for A-level performances in 2012 were awarded to the following on the basis of nominations from the examining bodies:

Frampton Prize:

OCR:	Jack Barden de Lacroix (Hampton School, Middlesex)
AQA:	Nicholas Hudson (Notre dame High School, Sheffield) and Georgia Perry (St Mary's Calne, Wiltshire)
WJEC:	Angharad Gilbey (Penglais Comprehensive School, Aberystwyth)

Beazley Prize:

CCEA:	Aaron Crossey (Bangor Grammar School)
SQA:	Alice Williamson (George Watson's College, Edinburgh)

The Director of the IHR announced the winners of the Pollard Prize 2012 awarded annually to the best postgraduate student paper presented in a seminar at the IHR, and the Sir John Neale Prize for the best essay on the study of 16th century England by a postgraduate student.

The Pollard Prize for 2012 was awarded to Marie Legendre (University of Oxford) for 'Not Byzantine nor Islamic? The Duke of the Thebaid and the formation of the Umayyad State' (paper given to the Early Middle Ages seminar). The article will appear in *Historical Research* in 2014.

The runner up was Anish Vanaik (University of Oxford) for 'Representing commodified space: maps, leases, auctions and 'narrations' of property in Delhi c.1900–47' (paper given to the Metropolitan History Seminar).

The Sir John Neale Prize for 2012 was awarded to Joanne Paul (Queen Mary, University of London) for 'The Best Counsellors are the Dead: Counsel and Shakespeare's *Hamlet*'.

PUBLICATIONS COMMITTEE 2012–13

The Publications Committee remains responsible for the ongoing programme: Dr Emma Griffin represents the Society's interests on the *Studies in History* Editorial Board, while Dr Ian Archer edits *Transactions*, and they share responsibility for Camden volumes. Professor Stephen Taylor is Honorary Academic Editor of the Bibliography of British and Irish History (BBIH).

Transactions, Sixth Series, Volume 22 was published during the session, and *Transactions*, Sixth Series, Volume 23 went to press.

In the Camden, Fifth Series *Documents on Conservative Foreign Policy*, eds John Charmley, Geoff Hicks and Bendor Grosvenor (vol. 41) and *The Diary of Robert Woodford, 1637–1641*, ed. John Fielding (vol. 42) were published during the session.

Observing Vatican II: the Confidential Reports of the Archbishop of Canterbury's Representative Bernard Pawley, 1961–5, eds, Andrew Chandler and Charlotte Hansen (vol. 43), and *The Letters of Lady Anne Bacon*, ed. Gemma Allen (vol. 44) went to press for publication in 2012–13.

There has been some interruption in the flow of proposals for new volumes, and while several have come in during recent months, the Society would welcome more. Although the series relates to texts on British history, our interpretation is quite catholic, and proposals relating to Britain's connections with the wider world are welcome.

The *Studies in History* Editorial Board continued to meet throughout the year. The second series continues to produce exciting and widely discussed volumes (one of the 2011 titles, Samantha Williams' *Poverty, Gender and Life-Cycle under the English Poor Law, 1760–1834*, attained the distinction of featuring on the *Today* programme on BBC Radio 4). The following volume went to press during the session for publication in 2013:

o *The Irish Rebellion of 1641 and the Wars of the Three Kingdoms*, Eamon Darcy

The series has a number of manuscripts under development with their authors for publication, and continues to receive a steady flow of proposals. During the course of the year it was decided that the Society should offer its authors a contract at an earlier stage in the development of their volumes in recognition of the importance of commitments to the career development of many early career scholars.

The Society acknowledges its gratitude for the continuing subventions from the Economic History Society and the Past & present Society to the *Studies in History* series.

As in previous years, volumes in the *Camden* and *Studies in History* Series were offered to the membership at a favourably discounted price. Many Fellows and Members accepted the offer for volumes published during the year, and the advance order for further volumes to be published in the year 2013–2014 were encouraging. Boydell and Brewer's decision to republish a number of titles in a paperback format has proved extremely successful and it is intended to extend the selection from the backlist that will be made available in this form. Next year will see some of the series become available as e-publications for the first time, and the Committee is evaluating the likely the impact of developments in open access publishing on its series.

During 2013 the Bibliography of British and Irish History (BBIH) continued to develop smoothly, thanks primarily to the work of Peter Salt, Simon Baker and the team of academic section editors. Around 14,000 records have been added to the database over the past twelve months and Brepols (our publisher) continues to make minor improvements to the user interface. The new Project Board, bringing together the academic project team, Brepols and representatives of various user groups, met a second time and provided further useful feedback and advice on the development of the Bibliography.

Finance

FINANCE COMMITTEE 2012–13

The Finance Committee approves the Society's accounts each financial year and its estimates for the following year. This year, as before, the accounts were professionally audited by Kingston Smith. They are presented elsewhere in *Transactions,* together with the Trustees' Annual Report.

The Society's expenditure was broadly in line with estimates. Income was somewhat higher than anticipated, due once again to greater than expected revenue from the joint publishing agreement with Cambridge University Press (as a result of the on-going sales of the new digital archive). The Society is declaring a surplus of £21,599 for the year 2012–13.

The Society has run a surplus for a number of years, which has allowed it to build up a significant cash reserve. Finance Committee recognises that the coming years will be much more challenging financially than recent years, particularly as the windfall income from the digitisation component of the publishing agreement with Cambridge University Press declines sharply. In addition the Society is now committed to a thorough overhaul of its communications strategy and its back-office functions that will require considerable expenditure. It is for this reason that the Society anticipates continuing to hold a substantial cash reserve in the expectation that it will be drawn down in future years to cover a series of planned in-year deficits. The deficit for financial year 2013–14 is likely to be particularly substantial given that much of the anticipated expenditure will occur in this financial year.

The value of the Society's investments rose to £2.62 millions in June 2013, an increase from the previous year's figure of £2.36 million. The return on investments is benchmarked against the APCIMS Balanced (Total Return) index. The Society's portfolio is invested for the long-term and members of Finance Committee are confident that the current spread of investments is appropriate. Finance Committee will in 2013–14 be undertaking a review of investment strategy.

Council records with gratitude the benefactions made to the Society by:

- o Professor G Alderman
- o Dr G Bakker
- o The Bibliographical Society
- o Dr G F Burgess
- o Professor J A Cannon
- o Professor C R Cole
- o Lord Cormack
- o Dr H Dawson
- o Professor M Dhada
- o Mr A Dighton
- o Dr P Du Plessis
- o Economic History Society
- o Professor Sir Geoffrey Elton
- o Dr J P Fox
- o Professor Dr A Gestrich
- o Dr W P Griffith
- o Dr R P Hallion
- o Miss B F Harvey
- o Mr A J Heesom
- o Dr P J W Higson
- o Ms E Josephs

- Professor E J King
- Professor A H M Kirk-Greene
- Dr M Lynn
- Professor S E Marks
- Professor P J Marshall
- Professor J Mayo
- Professor S N Mukherjee
- Past & Present Society
- Sir George Prothero
- Lieutenant Colonel Dr H E Raugh
- Dr L Rausing
- The Rausing Trust
- Miss E M Robinson
- Dr Z E Rohr
- Dr K W Schweizer
- Professor Lord Smith of Clifton
- Professor D P Smyth
- Dr A R Summers
- Dr G P Tapsell
- Dr E R Turton
- Professor J P Von Arx
- Mr T V Ward
- Mr F R Welsh
- Mr A Yavari

MEMBERSHIP COMMITTEE 2012–13

The following were elected to the Fellowship:

Clare Anderson, MA, PhD
Scott M Anthony, BA, MA, PhD
Catherine Armstrong, BA, MA, PhD
Paul W L Arthur, BA, PhD
Joanne Bailey, BA, MA, PhD
Frederick D Baldwin, BA, MPhil
Manuel B Paz, PhD
Nick Barratt, BA, PhD
Julie Barrau, BA, MA, PhD
Crispin Bates, MA, PhD
Robert W F Beaken, BA, STh, MA, PhD
Kevin Bean, BA, PGCE, MA, PhD
Edward J Beasley, BA, MA, PhD
Mike Benbough-Jackson, BA, MA, PhD
Huw Bennett, BSc, MSc, PhD
Tom H Blaen, BA, MA, PhD, AHEA

Fay Bound Alberti, BA, MA, PhD

Alixe Bovey, BA, MA, PhD, PGCHE

Esther Breitenbach, MA, PhD

Christopher J Brooke, BSc, PhD

George H Brown, PhD

Ambrogio A Caiani, BA, MA, PhD

Christopher P Callow, BA, PhD

Stuart Carroll, PhD

Emma Cavell, BA, MA, DPhil

Sabine Chaouche, MA, PCTHE, PhD

Ulrich Charpa, PhD

Stuart A Clewlow

Catherine Clinton, PhD

James Connor, BSc, MA, PhD

Rosalind H Crone, BA, MPhil, PhD

Peter Darby, BA, MA, PhD

Douglas E Delaney, PhD

Lucy Delap, PhD

Mark J R Dennis, MA

Hanna E Diamond, BA, MA, PhD

Andrew R Dilley, BA, M.St, DPhil, PGCAP, FHEA

Donald L Drakeman, AB, JD, MA, PhD

Paul J Du Plessis, BA, MA, LL.B, PhD

Aaron Edwards, BA, MSc, PhD, PGCE

Heather L W Ellis, BA, MPhil, DPhil

Martin J Farr, BA, PhD

Lori A Ferrell, BLS, MA, MPhil, PhD

Peter Frankopan, MA, MPhil, DPhil

Alexandra M Gajda, BA, DPhil

Andrea M Galdy, MA, PhD

Elizabeth A Gemmill, BA, PhD, MA by special resolution

Shirli Gilbert, B.Mus, M.St., DPhil

Christopher R Gilley, MA, MA, PhD

Peter W Gray, BSc, LL.B, MPhil, PhD

Dominic F Green, BA, MA, PhD

Francesco Guidi-Bruscoli, MA, PhD

Polly Ha, BA, PhD

Simon D Hall, BA, MA, PhD

Elizabeth Harvey, BA, DPhil

Joel Hayward, ZDaF, BA, MA, PhD

Christopher R Hilliard, BA, MA, PhD

Jane Humphries, BA, PhD

Arnold Hunt, BA, PhD

Richard Huzzey, MA, M.St, DPhil

Edward A Impey, BA, DPhil
William M Jacob, MA, LL.B, PhD
Andrew Jennings, PhD
Paul J E Kershaw, BA, MPhil, PhD
Zoe Knox, BA, PhD
Alastair M Kocho-Williams, BA, MA, PhD
Harshan Kumarasingham, BA, MA, PhD
Christopher R Kyle, BA, MA, PhD
L. Calvin Lane, BA, MTS, PhD
Mak Lanver, BA, MA, PhD
Sjoerd Levelt, MA, MPhil, PhD
Nicholas Lewkowicz, BA, MA, PhD
Paul Lim, BA, ThM, PhD
Marisa Linton, BA, MA, PhD
Suzannah R G Lipscomb, MA, M.St, DPhil
Julia Lovell, BA, MPhil, PhD
Michael J Lyon, B.Ed, MA, PhD
Anna K Maerker, MPhil, MA, PhD, FHEA
Alastair J Mann, BA, PhD
Steven N Mason, BA, MA, PhD
Deborah H Mawer, BMus, LRAM, FHEA, PhD
Mark McCarthy, BA, PhD
Sean McGlynn, BA, MA, PGCE
Stephen Meredith, BA, MA, MSc, PhD
David R Monger, BA, MA, PhD
Renaud Morieux, PhD
Miriam Muller, BA, MPhil, PhD
Elaine Murphy, BA, M.Litt, PhD
Hannah Newton, BA, MA, PhD
Gillian O'Brien, BA, MA, PhD
Ian M O'Donnell, MA, MPhil, PhD, LLD
Jan Palmowski, BA, DPhil
Jan Plamper, PhD
Matthew C Potter, BA, MA, PhD
Simon J Pulleyn, MA, DPhil
Kathrine M Reynolds, BA, MSc, PhD
Giorgio Riello, Laurea in Economics, PhD
Nicole Robertson, BA, MA, PhD
Emily A Robinson, MA, PhD
Simon Roffey, BA, MRes, PhD
Mark C Roodhouse, BA, MSc, PhD, PGCAP
Eve Rosenhaft, BA, PhD
Michael A Rutz, PhD
Boyd S Schlenther, BA, MA, PhD

Matthew J Shaw, DPhil
Daniel Siemens, PhD
David Simpkin, BA, MA, PhD
Mark B Smith, BA, MA, PhD
Scott A Sowerby, PhD
Colin Storer, BA, PhD
Matthias Strohn, M.St., DPhil
Antony D Taylor, BA, MA, PhD
James W Taylor
Nicholas Temple, MA, PhD, Dip.Arch, RIBA
Dora F Thornton, MA, PhD
Ulrich Tiedau
Elizabeth C Tingle, BA, DPhil, PGCE
Vishwa D Tripathi, BA, PGADBA, PhD by Published Works
Joan Tumblety, BA, PhD
Alison Twells, BA, PGCE, PhD
Chad Van Dixhoorn, BA, Mdiv, ThM, PhD
Brodie Waddell, BA, MA, PhD
Jonathan M Walker, MA, PhD
David Walsh, BA, MSc, PhD
Benjamin J Weinstein, BA, MA, PhD
Richard S J Willis, BSc, MPhil, PhD, FCP
Matthew G Yeo, MA, PhD

Over the year ending on 30 June 2013, 127 Fellows and 131 Members were elected, and the total membership of the Society on that date was 3,377 (including 2,040 Fellows, 652 Retired Fellows, 77 Emeritus Fellows, 78 Corresponding and Honorary Fellows, 12 Honorary Vice Presidents, 41 Associates and 477 Members).

The following were announced in the Queen's Honours Lists during the year:

Professor Richard J Evans – Fellow - KBE for Services to Scholarship.
Professor Hew Strachan – Fellow - KBE for Services to the Ministry of Defence.
Professor Aled Jones – Fellow - was appointed the Librarian of the National Library of Wales.
Council was advised of and recorded with regret the deaths of 1 Honorary Vice-President, 5 Fellows, 18 Retired Fellows, 1 Corresponding Fellow, 1 Life Fellow and 1 Member.

Professor R Ashton   Retired Fellow
Professor G R Batho   Retired Fellow

Professor J M Bean	Fellow
Professor J Brown	Fellow
Professor J H Burns	Honorary Vice-President
Dr M Chibnall, FBA	Retired Fellow
Dr C Cooper	Member
Professor F M Crouzet	Corresponding Fellow
Professor C M Crowder	Retired Fellow
Professor R W Bushaway	Fellow
Professor R B Dobson	Retired Fellow
Mr K Emsley	Retired Fellow
Professor P H J H Gosden	Retired Fellow
Professor J W Hiden	Retired Fellow
Dr P J W Higson	Fellow
Professor E W Ives	Retired Fellow
Professor D Jenkins	Retired Fellow
Professor G E Jones	Retired Fellow
Dr M H Jones	Retired Fellow
Dr M H Keen, OBE	Fellow
Mrs L Le Claire	Retired Fellow
Professor G H L Le May	Retired Fellow
Professor W Rodney	Retired Fellow
Professor C T Stannage	Retired Fellow
Dr E G Thomas	Retired Fellow
Dr J Wall	Retired Fellow
Lt Cmdr D W Waters	Life Fellow

The Society exchanged publications with 15 societies, British and foreign.

Representatives of the Society

- The representation of the Society upon other various bodies was as follows:
  - o Dr Julia Crick on the Joint Committee of the Society and the British Academy established to prepare an edition of Anglo-Saxon charters;
  - o Professor Claire Cross on the Council of the British Association for Local History; and on the British Sub-Commission of the Commission Internationale d' Histoire Ecclesiastique Comparée;
  - o Professor Colin Jones on the board of the Panizzi Foundation and the Advisory Council of the Committee for the Export of Objects of Cultural Interest;
  - o Professor Chris Whatley on the Court of the University of Stirling
  - o Professor Vanessa Harding on the Board of the British Records Association

Grants

RESEARCH SUPPORT COMMITTEE 2012–13

The Committee met five times in the course of the year to distribute research funds to early career historians (primarily research students but also recent PhDs not yet in full time employment) through a process of peer review. In total, the committee made 166 awards to researchers at over 150 different institutions, of which 18 grants were to support research within the UK, 45 to support research outside the UK, 50 to support the attendance of advanced doctoral students at conferences to deliver papers, and one, the Martin Lynn Scholarship, to support research in Africa. In addition, it made awards to 52 conference and seminar organisers to support the participation and attendance of early career researchers at their events and to fund sessions designed to develop students' skills for academic employment. The topics funded by the Committee reflect the Society's contribution to a wide spectrum of sub-fields within the historical discipline, as well as to interdisciplinary research with a substantial historical component. Successful applicants' end of award reports confirm that Society funding significantly enhances the opportunities for early career researchers to conduct original archival research and to gain feedback on their work in international settings. The quality of applications is impressively high and regretfully we are unable to offer awards to all the excellent applications from eligible candidates we receive. In the last year, however, the funds available to support these Society schemes have been enhanced by generous grants from *History Workshop Journal* and *Past & Present*, each of £5000. Awards made under the *HWJ* grant prioritise self-funded PhD students, not in receipt of research council or other institutional funding; awards made the *P&P* grant allow us to provide support to researchers regardless of nationality. The Society expresses its deep gratitude to these journals for their help in assisting our initiatives in this area.

The coming year will see a significant overhaul of the way in which the application process is administered, coinciding with the development of the Society's new website. It is hoped too, that the new website will enable the Society to publicise the outcomes of the research it funds and to highlight the ways in early career researchers have benefited from the Society's support.

For the academic year 2012–13, the Royal Historical Society Centenary Fellowship was awarded to Emilie Murphy (University of York) for research on 'Music and post-Reformation English Catholics 1575–1640'. The Society's P J Marshall Fellowship was awarded to Stewart McCain (University of Oxford) for research on 'The Language Question under Napoleon'.

Travel to Conferences

o Angela Ballone, University of Liverpool
Histories and Memories of Early Modern Popular Revolts in Oral
Culture Conference, Caen Basse-Normandie, France, 3rd-5th April
2013
o Nicholas Barnett, Liverpool John Moores University
Britain and the World Conference 2013. University of Texas, USA,
28th-30th March 2013
o Katherine Basanti, University of Aberdeen
On the Edge 2013: Transitions, Transgressions and Transformations
in Irish and Scottish Studies, Simon Fraser University, Vancouver,
Canada, 19th-23rd June 2013
o Olga Bertelsen, University of Nottingham
The 44th ASEEES Annual Convention (Slavic, East European, or
Eurasian Studies), New Orleans, USA, 15th-18th November 2012
o Harman Bhogal, Birkbeck, University of London
Demons and Illness: Theory and Practice from Antiquity to the Early
Modern Period, University of Exeter, UK 22nd-24th April 2012
o Katherine Buchanan, University of Stirling
The Problematical 'Towerhouse', Amersfoort, Netherlands, 17th-18th
August 2013
o Imogen Clarke, University of Manchester
24th International Congress of History of Science, Technology and
Medicine
University of Manchester, 21st-28th July 2013
o Justin Colson, Institute of Historical Research
North American Conference on British Studies, Montreal, Canada,
9th-11th November 2012
o Nicola Cowmeadow, University of Dundee
North Atlantic Conference on British Studies, Montreal, Canada, 9th-
11th November 2012
o Rosie Doyle, University of St Andrews
International Congress of Americanists, Vienna, Austria, 15th-20th July
2012
o Cynthia Fry, University of St Andrews
Splendid Encounters: Diplomats and Diplomacy in Europe, 1500–1750
Polish Academy of Science, Warsaw, Poland, 20th-21st September 2013
o George Gilbert, University of East Anglia
44th Annual Convention of the Association of Slavic, Eastern European
and Eurasian Studies, New Orleans, USA, 15th-18th November 2012
o Marco Giudici, Bangor University
War and Displacement Research Network Spring Conference,
Munich, Germany, 3rd-4th May 2013

o Allison Goudie, University of Oxford
  La miniature en Europe, Institut de France, Fondation Simone et Cino del Duca Paris, France, 11th-12th October 2012
o Jessica Hammett, University of Cambridge
  Voluntary Action Historical Society, Fifth Annual Conference, University of Huddersfield, 10th-12th July 2013
o Eliza Hartrich, University of Oxford
  European Association for Urban History: 11th International Conference on Urban History, Prague, Czech Republic, 29th August - 1st September 2012
o Paul Huddie, Queen's University Belfast
  On the edge: transitions, transgressions, and transformations in Irish and Scottish studies, Simon Fraser University, Vancouver, Canada, 19th-23rd June 2013
o Grace Huxford, University of Warwick
  Social History Society Conference, University of Leeds, UK, 25th-27th March 2013
o Leslie James, London School of Economics
  African Studies Association Annual Conference, Research Frontiers in the Study of Africa, Philadelphia, USA, 23rd November - 2nd December 2012
o Anna Jenkin, University of Sheffield
  Gender and Sexuality in the Crime Genre, University of Galway, 21st-22nd June 2013
o Christopher Jeppesen, University of Cambridge
  British Scholar Society – Britain and the World, University of Texas, Austin, USA, 28th-30th March 2013
o Emily Jones, University of Oxford
  On Liberties: Victorian Liberals and their Legacies, Gladstone's Library, Hawarden, 3rd-5th July 2013
o Hanna Kilpi, University of Glasgow
  International Medieval Congress Leeds 2013, University of Leeds, UK, 1st-4th July 2013
o Kimberley-Joy Knight, University of St Andrews
  Australian & New Zealand Association for Medieval & Early Modern Studies Conference: 'Cultures in Translation', Melbourne, Australia, 12th-16th February 2013
o Chloe Kroeter, King's College, Cambridge
  Writing Against the Grain: Dissent, Minorities and the Press in History, Kingston University, London, 16th-17th November 2012
o James Lees, University of Cambridge
  Clemens, Wenzeslaus 200 Jahre Todestag Symposium [Bicentary Symposium for the death of Clemens Wenzeslaus], Trier, Germany, 16th-17th November 2012

- Jamie Miller, University of Cambridge
  African Studies Association Annual Conference, Philadelphia, USA, 29th November - 2nd December 2012
- Stuart Minson, University of Oxford
  North American Conference on British Studies, Montreal, Canada, 9th-11th November 2012
- Joel Morley, Queen Mary, University of London
  War and Memory: artistic and cultural representations of individual, collective and national memories in C20th Europe at War, Warsaw, Poland, 7th-9th September 2012
- Peter Morton, University of Edinburgh
  Qui Sum? Provincialis? Manifestations Identiaires dans le cadre supra-civique. Les identités provinciales et regionales, Dijon, France, 10th-12th June 2013
- Emilie Murphy, University of York
  Music and Theology in the European Reformations, Leuven, Belgium, 19th-21st September 2012
- Emilie Murphy, University of York
  What is Early Modern English Catholicism?, Durham University, 28th June - 1st July 2013
- Fergus Oakes, University of Glasgow
  Leeds International Medieval Congress, University of Leeds, UK, 1st-4th July 2013
- Angel-Luke O'Donnell, University of Liverpool
  Empire and Imagination in Early America and the Atlantic World, Bayreuth Institute, Germany, 13th-15th December 2012
- Timothy Rogan, University of Cambridge
  North American Conference on British Studies, Montreal, Canada, 9th-11th November 2012
- Susan Royal, Durham University
  Sin and Salvation in Reformation England, The Shakespeare Institute, Stratford-upon-Avon, 26th-28th June 2013
- Jade Shepherd, Queen Mary, University of London
  North American Conference on British Studies, Montreal, Canada, 9th-11th November 2012
- Scott Siggins, University of East Anglia
  National Convention of the Association for Slavic, East European and Eurasian Studies, New Orleans, USA, 15th-18th November 2012
- Blair Smith, University of Dundee
  American Historical Association 127th Annual Conference, New Orleans, USA, 3rd-6th January 2013
- Claudia Soares, University of Manchester
  North American Conference on British Studies, Montreal, Canada, 9th-11th November 2012

- Ljubica Spaskovska, University of Exeter
  Trust and Distrust in the Eastern Bloc, 1956–1991, University College London, 4th-5th July 2013
- Stephen Spencer, Queen Mary, University of London
  Sourcing Emotions in the Medieval and Early Modern World, Perth, Australia, 17th-29th June 2013
- Marjolein Stern, University of Nottingham
  15th International Saga Conference, Aarhus, Denmark, 5th-11th August 2012
- Kate Stevens, University of Cambridge
  Pacific Historical Association Conference, Wellington, New Zealand, 6th-8th December 2012
- Nicolas Stone Villani, University of Oxford
  The Place of Renaissance Humanism in the History of Philosophy, Groningen, Netherlands, 13th-15th June 2013
- Florence Sutcliffe-Braithwaite, University of Cambridge
  5th Christina Conference on Gender Studies, Helsinki, 23rd-25th May 2013
- Pheroze Unwalla, SOAS
  2012 Middle East Studies Association Annual Meeting, Denver, US, 17th-20th November 2012
- Victoria Van Hyning, University of Sheffield
  Renaissance Society of America, San Diego, California, USA, 4th-6th April 2013
- Darren Wagner, University of York
  Canadian Society for C18th Studies Annual Conference, Edmonton, Canada, 18th-20th October 2012
- Faridah Zaman, University of Cambridge
  22nd European Conference on South Asian Studies, Lisbon, Portugal, 25th-28th July 2012

Research Expenses within the UK

- Katherine Allen, University of Oxford
  Archives in London, September 2012
- Alex Brayson, University of York
  Archives in London, July - August 2012
- William Butler, University of Kent
  Archives in Belfast, Northern Ireland, 15th-25th April 2013
- Carly Collier, University of Warwick
  Archives in Norwich and Aberdeen, March 2013
- Jennifer Depold, University of Oxford
  Archives in Worcester, Lincoln and Manchester, June - July 2013

o Stephanie Duensing, University of Manchester
Archives in London, October 2012 - March 2013
o Fiona Duncan, University of Stirling
Archives in London, October 2012
o Justin Fantauzzo, University of Cambridge
Liddle Collection, University of Leeds, 4th-18th December 2012
o James Freeman, University of Cambridge
Archives in Warminster, London and Cambridge, October - December 2012
o Janette Garrett, Teesside University
Archives in London, October 2012
o Anna Gurun, University of Dundee
Archives and interviews in London, August - September 2012
o Sally Osborn, University of Roehampton
Archives in Hereford, Taunton, Warwick and Preston, June – July 2013
o Edward Owens, University of Manchester
Archives in Windsor, Brighton, Lewes, Gloucester and London, December 2012 - January 2013
o Michael Robinson, University of Liverpool
Archives in Belfast, July 2013
o Sheng-Chi Shu, University of Cambridge
Archives in London, 3rd December 2012 – 25th January 2013
o Samuel John Tranter, University of St Andrews
Archives in London, 1st-30th June 2013
o Marie Ventura, University of St Andrews
Archives in London and Cambridge, 17th-26th January 2013
o Thomas Wright, University of York
Archives in Birmingham, Cambridge, Edinburgh and Hull, August 2012

Research Expenses outside the UK

o Rachael Abbiss, University of Chester
Archives in Boston, Cambridge and Worcester, Massachusetts, USA, 2nd-7th January 2013
o Rakesh Ankit, University of Southampton
Archives in Washington, Missouri, Boston and Connecticut, 27th July - 2nd September 2013
o Ivor Bolton, University of Birmingham
Oral interviews in Berlin, Leipzig and Eisenhuttenstadt, 1st-31st August 2013
o Louisa Cantwell, University of Cambridge
Archives and oral interviews in Botswana and South Africa, 24th June - 10th September 2013

- William Carruthers, University of Cambridge
  Archives in Philadelphia, USA, 2nd-9th December 2012
- Rosalind Coffey, LSE
  Archives Pretoria, Johannesburg, South Africa, 16th April - 10th May 2013
- John Condren, University of St Andrews
  Archives in Genoa, Mantua, Parma and Turin, Italy, May - July 2013
- Claire Connor, University of Bristol
  Archives in Melbourne Victoria, Australia, January - April 2013
- Poppy Cullen, University of Durham
  Archives in Nairobi, Kenya, 4th-26th January 2013
- Rabia Dada, University of Leeds
  Archives in Karachi and Lahore, Pakistan, 1st-14th May 2013
- Jan-Arend De Graaf, University of Portsmouth
  Archives in Paris, France, 25th March - 20th April 2013
- Maximilian Drephal, University of Loughborough
  Archives in New Delhi, India, 14th December 2012 - 6th January 2013
- Macdara Dwyer, King's College, London
  Archives in Dublin, 22nd-29th April 2013
- Justin Fantauzzo, University of Cambridge
  Archives in Poughkeepsie, New York, 1st-6th July 2013
- Alex Ferguson, University of Southampton
  Archives in Maryland, USA
- Alice Freeman, University of Oxford
  Archives in Tokyo, Japan, 3rd June - 19th July 2013
- Agnibho Gangopadhyay, University of Oxford
  Archives and interviews in India, August 2012 - October 2013
- Flavia Gasbarri, King's College London
  Archives in Pretoria, South Africa
- Shantelle George, SOAS
  Archives and interviews in Grenada, January 2013
- Daisy Gibbs, UCL
  Archives in Paris, France, 2nd September - 2nd December 2013
- Jennifer Griffiths, University College London
  Archives in St Petersburg and Moscow
- James Heath, University of Warwick
  Archives in Louisville, Kentucky, USA, 17th-29th June 2013
- Garrick Hileman, London School of Economics
  Archives in New York, USA, December 2012
- Anna Jenkin, University of Sheffield
  Archives in Paris, France, 17th- 24th March 2013
- Gillian Kennedy, King's College London
  Interviews in Cairo, Egypt, October - November 2012

- o Simon Mee, University of Oxford
  Archives in Frankfurt and Dortmund, Germany, 30th June - 11th August 2013
- o David Napolitano, University of Cambridge
  Archives in Florence and San Gimigano, December 2012
- o Meleisa Ono-George, University of Warwick
  Archives in Kingston, Jamaica, 1st May - 20th June 2013
- o Anna Orofino, Swansea University
  Archives in Valladolid-Castilla y Leon, Spain, 11th-15th June 2013
- o Dhwani Patel, King's College London
  Archives in Rome, Italy, October 2012
- o Selina Patel, Newcastle University
  Archives in Rio de Janeiro and Salvador, Brazil, 30th March - 22nd December 2013
- o Carin Peller Semmens, University of Sussex
  Archives in Baton Rouge, Louisiana, USA, 9th May - 27th June 2013
- o Aaron Rietkerk, London School of Economics
  Archives in Stockholm, Sweden, 2nd-5th April 2013
- o Bartley Rock, UCL
  Archives in Russia, October 2012 - April 2013
- o Mara Sankey, University College London
  Archives in Raleigh-Durham, North Carolina; Princeton, New Jersey; and Washington D.C, USA, 22nd April - 9th June 2013
- o Nancy Thornley, University of Leeds
  Archives and interviews in Uganda, November 2012
- o Elisabetta Tollardo, University of Oxford
  Archives in Switzerland, August - September 2012
- o Gabor Toth, University of Oxford
  Museums, libraries and site visits in Italy, September - October 2012
- o Imaobong Umoren, University of Oxford
  Archives in Paris and Aix-en-Provence, France, March 2013
- o Mark Walmsley, University of Leeds
  Archives at Emory University, Atlanta, GA, USA, 4th February - 27th March 2013
- o Maarten Walraven, University of Manchester
  Archives in Duisburg, Dusseldorf, Hamm and Essen in Germany, January 2013
- o Mark Whelan, Royal Holloway, University of London
  Archives in Munich, Germany, 17th-22nd March 2013
- o Malgorzata Wloszycka, University of Southampton
  Archives, oral interviews and observation in Mszana Dolna, Krakow and Warsaw, Poland, 24th August - 1 September 2013
- o Fei Yan, University of Oxford
  Archives in Stanford, USA, 1st August - 1st September 2013

o James Yeoman, University of Sheffield
Archives in Spain, August - September 2012

Conference Organisation

o Patrick Andelic
Historians of the Twentieth Century United Stated (HOTCUS)
Annual Conference, Northumbria University, Newcastle, 5th-7th July
2013
o Jason Berg
Networks and Neighbours: A Symposium on Early Medieval
Correlations, University of Leeds, 27th-28th June 2013
o Edward Browne
Elites in Discord in North-West Europe, c.900-c.1500, University of
Aberdeen, 10th October 2013
o Alison Carrol
A Century Later: New Approaches to French History, 1914–1945,
Maison Francaise, Oxford (organized by Birkbeck College/Brunel
University), 21st June 2013
o Roberta Cimino
Politics and Texts in Late Carolingian Europe, c.870–1000, St Andrews
Institute of Mediaeval Studies, 8th-9th July 2013
o Patrick Clibbens
The Savage State?: Violence in Nationalism and Nation-building
(Graduate symposium), University of Cambridge, 8th June 2013
o Tom Cutterham
Charles Beard, Economic Interpretation and History, Rothermere
American Institute, Oxford, 22nd-23rd April 2013
o Rachel Douglas
The Black Jacobins Revisited: Rewriting History, International Slavery
Museum, Liverpool and Bluecoat Arts Centre, 27th-28th October 2013
o Gian Ghirardini
Association for the Study of Modern Italy Postgraduate Summer
School, University of Reading, 26th-28th June 2013
o Meggen Gondek
Runes, Monuments and Memorial Carvings International Research
Network Workshop, University of Chester, 8th-11th April 2013
o Tim Grady
o Minorities and the First World War, University of Chester, 14th-15th
April 2014
o Clare Griffin
Trading Medicines: the global drug trade in perspective, London
School of Economics, 10th January 2014

- Mark Hailwood
  History from below in the 21st century, Emmanuel College, Cambridge, 3rd July 2013
- Niall Hodson
  Translation and the Circulation of Knowledge in Early Modern Science, The Warburg Institute, London, 28th June 2013
- Katherine Hunt
  Working it out: a day of numbers in early modern writing, Birkbeck, University of London, 18th May 2013
- Grace Huxford, Elodie Duche
  Representations of Prisoner of War Experience, University of Warwick, 9th November 2013
- Yvonne Inall
  Iron Age Research Student Symposium, Universities of Bradford and Hull, 6th-9th June 2013
- Melissa Julian-Jones
  'In the Hands of God's Servants': the Power of the Bishop in Europe 1100–1300, Cardiff University, 23rd-24th May 2013
- Hanna Kilpi
  Conflict and Rebellion in the North Sea World: Creating, managing and resolving conflict in the 12th – 13th centuries, University of Glasgow, 9th-10th April 2014
- Martha Kirby
  Defining Decades: Key Moments in History, Dundee, 15th-16th June 2013
- Jessica Knowles
  Durham, UEA, KCL and York Postgraduate Conference 2013, University of York, 19th-20th July 2013
- Elisabeth Leake
  Negotiating Independence: new directions in the histories of decolonisation and the Cold War, Trinity College, Cambridge, 3rd-4th May 2013
- Kevin Linch
  War, Society and Culture in Britain, c.1688–1830: New Perspectives, University of Leeds, 4th-5th July 2013
- Giorgio Lizzul
  The Fourth London Graduate Conference in the History of Political Thought: 'Global Order and Disorder in the History of Political Thought', Senate House, London, 3rd-4th June 2013
- Tracey Loughran
  Infertility in History, Science and Culture, University of Edinburgh, 3rd-5th July 2013
- Robin Macdonald
  Sensing the Sacred; Religion and the Senses, 1300–1800, University of York, 21st-22nd June 2013

o Jessica Moody
Little Britain's Memory of Slavery: the local nuances of a 'national sin', University College London, 13th-14th September 2013

o Frank Muller
Monarchical Succession and the Political Culture of 19th-Century Europe, University of St Andrews, 30th-31st August 2013

o Kevin Passmore
Annual Conference of the Society for the Study of French History, Cardiff University, 30th June - 2nd July 2013

o Catriona Pennell
The First World War in the Classroom: A Teacher Academic Exchange, IHR, Senate House, London, 18th-19th February 2013

o Malcolm Petrie
Politics and the Public in Scotland, c.1300–2000, Institute of Scottish Historical Research, University of St Andrews, 13th-14th June 2013

o Catherine Rider
Demons and Illness: Theory and Practice from Antiquity to the Early Modern Period, University of Exeter, 22nd-24th April 2013

o Thomas Smith
Power Manifest: Structures and Concepts of Ecclesiastical Authority in the High to Late Middle Ages, Institute of Historical Research, London, 20th June 2013

o Abigail Stevenson
Revealing Records V, King's College London, 24th May 2013

o Laura Tompkins
Gender and Transgression in the Middle Ages, St Andrews Institute of Mediaeval Studies, 2nd-4th May 2013

o Emma Vickers
Lessons of War: Gender History and the Second World War, University of Lancaster, 12th-13th September 2013

o Alexandra Walsham
Record Keeping in the Early Modern World, Centre for Research in the Arts, Social Sciences and Humanities, Cambridge, 9th-11th April 2014

o Mark Whelan
Speaking in Tongues: Language, Communication and Power in the Middle Ages, Institute of Historical Research, London, 14th June 2013

o Sarah Wood
Beyond History: a History Lab North West Interdisciplinary Workshop, University of Manchester, 1st November 2013

o Elena Woodacre
Kings & Queens II: Making Connections, University of Winchester, 8th-9th July 2013

- Armin Yavari
  Symposia Iranica: First Biennial Iranian Studies Graduate Conference, University of St Andrews, 13th-14th April 2013
- Deborah Youngs
  Anchorites in their Communities, University of Wales Conference Centre, Gregynon, Newtown, Powys, 22nd-24th April 2014

Martin Lynn Scholarship

- Temilola Alanamu, University of Exeter
  Archives in Nigeria, September - December 2012

Royal Historical Society Postgraduate Speakers Series

- Queen's University Belfast
- Newcastle University
- Bangor University
- University of Huddersfield
- University of St Andrews
- University of Birmingham
- University of Exeter
- University of Reading
- University of Leicester
- University of Wolverhampton

FINANCIAL STATEMENTS
FOR THE YEAR ENDED
30 JUNE 2013

THE ROYAL HISTORICAL SOCIETY REFERENCE AND ADMINISTRATIVE INFORMATION

Members of Council:

Professor C D H Jones, BA, DPhil, FBA	President - Officer (to November 2012)
Professor P Mandler, BA, AM, PhD	President - Officer (from November 2012)
A Smith, BA, MA, PhD	Honorary Secretary – Officer
I W Archer, MA, DPhil	Literary Director - Officer
Professor R A Burns, MA, DPhil	Literary Director - Officer (to November 2012)
E Griffin, Ba, MA, PhD	Literary Director - Officer (from November 2012)
Professor M J Hughes, BA, MSc, PhD .	Honorary Treasurer - Officer
Professor J C Fox, BA, PhD	Honorary Director of Communications – Officer (from November 2012)
E Griffin, BA, MA, PhD	Honorary Director of Communications – Officer (to November 2012)
Professor S J C Taylor, MA, PhD	Honorary Academic Editor - BBIH - Officer
R Baldock, BA, PhD	Vice President
Professor R A Burns, MA, DPhil	Vice President (from November 2012)
Professor M C Finn, BS, PhD	Vice President (to November 2012)
Professor C C Kidd, BA, Dphil	Vice President
Professor P Mandler, BA, AM, PhD	Vice President (to November 2012)
Professor N A Miller, PhD	Vice President (from November 2012)
Professor A Pettegree, MA, Dphil	Vice President
Professor A M Walsham, BA, MA, PhD, FBA	Vice President (from November 2012)
Professor S F Barton, BA, MA, DPhil	Councillor (to November 2012)
Professor J M Cornwall, PhD	Councillor (to November 2012)
Professor S Dixon, MA, PhD	Councillor
Professor D M Feldman, BA, PhD	Councillor
Professor K C Fincham, MA, PhD	Councillor
Dr L Fischer, BA, PhD	Councillor
Professor J S Henderson, BA, MA, PhD	Councillor (from November 2012)
J J Lewis, BA, PhD	Councillor
Professor A J Musson, BA, MusB, LLM, PhD	Councillor
Professor M J Stoyle, BA, DPhil	Councillor (from November 2012)
Professor P Summerfield, BA, MA, DPhil	Councillor (from November 2012)
A T Thacker, MA, DPhil, FSA	Councillor
Professor C A Whatley, BA, PhD	Councillor (to November 2012)
Professor P A Williamson, PhD	Councillor
Professor D R Wootton, MA, PhD	Councillor

Executive Secretary:	S E Carr, PhD
Administrative Secretary:	M F M Ransom, BA J Gerson, PhD (maternity leave cover)
Registered Office:	University College London Gower Street London WC1E 6BT
Charity registration number:	206888
Auditors:	Kingston Smith LLP Chartered Accountants Devonshire House 60 Goswell Road London EC1M 7AD
Investment managers:	Brewin Dolphin 12 Smithfield Street London EC1A 9BD
Bankers:	Barclays Bank Plc 27 Soho Square London W1A 4WA

THE ROYAL HISTORICAL SOCIETY
REPORT OF THE COUNCIL (THE TRUSTEES)
FOR THE YEAR ENDED 30 JUNE 2013

The members of Council present their report and audited accounts for the year ended 30 June 2013. The information shown on page 1 forms a part of these financial statements.

STRUCTURE, GOVERNANCE AND MANAGEMENT

The Society was founded on 23 November 1868 and received its Royal Charter in 1889. It is governed by the document 'The By-Laws of the Royal Historical Society', which was last amended in June 2010. The elected Officers of the Society are the President, six Vice-Presidents, the Treasurer, the Secretary, the Director of Communications, not more than two Literary Directors and the Honorary Academic Editor (BBIH). These officers, together with twelve Councillors constitute the governing body of the Society, and therefore its trustees. The Society also has two executive officers: an Executive Secretary and an Administrative Secretary.

Appointment of Trustees

The identity of the trustees is indicated above. All Fellows and Members of the Society are able to nominate Councillors; they are elected by a ballot of Fellows. Other trustees are elected by Council.

The President shall be *ex-officio* a member of all Committees appointed by the Council; and the Treasurer, the Secretary, the Director of Communications, the Literary Directors and the Honorary Academic Editor shall, unless the Council otherwise determine, also be *ex-officio* members of all such Committees.

In accordance with By-law XVII, the Vice-Presidents shall hold office normally for a term of three years. Two of them shall retire by rotation, in order of seniority in office, at each Anniversary Meeting and shall not be eligible for re-election before the Anniversary Meeting of the next year. In accordance with By-law XX, the Councillors shall hold office normally for a term of four years. Three of them shall retire by rotation, in order of seniority in office, at each Anniversary Meeting and shall not be eligible for re-election before the Anniversary Meeting of the next year.

At the Anniversary Meeting on 23 November 2012, the President retiring under By-law XVI was Professor C Jones; Professor P Mandler was elected in his place. The Vice-Presidents retiring under By-law XVII were Professor M Finn and Professor P Mandler; Professor A Burns and Professor A Walsham were elected in their place. The Members of Council retiring under By-law XX were Professor S Barton, Professor J Cornwall and Professor C Whatley. In accordance with By-law XXI, Professor J Henderson, Professor M Stoyle and Professor P Summerfield were elected in their place.

Trustee training and induction process

New trustees are welcomed in writing before their initial meeting, and sent details of the coming year's meeting schedule and other information about the Society and their duties. They are advised of Committee structure and receive papers in advance of the appropriate Committee and Council meetings, including minutes of the previous meetings. Trustees are already Fellows of the Society and have received regular information including the annual volume of *Transactions of the Royal Historical Society* which includes the annual report and accounts. They have therefore been kept apprised of any changes in the Society's business.

MEMBERSHIP COMMITTEE:	Professor C Kidd – Chair
	Professor S Barton (to November 2012)
	Professor K Fincham
	Professor P Williamson
	Professor P Summerfield (from November 2012)
RESEARCH SUPPORT COMMITTEE:	Professor M Finn – Chair (to November 2012)
	Professor A Walsham – Chair (from November 2012)
	Professor M Cornwall (to November 2012)
	Professor S Dixon (from November 2012)
	Professor D Feldman (to November 2012)
	Dr J Lewis (from November 2012)
	Professor N Miller – (to November 2012)
	Professor M Stoyle (from November 2012)
	Dr A Thacker (To November 2012)
	Professor D Wootton (from November 2012)

Risk assessment

The trustees are satisfied that they have considered the major risks to which the charity is exposed, that they have taken action to mitigate or manage those risks and that they have systems in place to monitor any change to those risks.

OBJECTS, OBJECTIVES, ACTIVITIES AND PUBLIC BENEFIT

The Society has referred to the guidance in the Charity Commission's general guidance on Public Benefit when reviewing its aims and objectives and in planning its future activities. In particular, the trustees consider how planned activities will contribute to the aims and objectives they have set.

The Society remains the foremost society in Great Britain promoting and defending the scholarly study of the past. The Society promotes discussion of history by means of a full programme of public lectures and conferences, and disseminates the results of historical research and debate through its many publications. It also speaks for the interests of history and historians for the benefit of the public.

The Society offers grants to support research training, and annual prizes for historical essays and publications. It produces (in conjunction with Brepols Publishers and the Institute of Historical Research) the Bibliography of British and Irish History, a database of over 534,000 records, by far the most complete online bibliographical resource on British and Irish history, including relations with the empire and the Commonwealth. The Bibliography is kept updated, and includes near-comprehensive coverage of works since 1901 and selected earlier works.

The Society's specific new objectives for the year are set out in 'Plans for Future Periods' below.

The Society relies on volunteers from among its Fellows to act as its elected Officers, Councillors and Vice-Presidents. In many of its activities it also relies on the goodwill of Fellows and others interested in the study of the past. It has two salaried staff, and also pays a stipend to the Series Editor of Studies in History and to certain individuals for work on the Society's Bibliography.

ACHIEVEMENTS AND PERFORMANCE

Grants

The Society awards funds to assist advanced historical research by distributing grants to individuals. A wide range of individuals are eligible for these research and conference grants, including all postgraduate students registered for a research degree at United Kingdom institutions of higher education (full-time and part-time). The Society also considers applications from individuals who have completed doctoral dissertations within the last two years and are not yet in full-time employment. The Society's Research Support Committee considers applications at meetings held regularly throughout the year. In turn the Research Support Committee reports to Council. This year the grants budget was £45,000.

The Society was also able to award its Centenary and Marshall Fellowships this year. Those eligible are doctoral students who are engaged in the completion of a PhD in history (broadly defined) and who will have completed at least two years' research on their chosen topic (and not more than four years full-time or six years part-time) at the beginning of the session for which the awards are made. Full details and a list of awards made are provided in the Society's Annual Report.

Lectures and other meetings

During the year the Society held meetings in London and at universities outside London at which papers are delivered. Lectures are open to the public and are advertised on the website. In 2012–13 it sponsored sessions at the University of Southampton and the University of Leicester. It continues to sponsor the joint lecture for a wider public with Gresham College. It meets with other bodies to consider teaching and research policy issues of national importance. Together with The National Archives, it organised the annual Gerald Aylmer seminar, between historians and archivists. Full details are provided in the Annual Report.

Publications

During 2012 – 2013 the RHS has delivered an ambitious programme of publications – a volume of *Transactions*, two volumes of edited texts in the *Camden* Series and further volumes in the *Studies in History* Series have appeared. It has continued its financial support for the Bibliography of British and Irish History. The Bibliography is offered to all universities at institutional rates, and made available free to members consulting it at the Institute of Historical Research. The Society's membership who are not attached to an academic institution are now able to subscribe to the Bibliography at a preferential rate payable on top of the normal subscription.

Library

The Society continues to subscribe to a range of record series publications, which, with its other holdings, are housed either in the Council Room or in the room immediately across the corridor, in the UCL History Library. A catalogue of the Society's private library holdings and listings of record series and regional history society publications (Texts and Calendars) are available on the Society's website.

Membership services

In accordance with the Society's 'By-laws', the membership is entitled to receive, after payment of subscription, a copy of the Society's *Transactions*, and to buy at a preferential rate copies of volumes published in the *Camden* series, and the *Studies in History* series. Society Newsletters continue to be circulated to the membership twice annually, in an accessible format. The membership benefits from many other activities of the Society including the frequent representations to various official bodies where the interests of historical scholarship are involved.

Investment performance

The Society holds an investment portfolio with a market value of about £2.62 million at 30 June 2013 (2012: £2.36 million). It has adopted a "total return" approach to its investment policy. This means that the funds are invested solely on the basis of seeking to secure the best total level of financial return compatible with the duty to make safe investments but regardless of the form the return takes. The total return strategy does not make distinctions between income and capital returns. It lumps together all forms of return on investment – dividends, interest, and capital gains etc – to produce a "total return". Some of the total return is then used to meet the needs of present beneficiaries, while the remainder is added to the existing investment portfolios to help meet the needs of future beneficiaries. The Society will be considering over the coming months whether this strategy remains the most appropriate at the current time, and any changes will be detailed in next year's report.

During the year Brewin Dolphin plc continued to act as investment managers. They report all transactions to the Honorary Treasurer and provide regular reports on the portfolios, which are considered by the Society's Finance Committee which meets three times a year. In turn the Finance Committee reports to Council. A manager from Brewin attends two Finance Committee meetings a year.

The Society assesses investment performance against the FTSE APCIMS Balanced (Total Return) index. The Society can afford to take a long view of its investment portfolio and is confident that the investment strategy remains prudent. The Society has a policy of not drawing down more than 4% of the market value of the portfolio (valued over a 3-year rolling period). The drawdown in 2012–13 was around 3% (measured against the portfolio value at year end).

FINANCIAL REVIEW

Results

The Society generated a surplus of £21,599 (2011–12 £100,868), before gains on investments. This surplus was once again accounted for by higher than expected income from Society's joint publishing agreement with Cambridge University Press due to on-going sales of the digital archive. Subscription income was slightly increased over the previous year. There was a slight decline in investment income compared with 2011–12 (although as noted earlier the capital value of the portfolio increased). Expenditure in 2012–13 was slightly higher than the previous year (in part due an increase in grants made as well as moderate inflation-driven cost rises). The Society continues to bear substantial costs for the production of the Bibliography of British and Irish History. The cost to the Society is estimated to be around £25,000 over the next year. The Society maintains a very significant cash reserve as a result of the accumulated surplus of the previous few years. The Society expects to enter a period over the next few years when it declares significant in-year deficits which will be funded by part of this accumulated surplus (see below).

Fixed assets

Information relating to changes in fixed assets is given in notes 5 and 6 to the accounts.

Reserves policy

Council has reviewed the reserves of the Society. To safeguard the core activities in excess of the members' subscription income, Council has determined to establish unrestricted, general, free reserves to cover three years operational costs (approximately £750,000). Finance Committee will be reviewing its reserves policy in the coming year.

The Society's restricted funds consist of a number of different funds where the donor has imposed restrictions on the use of the funds which are legally binding. The purposes of these funds are set out in Notes 10–13.

PLANS FOR FUTURE PERIODS

It was noted last year that Council plans to develop a new communications strategy in order to improve communication with both its membership and the general public. This will incur considerable expenditure in financial year 2013–14 when the Society expects to record a significant deficit. Council will also continue to monitor closely how policy and funding changes at the national level are likely to impact on the work of historians. It will also continue to monitor the challenges currently faced by local archives in an uncertain funding environment. Council continues to pay considerable attention to current policy initiatives that affect the teaching of History in schools and colleges. It will continue to offer support for wide-ranging seminar/lecture events outside London each year, some to be held at universities, and some run by consortia of local universities and other academic institutions. Council will continue to review the role, function, and membership of its committees.

The Society intends to maintain its current high level of financial support for postgraduate and other young historians (in part thanks to the generous support of *History Workshop Journal* and *Past and Present*). It will continue to support the stipends for the Centenary and Marshall Fellowships (and will continue to be involved in the selection procedure for the Fellowships, organised by the Institute of Historical Research). As noted above, the Society anticipates running deficits in future years in order to fund these developments and its other activities, following a period in which it has built up a cash surplus.

STATEMENT OF COUNCIL'S RESPONSIBILITIES

The Council is responsible for preparing the Trustees' Report and the financial statements in accordance with applicable law and United Kingdom Accounting Standards (United Kingdom Generally Accepted Accounting Practice.)

The law applicable to charities in England & Wales requires the Council to prepare financial statements for each financial year which give a true and fair view of the state of the affairs of the charity and of the incoming resources and application of resources of the charity for that period. In preparing these financial statements, the Council is required to:

- select suitable accounting policies and then apply them consistently;
- observe the methods and principles in the Charities SORP;
- make judgements and estimates that are reasonable and prudent;
- state whether applicable accounting standards have been followed, subject to any material departures disclosed and explained in the financial statements;
- prepare the financial statements on the going concern basis unless it is inappropriate to presume that the charity will continue in business.

The Council is responsible for keeping proper accounting records that disclose with reasonable accuracy at any time the financial position of the charity and enable them to ensure that the financial statements comply with the Charities Act 2011, the Charity (Accounts and Reports) Regulations 2008 and the provisions of the Royal Charter. It is also responsible for safeguarding the assets of the charity and hence for taking reasonable steps for the prevention and detection of fraud and other irregularities.

The Council is responsible for the maintenance and integrity of the charity and financial information included on the charity's website. Legislation in the United Kingdom governing the preparation and dissemination fo financial statements may differ from legislation in other jurisdictions.

In determining how amounts are presented within items in the statement of financial activities and balance sheet, the Council has had regard to the substance of the reported transaction or arrangement, in accordance with generally accepted accounting policies or practice.

AUDITORS

Kingston Smith LLP have indicated their willingness to continue in office and a proposal for their re-appointment will be presented at the Anniversary meeting.

By Order of the Board

. . . .

Honorary Secretary

Dr A Smith

27 September 2013

INDEPENDENT AUDITORS' REPORT TO THE TRUSTEES OF THE ROYAL HISTORICAL SOCIETY

We have audited the financial statements of The Royal Historical Society for the year ended 30 June 2013 which comprise the Statement of Financial Activities, the Balance Sheet and the related notes. The financial reporting framework that has been applied in their preparation is applicable laws and United Kingdom Accounting Standards (United Kingston Generally Accepted Accounting Practice).

This report is made solely to the charity's trustees, as a body, in accordance with Chapter 3 of Part 8 of the Charities Act 2011. Our audit work has been undertaken so that we might state to the charity's trustees those matters which we are required to state to them in an auditors' report and for no other purpose. To the fullest extent permitted by law, we do not accept or assume responsibility to any party other than the charity and charity's trustees as a body, for our audit work, for this report, or for the opinions we have formed.

Respective responsibilities of trustees and auditor
As explained more fully in the Trustees' Responsibilities Statement, the trustees are responsible for the preparation of financial statements which give a true and fair view. We have been appointed as auditors under section 145 of the Charities Act 2011 and report in accordance with that Act. Our responsibility is to audit and express an opinion on the financial statements in accordance with applicable law and International Standards on Auditor (UK and Ireland). Those standards require us to comply with the Auditing Practices Board's Ethical Standards for Auditors.

Scope of the audit of the financial statements
An audit involves obtaining evidence about the amounts and disclosures in the financial statements sufficient to give reasonable assurance that the financial statements are free from material misstatement, whether caused by fraud or error. This includes an assessment of: whether the accounting policies are appropriate to the charity's circumstances and have been consistently applied and adequately disclosed; the reasonableness of significant accounting estimates made by the trustees; and the overall presentation of the financial statements. In addition we read all the financial and non-financial information in the Annual Report to identify material inconsistencies with the audited financial statements. If we become aware of any apparent material misstatements or inconsistencies we consider the implications for our report.

Opinion on the financial statements
In our opinion the financial statements:

- give a true and fair view of the state of the charity's affairs as at 30 June 2013 and of the charity's incoming/outgoing resources and application of resources for the year then ended; and
- have been properly prepared in accordance with United Kingdom Generally Accepted Accounting Practice applicable to Smaller Entities; and
- have been prepared in accordance with the requirements of the Charities Act 2011.

Matters on which we are required to report by exception
We have nothing to report in respect of the following matters where the Charities Act 2011 requires us to report to you if, in our opinion:

- the information given in the Annual Report is inconsistent in any material respects with the financial statements; or
- sufficient accounting records have not been kept; or
- the financial statements are not in agreement with the accounting records and returns; or
- we have not received all the information and explanations we require for our audit; or
- the trustees were not entitled to prepare the financial statements in accordance with the small companies regime and take advantage of the small companies exemption in preparing the Trustees' Annual Report.

Devonshire House
60 Goswell Road
London EC1M 7AD

Kingston Smith LLP
Statutory auditor

Date:

Kingston Smith LLP is eligible to act as auditor in terms of Section 1212 of the Companies Act 2006.

THE ROYAL HISTORICAL SOCIETY

STATEMENT OF FINANCIAL ACTIVITIES
FOR THE YEAR ENDED 30 JUNE 2013

	Note	Unrestricted Funds £	Endowment Funds £	Restricted Funds £	Total Funds 2012 £	Total Funds 2011 £
Incoming Resources						
Incoming resources from generated funds						
Donations, legacies and similar incoming resources	2	10,248	–	–	10,248	10,612
Investment income	6	73,308	–	–	73,308	79,670
Incoming resources from charitable activities						
Grants for awards		–	–	12,000	12,000	13,100
Grants for publications		5,000	–	–	5,000	5,000
Subscriptions		113,374	–	–	113,374	110,499
Royalties		88,460	–	–	88,460	127,335
Other incoming resources		3,432	–	–	3,432	1,394
Total Incoming Resources		293,822	–	12,000	305,822	347,609
Resources Expended						
Cost of generating funds						
Investment manager's fees		11,634	–	360	11,994	11,619
Charitable activities						
Grants for awards	3	66,048	–	13,093	79,141	73,252
Lectures and meetings		16,627	–	–	16,627	15,806
Publications		95,364	–	–	95,364	68,573
Library		6,438	–	–	6,438	7,155
Membership services		53,961	–	–	53,961	50,793
Governance		20,698	–	–	20,698	19,543
Total Resources Expended	4a	270,770	–	13,453	284,223	246,741
Net Incoming/(Outgoing) Resources before transfers		23,053	–	(1,453)	21,599	100,868
Gross transfers between funds		1,096		(1,096)	–	–
Net Incoming / (Outgoing) Resources before gains		24,149	–	(2,549)	21,599	100,868
Other recognised gains and losses						
Net gain / (loss) on investments	6	269,948	8,349		278,297	(166,934)
Net Movement in Funds		294,096	8,349	(2,549)	299,896	(66,066)
Balance at 1 July		2,556,491	68,936	4,991	2,630,418	2,696,483
Balance at 30 June		2,850,587	77,285	2,442	2,930,314	2,630,418

The notes on pages 11 to 18 form part of these financial statements.

THE ROYAL HISTORICAL SOCIETY

BALANCE SHEET AT 30 JUNE 2013

	Note	2013 £	2013 £	2012 £	2012 £
FIXED ASSETS					
Tangible assets	5		455		568
Investments	6		2,618,996		2,358,108
COIF Investments			81,812		81,209
			2,701,263		2,439,885
Current Assets					
Debtors	7	13,074		11,018	
Cash at bank and in hand		255,247		216,668	
		268,322		227,687	
Less: Creditors					
Amounts due within one year	8	(39,271)		(37,154)	
Net Current Assets			229,051		190,533
Net Assets			2,930,314		2,630,418
Represented By:					
Endowment Funds	10				
A S Whitfield Prize Fund			51,702		46,136
The David Berry Essay Trust			25,583		22,800
Restricted Funds	11				
A S Whitfield Prize Fund			677		2,060
P J Marshall Fellowship			1,157		–
The David Berry Essay Trust			608		1,931
The Martin Lynn Bequest			–		1,000
Unrestricted Funds					
Designated - E M Robinson Bequest	12		130,949		117,904
General Fund	13		2,719,638		2,438,587
			2,930,314		2,630,418

The accounts have been prepared in accordance with the Financial Reporting Standard for Smaller Entities (effective April 2008).

The notes on pages 11 to 18 form part of these financial statements.

The financial statements were approved and authorised for issue by the Council on and were signed on its behalf by:

....
Professor P Mandler – **President**   Professor M J Hughes – **Honorary Treasurer**

THE ROYAL HISTORICAL SOCIETY

NOTES TO THE FINANCIAL STATEMENTS
FOR THE YEAR ENDED 30 JUNE 2013

1. ACCOUNTING POLICIES

Basis of Accounting
These financial statements have been prepared under the historical cost convention and in accordance with the revised Statement of Recommended Practice (SORP 2005) "Accounting and Reporting by Charities" and applicable accounting standards.

The following principal accounting policies, which are unchanged from the previous year, have been consistently applied in preparing the financial statements.

Incoming Resources
All incoming resources are included in the Statement of Financial Activities (SOFA) when the charity is legally entitled to receipt and the amount is quantifiable.

Grant income
Grant income is deferred only where the donor has specified that it may only be used for a future period or has imposed conditions that must be met before the charity has unconditional entitlement to the grant.

Subscription income
Subscription income is recognised in the year it became receivable with a provision against any subscription not received.

Donations and Other Voluntary Income
Donations and other voluntary income are recognised when the Society becomes legally entitled to such monies.

Royalties
Royalties are recognised on an accruals basis in accordance with the terms of the relevant agreement.

Resources expended
All expenditure is accounted for on an accruals basis and has been classified under headings that aggregate all costs related to the category. Wherever possible costs are directly attributed to these headings. Costs common to more than one area are apportioned on the basis of staff time spent on each area.

Grants Payable
Grants payable are recognised in the year in which they are approved and notified to recipients.

Cost of generating funds
The costs of generating funds are those costs of seeking potential funders and applying for funding.

Allocation of costs
Indirect costs are those costs incurred in support of the charitable objectives. These have been allocated to the resources expended on a basis that fairly reflects the true use of those resources within the organisation.

Governance costs
Governance costs are those incurred in the governance of the charity and are primarily associated with the constitutional and statutory requirements.

Library and Archives
The cost of additions to the library and archives is written off in the year of purchase.

Pensions
Pension costs are charged to the SOFA when payments fall due. The Society contributed 12.5% of gross salary to the personal pension plan of two of the employees.

Investments
Investments are stated at market value. Any surplus/deficit arising on revaluation is included in the Statement of Financial Activities. Dividend income is accounted for when the Society becomes entitled to such monies.

Depreciation
Depreciation is calculated by reference to the cost of fixed assets using a straight line basis at rates considered appropriate having regard to the expected lives of the fixed assets. The annual rates of depreciation in use are:

Furniture and equipment	10%
Computer equipment	25%

Funds

Unrestricted:
These are funds which can be used in accordance with the charitable objects of the Royal Historical Society at the discretion of the trustees.

Designated:
These are unrestricted funds which have been set aside by the trustees for specific purposes.

Restricted:
These are funds that can only be used for particular restricted purposes defined by the benefactor and within the objects of the charity.

Endowment:
Permanent endowment funds must be held permanently by the trustees and income arising is separately included in restricted funds for specific use as defined by the donors.

The purpose and use of endowment, restricted and designated funds are disclosed in the notes to the accounts.

2. Donations and Legacies

	2013 £	2012 £
Donations via membership	6,540	5,336
Gladstone Memorial Trust	600	600
Martin Lynn scholarship	–	1,000
Sundry income	–	587
Gift Aid reclaimed	3,108	3,089
	10,248	10,612

3. Grants for Awards

	Unrestricted Funds £	Restricted Funds £	Total funds 2013 £	Total funds 2012 £
RHS Centenary Fellowship	11,000	–	11,000	12,100
Research support grants (see below)	40,145	1,000	41,145	32,838
A-Level prizes	600	–	600	400
AS Whitfield prize	–	1,000	1,000	1,000
Gladstone history book prize	1,000	–	1,000	1,000
P J Marshall Fellowship	2,863	10,843	13,706	15,963
David Berry Prize	–	250	250	250
Alexander Prize	250	–	250	250
Rees Davies Prize	–	–	–	100
Staff and support costs (Note 4a)	10,190	–	10,190	9,352
	66,048	13,093	79,141	
30 June 2012	57,902	15,350		73,253

During the year Society awarded grants to a value of £41,229 (2012 - £34,281) to 151 (2012 - 139) individuals.

Grants Payable

	2013 £	2012 £
Commitments at 1 July	5,862	7,305
Commitments made in the year	68,951	63,901
Grants paid during the year	(68,951)	(65,344)
Commitments at 30 June	5,862	5,862

Commitments at 30 June 2013 and 2012 are included in creditors.

4a. Total Resources Expended

	Staff costs £ (Note 4b)	Support costs £ (Note 4c)	Direct costs £	Total £
Cost of generating funds				
Investment manager's fee	-	-	11,994	11,994
Charitable activities				
Grants for awards (Note 3)	6,509	3,681	68,951	79,141
Lectures and meetings	6,509	1,780	8,338	16,627
Publications	11,571	7,120	76,673	95,364
Library	2,893	1,780	1,766	6,438
Membership services	36,159	17,801	-	53,961
Governance	8,678	3,560	8,460	20,698
Total Resources Expended	72,318	35,722	176,182	284,223
30 June 2012	68,693	31,697	146,349	246,741

4b. Staff Costs

	2013 £	2012 £
Wages and salaries	59,731	55,988
Social security costs	5,528	5,729
Other pension costs	7,058	6,976
	72,318	68,694

4c. Support Costs

	2012 £	2011 £
Stationery, photocopying and postage	14,743	16,861
Computer support	2,816	1,425
Insurance	1,084	1,032
Telephone	296	311
Depreciation	113	113
Other	16,549	11,955
	35,601	31,697

The average number of employees in the year was 3 (2012 - 2). There were no employees whose emoluments exceeded £60,000 in this year or in the previous year.

During the year travel expenses were reimbursed to 22 (2012: 22) Councillors attending Council meetings at a cost of £4,206 (2012 - £5,566). No Councillor received any remuneration during the year (2012 - £Nil).

Included in governance is the following:

	2013 £	2012 £
Auditor's Remuneration – current year	8,460	8,130

5. Tangible Fixed Assets

	Computer Equipment £	Furniture and Equipment £	Total £
Cost			
At 1 July 2012	33,224	1,134	34,358
At 30 June 2013	33,224	1,134	34,358
Depreciation			
At 1 July 2012	33,224	566	33,790
Charge for the year	–	113	113
At 30 June 2013	33,224	679	33,903
Net Book Value			
At 30 June 2013	-	455	455
At 30 June 2012	-	568	568

All tangible fixed assets are used in the furtherance of the Society's objects.

6. Investments

	General Fund £	Designated Robinson Bequest £	Whitfield Prize Fund £	David Berry Essay Trust £	Total £
Market value at 1 July 2012	2,169,461	117,904	47,161	23,582	2,358,108
Additions	625,907	34,017	13,607	6,803	680,334
Disposals	(641,924)	(34,887)	(13,955)	(6,977)	(697,743)
Net gain on investments	256,033	13,915	5,566	2,783	278,297
Market value at 30 June 2013	2,409,477	130,949	52,379	26,191	2,618,996
Cost at 30 June 2013	1,958,833	106,458	42,583	21,292	2,129,166

	2013 £	2012 £
UK Equities	1,156,070	1,160,664
UK Government Stock and Bonds	361,242	469,889
Overseas Equities	994,381	690,345
Uninvested Cash	107,303	37,211
	2,618,996	2,358,109
Dividends and interest on listed investments	72,585	78,693
Interest on cash deposits	723	977
	73,308	79,670

7. Debtors

	2013 £	2012 £
Other debtors	11,296	6,632
Royalty debtor	840	3,448
Prepayments	938	938
	13,074	11,018

8. Creditors: Amounts due within one year

	2013 £	2012 £
Sundry creditors	16,563	15,325
Taxes and social security	1,171	1,565
Subscriptions received in advance	5,703	4,814
Accruals and deferred income	15,834	15,450
	39,271	37,154

Included within Sundry creditors is an amount of £577 (2012: £582) relating to pension liabilities.

9. Lease Commitments

The Society has the following annual commitments under non-cancellable operating leases which expire:

	2013 £	2012 £
Under 1 year	–	–
Within 1 – 2 years	–	–
Within 2 – 5 years	7,080	5,900

10. Endowment Funds

	Balance at 1 July 2012 £	Investment Gain £	Balance at 30 June 2013 £
A S Whitfield Prize Fund	46,136	5,566	51,702
The David Berry Essay Trust	22,800	2,783	25,583
	68,936	8,349	77,285

A S Whitfield Prize Fund

The A S Whitfield Prize Fund is an endowment used to provide income for an annual prize for the best first monograph for British history published in the calendar year.

The David Berry Essay Trust

The David Berry Essay Trust is an endowment to provide income for annual prizes for essays on subjects dealing with Scottish history.

11. Restricted Funds	Balance at 1 July 2012 £	Incoming Resources £	Outgoing Resources £	Transfers £	Balance at 30 June 2013 £
A S Whitfield Prize Fund	2,060	–	(1,240)	(143)	677
P J Marshall Fellowship	–	12,000	(10,843)	–	1,157
The David Berry Essay Trust	1,931	–	(370)	(953)	608
Martin Lynn Bequest	1,000	–	(1,000)	–	–
	4,991	12,000	(13,453)	(1,096)	2,442

The transfer from the Restricted fund to the general fund represents a correction to the fund balances arising from the investment portfolio analysis.

A S Whitfield Prize Fund Income

Income from the A S Whitfield Prize Fund is used to provide an annual prize for the best first monograph for British history published in the calendar year.

P J Marshall Fellowship

The P J Marshall Fellowship is used to provide a sum sufficient to cover the stipend for a one-year doctoral research fellowship alongside the existing Royal Historical Society Centenary Fellowship at the Institute of Historical Research.

The David Berry Essay Trust Income

Income from the David Berry Trust is to provide annual prizes for essays on subjects dealing with Scottish history.

The Martin Lynn Bequest

This annual bequest is used by the Society to give financial assistance to postgraduates researching topics in African history.

12. Designated Fund	Balance at 1 July 2012 £	Incoming Resources £	Outgoing Resources £	Investment Gain £	Transfers £	Balance at 30 June 2013 £
E M Robinson Bequest	117,904	3,629	(4,500)	13,915	–	130,949

E M Robinson Bequest

Income from the E M Robinson Bequest is to further the study of history and to date has been used to provide grants to the Dulwich Picture Gallery.

13. General Fund

	Balance at 1 July 2012 £	Incoming Resources £	Outgoing Resources £	Investment Gain £	Transfers £	Balance at 30 June 2013 £
	2,438,587	290,193	(266,270)	256,033	1,096	2,719,638

The transfer from the Restricted fund to the general fund represents a correction to the fund balances arising from the investment portfolio analysis.

14. Analysis of Net Assets between Funds

	General Fund £	Designated Fund £	Restricted Funds £	Endowment Funds £	Total £
Fixed assets	455	-	-	-	455
Investments	2,409,477	130,949	1,285	77,285	2,618,996
COIF investments	81,812	-	-	-	81,812
	2,491,744	130,949	1,285	77,285	2,701,263
Current assets	267,165	-	1,157	-	268,322
Less: Creditors	(39,271)	-	-	-	(39,271)
Net current assets/(liabilities)	227,894	-	1,157	-	229,051
Net Assets	2,719,638	130,949	2,442	77,285	2,930,314